Aging:
Continuity and Change

Robert C. Atchley

Scripps Foundation Gerontology Center
Miami University

Wadsworth Publishing Company
Belmont, California
A Division of Wadsworth, Inc.

Sociology and Gerontology Editor: *William Oliver*
Production Editor: *Robin Lockwood*
Designer: *Marilyn Langfeld*
Copy Editor: *Linda Purrington*
Technical Illustrator: *Brenda Booth*

The cover art is from *Japanese Design Motifs: 4,260 Illustrations of Heraldic Crests*, published by Dover Publications.

Photo Credits
Page 8: © Glenn Rand; 11: Courtesy, Western Gerontological Society; 14: © Glenn Rand; 21: S.R. Spangenberg, Western Gerontological Society; 31: © Glenn Rand; 45: © Glenn Rand; 56: Leon Pastalan, with permission; 60: Courtesy, Scripps Foundation Gerontology Center; 63: Sally Wagner, Western Gerontological Society; 70: © Glenn Rand; 81: © Glenn Rand; 92: Courtesy, Scripps Foundation Gerontology Center; 97: © Glenn Rand; 109: © Glenn Rand; 112: Courtesy, Scripps Foundation Gerontology Center; 123: © Glenn Rand; 128: © Glenn Rand; 141: © Glenn Rand; 144: © Glenn Rand; 156: Courtesy, Scripps Foundation Gerontology Center; 165: © Glenn Rand; 169: Courtesy, Scripps Foundation Gerontology Center; 176: Jonathan Prince, Western Gerontological Society; 181: Courtesy, Scripps Foundation Gerontology Center; 189: © Glenn Rand; 205: © Glenn Rand; 211: Alice Leveston, Western Gerontological Society; 221: © Glenn Rand; 223: © Glenn Rand; 241: Courtesy, Scripps Foundation Gerontology Center; 248: Courtesy, Western Gerontological Society; 254: Courtesy, Scripps Foundation Gerontology Center; 262: Courtesy, Western Gerontological Society; 277: © Glenn Rand; 289: Sharron Bentley, Western Gerontological Society.

Printed in the United States of America

1 2 3 4 5 6 7 8 9 10—87 86 85 84 83

ISBN 0-534-01417-8

Library of Congress Cataloging in Publication Data

Atchley, Robert C.
   Aging, continuity and change.

   (Lifetime series in aging)
   Bibliography: p.
   Includes index.
   1. Aging—Social aspects.   2. Aged—Psychology.
3. Life cycle, Human—Social aspects.   I. Title.
II. Series.   [DNLM: 1. Aging.   2. Aged.   WT 100 A863a]
HQ1061.A778   1983   305.2'6   82-23683
ISBN 0-534-01417-8

This book is dedicated to the
Complete Teacher in all of us.

Lifetime Series in Aging

Contents

Part Four   Aging Produces Changes and Challenges   215

Preface

This book began from the idea of a brief edition of *The Social Forces in Later Life* that could be used in courses for people involved in direct services.

The more I thought about it, the less appropriate that seemed. What was needed was not simply a shorter book but an entirely different kind of book; one that would center around creating empathy and providing information for diagnosis and helping.

Accordingly, there is much more in this book on the inner experience of aging than in most texts, there are many more case examples, and there is more emphasis on the application of knowledge. There is also an extended treatment of compensation and continuity and how they fit into the adaptation process.

The preface is where authors get to acknowledge others for their contributions. The first draft of the book was reviewed for style by John Cobb, who made literally hundreds of suggestions that helped me identify points that needed examples or clarification. Robin Lockwood took the book smoothly through the production process, including very solid editing by Linda Purrington. It's a genuine pleasure to work with people who appreciate high-quality results as much as I do. I feel that this book is very much a team effort.

Many authors thank their families for doing without them while a book is being written, but I never really felt before that my family suffered while I was writing. This time is different, and I want to acknowledge Sheila Miller and Christopher Atchley for being willing and able to do without me in the winter and spring of 1982.

I have many colleagues who over the years have guided, challenged, and encouraged me. These include Sheila Miller, Suzanne Adlon, Lillian Troll, Ted Wagenaar, Kay Phillips and Marty Jendrek. Fred Cottrell taught me to keep my feet on the ground while my mind was on theory. Dave Lewis taught me that science and humanism could be done at the same time. Millie Seltzer taught me the incredible power of unwavering support. Carl Adlon taught me who is using all of this. I have truly been blessed by each of these people.

Everything I do in my profession is made easier by the office staff of the Scripps Foundation: Debbie Rumpler, Joan McLaughlin and Thelma Carmack. Their dedication and good humor are contagious.

Part One

Perspectives

In Part One we will look at what aging is, what some of its physical and mental results are, and why it is an important area to study. This part of the book provides you with an overview of aging and the aged that is an important foundation for the parts that follow.

Chapter 1

Introduction

People have a variety of reasons for wanting to know about aging. A look around one of my classes usually reveals most of them. For example, there's Stan. He's in his late 50s and teaches English in a local high school. He is interested in aging because he sees it happening to him and wants to understand it better. Ann is a music major who is in the class because her parents are on the eve of retirement and she thought she might pick up some ideas that might help them. Bill is a pre-med student whose advisor told him that he ought to know something about the social aspects of aging. Jenny is a counseling major who wants to know more about older people in case she has to serve them. Brad worked as a volunteer in a nursing home and got interested in aging. Paula is a social gerontology major.[1] She's already committed—at least for now—to employment in the field of aging. This is just the first of several courses in aging that she will take. She hasn't yet decided whether she wants to serve the elderly directly or whether she would prefer program administration. The courses she takes will help her decide. Jim is a sociology major who plans to go on to graduate study and eventually do research. He thinks he might be interested in research on aging. Annette already has a job in the field of aging. She's an activities coordinator for a senior citizen's center, and frankly she doesn't feel that she knows enough about aging or older people to do her job as well as she should. And then there's Molly, who needed a course that met on Monday night. No doubt you have a reason for studying aging that is just as unique as any of these.

---

[1] *Social gerontology* is the study of the nonbiological aspects of aging.

What Do You Need?

Regardless of your motive for studying aging, to achieve a basic understanding of aging you need

△ *Concepts* you can use to organize your thoughts, observations, and communications.

△ *Factual information* to provide you with points of comparison and a means for putting your specific experiences into an overall context.

△ *Understandings* of how the various aspects of aging interact within an individual's life to produce a dynamic and only sometimes predictable process.

△ *Examples* to bring concepts, information, and understanding alive in your mind, to make them practical.

Concepts are human inventions, mental tools created for a purpose. Like all tools, concepts must be designed precisely if we are to understand thoroughly what they represent. The field of aging contains many concepts, such as *life course,* that will be new to you. Fortunately, although the terms may appear strange, the content of the new concepts will usually be familiar. For example, you are already familiar with the idea that there is an appropriate time in life to experience various events and to do various kinds of activities. There is a time to begin school, a time to begin dating, a time to marry, a time to begin an occupational career, a time to retire, and so on. The life course concept involves organizing these "normal" times into a sequence. Thus, a life course is an ideal sequence of events people are expected to experience and positions they are expected to occupy as they mature and move through life. As we shall see later, there are many versions of "ideal sequence," all of which can be called *life courses.*

In addition to learning new concepts about aging, you must also refine and sharpen many concepts that you have already been introduced to. For example, you are probably familiar with the concept of *self,* and you probably have learned that the self is developed in interaction with other human beings. But what if the self is already well developed, as is true of many older people? In this case you need some new ideas about how people *maintain* and *defend* their self-concepts.

Finally, some of your concepts about aging probably need to be replaced with better ones—better in the sense of being more accurate and useful. For example, many people believe that mental confusion in older people is caused by a condition called *senility* that is a typical result of biological aging. However, researchers have found that mental confusion in older people can stem from a number of causes, that much of it can be reversed, and that permanent and progressive brain damage is caused by a specific disease that is not confined to the old and that is not a normal part of the aging process. Thus, it is better to replace the concept of senility as a process of aging with the concept of organic brain disease as a chronic condition that is more common among older people but that can afflict individuals of any age.

Your *factual information* about aging needs to be *representative*. Most of us get quite a bit of information from our everyday experience, and that information is often correct—*as far as it goes*. The problem is that our everyday lives do not expose us to a cross-section of all types of people or situations, even though it may seem that they do. For example, suppose someone asks, "Do people have difficulty adjusting psychologically to retirement?" And suppose we have a group of four people who are asked to respond to this question. The first is a psychiatrist who, after all, should know a lot about psychological adjustment. She says, "Yes. I see many people who are very distressed about retirement." The second is director of a planned retirement community who has lots of experience with retired people. He says, "No. In my ten years at Covebrook Center, I have seen only two people who had a significant problem in adjusting to retirement." The third is director of a senior center who says, "Yes. Many of the people who come to the center are quite anxious. They feel cut adrift and unsure of what to do." Another senior center director says, "That's interesting. At my center the people are all retired from Xenon Corporation, and they are *all* delighted with retirement!" What response can we believe? The problem is that the experience of each person is *selective*. The psychiatrist has little experience of people who don't have adjustment problems—they do not need her services. The retirement community director sees people who are healthy, wealthy, and committed to an active life-style. The senior center directors' conflicting views reflect the fact that senior centers differ quite a bit in terms of the social, ethnic, occupational, regional, and community backgrounds of their clientele.

Information collected through scientific research has at least two major advantages over information gathered from everyday experience. Social scientists examine samples of people or situations that can be *evaluated* in terms of how representative they are. This evaluation provides a basis for *weighing* evidence from various sources. For example, suppose we found five studies of retirement adjustment: two based on national samples of households, one based on a sample of people retired from a government agency, one based on a sample of people who live in a small community in the South, and one based on a sample of unknown origin. *All other things being equal*, the two national studies would get the greater weight because they better represent the national experience.

The second advantage of scientific information is that the *procedures* used to collect the information and arrive at conclusions based on it are explicit. This specificity gives us another tool that can be used to weigh the evidence. Weighing scientific evidence requires experience and practice and is one of my major jobs as author of this book. The facts seldom speak for themselves. They need to be interpreted and put into context. And by watching how it is done in this book, you can learn more about how to do it yourself.

In addition to learning new factual information, you will face the problem of what to do with old information. No one likes to be wrong, and much of what passes for information about aging in everyday life is inaccurate. When you look at any piece of information, there are two basic questions to ask: "Is it true?" and "How often is it true?" Very seldom is a "truth" always true. An important part of your knowledge concerns proportion—the *relative* frequency with which a phenomenon occurs. Thus, our earlier question was poorly phrased. It should not be categorically "Do people have difficulty adjusting psychologically to retirement?" but rather "How common is difficulty in adjusting psychologically to retirement?" The best general answer is that about 10 percent of people who retire find the adjustment psychologically difficult and 90 percent do not. Some of what you now think about aging will turn out to be completely incorrect. But more often you will only need to adjust your ideas about proportions. This mental housecleaning may be an uncomfortable process, especially if you tend to hold strongly to your beliefs.

To understand something, you must grasp its underlying logic—you must know its parts and how they relate to form an operating whole. No matter whether we are concerned with biological aging, psychological aging, or social aging, the underlying logic must be known if we are to understand what is happening. For example, as people grow older they often become less involved in the activities of organized groups. Why? As we shall see, there are at least two important underlying dimensions to this pattern. First, as people grow older they are often less interested in taking responsibility in groups because the obligations interfere with their hardwon freedom. And second, as people grow older organizations are less likely to seek them to take positions of responsibility. Thus, to increase the involvement of older people in organizations would require *both* a change in older people's motivation to participate *and* greater willingness among organizations to recruit older people for responsible positions. Your study of aging should give you an effective set of understandings of how various aspects of aging operate in the lives of aging individuals.

A basic understanding of aging also requires concrete examples. Abstractions and general information allow the connectedness of things to be seen in an *intellectual* way, but for this intellectual understanding to have value it must help people see that connectedness in a *practical* way. Throughout this book are many illustrations of concrete situations that led to the development of ideas, illustrations of what the ideas imply for specific situations, and examples of how concepts are linked in everyday life.

You should come away from your study of aging with a sense of the issues—the major points of contention. For example, is chronological age a good predictor of performance? Is mandatory retirement justified? Is the Social Security program adequate? Are older people neglected by their families? Should programs be for all older people or just for the needy? These and many other issues need to be raised and discussed.

Benefits of Studying Aging

Knowledge of aging can improve your interactions with aging or older people by helping you see the world from their viewpoints. Studying aging cannot tell you what a particular older person's viewpoint is but it can show you that older people vary so widely on so many dimensions that stereotypes of older people's viewpoints are not very useful as a basis for action. It can help you be open to their point of view. And a study of aging can also motivate you to find out enough about an aged person to have a basis for genuine empathy.

Empathy is essential if you want to serve older people effectively. *Serving the elderly is mainly a process of assisting competent people to pursue goals of their own choosing.* Understanding their goals requires both knowledge of the other person and skill in setting aside your own viewpoint so that it does not interfere with your ability to see theirs.

Knowledge about aging can also improve your ability to make sound decisions, whether they be decisions about your own life, decisions about what social policies are needed, decisions about what programs need to be developed, or decisions about whether current programs are operating effectively.

What Is Aging?

Aging is a broad concept that includes *physical* changes that occur in our bodies over adult life, *psychological* changes in our minds and in our mental capacities, and *social* changes in how we are viewed, what we can expect, or what is expected of us. The study of aging also includes the *effects on societies or groups* of having members who are aging.

It is common to think of human life in terms of a period of *maturation* in which the person develops, a period of *maturity* in which the person exercises his or her full powers, and a period of *aging* in which the person gradually diminishes. This view is based on the biological characteristics of life in both animals and plants. But such a view of human aging is too simplistic. Even biological aging is the result of many processes that progress at different rates. For example, the kidneys typically show diminished functioning much sooner than the skin does. In addition, we achieve maturity for different physical functions at different ages. For instance, we usually reach sexual maturity several years before we reach our full height. To confuse matters further, most physical functions vary quite a bit among individuals at all stages of life.

When we examine the psychological effects of the passage of time in adulthood, we find that some dimensions diminish with aging, others in-

crease, and some remain relatively constant throughout adulthood. For example, visual acuity generally declines with age, vocabulary usually increases, and habits tend to remain relatively constant throughout adulthood. Variability is as great or greater for psychological aging than it is for physical aging.

On the other hand, defining social aging is largely an arbitrary process of defining what is appropriate or expected of people of various ages, based very loosely on information about what people of various ages are typically capable of. Thus, school begins at age 6, even though most children are quite capable of beginning sooner and many do. Airline pilots must retire at age 60 even though most are still quite capable of continuing. The age when young people are considered old enough to marry varies from age 13 to 16 in Appalachia, to 25 to 30 in Chinatown. As a result, social aging adds yet another dimension of variability to an already complex problem.

Aging is not one process but many, and it has many possible outcomes, some positive and some negative. On the one hand, aging increases the amount of experience one can have and thus brings opportunities to gain wisdom or to become quite skilled at subtle arts and crafts ranging from politics to music. Wisdom and experience can give an older person the kind of long-range perspective that is invaluable in an advisor. Older people can also be keepers of tradition. They have information about many unrecorded events that have happened over the years in families, workplaces, communities, and the nation. Aging can also bring personal peace and mellowing. Later life can be a time of extraordinary freedom and opportunity once the heavy responsibilities of employment and of child rearing are set aside. On the other hand, aging for some people is a losing proposition. They may lose physical or mental capacities, they may lose their good looks, they may lose the opportunity for employment and the income that goes with it, they may outlive their spouse and friends, or they may lose their positions in organizations. *Aging is neither predictably positive nor predictably negative.* For some it is mainly positive, for others it is mainly negative, and for still others it is somewhere in between.

How aging is viewed by society reflects the two-sided nature of aging. In some quarters, such as politics, the advantages of age are stressed. In others, such as industrial employment, the disadvantages are emphasized. In still others, such as in the family, both sides are accepted. And the emphasis changes over time. For example, in the early days of the United States aging was much more likely to bring infirmity than now. Yet older men were in charge. They made the laws, led the troops, ran the enterprises, and set the moral tone for the country. The fact that this responsibility was difficult for most older men to bear physically was seen as less important than the contribution they could make (Fischer, 1978). The rationale for this patriarchy was founded in the European aristocratic tradition.

However, the egalitarian ideology that swept through Europe and America in the nineteenth century brought with it a new order based on achievement rather than on inherited or ascribed position. The negative side of aging took on more importance as competition, productivity, and efficiency replaced tradition as the dominant values of the marketplace. It was not that aging always produced incapacity. Aging only had to produce incapacity *sometimes* to put older workers at a disadvantage in a labor market glutted by European immigrants and migrants from agricultural areas. And forced retirement in the absence of pensions meant poverty for huge numbers of older Americans. By the 1930s, the number of older people living in poverty was enormous. Aging came to be equated with poverty and shabbiness.

But then the pendulum began to swing the other way. The Social Security program began to deliver pensions in 1940. A national welfare program for the elderly was established. In 1948 private pensions were declared legal as a point of collective bargaining between unions and management. In 1961 the White House Conference on Aging directed political attention to the inequities suffered by older Americans. In 1965, the Older Americans Act was passed, which led to the development of comprehensive service programs for older Americans. Medicare was enacted in 1966 to provide health care financing for most older people. The 1972 amendments to the Older Americans Act created a national network of services. The Age Discrimination Act of 1975 outlawed age discrimination in all programs receiving federal funds. In 1978 the mandatory retirement age was raised to 70.

The fact that there is still much room for improvement should not be allowed to obscure the fact that vast improvements in the situations of older Americans have occurred over the past 40 years. The important point here is that whether aging is seen as good or bad is not inherent in the processes of aging or their outcomes but is a product of the prevailing social ideology. What that ideology will be in the future is uncertain, but the past 30 years are a history of movement toward a more positive view of aging and the aged.

The double-edged nature of aging can also be found in the current literature on aging. Some researchers emphasize the negative aspects of aging. They focus on sickness, poverty, isolation, and demoralization. The theories they develop seek to explain how people arrive at such an unhappy state. And they tend to see aging as a social problem. Other researchers emphasize the positive. They look at the elderly and see that most have good health, frequent contact with family members, adequate incomes, and a high degree of satisfaction with life. The theories they develop try to explain how aging can have such positive outcomes. They see the social problems of aging as applying to only a minority of the elderly. Because aging can have both positive and negative outcomes, neither side is wrong. Certainly both kinds of outcomes exist, and understanding both kinds of outcomes is important. However, it is also important to acknowledge that *positive outcomes outnumber the negative by at least two to one.*

The dual nature of aging is reflected in the fact that aging is both a social problem and a tremendous social achievement. For a significant minority of older Americans, the system does *not* work. They have difficulty securing adequate incomes, work, social services, adequate health care, and better housing and transportation. That these difficulties recur regularly certainly represents a significant social problem. Yet for the majority of older Americans, the system does work. They are in good health, have modest but adequate retirement pensions, own their own homes, drive their own cars, and need little in the way of social services. And *the fact that most elderly people do not need assistance makes it possible to do something for those who do.*

Who Are the Aging and the Aged?

Aging begins long before it becomes obvious. But to use age as a social attribute, it is necessary to identify *indicators* of aging. Aging can be defined by chronological age, functional capacity, or life stage.

Birth certificates provide a clear means of assessing *chronological age.* Chronological age definitions arose out of a need to set a point at which

rules and policies should be applied and to separate those people who were eligible for benefits from those who were ineligible. However, because the relationship between chronological age and the results of aging is not very strong, all chronological definitions misclassify a large proportion of the population. For example, age 65 is the most commonly used chronological age for classifying people as aged or elderly. At this age people are eligible for full retirement benefits from Social Security, and 65 is the age of eligibility for Medicare.

The rationale for using age 65 was in part that mandatory retirement most commonly occurred at 65, so this was the point at which people needed retirement benefits and assistance in financing health care. Yet thousands of people become unable to work due to poor health *prior to* age 65, and thousands more continue employment *after* age 65. Even though there has been some provision made for early retirement at age 62, workers who retire early are penalized by getting lowered benefits. And those who delay retirement beyond 65 are not given a proportionate benefit increase. Thus, the use of age 65 as the age for defining need for certain programs includes people (such as the employed) who do not need the programs and excludes people (such as those who are under 62 and in ill health) who do need the benefits the program provides. These are the costs of using chronological age, and sometimes the costs outweigh the benefits of easy administration. Ask anyone who would like to work longer in order to earn a higher Social

Security retirement benefit but can't because the program is dominated by the idea of 65 as *the* retirement age.

The problem is compounded by the fact that many different chronological ages are used to define "older." At age 45, a worker is defined as "older" by the U.S. Department of Labor. At age 62, people become eligible to live in housing for the elderly. At age 60, widows become eligible for early retirement under Social Security. And these examples are taken from only a few government programs. The range in all government and local community agencies is amazing. The result is a confusing hodge-podge of definitions that hardly reflect consensus about when individuals typically become old. Nevertheless, age 65 remains dominant as the legal definition of when a person becomes "older," so it also dominates as the most often-used research definition of the point at which people become aged, older, or elderly.

Functional definitions rely on observable individual attributes to assign people to age categories. Appearance, mobility, strength, coordination, and mental capacity are examples of such attributes. Gray hair, wrinkled skin, and stooped posture are commonly used general criteria for categorizing people as old. Adults who move stiffly, tentatively, and with poor coordination exhibit the physical frailty that we associate with old age. And people who are very forgetful, sometimes confused, and hard of hearing have some of the psychological frailties associated with old age. Anyone who has all these attributes is undoubtedly old regardless of chronological age. Fortunately, only a very small percentage of people has even a few of these attributes; therefore, classifying people into age categories based on functional attributes is an uncertain process in most cases. In addition, functional age definitions vary from environment to environment. For example, one may become a functionally old pro tennis player as early as age 30 or 35, whereas one may remain a functionally capable judge at age 90. Because they are so difficult to assess, functional age definitions are seldom used in research, legislation, or social programs. Nevertheless, we do use them in our everyday lives to get a general feeling of where to place people along the functional age continuum.

Very often we combine physical attributes with social ones to categorize people into broad *life stages* such as adolescence, young adulthood, adulthood, middle age, later maturity, or old age. *Middle age* is the life stage in which most people first become aware that physical aging has noticeably changed them. They become aware that they have less energy than they used to, and they often begin to look for less physically demanding activities. Recovery from exertion takes longer. Chronic illness becomes more prevalent. Vision and hearing begin to decline.

Job careers often reach a plateau of routine performance in middle age. Offspring leave their parents' households to begin their own. Married couples often grow closer. People sometimes make "midcareer" job changes, and women who have raised children often increase their involvement in paying jobs. Retirement in middle age with no continuation of employment is becoming more prevalent. Middle age is also a time when people begin to experience deaths of people close to them, particularly their parents. Women sometimes become widows in middle age.

Middle age is a stage marked primarily by social transitions—at home, on the job, in the family. Significant physical transitions usually come later. Most people find middle age to be an exciting time of life. Many of its transitions involve opportunities to lead a more satisfying and sometimes less hectic life. For a few, however, middle age brings irreplaceable losses.

Chronologically, this stage usually begins around age 40, but individuals vary a great deal in terms of when they or others around them perceive that they are symptomatically middle-aged. Nevertheless, middle age is the stage at which people become part of the *aging* population (as opposed to the *aged* population).

In *later maturity*, the declines in physical functioning and energy availability that begin in middle age continue. Chronic illnesses become more common. Activity limitations become more prevalent. But even in this stage, most people continue to be relatively active adults. Mortality begins to take its toll among family and friends. Most such deaths are not associated with long chronic illnesses but instead are typically the result of acute episodes of cardiovascular disease. Deaths of family members or friends often bring home the fact of one's own mortality.

The major changes associated with later maturity are also social. Retirement typically occurs during this stage. For most people this is a welcome and beneficial change, but it usually brings a reduction in income. By contrast, a sizable percentage of women become widows during this stage, and although most manage to adjust to widowhood, adjustment is seldom easy. Deaths of friends and relatives begin to reduce noticeably the size of the everyday social environment.

Despite the aura of loss that typifies later maturity, most people retain a fair measure of physical vigor, which—coupled with freedom from responsibilities—makes later maturity one of the most open and free periods of the life course for those prepared to take advantage of it. Chronologically, this stage usually begins in the early 60s.

Old age is the beginning of the end. It is characterized by extreme physical frailty. Mental processes slow down, and organic brain disease becomes more common. People think a lot about themselves and their pasts, and try to find meaning in the lives they have led. In old age, the individual feels that death is near. Activity is greatly restricted. Social networks have been decimated by the deaths of friends and relatives and by the individual's own disabilities. Institutionalization is common at this stage. This stage of life may not be very pleasant, at least externally. Middle age and later maturity are defined mainly in terms of social factors such as the empty nest or retirement; old age is defined in terms of the physical frailty that accompanies advanced aging. Chronologically, the onset of old age typically occurs in the late 70s, but there are many people in their 80s who show no symptoms of old age.

These stages of later life are based on sets of characteristics that seem to be related in many cases. Seldom does a particular individual show each

and every symptom typical of a given phase. Moreover, these categories are based on characteristics other than chronological age. People may have the characteristics of old age at a number of chronological ages. One person may be in old age at 55, and another may be in later maturity at 85.

I use the terms *midlife* and *middle age* to refer to people who are in their 40s, 50s, and early 60s. The *aged, elderly,* and *older people* are used interchangeably to refer to people who are 65 or over. As I said earlier, these chronological definitions misclassify some people, but they are necessary in order to summarize information and make comparisons. Just remember that I am using them for convenience and that they have only limited value in helping us relate to specific individuals.

Not One Experience, But Many

Variety is a key idea to remember throughout your studying of aging. If we were to begin with a group of 1,000 high school freshmen and follow them throughout their lives, we would find that they become more unlike one another with each passing year. Some of these differences are created by differing physical attributes such as athletic ability or mental attributes such as problem-solving ability or mechanical aptitude. Others are due to emerging personality factors such as dominance-submissiveness or need for achievement. Still other differences are caused by the different sex roles assigned to males and females. People also vary widely in terms of their values, beliefs, or aptitudes, often according to the social class, race, ethnic group, size of community, or region of the country in which they grew up. Of course, we do share things in common—such as language, or political orientation, or economic philosophy. But we are an extremely pluralistic society, and aging is a highly variable set of processes that make for a huge variety of possible experiences and outcomes.

Our challenge is to identify those dimensions of aging that can best organize the vast chaos represented by the individual experiences of millions of people from all walks of life. Fortunately, although there is no denying the great variety in the older population, certain processes, events, transitions, and outcomes are common to just about everyone. And there are areas of life where we can discover the *relative* proportions of people who have various kinds of essentially similar situations.

The process of generalization is necessary for gaining an overview, but it always glosses over many exceptions—sometimes important ones. Please remember that not all your experiences have to match a particular generalization in order for it to be true *in general*. For example, it is true that a large majority of the elderly have children living nearby and are in frequent contact with them. But my next-door neighbor, who is an 84-year-old widower with no children, is an important exception.

Plan of the Book

This book is organized from the viewpoint of the aging individual. It begins with various concepts and theories that can be used to look at individual aging. Basic physical aspects of aging such as changes in sight and hearing or susceptibility to illness and disability are then considered. Next, it looks at the inner experience of aging—ideas, orientations, and the experience of personal effectiveness, autonomy, or vulnerability. Attention is then directed to how aging influences the ability to meet needs for income, housing, health care, and transportation. Next, it looks at how aging affects the use of time—employment, leisure activities, group activities, education, religion. How aging affects one's relationships with others is then considered. Transitions associated with age in the family (child launching (the empty nest), widowhood, divorce, remarriage), changes in employment (career change, employment problems, retirement), and changes in living arrangements (changes within households and changes of household, or migration) are discussed next, followed by various ways to look at adaptation to individual aging. Finally, aging as a social problem is considered, and some of the important issues for society are identified.

Throughout most of the book, there are several recurrent themes:

△ The elderly are typically capable.

△ Aging is usually both positive and negative.

△ Aging is influenced significantly by sex, social class, and minority
    group status.

I have chosen the individual as the focal point of this introduction to
aging because I think this approach is the most relevant to the largest number of people. Nevertheless, you should be aware that there are important
topics that it does not cover, primarily those dealing with society's institutions and how they respond to the aging population. The research issues,
economics, politics, or social policies of aging receive relatively little attention here.[2]

Summary

There are many motives for studying aging. But regardless of motive,
you need concepts that you can use to organize your thoughts, observations and communications, factual information to provide points of comparison, understandings that will allow you to see how various aspects of
aging are connected, and examples to bring these concepts, facts, and
understandings alive. Studying aging can have three major benefits: improved interactions with aging people as a result of your better understanding of them, increased ability to empathize with aging people, and
improved ability to make decisions about your own life and the lives of
others you encounter.
    Aging is not one process but many. It occurs at the physical, psycho-
logical, and social levels. Aging is quite variable both within a particular
individual and among separate individuals. The results of aging are not
predictably either positive or negative. Whether aging has good or bad results depends not only on what changes occur in the individual but also on
the social ideology of the era in which the person grows old.
    Aging can be measured by the calendar, by assessments of various
functions, or by life stages. Chronological definitions are by far the most
commonly used in rules or laws, but in everyday interaction we often define
age by functional capacity or by life stage such as middle age, later maturity,
or old age.
    As you continue your study of aging remember these basic points:

---

[2] Readers interested in these topics should look at another of my books, *The Social Forces
in Later Life: Introduction to Social Gerontology*, 3rd ed. (Belmont, Calif.: Wadsworth, 1980).

△ Aging is not one experience but many.

△ The elderly are typically capable people.

△ Aging usually has both positive and negative results.

△ Aging is greatly affected by the person's sex, social class, minority group status, the region of the country in which they live, the size of community in which they live, and the social ideology of the era in which they grow older.

As a result, the aging of any particular individual is a mystery to be discovered rather than a fact to be assumed.

Chapter 2

Three Ways to
Look at Aging

There is no way to make aging a simple subject, because the processes of aging are embedded in the whole of human life. Nevertheless, conceptual overviews of the basic dimensions or facets of aging can provide a context for the details. Understanding requires that we be able both to *differentiate* phenomena by means of various types and categories and also to *integrate* our specific observations into a coherent whole by means of guiding principles. *Typologies* help us with differentiation, and *theories* supply the guiding principles for integration.

Typologies and theories about aging are quite plentiful—so plentiful in fact that they themselves need to be organized and related to one another. This chapter examines three broad classes of perspectives on aging: physical, psychological, and social. Each of these perspectives approaches aging from a different viewpoint. In addition, multiple viewpoints exist *within* these basic perspectives.

I know that it must seem frustrating to have so many different approaches to aging, but each serves a purpose. And the more approaches you are familiar with, the more tools you have for diagnosing and understanding specific situations. For example, when I started to study aging, I thought that retirement meant losing one's purpose in life and that it almost always led to psychological distress. I therefore set out to document the damage that retirement did to women's self-concepts. I began with interviews of women who were retired from careers as schoolteachers. Imagine my surprise when in interview after interview I found that the women were not at all distressed about retirement; indeed, most were delighted with it. I needed another theory about retirement. Based on my interviews, I knew that these women still viewed themselves as teachers and that their identities had not been damaged by retirement. Yet some adjusted better to retirement than others.

19

Why? I began to focus on the idea of retirement as planned change, reasoning that planned changes might be smoother than unplanned ones. Sure enough, those women who were able to retire on their own planned schedule adjusted to retirement much sooner than those who retired unexpectedly. Both groups were well adjusted to retirement after a year, but the "on schedule" group got there sooner. I later tested this theory on men as well as women, on other occupational groups, and even on other types of life changes, such as widowhood. I consistently found that being able to anticipate and plan for a life change is very definitely related to making a smooth transition.

Theories are not just something intellectuals play with. They are dynamic ideas of what is going on, and why, that can be used to inform action. For example, if you are concerned with assisting employees to make a smooth transition into retirement, then the theory just given suggests various actions. For one thing, planning for retirement should make the transition smoother. Another implication is that employers should do all they can to help employees schedule retirement well in advance.

Perspectives on Physical Aging

Ideas about physical aging are tied to the concept of the *life span*—the length of life that is biologically *possible* for a given species. Among animals there are wide variations in life span, and these variations are thought to be programmed into the genetic makeup of the species. The life span of human beings is about 120 years. Of course, the life span is the maximum genetically possible length of life. *Life expectancy* is the average length of life that would occur under current mortality rates. For example, under mortality conditions in 1900 in the United States, the average length of life that could be expected was 46 years. Under conditions prevailing in 1975, life expectancy had risen to 72 years. Indications are that by the year 2000 life expectancy may approach 85 years (Fries, 1980).

The significance of physical aging is what happens to the human body *during* the life span. As mentioned in the previous chapter, human bodies go through a period of *maturation,* during which the body grows and develops to its peak level of functioning; a period of *maturity,* during which physical functioning remains at peak levels; and a period of *aging,* during which the body gradually loses its capacity for peak performance. Each of the body's systems and organs is on a slightly different schedule for maturation, the duration of maturity, and the point of onset and rate of aging.

Although this framework is useful for guiding the work of physiologists, it needs to be modified slightly to meet the needs of social gerontology. We are not as interested in aging's effects on *peak* physical performance as we are in its effects on ability to perform physically at a level that will support a typical adult life-style. We also want to take into account the availability of ways to *compensate* for effects of aging. Thus, we are interested more in ability to perform to a socially defined minimum rather than to a

physiologically defined maximum. An example may help bring home this important difference in perspectives.

In the state of Ohio, where I live, an adult must have distance visual acuity of 20/40 or better in order to get an unrestricted driver's license. Because driving a car is a common task where visual acuity is especially important, it represents a good way to illustrate the physical effects of aging. As Figure 2-1 shows, the percentage of people with uncorrected distance vision of 20/40 or better increases slightly from age 20 to 40 and then declines sharply until age 70, when it levels off. Aging reduces the percentage with 20/40 or better vision from over 90 percent at age 40 to just 30 percent at age 80. This age difference is substantial, and it affects a large proportion of people. However, if we look at *corrected* vision we get a different picture. By age 60, more than 90 percent of people are still visually eligible for unrestricted driving, and at age 80, seven out of ten older people are still visually eligible for an unrestricted license. And at age 80, another 15 percent are visually eligible for "daytime only" driving. Although I won't try to minimize the problems of becoming visually ineligible to drive, it is obvious that

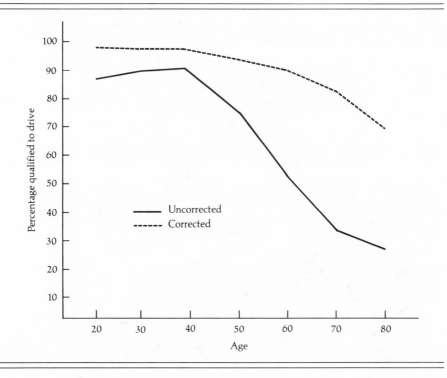

FIGURE 2-1 Percentage of People Visually Qualified to Drive, for Corrected and Uncorrected Vision.   Source: Roberts (1968:10).

compensating glasses can *substantially* minimize the social consequences of age changes in vision.

Thus, although the maturation-maturity-aging view of physical aging is generally valid, for social gerontology we are interested in functional measures of physical aging that allow for compensating mechanisms such as corrective lenses, hearing aids, or medication. And when we look at compensable age changes, the physical decrements due to aging are substantially reduced in many cases. I am not saying that aging brings no decrements. It does. However, if we look at the minimum level of functioning required of a typical adult, then social impairments resulting from aging do not become widespread until well after age 75.

Perspectives on Psychological Aging

Psychology includes the study of mental processes such as thinking, creativity, and problem-solving. Psychology is also concerned with the mind: the nature and content of consciousness, and the role of consciousness in behavior. It is concerned with interchanges between the person and the physical or social environment. It is concerned with the person's adaptations to both internal experiences and external experiences of the world. With this breadth of coverage—and the preceding list of topics is by no means complete—it is not surprising that there are many views of the nature of psychological aging and its results.

We will look at two of the major perspectives that have been used to study the psychology of aging. The first involves the study of various separate mental dimensions such as perception or intelligence. This perspective is useful for developing a basic factual description of aging's effects on specific mental processes such as hearing or problem solving. The second is a more global perspective, called *human development*, which looks at the mind and its various dimensions as an evolving whole. This second perspective is useful for gaining insights into aging's effects on the interaction between mental processes, subjective experiences, and adaptive strategies on the one hand and the individual's social environment on the other. For example, as they age, men tend to be less motivated by the prospect of achievement. This decline sometimes conflicts with what is expected of them on their jobs and requires that they develop an adaptive strategy.

Aging and Separate Psychological Functions

Processes such as perception, motor coordination, and reaction time have obvious ties to physical aging. They depend on sensory organs, neurological transmission, and muscular capacities to take in information, process it, and coordinate action based on it. The maturation-maturity-aging model is supported by research, which shows general declines with age in psychophysiological functioning.

However, when we begin to consider "higher" mental processes such as intelligence, learning, memory, creativity, thinking, and problem solving, the dependence on biological functioning is not as direct and the effects of aging are much less clear-cut. Take intelligence, for example. For a long time people thought that intelligence declined with age, and the scoring formulas for standardized intelligence tests contained an "age credit" that allowed for the fact that older people usually scored lower on such tests. However, in the 1970s research began to appear that was based on studies of various aspects of intelligence in the same people over time. When mental abilities were divided into those that are based on neurological processes in the central nervous system such as visual flexibility versus those that are based on learned abilities to evaluate or diagnose or solve problems, an interesting difference appeared. Learned abilities increased over time for adults of all ages, while biologically based abilities declined for all adults over 40 (Nesselroade, Schaie, and Baltes, 1972). Figure 2-2 shows how these processes probably work across the life span. There is no decrement in learned abilities, and the decline in overall ability is due to

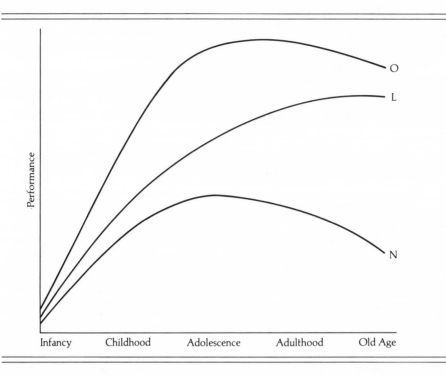

FIGURE 2-2 Development of Overall Mental Ability (O), Learned Mental Ability (L), and Mental Ability based mainly on Neurological Processing (N). Source: Adapted from Horn (1970:465).

declines in functioning within the central nervous system. Functions that are closely linked to biological functioning are negatively influenced by age, and those based on learning and experience are not. Thus, the maturation-maturity-aging view of aging is not appropriate for mental abilities that rest on prior learning and experience. In these areas, models based on stability or increment are more accurate.

Aging and Human Development

Human development theories are concerned with personality and self across the life span. The self is your perception of yourself—what you think you are like, what you think you should be like, and how you feel about the fit between the two. Personality is how you appear to others, especially your attitudes, values, beliefs, habits, and preferences. Scholars have looked at personality and self throughout life in terms of both stages and processes. The literature on human development and aging probably has more theories and concepts than any other, and even summarizing all of them lies beyond the scope of this book. Instead, I provide prominent examples of various types of theories.

Stage Theories of Human Development

The idea that people go through stages of development has been around a long time. Perhaps the most influential theory of stages of adult development was formulated by Erik Erikson (1963). Erikson's theory is mainly concerned with how people develop an identity in childhood and adolescence, but he also considered development in old age. To Erikson, identity is formed on a foundation of trust, autonomy, initiative, and industry. These qualities, developed in childhood, allow individuals to form a view of themselves as capable, worthwhile, and safe. People who do not develop these qualities have difficulty trusting others, have doubts about their abilities and feel guilt about their poor performance, feel inferior to others, and feel no basis for confidence in their ability to face the changes brought on by adulthood. Obviously, these two extremes are end points of a continuum along which individuals can vary considerably in terms of bringing a strong sense of positive identity into adulthood and later on into old age.

According to Erikson, in early adulthood the main issue in human growth and development is learning to establish *intimacy*—close personal relationships such as friend or mate. This process involves learning to unite one's own identity with that of another person. People who do not learn to develop intimacy remain isolated, relating to others but never having a sense of unity with them. In middle adulthood, the issue is *generativity* versus *stagnation*. Generativity is the ability to support others, particularly one's children and other members of younger generations. It involves caring and concern for younger people and also an interest in making a contribution to the world one lives in. Stagnation results when an individual does not learn to contribute to others. It is typified by a lack of interest in others, especially the young, a feeling of having contributed nothing, and the appearance of just going through the motions. In late adulthood, the issue is what Erikson calls *ego integrity* versus *despair*. Integrity involves being able to look at one's life as having been meaningful and being able to accept one's self as a whole being having both positive and negative dimensions, without being threatened by this acceptance. Integrity provides the basis for approaching the end of life with a feeling of having lived completely. Despair is the result of rejecting one's life and oneself and the realization that there is not enough time left to alter this assessment. The person is prone to depression and afraid of death.

Erikson's theory is both incremental and contingent. That is, life is a process of continuous growth provided one adequately resolves the issues of life's successive stages. In order to develop intimacy, one must first have developed a positive identity. In order to develop generativity, one must have the capacity for intimacy. And in order to develop integrity, one must have the feelings of connectedness and contribution that come from intimacy and generativity. This progression of human growth is closely tied to chronological age in childhood by the expectations of home and school, but in adulthood the individual is freer to move at his or her own pace. Thus, although generativity may be typically something people are learning in middle adulthood and certainly something they are supposed to be learning, many people are still trying to learn to deal with identity or intimacy and they feel irritated by demands that they exhibit generativity.

Erikson's theory is most useful for what it suggests rather than for its scientific validity. Indeed, many of the concepts in the theory, such as integrity or self-acceptance, are so difficult to measure that it may never be possible to test the theory scientifically. Nevertheless, Erikson's framework provides us with a tool for relating to people. By listening to them, we may get a sense of where they stand on the issues Erikson raised, which in turn may help us understand not only their behavior but also their priorities and their aspirations.

Mrs. Y's case is an example. Mrs. Y was in her late 60s when I first encountered her. She was an attractive, gregarious woman, and the stories she told usually affirmed basic values such as self-reliance or family responsibility. However, she had a problem in believing that her son would stick by her if she should become disabled, and as a result she felt insecure about her future. On the surface, her fear seemed unfounded. Her son kept close contact with her. He lived close by, and he seemed willing to provide for his mother's needs.

In the process of our talks, it came out that Mrs. Y's father had been an alcoholic whose erratic behavior had created many problems for Mrs. Y as a child. Although she loved her father, she did not feel that she could trust him. This same pattern of difficulty in establishing trust came up over and over again as she described her relationships with her former husband and her various friends. She was always fearful that people were going to betray her trust, and as a result she did not trust people. The problem with her son was just one example of a general personality pattern. Thus, Erikson's theory about the point in life where people learn to trust helped me to ask the questions needed to uncover the basis of Mrs. Y's fear and her difficulty in establishing satisfying long-run relationships. Knowing this, Mrs. Y's fears no longer seemed mysterious.

Levinson et al. (1978) also developed a stage theory of adult development. To Levinson, the main work of adulthood is to structure one's life in such a way as to enhance it. Like Erikson, Levinson noted the importance of intimacy and added occupational development as an important issue in early adulthood. Levinson extended Erikson's concept of generativity in middle adulthood by adding *mentoring*—a relationship in which a middle-aged adult serves as a combination parent figure and friend to a young adult.

Process Theories of Human Development

For many psychologists, human development does not involve discrete stages but instead is the result of the continuous operation of various processes of development. Riegel (1975, 1976) contends that human development arose out of a dialectic process resulting from contradictory ideas or actions produced by the constant changes occurring in the person and his or her environment. These contradictions are not deficiencies to be corrected but invitations to a new level of integration. For example, I might notice that at times I am cautious and at other times I am adventuresome. Accepting both views as valid parts of myself is a higher level of integration than putting them in opposition to one another and trying to make myself be only one or the other. Thus, "developmental and historical tasks are never completed. At the very moment when completion seems to be achieved, new questions and doubts arise in the individual and in society" (Riegel, 1976:697). To Riegel, the process of development is thus a process of resolving the doubts, questions, and contradictions that constantly flow through our consciousness. Riegel's theory is insightful in its focus on the everyday character of development. However, it says very little about the specific mechanisms for achieving the necessary resolution.

Whitbourne and Weinstock (1979) address more specifically the dynamics of continuous development. They argue that adult identity is an integration based on a person's knowledge about his or her physical and mental assets and liabilities, ideas (motives, goals, and attitudes), and social roles.[1] Identity serves to organize the interpretation of experiences—the assignment of subjective meaning to them. And identity can be modified by experience. The day-to-day contradictions that appear between the identities we bring to experience and the feedback we get from experience can be responded to in numerous ways. If the person is flexible about the content of his or her identity, then identity is a theory of the self that is constantly being tested, modified, and refined through experience (Kelley, 1955). To the extent that one's observations of oneself are honest, the theory gets better as time goes on. That is, the results our identities lead us to expect are the results we get. For example, my identity includes the idea that I am a capable speaker. Observation of myself as a speaker over several years has led me not only to predict that I can be a successful speaker but also to identify the conditions I must meet in order for success to happen. If I prepare myself by organizing my thoughts and by having the material for the speech well in hand, have a good understanding of what kinds of people will be in the audience, pay close attention to the audience response to govern the timing of my delivery, and present the speech with energy and enthusiasm, I can be reasonably sure that any speech I give will be successful. I did not get this theory from a book on public speaking. I developed it from my own experiences. And the more times the theory works, the greater my confidence in it and the greater my unwillingness to change it.

When I first started giving speeches, I often got so nervous that I could hardly speak. A large part of my anxiety was my lack of confidence about the results. I simply did not yet have faith in my theory of speaking. Over ten years of giving speeches, I developed a set of tried and true principles that now allow me to speak with confidence and assurance. But believe me,

---

[1] *Social role* is defined in detail later in this chapter.

I had to endure a lot of fear over these years to arrive at this happy state of affairs. A large measure of human growth involves living with doubts and fears while we develop the knowledge and skills necessary to perform at a personally satisfying and socially successful level.

Once skills are developed, we tend to *maintain* them by practicing them. A good bit of luck may also be involved. For example, speakers sometimes encounter members of the audience who are vocally hostile to the message being presented. What we make of such an experience—how we integrate it into our theory of speaking—depends a lot on how well developed our theory is at the time it happens. If a hostile encounter had happened to me at the beginning of my career, I might have given up speaking. I might have interpreted the incident as meaning that I was in the wrong line of work. Fortunately, for me, the first occurrence came much later. I was giving a speech I had given several times before with good success. My theory about myself as a speaker was well tested, and I simply *interpreted* the incident as an isolated experience that had no relation to my theory of speaking.

Sometimes people develop an identity but refuse to test it. They use their identity to decide how to act, but they do not let the results modify their ideas about themselves. For example, Mr. G thought of himself as a good teacher. In his discussions with colleagues, he would often talk about how rewarding teaching was for him and how well the students responded to his teaching. In fact, he was a frightful teacher. His "lectures" consisted of anecdotes about when he was in graduate school. Students complained bitterly about his poor organization, inconsistent standards for evaluating student work, and heavy reliance on irrelevant films. Students registered for his classes because he was the only professor teaching a course that many students were required to take. Mr. G maintained his erroneous theory of himself as a teacher by several means. He completely ignored negative feedback from students and other faculty to whom disgruntled students complained. He never allowed himself to be included in the campus-wide course-professor evaluation program. He required students to attend class. Eventually the gap between his own interpretation of the situation and everyone else's led to a confrontation in which Mr. G was removed from his job. Even now, Mr. G says that what happened to him was the result of campus politics and that he was fired because other faculty were jealous of his achievements with students.

Other people never quite develop a firm identity that could be tested. They don't quite know what to expect of themselves in various situations, and the result is that they behave in an inconsistent and confused way.

Aging affects the stability of identity in several important ways. First, the longer one has an adult identity, the more times one's theory of self can be tested across various situations. This experience usually results in a stable personal identity that stands up well to the demands of day-to-day living. Second, the reduction in social responsibilities associated with later adulthood can reduce the potential for conflict among various aspects of identity. For example, while he was chief financial officer for a local company, Mr. A was a dour man who rarely smiled. The "sober" identity that he saw as being required in his job carried over to much of the rest of his life. After retirement, Mr. A seemed like a new man. He smiled frequently and even laughed out loud from time to time. He rated retirement as the best time of his life, perhaps because it freed him to reach a better match between what he saw himself as *being* and what he was *doing*. He could relax at last. Third, aging for most people means continuing familiar activities in familiar environments. Most have long since developed skill and accumulated accomplishments in these arenas. All they need do now is *maintain* them.

The identity perspective also provides a basis for predicting when change might reach crisis proportions. When change in either the individual or the environment is so great that it cannot be integrated without a fundamental reorganization of one's theory of self, an identity crisis results. An identity crisis in these terms means reassessing the very foundations of one's identity. The changes that precipitate the crisis may occur in the individual or in the social situation. Consider these examples:

△ Mr. F has learned that within six months to a year he will be totally blind.

△ Mrs. T's husband died six weeks ago. They had been married 47 years.

△ Mr. M retired from teaching after 41 years.

△ Mrs. B has become increasingly frail. After 16 years of living alone as a widow, she must move in with her divorced, middle-aged daughter.

None of these changes need automatically trigger an identity crisis. Whether an identity crisis occurs depends on how central the dimension is to the individual and whether the change was anticipated. Profound physical changes usually have less ambiguous outcomes than social changes. Going blind would be a profound adjustment for most of us. But how much Mrs. T is affected by her husband's death depends how her relationship with him has fit into her identity. If they were inseparable companions whose selves were completely intertwined, or if theirs had been a marriage of convenience that had endured mainly by force of habit, makes a lot of difference in whether his death brings on an identity crisis in his wife. Mr. M may well be able to give up teaching easily if he feels that he has completed what he set out to do as a teacher and that it is time to move on. He may not be able to leave easily if he is being forced to retire when he feels he still has something to contribute. How Mrs. B resolves her dilemma depends on how she feels about being dependent—what it implies for her identity— particularly in her relationship with her daughter. Identity crises are not produced by events alone—they stem from the interpretation of events in the context of a particular identity.

Social Aspects of Aging

Individuals' lives are also structured by their social environments. We interact with one another not only as individuals but as role players. And the roles we play are organized sequentially into a life course tied to age or life stage. In addition, social processes such as socialization involve the individual with his or her social world. All these aspects of the social environment can be influenced by age.

Social Roles

Social roles are important, because individuals often define themselves in terms of these roles and their places in society are determined by them. *Roles* are the expected or typical behavior associated with positions in the organization of a group. Positions and the roles that go with them usually have labels such as *mother, teacher, senator, milling machine operator, volunteer, moviegoer,* and so on.

Obviously, we do not behave as isolated role players. We behave in relation to others in *role relationships.* That is, in the organization of a group, the various positions are related to one another in specified ways *regardless* of who the people are who occupy the positions. For example, teachers assign work and evaluate the results, and students do work and aim for a positive evaluation of it in the vast majority of cases. This much we can know in advance without knowing who the actual role players are.

A large part of everyday life consists of human relationships that are structured at least partially by the social roles and positions of the various actors. But in everyday life the action is much more like improvisational theater, in which the characters and dialogue are made up right on stage, than like formal theater, in which the action is predetermined. An example may help make this clearer.

Suppose you are a student and I am your teacher for a course on aging. When we first meet, we both have general ideas of what we can expect from each other. For example, you may expect that I already know a lot about aging and that I will use that knowledge to structure an educational experience for you. You might also expect me to evaluate your progress. I might expect that you have relatively little systematic knowledge about aging but are intelligent and interested in the subject and willing to work to improve your knowledge.

These general ideas would serve as the background for our initial interactions, but almost immediately we would begin to incorporate *personal* information into our expectations for our *specific* relationship. You might discover that I am relatively easygoing and have a good sense of humor. I might find that you are conscientious and inquisitive and that you write well. We would each gradually modify and refine our expectations for both ourselves and the other to take an increasing amount of personal informa-

tion into account. The pace of this process would depend on the willingness of each of us to disclose personal information. The longer we kept at this process, the more personalized our relationship would become. Thus, its *duration* is one of the most important aspects of any role relationship.

Aging and Social Roles

When life is filled with relatively new relationships, as in young adulthood, we are uncertain about what to expect from others and what we think they expect from us. But when life is filled with relationships of long standing, there is a large component of *security* in knowing what to expect—even if the relationship is not all that we might wish it to be. In middle age and later life, most role relationships for most people are long-standing relationships that are highly personalized.

For example, on the day I wrote this section I was 42 years old, which probably qualified me as middle-aged. I had breakfast with my son, with whom I have lived for 14 years. Then I went to my office, where I talked briefly with the office staff. The office manager has worked with me for 7 years, and I have known the secretaries more than 5 years each. I talked with a third-year student about her thesis. I had lunch with colleagues of more than 10 years each. My only contact with a stranger was a phone conversation to confirm a speech I was scheduled to give the following week. In my entire day, I never once thought about what someone else might be expecting of me or what to expect of them. I knew the people well, and they knew me. I felt comfortable with them and they with me.

Age is not a position in the structure of a group.[2] Along with other individual attributes such as sex, social class, or race, age is used to determine eligibility to occupy various positions, to evaluate the appropriateness of various positions for specific people, and to modify the expected behavior for an individual in a specific position. Let us look at each of these uses of age in turn.

In adulthood, advanced age occasionally makes people eligible for valued positions such as *retired person*, but more often it makes them ineligible to hold positions they value. Whether we are merely *assigned* to the positions we occupy, or whether we must have the opportunity to *achieve* them, or whether we *select* them, we do not simply occupy or take over or retain positions. They are usually available to us as a result of our having met certain criteria. In most societies, particular positions, rights, duties, privileges, and obligations are set aside for children, adolescents, young adults, the middle-aged, and the old. In our culture, the primary eligibility criteria are health, *age*, sex, social class, ethnicity, color, experience, and educational achievement. These criteria may be gradually modified and personalized in some cases, but overall these attributes govern eligibility in the prescribed ways.

As we pass through life, the field of positions for which we are eligible keeps changing. Young boys can legitimately be members of a neighborhood gang, pupils, and not employed—all things they cannot be as adults. As young men, they can be auto drivers, barflies, and voters—all things they cannot be as children. As older adults, they can be retired, be great-grandfathers, or pretend to be deaf—all things they cannot do as young adults. Of course, age also works negatively. For example, older people are often prevented from holding jobs, even if they want to.

In addition to eligibility, age influences the suitability of particular roles for particular people. For example, when I was 39 I began competing in local cross-country motorcycle races. Most of my friends thought I was crazy, and nearly everyone expressed disapproval either by saying that *they* would certainly never do anything that dangerous *at my age* or by nonverbal signals such as disapproving facial expressions. But no one laughed, although laughter was definitely the most appropriate response given my riding skill.

[2] There are others who would disagree with me on this assertion. See Riley et al. (1972).

Interestingly, the other racers of all ages encouraged me. These reactions illustrate, of course, that the age standards of the general society may not be adopted by all subgroups within the society. And this tendency, in turn, shows why both older people and younger people often restrict their interactions to subgroups that approve of their choices of roles.

Age also serves to *modify* what is expected of people in particular positions. Young people are often dealt with leniently in adult positions because of their inexperience. For instance, young adults often show too much impatience with others on the job. Such behavior is generally tolerated by their supervisors and is attributed to inexperience rather than to a character flaw. The same amount of impatience from a middle-aged worker would not be tolerated as long or as well. In old age, the standards may also be different. For example, an 86-year-old father is allowed to be more dependent in his relationships with his offspring than a 56-year-old father is.

Cumulative Effects

Positions that adults hold or have held provide various degrees of access to advantages such as prestige, wealth, or influence. Highly rewarded positions can be obtained either through family background or individual initiative or both. But despite the rhetoric that ours is an open class system in which one can rise from rags to riches, in reality only a tiny minority of people ever move out of the social class into which they were born.

Growing older in an advantaged social position generally means being able to accumulate personal wealth and prestige. People do not become wealthy, revered, or influential just by becoming old, but by occupying an advantaged position for a number of years. Former President Eisenhower had a great deal of prestige and influence in old age, not because he was old but because he had been both a president and a military chief. A great many of the richest and most influential Americans are old, but their age is not the reason why they are rich or influential.

In fact, their wealth and influence *discounts* their age in the sense that rich and powerful people are much less likely than others to be disqualified from participation purely on account of age. Age disqualification happens mainly to people who are already disadvantaged.

One can also be advantaged by having *exceptional* skills. Great writers, musicians, artists, therapists, diplomats and others can use their skills to offset their age and to avoid being disqualified. Segovia, Picasso, Jung, or Harriman never had to worry about age discrimination—their talents remained in demand. Other people find that age often offsets ordinary skills and leads to disqualification.

Some of the disqualifying character of age is related to erroneous beliefs about the predictability of age's effects on performance. But some is related to the scarcity of leadership positions, the desire of younger people to acquire them, and the willingness of older people to give up responsibilities.

The Life Course

As mentioned earlier, the life course is an idealized and age-related progression or sequence of roles and group memberships that individuals are expected to follow as they mature and move through life. Thus, there is an age to go to school, an age to marry, an age to "settle down," and so forth. For example, Neugarten et al. (1965) found considerable consensus among adults that people should marry in their early 20s and that men should be settled in a career by the time they are 24 to 26.

But the life course in reality is neither simple nor rigidly prescribed. For one thing, various subcultures (whether based on sex, social class, ethnicity, race, or region of the country) tend to develop unique ideas concerning the timing of the life course. For example, male auto workers tend to favor retirement in the mid-50s while physicians tend to prefer the late 60s. In addition, even within subcultures, there are often several alternatives. For instance, having made a decision to attend college, a young person often has a wide selection of types of institutions from which to choose. Thus, like a road map, the abstract concept of the life course in reality is composed of a great many alternative routes to alternative destinations.

As people grow older, their accumulated decisions about various life course options produce increased differentiation among them. Although very late in life options may diminish somewhat because of social and physical aging, the older population is considerably more differentiated than the young.

Yet even with the increased complexity of the life course with age, certain generally accepted standards serve as a sort of master timetable for the entire population. Even though there are many exceptions and variations, most Americans start school, finish school, get married, have children, experience the "empty nest," and retire, each within a span surrounding a particular chronological age, the age at which these events are *supposed* to happen. Most of us spend our lives reasonably on schedule, and when we get off schedule we are motivated to get back on again (Neugarten and Datan, 1973).

Figure 2-3 shows, very roughly, how the life course stages are related to chronological age, occupations, the family and education. More dimensions could be added but the important point is that various social institutions tend to prescribe their own career cycles and that these cycles are related to the various life stages.

The various stages of the life course are made real for the individual in three ways. First, they are related to more specific patterns such as the occupational career or family development. Second, specific expectations or age norms accompany various life stages. And finally, people are forced to make particular types of choices during given phases of the life course.

Age Norms

Age norms tell us what people in a given life stage are allowed to do and to be, and what they are required to do and to be. Age norms sometimes operate very generally to specify dress, personal appearance, or

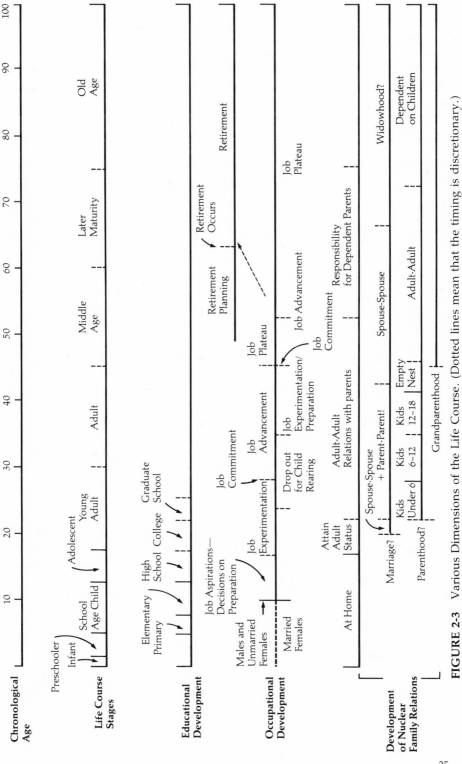

FIGURE 2-3 Various Dimensions of the Life Course. (Dotted lines mean that the timing is discretionary.)

demeanor in a wide variety of social roles. Other age norms govern approach, entry, incumbency, and exit from social roles, groups, or social situations (Atchley, 1975b). Many age norms come down to us through tradition. On the other hand, legal age norms are often the result of compromise and negotiation. A series of assumptions underlie age norms. These assumptions, often uninformed, concern what people in a given life stage are capable of—not just what they *ought* to do, but what they *can* do. Thus, both children and older people experience limited opportunities because others assume that they are not strong enough, not experienced or educated enough, or not capable of adequately mature adult judgments.

For instance, older workers are passed by for training opportunities because "You can't teach an old dog new tricks." Older job applicants are passed over on the assumption that people aged 60 have too few years left to work to warrant investing in them. By the same token, young adults are passed over because they "don't have enough experience."

Sometimes age norms make useful and valid distinctions. For example, few of us would want to drive automobiles if 6-year-olds were allowed to take to the roads. But beginning with adolescence it becomes increasingly difficult to justify the essentially arbitrary nature of many age norms. And the greater the gap between the actual level of individual functioning and the level implied by the age norm, the more likely that age norms will be seen as unjust.

I once attended a workshop called "Growing Older." About half of the 250 people there were over 60, and about a fourth were under 35. A man of about 65 said, "I get tired of people taking one look at me and assuming that I'm too old to be able to handle responsibility. I volunteered for responsibility, and, damnit, that's what I want!" A young man of about 25 said, "I've been supervising employees at the plant for six years now. I do a good job, and I get respect from the men who work under me, even the older ones. But every time I put in for a promotion, I'm told I don't have enough experience. I'm tired of hearing it." Both men were expressing their frustrations about what they saw as the injustices of age norms.

Various mechanisms secure conformity to age norms. People are taught early in life by their parents, teachers, and peers how to apply age norms to themselves. If they do not conform, friends, neighbors, and associates can be counted on to apply informal pressures. In the formal realm, regulations bring bureaucratic authority to bear. And finally, laws put the full power of the state behind age norms. For example, the idea of retiring by age 70 is supported at every level along this continuum.

Decision Demands

The sometimes chaotic nature of the alternatives presented by various life courses has been mentioned earlier. This chaos is minimized to some degree by age, sex, social class, ethnicity, and so forth. But how do people get into *specific* situations? It is impossible to assign people to each and every niche in complex, rapidly changing societies. Decision demands force the individual to work within the system to find a slot in the social organization.

Decision demands require that selections be made from an age-linked field of possibilities.[3] For example, after completing preparatory education, young adults usually enter a period of job experimentation. The field of possibilities expands dramatically immediately after graduation (certification) and continues to expand while the individual gains job experience. But there is an increasing expectation that people will find positions of employment into which they will settle; during this period the field of jobs for which they are eligible may slowly contract. Contraction also occurs as jobs are selected by others of similar age and experience. For many jobs, career tracks are difficult to begin after age 45.[4] For others, it is difficult to break in after age 35.

Decision demands tend to be concentrated in the first half of the life course. That is, individuals are *required* to make choices and select their "career tracks" in all sorts of areas—education, employment, family, community, voluntary associations, and so on. Life-styles developed before or during middle age tend to persist as long as health and money hold out. Thus, middle-aged people who want to switch tracks or get involved in new areas often must confront the fact that the available slots were taken earlier by their age peers.

On the other hand, those middle-aged people who do retrain and switch careers often find that their new careers develop at an accelerated rate compared to those younger people starting at the same time. This acceleration is probably due to their greater maturity and general experience plus the underlying notion that a person's position in an organization should match his or her life stage. More research is needed on this phenomenon.

Social Processes

Socialization is a group of processes through which a group encourages and/or coerces its members to learn and conform to its culture—the distinctive way of life of the group. It is society's means for creating capable participants. *Acculturation* is the actual learning of a culture. Much of what we seek to learn through acculturation is aimed at making us more effective role players. Some social scientists use the term *socialization* to refer to both (1) the action initiated by the group toward the individual *and* (2) the individual's response to it. To the individual, socialization and acculturation are important prerequisites for getting whatever society has to offer. If people know and understand the social system, they can potentially put the system to use. If they do not understand the way of life where they live, their lives can be confusing and unpredictable. Thus, people are usually motivated to become acculturated.

[3] For a more detailed discussion of decision demands, see Atchley (1975b).
[4] The term *career* as used here refers to experience in any particular role attached to an ongoing group.

For society, socialization produces a measure of continuity from one generation to another. After all, society needs new participants, and socialization is a major process through which society attracts, facilitates, and maintains participation. The efforts of the group to help individuals learn the system range from formal, structured programs in which the group is responsible for the outcome to unstructured, informal processes in which the individual is responsible for the outcome. For example, families are expected to teach children to speak, and schools are expected to teach children to read and write. On the other hand, adults must generally find out on their own how to locate a physician.

Age affects what the individual is expected to know and what he or she needs to know in order to be an effective participant in society. Early in life, the emphasis in socialization is on learning language and customs; then it shifts to preparing for adult social roles. In adulthood, expectations gradually shift toward self-initiated acculturation; that is, adults often recognize their need for knowledge and skills and go after them without waiting to be told (Brim, 1968). At the same time, fewer publicly supported, formal opportunities exist for socialization in adulthood compared to the opportunities that exist for young people.

Rosow (1974) has argued that because norms for the aged do not exist there is nothing to socialize the aged *to*. Although this argument may be accurate in terms of formal socialization, its applicability is questionable in terms of acculturation. Older people often have few required contacts with the general community. They associate primarily with people they know and who know them. In addition, most older people continue to function mainly in roles they have occupied for many years. The point is that most roles older people play are roles they have been socialized to for a long time. Aging often results primarily in adjusting the nuances of role playing rather than its basic structure.

Most societies pay little attention to their adult members' needs for maintenance or renewal of their knowledge or skills. In this age of the computer, for example, where do middle-aged or older adults go to learn how to use this new way of dealing with information? As we shall see later, this pattern seriously hampers the ability of some older members of society to remain integrated in the society, particularly in terms of the knowledge and skills required for employment. If older people need information and skills that are necessary for participation in society but that cannot be secured by older people themselves, then the socialization processes in the society are not adequate.

Much adult acculturation comes from experience. For example, Kohlberg (1973a) points out that the moral development of young people is mainly cognitive and symbolic. But in order for the person to develop what Kohlberg calls *principled thinking*—"principles to which the society and the self *ought to be committed*" (1973a:194)—it is not enough merely to "see" the principles. The person must also experience sustained responsibility for the welfare of others and experience having to make irreversible moral choices. A similar process occurs in other areas of life, such as mate selection, career choice, choice of residence, and so on. The adult develops life principles—a philosophy of life—in a dialectic process between what is known, what is experienced, and his or her personality. And, theoretically at least, the longer one lives, the greater the opportunity for this dialectic to produce refinements in one's approach to living.

For instance, it is one thing to know intellectually that telling lies is wrong, and it is quite another to have experienced the results of having lied. When we are young, it is difficult to believe that all of the do's and don'ts we are taught are necessary. As we get older, our experiences give us a fuller understanding of why rules exist. Older people are often more committed to basic moral principles compared to the young, not because they are rigid but because life has taught them the value of following the rules.

The process of *anticipation* involves learning the rights, obligations, resources, and outlook of a position one will occupy in the *future*. To the extent that the future position is a general one, it need not represent an unknown. Through fantasies, it is possible to anticipate what the future will hold, identify potential problems, and to prepare in advance (Atchley, 1976). The role changes common to later life can often be anticipated, thus smoothing the process of transition.

However, many roles we take up in later life have a degree of vagueness that allows some flexibility in playing them but at the same time hinders anticipation. Such roles are not "packaged," as roles that young people play are. For example, the role of high school student is much more clearly defined than the role of retired person. As a result, older people must often negotiate the rights and duties of their positions with significant other people in their environment. Thus, in late adulthood, acculturation—learning or relearning how to function in one's social milieu—depends heavily on the characteristics of others with whom the older person must negotiate. The attitudes of others concerning who the older person is becoming are probably crucial to the content of acculturation in later life. As images of aging become less stereotyped in American culture, the outcome of these negotiations can be expected to become more positive.

Social roles, even the specific ones such as mother or teacher, tend to be defined in terms that allow room for interpretation. *Adaptation* to roles is a process of fitting role demands to the individual's capabilities. Negotiation—the interpersonal aspect of this adaptation—takes place between role players. This process of tailoring the role to fit the individual and the situation means that it is impossible to describe *the* role of *the* grandfather. We can only describe some of the similarities and differences we find when we look at how grandfathers play their roles and what these similarities or differences are related to.

Thus, through socialization society tells its members that retirement is normal and that it should occur at around age 65. Through acculturation, an individual comes to *believe* that retirement is normal and that it should occur at around age 65. Through anticipation, the individual identifies potential problems associated with retirement and tries to solve them in advance. Once the individual retires, the process of adaptation involves tailoring the rather vague retirement role to fit the needs of the individual. Part of this process may involve negotiations between spouses about what the retirement role will consist of and how it will influence their life together.

Summary

There are three basic ways to look at aging. It can be viewed as a biological phenomenon involving maturation, maturity, and decline of the body and its various functions. Aging can also be viewed as a process of mental development that involves a great deal of continuity in functioning, some declines in functioning, and some increases in functioning. Or aging can be viewed as a socially defined phenomenon in which chronological age is used to define people's capabilities and opportunities. All these approaches are true, and all are limited. In combination, they provide concepts that can be used to better understand aging.

The physical model of aging as a process of maturation, maturity, and decline is useful for guiding the work of physiologists, and it tends to accurately describe what happens to various bodily functions in general over the life span. But for our purposes the maturation-maturity-aging model has two serious limitations. First, because there is so much variability among people and between functions even within the same person, the model is not very useful for telling us what to expect in specific cases. Second, because many declines in physical functions can be completely or partially compensated for, the model very greatly overestimates the effects of aging on social functioning. Social impairments due to aging do not become widespread until well after age 75.

Psychological aging can be viewed either as a process of change in specific mental factors such as memory or motor coordination, or as a more global process of evolution in the mind and its various dimensions. From the perspective of specific traits, aging has variable results. Functions such as vision, reaction time, or memory that have a strong dependence on the body and its level of functioning are much more likely to decline with age than are learned functions such as vocabulary, creativity, or problem solving that depend more on the mind and are more easily maintained by practice. Some mental functions increase steadily with age, some remain relatively constant, and some decline. Therefore, the effects of aging on mental capacities cannot be assumed to follow any single pattern.

From the human development perspective, aging can be viewed either as a process of moving through several discrete stages or as a continuous process of unfolding. Erikson's is the most often-used stage theory. It assumes that humans evolve through a building-block approach of establishing capability, worth, and safety by confronting a predictable series of life issues. The first is intimacy versus isolation and is usually resolved in early adulthood. The second is generativity versus stagnation, which is often an issue of middle adulthood. The final issue, ego integrity versus despair, is usually an issue of later life. Erikson's theory is useful in helping to identify where people are in the developmental process. It is less useful as a means of predicting the central issues of a person's life.

Process theories of human development view aging as a matter of continuously taking in information about the self, interpreting that information in light of a theory of self, and refining the theory based on experience. The concern here is with identity and how it evolves over the life span. Aging can solidify the theory of self by providing a large amount of experience about the self. The reduction in job and parenting responsibilities that often accompanies aging can reduce the potential for conflict among the various aspects of identity. Aging is more a process of identity maintenance than a process of identity formation. Identity crises result from age changes in the individual or the environment that cannot be accommodated without a complete reorganization of the person's self-concept. No life change predictably causes identity crises. Identity crises result from the individual's interpretation of life events.

Social aging involves the use of age by society to assign people to positions and opportunities based on their chronological age or life stage. Age is used to determine eligibility, evaluate appropriateness, and modify expectations with respect to various positions in society. Positions in groups and the roles and relationships that go with them largely define the participation of people in their society. At the beginning, we tend to play roles rather formally, but the longer we have been in a role the more personalized the role becomes and the more comfortable we are in it. Aging is a socially satisfying process to many people because it increases the duration and therefore the security of their role relationships. Holding an advantaged social position for a long time can also result in an accumulation of advantages such as wealth, prestige, and influence. Holding a position for a long time can also lead to the development of exceptional skills that can be used to offset the disqualifying character of older age as an eligibility criterion.

The life course is an ideal sequence of roles a person is expected to play as he or she moves through life. There are many versions of the life course, depending on the sex, ethnicity, or social class of the individual. The time schedule implied by the life course can also change over historical time, so that the ideal time to marry in one era may be much older than the ideal time to marry in another era, for example. As people grow older, their accumulated decisions about various life course options result in increased differentiation among them.

The life course determines the opportunities and limits for people in a given life stage and decision demands require people to make choices from among the options open to them. The older one gets within a given life stage, generally the narrower the range of options left.

The age norms used to allocate people to positions and roles are based loosely on ideas about what people of various ages are capable of as well as about what is appropriate for them. The greater the gap between the assumptions about functioning implied by the age norm and the actual level of functioning of the individual to whom the norm is applied, the more likely that the age norm will be seen as unjust.

Society conveys age norms through socialization, and individuals learn them through acculturation. As age increases, opportunities for formal socialization decrease. As adult experience increases, so does appreciation for the value of following rules. Anticipation allows people to prepare for and to smooth life transitions. Adaptation and negotiation processes allow people to fit themselves to new roles and vice versa.

In the previous chapter, I said that aging can have both positive and negative outcomes, and that it is mainly positive for most people, and that it is unpredictable for any given individual. The material in this chapter further illustrates why this is so. Variety among people increases with age as a result of biological, psychological, and social processes that operate differentially.

No single model or set of assumptions about the effects of aging can capture the reality of aging. Yet the perspectives given in this chapter provide you with a rich source of ideas that you can use to organize your thoughts, observations, and communications about aging.

Chapter 3

What Are the Facts about Aging?

Beliefs about physical and mental changes that result from aging are used to develop and justify ideas about appropriate behavior both for the aged themselves and of others toward them. Throughout this book, we will be constantly trying to establish whether various social patterns exist because of the *actual* limitations imposed by age, or because of *presumed* limitations that have no basis in fact. To do this, we must have at least a *general* idea of what the basic "facts" of aging are.[1]

Most of us are uncomfortable about physical aging because it must ultimately lead to death. And because much of physical aging is decremental, we may fear that death will be preceded by a lengthy period of physical and mental misery. Moreover, when we look at how physical aging has affected the appearance, alertness, or agility of the older people we see, it is difficult to imagine that such people could lead happy and satisfying lives.

Let me assure you that although it is true that we will all eventually die, the vast majority of us will live long and full lives without *ever* experiencing lengthy periods of disability or dependency. Also remember that there is little about a healthy, vital older person that would cause you to notice him or her. For instance, when you go into a supermarket, do you notice the healthy older people there? Probably not. Nothing about them attracts your attention. They move about at the same pace everyone else does, their posture and alertness is similar to those of other adults. But what about the frail or disabled older person? There is plenty to notice about them. They move slowly or with difficulty. They may need assistance in the

---

[1] For a more detailed discussion of physical aging, see Atchley (1980b).

checkout line. Often they are accompanied by someone who assists them in making their selections, managing the grocery cart, and so on. Frail older people also look different compared to those who are healthy. They often have bent posture; they look as if what they are doing is an effort. But if the thousands of older people that I have studied are telling the truth, it is quite typical to endure physical aging and still feel that life is meaningful and satisfying. Keep this in mind as we review the basic facts about physical and mental aging.

What Is Physical Aging?

Physical aging is the result of many physical processes that gradually decrease the *viability* and increase the *vulnerability* of the body.[2] As we age, the balance of conditions necessary to sustain life becomes more precarious. This fragility can be seen at every level—cells, molecules, tissues and organs, and the control systems of the whole body. In addition, the ability of our bodies to fend off disease decreases as we age.

But even though there is a genetically determined maximum life span for our species, it is also clear that both heredity and environment can substantially alter this species-wide maximum. Rates of physical aging vary greatly from individual to individual. Moreover, as noted earlier, various tissues, organs, systems, and functions age at varying rates even within the same individual. Thus, as a group of age peers increases in age so do physical and mental variations among the individuals. In short, although we can specify generally what physical aging is, we cannot predict *when* it will occur for a particular function in a particular individual or the *rate* at which the change will occur.

Physical and mental aging affect the functioning of our minds and bodies in many ways. Physical aging alters the amount of energy we can mobilize; affects our stature, mobility, and coordination; alters our physical appearance; and increases our susceptibility to physical and mental illness. Mental aging influences our ability to get, process, and act on information.

As we look at these various kinds of changes in detail, we need to ask three basic questions:

1. What usually happens?

2. Can decrement be prevented, treated, reversed, or compensated for?

3. What are the *social* consequences of the typical change?

---

[2] For a more detailed discussion, see Atchley (1980b).

Physical Energy

The amount of physical energy that a person has is a function of the body's capacity to deliver oxygen and nutrients throughout the body and to remove waste products. This process requires a vast amount of coordination among the various systems of the body. And because aging reduces both the body's capacity to coordinate its systems and the level of functioning of these systems, aging reduces the supply of physical energy that the body can mobilize.

For example, Shock (1977) reported that the ability to get oxygen into the blood peaks at about age 20, remains relatively high through about age 45, and then declines steadily. At age 80, the volume of oxygen that can be gotten into the blood is only about half as much as at age 40. Accordingly, although muscle strength remains relatively constant through age 70, maximum work output declines steadily after age 40 (Shock and Norris, 1970).

However, the socially important issue is the extent to which this decline interferes with typical social functioning. Shock (1977:655) reported that at low to moderate levels of physical work, age does not affect the ability to perform work. The only age effect was a somewhat longer time required to recover from work. Most work that American adults perform is in the low to moderate range and is thus well within the physical capacities of older adults who do *not* have disabling chronic conditions (at least 60 percent of the elderly).

But physical energy is more than simply the ability to perform work. It is also a function of drives and motivation. Drives are unlearned bodily states, frequently experienced as feelings of tension or restlessness, that make people want to act. When a person is hungry, for example, feelings of tension and restlessness do not have to be learned—they just appear. The sex drive is another important example.

One central theme of common nonsense about aging is that aging causes the sex drive to disappear. Masters and Johnson (1966) concluded that with regard to sex, the old adage "Use it or lose it" appears to be largely true. People who have sex often tend to maintain that pattern into late life. Women sometimes experience physical changes in their sex organs following menopause, and without treatment these changes can lead to painful coition and orgasm. This difficulty in turn can lead to a reluctance to engage in sex. However, this condition is *treatable* and is not a change in sex drive per se. For men, physical illness rather than a declining sex drive appears to be the most important biological factor influencing sexual behavior. For men who encounter a reduction in sexual behavior in later life, social factors such as the death of a spouse or institutionalization and psychological factors such as fear of failure play at least as important a part as physical aging.

Motives are closely related to drives. Drives are very generalized dispositions toward action. Superimposed on these generalized states are patterns of *learned behavior* that give specific direction to these general tendencies to act. Motives are thus specific, goal directed, and learned.

We know very little about motives, but what evidence there is indicates that capacity for motivation changes only slightly with age. Elias and Elias (1977:379) pointed out that, as a factor in poor performance, too much motivation can be as bad as too little. For example, much research on psychological functioning in later life is based on the performance of older people in laboratory situations. Often older research participants' desire to do well is so high that it interferes with their performance. And part of their desire to do well is based on their perception that the experimenters expect them *not* to do well. This problem also occurs in situations where older people are "tested" for job assignments. Sainer and Zander (1971) reported that older people would not volunteer if they had to go through any sort of testing procedure. However, with training, older people can be taught to perform well on most tests.

Stature, Mobility, and Coordination

Physical activity also depends on the structure of the body and on our ability to move effectively. As we grow older, we get shorter, partly because bones that have become more porous develop curvature and partly because some older people carry themselves with a slight bend at the hips and knees. A height loss of 3 inches is not uncommon. Older women are especially likely to find themselves too short to reach conveniently in environments where heights and widths are the common "adult standard." For example, standard kitchen cabinets, sinks, and counters tend to be too high and too deep.

Ability to move may also be influenced by aging. For example, we know that with age arthritis increases and that connective tissue in joints stiffens. However, we do not know how these changes influence ability to flex and extend arms, legs, or fingers. This is a major area in need of research.

We know much more about coordination. Physical coordination is a complex process that involves taking in sensory information, attaching meaning to it through perception, selecting appropriate action based on that perception, transmitting instructions to various parts of the body that need to act, and initiating action. Coordination depends on several body systems. Sensory systems provide information. Neurological systems transmit that information to the brain. Various parts of the brain handle perception and selection, initiation, and monitoring of action. Various muscle groups perform action under the control of the nervous system and the brain. In most cases, these separate functions occur in such rapid succession that the interval between sensation and response action is minute. This rapidity is especially true of practiced skills such as typing, playing a musical instrument, or operating familiar equipment.

Aging can influence coordination by influencing any of the systems that support physical activity. In fact, however, sensory systems and muscle groups are generally more than able to perform well into old age. Coordination and performance are much more likely to be influenced by age changes in the brain-based functions, especially by a slowdown in decision making related to performance (Welford, 1959:563).

For example, suppose a 70-year-old man is just learning to play the piano. His eyesight and sense of touch would probably be quite adequate to the task, as would his muscle tone and strength in his arms and fingers. His progress would be much more likely to be limited by the speed with which he could interpret notes and decide which keys to play and when. Chances are that he would have to go very slowly until the translation process became habitual. On the other hand, a 70-year-old man who had been playing the piano with skill for 60 years would probably encounter very little difficulty in continuing to play because his skills would be mainly automatic and would require very little conscious interpretation or decision making. The contrast between performance in practiced skills versus new skills is probably a main reason why many older people find little pleasure in trying to learn new skills that require physical coordination. Young people also experience frustrations in trying to learn new skills, but they do not have a large, contrasting backlog of much less frustrating practiced skills.

When older people must learn new skills, particularly those required for employment, they are able to do so. There is no scientific support for applying the old adage "You can't teach an old dog new tricks" to humans. Nevertheless, there are definite changes in observed physical coordination as the individual ages. The most important differences from the point of view of social functioning are in reaction time, speed and accuracy of response, and ability to make complex responses.

Reaction Time

Reaction time increases with age. This increase is very slight for simple tasks, such as answering true-false test items but becomes greater as the tasks get more complex. The more choices involved in the task, the longer it takes older people to react compared to the young. Botwinick (1978:204) has suggested that more cautiousness among older people compared to the young may play a big part in slowed reaction, because older people are perceptibly slower only when they have time to be cautious.

The slowing of reactions in older people may also result from a tendency toward care and accuracy. Older people tend to spend more than an average amount of time checking their results; therefore, part of their slowness may be the difference between the time required for *accuracy* and the time required for *certainty*.

Botwinick (1978:205) also pointed out that exercise, increased motivation, and practice can reduce the age effects of slowed reaction time. Extended practice may eliminate slowing completely. Finally, individual differences in reaction time are so great that, even with age changes, very many older people are quicker in responding than are many young adults.

Speed and Accuracy

Speed of movement also tends to decline with increasing age. In fact, when older people try to hurry, their control capabilities are often so poor that their movements appear jerky in comparison with the more fluid motions of younger people. For simple movements such as sewing, the slowing with age is very slight, whereas for complex movements such as typing, in which the same muscles must be more controlled, the slowing with age is generally more marked. However, remember that people are quite variable with respect to this and all other physical functions. Take the case of Mike Bachman, a 78-year-old printer who gained fame in 1922 illustrating how fast the then-new Linotype machine for setting type could be operated. When Mike sat at the Linotype, the foreman was kept busy providing trays fast enough to receive the set type from Mike's machine (Graebner, 1980:22–23).

These same observations apply to *accuracy*. Accuracy is a skill required to operate most kinds of equipment that require an operator. Accuracy of movement declines as the individual grows older unless more time is taken to compensate for the greater difficulty in controlling the response (Welford, 1959:584–599).

Although physical coordination generally declines with age, it is much less marked for *practiced* skills. Thus, older people are apparently more effective in processing and coordinating responses over well-established networks than they are at establishing new ones. It is possible for them to learn new skills, but it is easier to ply established ones. This tendency may be one important reason why older people seem to prefer "tried and true" methods rather than new ones.

Implications of Declines in Coordination

The implications of the foregoing are of interest in regard to (1) general social functioning and (2) job performance. In terms of general social functioning, age-related decrements do not affect a sizable proportion of the population prior to age 75 to 80. To begin with, continuity of life-style and habits means that most people continue to practice existing skills rather than to learn new ones. In addition, freedom from job demands means that learning, problem solving, and creative activity can be paced to suit the individual. Aging (as opposed to chronic disease or disability or generational differences) does not produce any significant limitations on social functioning. Even among older people who are residents of institutions, a large proportion exceed the minimum functional capacity necessary for adequate social functioning (Lawton, 1972).

Concerning job performance, Fozard and Carr (1972) pointed to the need for functional measures and to the inadequacy of chronological age as an index of potential job performance. Not all pertinent job skills are influenced by age; in those that are, the range of individual differences is too great to give much predictive power to age alone. Belbin and Belbin (1969) found that trainability tests consisting of small work samples were more effective in measuring job potential than were general tests of aptitude or ability. Fozard and Carr (1972) reported that both older workers and their employers consistently tended to overestimate the functional demands of jobs. Many older workers are currently being arbitrarily denied jobs on the assumption that beyond a certain chronological age people cannot perform adequately. The use of job-specific testing could result in better job performance at all ages, but such testing is unlikely to be used as long as there is a labor surplus (McFarland, 1973).

Physical Appearance

Wrinkled skin, "age spots," gray hair, and midriff bulge are common examples of age changes in appearance. Yet these changes do not predictably influence physical attractiveness. Certainly, if we take a narrow, idealistic view of physical beauty or attractiveness, then not very many people fit the bill at any age. But in terms of *practical* attractiveness—the ability to draw positive attention through one's physical appearance—there are plenty of unattractive 25-year-olds. And many people find that they become *more* attractive as they grow older. Aging rarely transforms a silk purse into a sow's ear. More often it provides interesting lines and the image of experience and "character." Nevertheless, people tend to fear what aging may do to their appearance, especially if they see their attractiveness as one of their major assets. Some people try to alter surgically the effects of aging on their appearance. The main reasons cited for having cosmetic surgery in middle age or later are job security, marital security, and social attitudes about their appearance (Wantz and Gay, 1981:154). For example, Mrs. G was divorced in her late 40s. In order to meet men with whom she might develop a relationship, she attended various functions sponsored by local "singles" groups. Very quickly she concluded that the men there were looking for "younger" women. She had surgery for a facelift and breast reduction. She was close to tears as she expressed her anguish to a support group: "I spent over $10,000 fixing up my body and nobody noticed!" Mrs. G was like a lot of us. She was impatient to "do something" about her problem, and as a result she decided perhaps prematurely that surgery was the solution. Most people who have Mrs. G's experience eventually meet someone else who finds them attractive, regardless of their age.

Most people tend to be preoccupied with physical aspects of attractiveness and to ignore other aspects. Yet many of the most attractive people attract with their enthusiasm, attention, and "personality." And these aspects of attractiveness can also improve with age. Nevertheless, some people experience aging as a loss of attractiveness, and this change can be difficult to deal with. Fortunately, most of us grow older with mates and friends who tell us by their actions that changes in physical appearance are not nearly as important as we have been led to think they are.

Susceptibility to Physical and Mental Illness

Health is a central factor in everyone's life. Most people are fortunate enough to be able to take good health for granted. However, poor health affects life satisfaction, participation in most social roles, and the way we are treated by others. In later life, declining health cuts across all social, political, and economic lines, although disabling illness is more common and occurs at earlier ages among people at the lower socioeconomic levels. Health becomes a major determinant of ability to participate in the family, the job, the community, and in leisure pursuits. And health needs absorb a larger amount and proportion of older people's incomes. A large proportion of the medical industry's facilities and services are geared toward meeting the needs of people with diseases and infirmities that are most common in old age.

We do not usually define health. Instead, we define illness, and health becomes the absence of illness—a malfunction or disorder that has a negative effect on the organism's ability to function. Illnesses can be classified either by their expected duration or by the magnitude of their effect on functioning. *Acute illnesses* or injuries are expected to be short-term or temporary. They include such conditions as the common cold or a sprained ankle. *Chronic illnesses* or injuries are expected to be long term or permanent. Examples include paralysis, amputation, diabetes, or emphysema.

Both acute and chronic illnesses can cause people to restrict their activities. *Minor disabilities* cause restrictions, but not in major activities such as employment, child care, or housework. For example, Mr. L has a chronic heart condition that limits his capacity to engage in vigorous physical exercise, but otherwise he leads a "normal" life at home and on the job. Mrs. P was born with a clubfoot. She wears a built-up shoe and walks with a pronounced limp, but this has not interfered with her ability to bear and rear three children. Now 67, she takes care of her granddaughter regularly. These cases are minor disabilities because although the conditions interfere with some kinds of activities, they do not interfere with major life roles. *Major disabilities* interfere with central life activities such as employment, going to school, or child rearing. People usually must have a major disability in order to qualify for disability benefits. For example, in order to qualify for Social Security disability benefits, a person must have a job-related disability that is expected to last at least a year. Disabilities can be mental as well as physical. For example, Mrs. A was an accountant. At age 59, she suffered a stroke. After three months, she had recovered completely, with one exception: she could no longer do arithmetic reasoning. As a result, she was occupationally disabled, and although her disability had physical origins, its only long-term result was mental.

Aging affects both (1) the kinds of illnesses people are likely to have and (2) the degree of limitations that illnesses or injuries cause. Compared to the young, older people are less likely to have acute conditions such as colds or flu but are more likely to have chronic conditions such as diabetes or allergies. Regardless of the type of condition, older people are more likely to be disabled by them than young people are.

Despite the high prevalence of chronic conditions among older people, only a small proportion are severely handicapped. Although nearly 86 percent of the older population has one or more chronic conditions, 54 percent are not limited in any way by them, and only about 14 percent are severely limited by them (Wilder, 1974). Thus, although the expected increase in chronic conditions among older people does occur, the proportion who escape serious limitation by these factors is surprisingly large. Even among those who are disabled by illness or injury, most are not permanently bedridden. This is not to say that chronic conditions are not serious problems for older people. Clearly, they are. The point is that for many people aging is not accompanied by serious illness or disability. For example, in 1967 there were over 10 million older Americans who reported no serious limitations in activity caused by health problems (Wilder, 1971:19).

Physical Illness

The major chronic physical illnesses that limit the activities of older people are heart conditions, arthritis, and visual impairment, and they affect 22, 20, and 9 percent of the elderly, respectively. Diabetes, cancer, and allergies are the other main chronic illnesses among older people.

Older people are also much more susceptible to injury from falls compared to younger people. Burnside (1981) found that falls were the leading cause of accidental death among people over 75. Older women are especially likely to fall. The most common cause of falls in the elderly is tripping or stumbling over something at home which is of course related to poor coordination or poor eyesight. However, many falls occur as a result of dizziness, which in turn is related to chronic illnesses such as high blood pressure (hypertension) and to the medications used to treat them.

Many health care professionals such as physicians and nurses assume that a certain amount of limiting illness is normal in an aging person. This assumption is absolutely untrue! Although limiting chronic conditions are common among older people, many of them are preventable, most are treatable, and all can be compensated for to some extent. And limiting physical illness is not *typical* of older people at any age. The next time you hear of a doctor telling an older patient to accept a certain amount of disability as a normal part of the aging process, get angry!

The social consequences of chronic conditions fall into two major categories: functional limits imposed by the illness and social limits imposed by other people's perceptions of the illness. Social limits are often much more severe than the actual physical limits. For instance, Dr. T suffered a heart attack at age 49. He was disabled for about six months. But it took him two years to convince his colleagues that he had recovered and that they could give him work to do. The major functional limit caused by illness in later life is in the area of employment. Parnes and Nestel (1981) found that 51 percent of the 2,016 men's retirements they studied were caused by poor health. Poor health is also by far the greatest limitation on participation in the community and on leisure pursuits. However, the proportion of older people affected in nonemployment areas is less than 20 percent.

Mental Illness

Mental disorders are also affected by age. *Functional mental disorders* have no apparent organic origin and range from serious conditions such as loss of reality contact to much less severe ones such as mild depression. The only functional disorder that is more likely to have its onset in later life is depression, usually in response to losses either in physical functioning or of social resources through death.

Dementia, or organic brain disease, is a particularly fearsome mental condition that is typified by mental confusion—loss of memory, incoherent speech, and poor orientation to the environment. It is often accompanied by poor motor coordination as well. Organic mental disorders can be either reversible or chronic. Because symptoms of both types are similar, diagnosis depends heavily on knowledge of prior health events. For example, if a doctor sees a patient with symptoms of organic brain disorder, before settling on a diagnosis he or she may check for malnutrition, find out what drugs the patient has been taking, and check for infections or diseases such as diabetes or hyperthyroidism. Any of these factors can cause reversible organic brain disorders. Reversible brain disorders can also accompany congestive heart failure, alcoholism, or stroke. If none of the possible causes of reversible organic brain disorders is present, then it is usually assumed that the patient has a chronic brain disorder. The prevalence of both types of organic brain disorders increases with age.

Chronic brain disorders fall into two categories: those caused by a deterioration of brain tissue and those caused by cerebral arteriosclerosis, which cuts off the blood supply to the brain. All chronic brain disorders involve a gradual deterioration of mental functions, but sometimes they also bring agitated behavior, depression, or delirium.

As the percentage of the older population that is very old increases, so will the prevalence of chronic organic brain disorders. Kay (1972) reports that 90 percent of first admissions to mental hospitals above age 75 are diagnosed as being the result of chronic brain disorders. Shanas and Maddox (1976) report that at age 65 only about 2 percent of the population has chronic organic brain disorders, while at age 80 about 20 percent does.

The implications of this trend are controversial. Wershow (1977:301) contends that most of these cases cannot be treated and that this situation raises various ethical questions:

> Must we be bound to keep alive as long as possible those poor souls who sit tied into their chairs, babbling incoherently, doubly incontinent, whose dining consists of having usually cold food stoked into them as rapidly as possible by overworked aides who must move on and stoke the next bed's patient? Is this living, much less living with dignity?

On the other side, Settin (1978) argues that no valid and practical test exists that can differentiate treatable organic brain disorders from the untreatable. In addition, Hellebrandt's (1978) observations provide a less stereotypic and more optimistic view of life for people with chronic organic brain disorders that have not reached the level of deterioration described by Wershow. He points out that most people suffering from this condition manage to live at home, cared for by family members and friends. Infections or other complicating diseases usually end life before the individual reaches a "vegetative existence."

Hellebrandt, himself 76, also describes life for sixteen patients with chronic organic brain disorders who lived in a locked ward in the convalescent facility of a large retirement village:

> Oblivious to their plight, without apprehension or concern, they move about at will, accepting the locked door with matter-of-fact aplomb on all but the most exceptional occasions. . . . The idea of the locked door may distress the visitor (or the reader) but it is a meaningless concept to virtually all patients deteriorated enough to require segregation in this unit. [Hellebrandt, 1978:68]

The average age of these patients was 85. They were generally coopera-
tive and in good general health. They were the most contented residents of
the nursing facility.

> They move about freely, often in pairs, showing evidence of concern one
> for another even though they never address each other by name and cannot
> identify the person with whom they are walking. . . . They are clean, neat, and
> groomed appropriately for the most part. On occasion they may wear two or
> three dresses at once. . . . The casual visitor would find the group deceptively
> normal.
>
> All patients in the locked ward are completely disoriented as to place,
> time, day, date, year, season, or holidays. They have a poor memory for
> ongoing events. . . . None know that their behavior is in any way aberrant.
> Neither do they realize that they have been institutionalized. [Hellebrandt,
> 1978:69]

On the Kahn-Goldfarb Mental Status Questionnaire, the group was
classifiable on the borderline between severe and moderately severe brain
damage. Yet much of what we consider human remained in these people—
the capacity to be concerned for others, friendliness, and optimism.

Caring for people who are disoriented is not easy. Student visitors
often are upset by patients' inability to remember them from one visit to the
next. Many visitors lack the patience required to listen to their incoherent
ramblings. Incontinence is disgusting to most people. And it is difficult to
regularly face the reality that if we live long enough, there is a one in five
chance that we ourselves will experience chronic organic brain disorders.

Getting Information

The *senses* are the means through which the human mind experiences
the world both outside and inside the body. The sensory process is not
particularly complex. Sensory organs pick up information about changes in
the internal or external environment and pass this information on to the
brain. All the input from the sensory organs is collected and organized in
the brain. The subjective result is called sensory experience.

The minimum amount of stimulation a sensory organ must experience
before sensory information is passed to the brain is called a *threshold*. All
individuals have their own thresholds for each sense. The higher the threshold, the stronger the stimulus needed to get information to the brain. For
example, some people require very little sound before they begin to hear,
while others require a considerable amount. In looking at the sensory processes as a function of age, we will be concerned both with changes in
threshold that occur with increasing age and with the complete failure of a
particular sensory process.[3]

---

[3] For a more detailed discussion of aging and sensory processes, see Botwinick (1978)
and Birren and Schaie (1977).

Vision

Increasing age decreases the ability of the eye to change shape and therefore to focus on very near objects. Hence, many older people find glasses necessary for reading, if for nothing else. The tendency toward far-sightedness increases about tenfold between age 10 and age 60, but does not appear to increase much more thereafter. Thus, close work of all kinds becomes more difficult without glasses, and bifocal or trifocal lenses are often very aggravating.

Proper focusing of the eye on the image requires both the proper quality and proper quantity of light. Because both these functions show a decline with increasing age, vision as a whole gets poorer. A large proportion of older people can compensate for poor focusing ability with glasses. But the eye of the average 60-year-old admits only about one-third as much light as the eye of the average 20-year-old, which means that greater levels of illumination are required by older people.

Older people seem to adapt to darkness about as fast as the young, but their level of adaptation is not nearly as good (Botwinick, 1978:145). This decline makes moving about in a dark house more dangerous for older people. In addition, poor adaptation to darkness can cause problems with night driving. This fact does not imply that older people should not drive at night—merely that they must exercise extra care when driving at night. It also means that others should be patient with older drivers at night.

Color vision also changes as the individual grows older. The lens of the eye gradually yellows and filters out the violet, blue, and green colors toward the dark end of the spectrum. The threshold for these colors increases significantly as people grow older, and it is much easier for older people to see yellow, orange, and red than to see the darker colors. For older people to get the same satisfaction from looking at colors in their surroundings that young people get, their environment must present more yellow, orange, and red, and less violet, blue, and green.

About 25 percent of the people over 70 have cataracts, a condition in which clouding of the eye's lens diffuses light, heightens sensitivity to glare, and impairs vision (Botwinick, 1978:144). As Figure 3-1 shows, to people with cataracts the world looks darker, objects are less distinguishable from one another, and visual acuity is often quite poor. Treatment involves surgically removing the lens and replacing it with a contact lens. This treatment generally improves vision, but requires a period of adjustment to a "new look."

The vast majority of the older population has corrected vision that is adequate for social functioning. The most common problem is inability to focus on near objects, which hampers ability to read (Botwinick, 1978:143). However, there are many exceptions to this general trend, because visual acuity is one of the most variable human senses.

Only a small percentage of older people are blind. Only 2.6 percent of Americans age 65 to 74 are blind, as compared to 8.3 percent of those age 75 or over (National Center for Health Statistics, 1959:9). Yet these people consti-

FIGURE 3-1 Simulated Effects of Increased Susceptibility to Glare and Reduced Visual Accuity Common to an Average 70-Year-Old. *Source: Original photographs by Leon Pastalan.*

tute a large proportion of the blind population. One California study found that 55 percent of the blindness in that state occurred after age 65 and that 85 percent occurred after age 45 (Birren, 1964:84). Thus, although blind people are a relatively small proportion, blindness is definitely related to age.

Hearing

Hearing is the second major sense. It involves detecting the frequency (pitch) of sound, its intensity, and the time interval over which it occurs. As people grow older, their reactions to frequency and intensity change, but there is no evidence to indicate that ability to distinguish time intervals changes significantly with age. Why these changes occur is not clear (Weiss, 1959).

Hearing loss begins about age 20. Very gradually, as they get older, people lose their ability to hear high frequencies and to discriminate among adjacent frequencies. Intensity threshold also changes with advancing age. Older people cannot hear some frequencies no matter how loud, but even within the range of pitch that they can hear, the intensity level necessary to produce hearing is greater, particularly for higher pitches (Botwinick, 1978:147). As a result, older people enjoy music with more low-pitched sounds and with uniform intensity. For example, organ music is popular because of the richness of its lower tones. Older people must play radios and televisions louder in order to hear them. Background noise is more distracting to older listeners than to the young (Botwinick, 1978:149).

Corso (1977) estimated that 13 percent of the elderly have severe hearing loss, but Botwinick (1978:146) cited some methodological research problems that may lead to overestimation of hearing loss. Apparently older people are more cautious and tend to report hearing things only when they are fairly sure that they have heard them. They also have more difficulty concentrating on hearing. Both these factors may lead to an overestimation of hearing loss among older adults.

After about age 55, a consistent sex difference appears in hearing ability. Up to that point, the prevalence of hearing loss is about equal for men and women, but after age 55 men show greater incidence of hearing loss than do women. Botwinick (1978:148) suggests that greater exposure to noise pollution on the job may be the cause of this differential.

Impaired hearing reduces the individual's capacity for interacting successfully with his or her environment. But impaired hearing does not always result when the sense of hearing declines. For example, if the individual still has good eyesight, he or she may be able to compensate for loss of the ability to hear speech by learning to read lips. But eyesight too begins to decline in the 40s. Thus, the incidence of impaired hearing increases sharply after age 45.

Hearing loss can have a major impact on speech communication. Age-related changes in ability to discriminate among sounds make speech more difficult to hear, especially when people talk fast, when there is background noise, and when there is sound distortion or reverberation (Corso,

1977:550). Among older people, 30 percent of men and 25 percent of women have difficulty hearing faint speech, and 5 percent of both men and women cannot hear even amplified speech (Corso, 1977:551). Hearing aids often can help, but they also can be frustrating in the presence of background noise because they tend to amplify it, too.

A decline of either sight or hearing can be partly compensated by the other, but when both decline simultaneously, as is so often the case among older people, a serious problem of adaptation to the environment occurs. Not only is the ability of these people to earn a living adversely affected, but those who deal with such people on a personal basis must learn to take these new limitations into account in order to help them make maximum use of their capabilities and opportunities.

Taste and Smell

As a sense, taste certainly can have a good deal to do with satisfaction. The evidence indicates that all four qualities—sweet, salt, bitter, and sour— show an increase in threshold after age 50. Nevertheless, it is unlikely that large changes in taste sensitivity occur before age 70. People in later life are apt to require more highly seasoned food to receive the same taste satisfactions they received when they were 20. They also seem to prefer tart tastes and to show less interest in sweets.

Research on the sense of smell is very sparse, but the evidence indicates little age change (Engen, 1977:560). Other factors such as smoking and air pollution seem to play a much bigger part than aging does.

Engen (1977:554) pointed out that the senses of taste and smell are of greater importance than the research on them indicates. These senses are major components in one's capacity to enjoy. They also make important contributions to one's capacity to survive. For example, taste is important in detecting spoiled food, and smell can alert people to the presence of smoke or natural gas.

Processing Information

The senses provide the means for assembling and classifying information, but not for evaluating or remembering it. Perception and memory are our major means of processing information.

Perception

The process of evaluating information gathered by the senses and of giving it meaning is called *perception*. Most research shows an age decrement in perception. One possible reason for this loss is that aging affects the speed with which the nervous system can process one stimulus and make way for the next. The "trace" of the initial stimulus in the nervous system interferes with ability to perceive subsequent stimuli. Thus, older people can be confused or irritated by visual images that change too rapidly.

Memory

There are essentially four types of memory. Short-term or immediate memory involves recall after very little delay, from as little as 5 seconds up to 30 seconds. This kind of memory is used to remember a telephone number between looking it up and dialing. Recent memory involves recall after a brief period, from one hour to several days. Remote memory is recall of events that took place a long time in the past but that have been referred to frequently throughout the course of a lifetime. Old memory is recall of events that occurred a long time in the past and that have not been thought of or rehearsed since.

Regardless of type, there are three stages of memory. Registration is the "recording" of learning or perceptions. In concept, registration is analogous to the recording of sound on a tape recorder. Retention is the ability to sustain registration over time. Recall is retrieval of material that has been registered and retained. Obviously, in any type of memory, a failure at any of these stages will result in no measurable memory.

There is an age deficit in memory of all types, but there appears to be a greater loss in short-term and recent memory than in remote or old memory, and the decline is less for rote memory than for logical memory. As age increases, the retention of things heard becomes increasingly superior to the retention of things seen, and use of both gives better results than the use of either separately.

Bright people are less susceptible to memory loss with increasing age than are their less intelligent counterparts, and some older people escape memory loss altogether. People who exercise their memories tend to maintain both remote and recent memory well into old age.

Mental Functioning

Sensation, perception, and memory are all very important for the functioning of the individual, yet in human beings as in no other animal these processes take a backseat to mental functioning. The term *mental functioning* refers to a large group of complex processes, subdivided for convenience into intelligence, learning, thinking, problem solving, and creativity.

Intelligence

When we think of intelligence, we usually imply both a potential and an actual ability. In practice, however, we always deal with measured ability. As many as twenty basic abilities go together to make up intelligence. Troll (1982:165) reported that abilities that require quick thinking such as

timed matching tasks decline steadily after about age 40. This decline is no doubt related to changes in response speed (referred to earlier). Tests of stored information such as vocabulary or general information may continue to increase to the end of life. Tests of logical abilities such as arithmetic reasoning often show a plateau throughout adulthood.

Baltes and Labouvie (1973:205–206) reviewed the literature on age and intelligence and concluded that individual differences are so great that age is of little predictive value. In addition, studies of intervention suggest that age changes can be altered, even in old age. They also concluded that although biological aging undoubtedly influences intellectual functioning, there has been a tendency to underestimate or ignore the impact of environments for older people that are not conducive to "intellectual acquisitions and maintenance." Botwinick (1978:230) concluded that, in terms of overall ability, education is much more important than age in explaining individual intellectual differences.

Learning

Learning is the acquisition of information or skills and is usually measured by improvements in task performance. When someone improves performance at a given intellectual or physical task, we say he or she has learned. All studies of performance indicate a decline in learning with age.

Clearly, however, factors other than learning ability affect performance. These factors include motivation, speed, intelligence, ill health, and physiological states. In practice, it is extremely difficult to separate the components of performance in order to examine the influence of learning ability, although a number of studies have attempted to do so. Because research to date has not been able to isolate learning ability from other causes of performance and because very little longitudinal research has been done on learning, we are in a poor position to say what effect age has on learning ability.

From a practical point of view, learning performance seems to decline as age increases, although the declines are not noticeable until past middle age. All age groups can learn. If given a bit more time, older people can usually learn anything other people can. Extra time is required both to learn information or skills and to demonstrate that learning has occurred. Tasks that involve manipulation of concrete objects or symbols, distinct and unambiguous responses, and low interference from prior learning are particularly conducive to good performance by older people.

Via intelligence, learning, and memory, human beings have at their disposal a great many separate mental images. Thinking, problem solving, and creativity all involve the manipulation of ideas and symbols.

Thinking

Thinking is the process of developing new ideas. It helps bring order to the chaos of data brought into the mind by perception and learning by differentiating and categorizing these data into constructs called *concepts* (Botwinick, 1968:156). Thus, thinking is the process we use to form concepts.

Older people seem to be particularly poor at forming concepts. Concept formation often involves making logical inferences and generalizations. Older people have been found to resist forming a higher-order generalization and to refuse choosing one when given the opportunity. All studies seem to agree that as age increases, ability at concept formation and its components declines.

Concept formation is not completely independent of other skills such as learning and intelligence, but at the same time it is not completely dependent on them either. A substantial part of the decline with age in measured ability to form concepts appears to be genuine.

Problem Solving

Problem solving is the development of decisions out of the processes of reason, logic, and thinking. Whereas thinking involves the differentiation and categorization of mental data, problem solving involves making logical deductions about these categories, their properties, and differences among them. Problem solving differs from learning in that learning is the acquisition of skills and perceptions, while problem solving is using these skills and perceptions to make choices.

In solving problems, older people are at a disadvantage if they must deal with many items of information simultaneously. They have more difficulty giving meaning to stimuli presented and have more trouble remembering this information later when it must be used to derive a solution. The number of errors made in solving problems rises steadily with age. This difficulty is why older people are often befuddled by forms they are asked to complete, particularly if the instructions are complex.

Older people take a long time to recognize the explicit goal of a particular problem. Their search for information is thus characterized by haphazard questioning rather than by concentration on a single path to the goal. They attain information randomly, have trouble separating the relevant from the irrelevant, and thus tend to be overwhelmed by a multitude of irrelevant facts. They also tend toward repetitive behavior, a tendency that can be disruptive in situations where the nature of problems and their solutions is constantly or rapidly changing. I once saw a group of older people involved in a simulation game called SIMSOC that attempts to simulate the way society operates. The game requires quick learning and problem solving. More than half of the older people quit in frustration within 30 minutes.

In general, the same trend of decline is observed with regard to problem solving that was observed in the other mental processes. However, Arenberg (1968) has shown that when abstract reasoning is required in relation to concrete tasks such as shopping, older people are in fact able to think at abstract levels. In addition, some data on the role of education indicate that older people whose jobs had trained them to perform deductions (for example, physicians) showed deductive ability comparable to younger colleagues (Cijfer, 1966). This finding suggests that sizable cultural and social factors may be operating in the data that have been the mainstay of our knowledge of the relationship between age and problem solving. Indeed, Kesler, Denney, and Whitely (1976) found that what had been presumed to be age effects in problem solving disappeared when education and nonverbal intelligence were controlled. Thus, those entering the older population now may be at less disadvantage compared to those who entered the older population twenty years ago.

Creativity

Creativity is unique, original, and inventive problem solving. The biggest problem in studying creativity is deciding whom to study—how to define creative people. Ratings by colleagues and psychological test scores have been used, but the most frequently used method is to count the number of publications produced by people. Most studies of age and creativity have shown a decline in both the quantity and the quality of creative output with age, but Dennis (1966) presented data showing that in some academic fields the average output declined scarcely at all through age 70. Clemente and Hendricks (1973) found no correlation between age at receipt of doctorates and six operational indices of publication output. Certainly individual exceptions are prevalent enough in every field and declines are gradual enough that no one should assume that older people automatically reach an end of their creativity, particularly at a given chronological age.

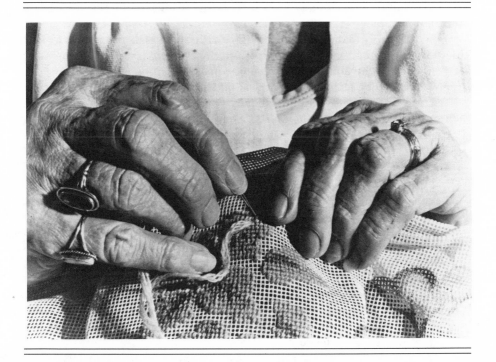

A crucial issue revolves around social supports of creative effort. Zuckerman and Merton (1972) point out that in science the political cards within the academic disciplines are stacked in favor of the older members of the discipline. Older scholars are overrepresented in committee posts, on proposal review committees, among journal referees, and so on. On the other side, however, pressure is placed on established scholars to move into supervisory and leadership positions, which often takes them away from their own individual work. In addition, seldom does an individual get to be "established" just by virtue of growing old. Crane (1965) suggests that motivation and selection of research topics are both very important. In academic competition, people fall by the wayside and fade into obscurity, but it is difficult to experience falling into obscurity unless you live long enough. These issues suggest that all sorts of social factors mediate whatever age changes may occur in pure creativity.

Implications of Mental Aging

As we have seen, mental aging is not a unitary process. Some functions decline with age, some remain relatively constant over the entire adult life span, and others improve steadily with age. The closer the tie to physical functioning the more likely a decline with age. Nevertheless, the variability in physical aging means that the results of mental aging are rarely predictable.

Getting information is a problem for only a small proportion of the elderly. Most can successfully compensate by using glasses or hearing aids. Age changes in the ability to process information can be minimized by continuing to practice skills such as thinking, problem solving, and creativity. Losses can be offset by compensating. For example, declining short-term memory can be offset by note taking. Learning can be improved by slowing down the pace of the material being presented.

Summary

In summary, biological aging alters the physical and mental capacities of the body and alters its appearance. It reduces the body's capacity to coordinate the various functions that are necessary for both performances and survival.

Aging is not a single process but many. And each process begins at different *ages* for different people and progresses at different *rates* for different people. Thus, chronological age is a poor predictor of the aging any individual will be experiencing.

Aging occurs *gradually* for the vast majority of people. In fact, most older people cannot identify the exact age at which they first experienced particular functional changes. The adjustments and compensations also tend to be made gradually.

Although aging gradually diminishes physical resources such as the ability to gather information and evaluate it, to think and solve problems, to mobilize energy, and to move quickly, smoothly, and accurately, the typical amount of decrement is not great enough to seriously hamper social functioning until the late 70s, and many people are not seriously limited by aging even in their 80s. The implication is that normal aging does not produce decrements that require society systematically to exclude older people from participation at the workplace or anywhere else.

Aging also increases the proportion of the population with disability, but it is important to remember that part of this increase is due to the living conditions people experienced earlier in life and to heredity, and that disability is not an inevitable or necessary part of aging. Tomorrow's older people may not be as likely to experience disability as today's.

Aging makes one more vulnerable to physical disabilities that include blindness, deafness, arthritis, and heart conditions. Generally, these conditions limit physical activity, while the capacity for mental participation remains. For such people, it is often necessary to make the effort required to take opportunities to them because they cannot physically get to the opportunities. Visitor programs, sheltered workshops, and Meals-on-Wheels are examples of things communities can do to create more opportunities for disabled people to participate.

Organic brain disease is the major mental disability that limits participation in later life. It occurs in only a small minority of cases, but when it
does, the greatest of understanding and maturity is required in those who
care for people afflicted with it.

Like other aspects of physical aging, serious disabilities are the exception rather than the rule. No more than about 20 percent of the older population is seriously hampered in terms of social functioning by physical aging
or illnesses associated with it. The proportion that is occupationally disabled
is higher because we tend to overestimate the physical demands of jobs and
have poor methods for making job reassignments.

Social continuity is an important force that minimizes the effects of
physical aging. To the extent that we remain in familiar relationships and
environments, our ability to rely on constantly practiced skills greatly offsets
whatever problems we might have in learning new ones. Long-standing
relationships can soften the impact of aging on physical appearance. And
physical disabilities can be somewhat offset by supports from a persistent
social environment. Of course, a corollary of this rule is that serious discontinuity in relationships and environments can make the effects of physical
aging even worse. This corollary is an important point to keep in mind.

Part Two

How Does
It Feel to
Grow Older?

We turn now to the inner experience of aging. If we are to understand aging people and relate to them effectively, we must have some capacity to see the world as they see it. This capacity involves having an appreciation of what it is like to experience negative messages about aging when you yourself are aging. How can people deal with such messages without becoming negative about themselves? Aging people have several ways to deal with this problem.

Adult identity in the United States is very strongly tied to the capacity to be independent and personally effective. In spite of numerous changes that most people would define as at least somewhat negative, most people are able to retain their feelings of independence and personal effectiveness well into old age. We will see how in Chapter 5.

Aging also can increase a person's sense of vulnerability. Aging increases the probability that a person might become disabled, dependent, or prey to exploitation. This is the subject of Chapter 6.

In the final chapter of this part, we will examine dying, death and grief and how they are related to aging. We will see that most older people are not as afraid of death as most younger people are but are more likely to experience grief.

Chapter 4

Dealing with Negative Messages about Aging

The personal meaning of aging to each of us is most profoundly shaped by our direct experience of it. Although we may learn a great deal from reading about aging, our direct experiences of aging, first in others and later in ourselves, are what create what aging means to us, in contrast to what aging means in our culture or to people in general. Nevertheless, it helps to have a framework that can be used to interpret these experiences and to begin to understand what others may be experiencing. Such a framework should be based as much as possible on factual information rather than on the un-grounded ideas about aging that are so prevalent in our society and even in the field of aging.

In order to understand what aging means to people, we need to look first at the various kinds of messages people get about aging. Some of these messages come from observing oneself. Many come from cultural attitudes, beliefs, and stereotypes that are expressed by others and maybe even held by ourselves. Messages about aging are also contained in the mass media. Finally, service providers often convey messages about aging to their clients.

The content of messages about aging is often negative and disparaging, yet the vast majority of the older population does not believe that the common conceptions of aging apply to them specifically, even though they may see these stereotypes as applicable to other older people. Once we understand the basic difference between what we learn from ourselves about aging compared to what we learn from others, our culture, the media, or service providers, we will then be in a position to explore the various mechanisms people use to deal with negative messages and the potential threat that they represent to one's concepts of self and personality. We also need to consider under what circumstances the individual's defenses might fail to protect him or her from negative effects of derogatory messages about aging.

Observing Ourselves

The experience of aging can be positive, negative, or both. The quality of the experience can also change over time. And the relationship between our objective circumstances and how we experience them is often tenuous. Some people experience many physical setbacks in later life and still retain a vital and hopeful outlook. Others are utterly defeated by seemingly trivial changes in circumstances. Some people never have the experience that aging has changed them. Others seize upon their age as an excuse to give up even when they have experienced few physical, mental, or social decrements. Thus, it is not merely a matter of what aging does to you but also of what you do with aging.

Probably the most remarkable aspect of physical aging is that most people do not experience it until quite late in life. Up until the late 70s or so, changes occur so gradually that we are scarcely aware of them. At age 60, author and feminist Simone de Beauvoir (1972:284) stated, "Our private, inward experience does not tell us the number of our years; no fresh perception comes into being to show us the decline of age." She went on to contrast aging with illness. Whereas our aging is usually gradual and barely perceptible, illness is much more obvious to us. When we are ill, we are usually more aware of it than anyone else, but when we age we are often less aware of it than others around us are. She quoted Mme. de Sevigne, who in 1687 said, "Providence leads us so kindly through all the different stages of our life that we hardly feel them at all. The slope runs gently down; it is imperceptible—the hand on the dial whose movement we do not see" (1972:287).

When we do become aware that we have changed, the cause of the change is not always clear to us. People sometimes confuse the effects of treatable illnesses with irreversible aging. Sometimes we think we have lost some function forever, and later the loss turns out to have been only temporary. Because aging can bring both positive and negative results, we may be aware that decrements are offset by increments. For example, declines in response speed may be offset by increased ability to concentrate on the task at hand.

In addition, we tend to grow older in familiar environments with familiar demands we have long since learned to meet. Only when we are confronted with new people or significant environmental change do we become aware that aging may have reduced our capacity to cope quickly with new situations. And even then we often cannot know whether the result is caused by aging or by the fact that our skills have become rusty.

The great social psychologist George Herbert Mead said that the self consists of *the I* and *the me*. *The I* is the actor, the entity that is aware of its own existence and the world around it. When I focus my awareness on my own body, mental life, or social characteristics, the result is *the me*—what I think and feel about myself as the object of my own attention.

What I have been saying so far in this chapter is that aging usually causes changes in *the me* that occur so gradually that *the I* does not notice or does not notice often. The changes are so slow and subtle that it seems more like an unfolding than an abrupt shift. Our past blends with and is part of our present—we recognize a consistency as being uniquely us.

Messages from Others

Part of *the me* comes from our own observations of ourselves and part comes from what we are told, both verbally and nonverbally, by others and by the mass media. Because I and my long-standing friends are aware of the multitude of my connections to *the me* of the past, we tend to see *the me* as having changed over the past fifteen years but in ways that are consistent with and in many ways an elaboration of what was always there.

Strangers do not have the benefit of this perspective. They may think my looks are only so-so and that aging may have harmed me in this respect.

But I and my friends know that my looks have improved and that compared to what I looked like when I was 25, aging has created a miracle!

Strangers are always willing to project a host of characteristics onto other strangers who happen to be older. Even family and friends can fall prey to this often unconscious process. For example, Harris and Associates (1975) compared the actual prevalence of problems in later life with what the general public thought the prevalence to be. The general public thought that "most people over 65" were poor and lonely, but only 12 percent of the elderly said that loneliness was a problem for them and only 15 percent said their incomes were inadequate. The public thought that most older people had problems with not feeling needed, whereas only 7 percent of the elderly had experienced this as a problem. Not *one* problem that a majority of the general public thought applied to most older people actually applied to even a quarter of the elderly.

Beliefs, Stereotypes, Attitudes, and Norms

Part of what people see when they look at aging people is a product of what is there, and part of it is influenced by what they have been taught to think is there. Ideas about what is true, what ought to be true, and how one typically feels about it are contained in our culture in the form of beliefs, stereotypes, attitudes, and norms.

Beliefs are assertions about what is true that are accepted and acted on often with no effort to assess their validity. To believe that retirement causes premature death means to accept this idea as true and to act as if it were true. Stereotypes are composites, usually made up of several beliefs about a category of people such as college students, widows, or the aged. Beliefs can be either accurate or inaccurate, while stereotypes are by definition both inaccurate and derogatory. For example, the belief that aging adversely affects sight is correct, but the stereotype that older workers are less effective than younger workers is inaccurate. *Whether beliefs or stereotypes are widely held or not has nothing to do with their accuracy.*

Research on general beliefs about the aged has shown that some of our beliefs are accurate, some are inaccurate, and some may or may not be accurate. For example, it is true that most older people need glasses to read, are able to learn new things, are not helpless, are more interested in religion, get love and affection from their children, and worry about money and health. It is *not* true that most older people are conservative, are lonely, usually live with their children, or repeat themselves in conversation. It may or may not be true that older people like to give advice, are good to children, are not bossy, are kind, or do not meddle in the affairs of others. Overall, *beliefs* about the aged are accurate about as often as they are inaccurate.

But *stereotypes* about the aged are negative in content, are inaccurate, and tend to reflect negative assessments of the results of aging. Aging is presumed to make people unattractive, unintelligent, asexual, unemployable, and mentally incompetent (Comfort, 1976). Stereotypes often provide justification for discrimination against the aged. For example, Rosen and Jerdee (1976a) found that prospective business managers rated older workers (age 60) lower than younger workers (age 30) on productivity, efficiency, motivation, ability to work under pressure, and creativity. Older workers were also seen as more accident prone and as having less potential. Not only were the older workers seen as less eager, but they were also seen as unreceptive to new ideas, less capable of learning, less adaptable, less versatile, and more rigid and dogmatic. On the plus side, older workers were seen as more reliable, dependable, and trustworthy and as less likely to miss work for personal reasons. This negative stereotype is mostly inaccurate. Older workers are more dependable and do miss work less often. But the rest of the stereotype either is demonstrably wrong or has never been tested. Nevertheless, this image is *imposed* on the older person who applies for a job, usually with poor results for the older person.

Attitudes are our likes and dislikes. They may develop out of purely personal preferences, but often they are a product of what we are *taught* to like or dislike. People who dislike aging or "older people in general" tend to do so because they associate aging with poor health, disability, and financial worries and because they presume negative effects of aging on productivity, achievement, and independence (Atchley, 1980b:257). The connection between erroneous beliefs and negative attitudes is obvious. However, only about 20 to 30 percent of the public has a negative attitude toward the elderly (McTavish, 1971). *Ageism,* like sexism and racism, is an unfair attitude based on stereotypes that are erroneously assumed to apply uniformly to all aging people.

Norms are ideas about what one's behavior in a particular situation *ought to be.* These too tend to be linked to beliefs and stereotypes. Thus, older people are sometimes *expected* to retire because others assume that they are less efficient, and widowed older people are sometimes *expected* not to want an intimate relationship because others assume that they are uninterested in sex. And old people are sometimes *expected* to let their children take over their financial affairs because others assume that they are no longer capable of managing for themselves.

Messages from the Mass Media

The mass media also serve as a source of images about aging and the aged. Television is the most important medium, and older people watch television more than any other age category does. How older people are portrayed on television is difficult to summarize because the portrayal varies greatly across major types of programs: daytime drama, prime time series, commercials, and news and documentary.

Generally, research on nighttime television series has shown that the proportion of older characters is what it ought to be—about 10 percent. However, research estimates vary from 1.5 to 13 percent because we are seldom given concrete clues to assess a character's age. Most studies have concluded that the elderly are often portrayed in a negative light in nighttime series. However, there is some evidence that the portrayal of the elderly has improved recently (Atchley, 1980b:258–259).

The news, on the other hand, brings us pictures of older people burned out of their homes, of frightful conditions in a nursing home, of an ambulance loading an elderly mugging victim, and so on. There is seldom any good news. Network and local news programs thrive on sensationalism and often try to create drama out of mundane events. Just once, I would like to hear a newscaster say, "Good evening. There is nothing you need to hear about today so we will use this time to bring you a special program entitled 'Treasures of the Louvre.' " There is nothing "newsworthy" about individuals and families who are successfully and quietly coping with the trivial (at least in the long run) conflicts of everyday life. Those older people who get news attention tend to be those who have a "problem" that can serve as a springboard for two of the newscasters' favorite games: "Can you believe this?" and "Ain't it awful!" The object of both games is to expose something that is either ridiculous, morally outrageous, or esthetically disgusting. Needless to say, the portrayal of older people or any other category in this system is seldom positive.

Yet even this tendency may be changing. There are so many news hours, television "magazines," and documentaries on the air that in recent times newscasters have resorted out of desperation to reporting on people who are doing good things and doing them well. And quite a few of these people are middle-aged or older.

Older people generally get favorable treatment in public affairs and talk shows (Harris and Feinberg, 1977). Older people who appear on these shows tend to be influential business leaders or politicians, or respected actors or creative artists. The criterion for being on these shows is having something to offer, and age is usually not a barrier. In the late 1970s, talk shows specifically aimed at the interests of older Americans began to appear. It probably is not a coincidence that public affairs and talk shows are the type of program most frequently watched by the elderly.

Commercials present a mixed picture of aging. Older characters appear in commercials in proportion to their share of the general population, but they tend to be concentrated in messages for health aids and food and absent from ads for clothing, appliances, cars, and cleaning products. Advertisers often use older characters as symbols of quality and tradition but not as often as potential buyers. But this tendency may be changing. Retirement incomes have improved significantly over the past two decades, and it is becoming recognized that older people are potential consumers. Sears, the nation's largest retailer, has begun using older models in its catalog, and commercials for travel are beginning to focus on active middle-aged and older people.

Magazine, book, and newspaper portrayals of aging and the aged have received much less research attention compared to television. Fictional portrayals of older people in women's magazines and in novels are much more often positive than negative (Schuerman et al., 1977; Sohngen, 1977). But the portrayals in nonfiction probably have the same negative biases found in television news. More research is needed on the images of aging presented in nonfiction, particularly in newspaper articles, magazine articles, nonfiction books, and biographies.

Messages from Service Providers

The 20 to 30 percent of the aged who come in contact with agencies that provide services to the elderly also encounter professional beliefs about the elderly, especially those who use services. There are two basic assumptions that can be used to design services for the elderly. One assumption is that the prospective clients are mostly capable individuals or couples who require assistance in some way—information, counseling, transportation, and so forth—in order to pursue their own personal goals more effectively. A second assumption is that older clients are incapable of self-determination—that they lack the physical, mental, social, or educational resources necessary to cope on their own with the demands of life. Some programs and services are based on the first assumption ("Assist the capable"), and some are based on the second ("Help the helpless").

Either of these assumptions can be valid *in some situations*. For example, the "Help the helpless" model is often appropriate in skilled nursing facilities with high proportions of bedridden patients or in wards of mental hospitals reserved for those with severe organic brain disease. The "Assist the capable" model is generally appropriate for public housing for the elderly. The important question is "What is the degree of fit between the assumption being used by the program and the characteristics of the people being served by it?" For example, research on housing has shown the importance of the fit between the person and his or her housing environment for the well-being of the person (Carp, 1976). Older people who want to live in a facility with organized programs of recreation benefit a great deal from being able to live in such a facility. On the other hand, people who do not want to live in such a facility may be depressed by having to live in one.

Yet indications are that a significant proportion of programs and services for the elderly are based on the wrong assumption. Research on the factual knowledge that service providers have about the elderly indicates that a large proportion are operating on the basis of stereotypes rather than facts (Brubaker and Barresi, 1980). Also, the policies that serve as the basis for programs are sold to legislatures and developed on the premise that a majority of the elderly are incapable (Estes, 1979). Although some of this "propaganda" may be necessary to get such policies and programs assigned a high priority, it may result in a self-defeating mismatch of program philosophy and client population. For example, many programs developed under the Older Americans Act assume that the elderly need someone to manage at least part of their lives.

This approach has a significant bearing on the messages being sent about themselves to older people who use these services. Although at least 70 to 80 percent of the elderly fit the "Assist the capable" assumption, if they are to get services they must often accept or at least put up with a paternalistic assumption that they are incapable. For instance, I once spent some time in a waiting room of our local welfare department. While I was seated there, a middle-aged clerk approached an elderly woman seated next to me, handed her a form, and then in a very loud voice went into a most tedious explanation of how to fill out the form—as if she were talking to a 10-year-old. When the clerk had left, the older woman, who had not uttered a word throughout, turned to me and said, "If you're over 65, they treat you like an idiot."

Dealing with Messages about One's Own Aging

There is no question that what others tell older people about themselves and about aging and the aged in general is sometimes based on stereotypes and delivered in a cruel and impersonal way. The same can be said for the media and for those who provide services.

But the crucial question is what aging people do with these messages—how these messages affect them. We also need to consider these impacts *in the context of* changes that are often going on in personality and self.

Age Changes in Personality

The term *personality* refers to what the individual typically thinks and feels and how the individual characteristically interacts with his or her physical or social environment. Personality develops out of an interaction between innate dispositions, capacities, and temperament on the one hand and the physical and social environment on the other. The individual actively participates in this process rather than simply being affected by internal or external forces beyond his or her control.[1]

Personality is difficult to study because it can be unique for each individual and because it is made up of hundreds of patterns of thought, motivation, and response. Each personality theory tends to focus on different aspects of personality, and each personality who uses personality theory tends to promote his or her focus as the most useful. This difficulty is further compounded by the fact that some theorists are primarily researchers and others are psychotherapists, both of whom look at very different samples of people for very different reasons. Another problem is that the object of study is the inner working of the mind, which cannot be directly observed (Back, 1976). For all these reasons, the scientific study of personality and aging has not advanced very far in terms of developing a specific profile of age changes in personality (Neugarten, 1977; Fiske, 1974).

Inward dimensions of personality that have been studied in relation to

[1] For alternative views of and assumptions about personality and how it is affected by aging, see Atchley (1980b:78–80).

aging include psychological dependency, dogmatism, cautiousness, ego strength, risk taking, introversion, hopefulness, need for achievement, creativity, and several others (Neugarten, 1977). Two themes emerge from these various studies: (1) there is continuity of personality[2] in that individual differences in typical thoughts, motives, and emotions tend to be maintained over time, and (2) the *only* internal dimension that changes systematically with age in nearly all studies of personality is introversion—turning one's interest and attention inward on the self rather than toward external objects and actions. Yet this turning inward seems more in the cause of self-acceptance and understanding and a yearning for what Erikson called *integrity* than for the purpose of social withdrawal.

In terms of adaptation patterns, there is a substantial controversy over whether, when, and how personality changes with age. Vaillant (1977) found numerous changes in men from young adulthood to middle age. These changes revolved around the successive life concerns of establishing intimacy, career consolidation, and developing a meaning for life. Livson (1976) found that "traditional" women (those who were nurturing and conventional conformists) showed a steady pattern of personality growth from adolescence to middle age while "independent" women (those who were ambitious and unconventional and whose satisfactions came from developing themselves rather than from attachment to others) found traditional women's roles constricting and a source of conflict in their 40s but by their 50s their social responsibilities were more in tune with their personalities. These findings suggest that early in adulthood personality may be adaptable, but that by late middle age personality becomes more stable.

Consistent with this picture, Neugarten et al. (1964) found that after middle age adaptation patterns show no significant changes with age. Neugarten concluded that after age 50, changes in health, finances, and marital status were more important influences on social adaptation than age changes in personality were. This pattern of stability in personality after middle age has been found by many investigators both in the United States (Schaie and Parham, 1976; Neugarten, 1977; Smith and Hall, 1964; Dennis, 1960; Thaler, 1956) and in West Germany (Thomae, 1975). Stability of personality in later adulthood is related to two factors. First, over time there is an "institutionalization" of personality (Neugarten et al., 1964). Individuals expect themselves to respond in ways that are consistent with their past histories. Second, they build up around themselves familiar social networks that facilitate dealing with the social world in habitual ways (Streib and Schneider, 1971). Stability is also supported by what happens to the self with advancing age.

Age Changes in the Self

The objective *self—the me* (as contrasted with the subjective *self—the I*) consists of what we think and feel about ourselves. It can be viewed in terms of four components. *Self-concept* is what we think we *are* like, the *ideal*

---

[2] Again, that there is continuity does *not* mean that there is not also change. The implication is simply that change occurs in the *context* of considerable continuity.

self is what we think we *ought to be* like, *self-evaluation* is a moral assessment of how well we live up to our ideal self, and *self-esteem* is whether we like or dislike ourselves and how much.

The self-concept and ideal self are often tied to the social positions we occupy, the roles we play, and the norms associated with personal characteristics such as sex, race, social class, and so on. These ties tend to be closer earlier in life compared to later.

To understand how aging may be different from maturation, we need to consider how the self works in young adults. In young adulthood, we play many roles, and it is often difficult to tell which is the role and which is us. Part of this difficulty comes from the fact that we seldom use written or verbal job descriptions or rules about roles to decide what to do in a particular role. Instead, we tend to base our behavior on what we have seen others do in that role—we try to imitate them. People who serve as the basis for how to perform a role are called *role models*. We also watch others' reactions to our performance and, if we want to improve the impression others have of our performance, we may gradually change the way we play the role (to the extent that we are able). We may attempt to change what others expect of us by introducing personal information about us, and at the same time others may be attempting to alter what we expect of them by the same process. This process of taking up roles, finding role models, dropping roles, and transforming roles in a wide variety of settings—jobs, family, community—is so common in early adulthood that it is often difficult to develop a firm sense of self. The self gets too mixed up with our roles.

Aging introduces a crucial variable into this confusing situation: *our role relationships increase in duration*. With this increase in duration, many people become aware that their current adult relationships are not what they want or are unrealistic given their capacities or interests. Over time, we can also become more astute at differentiating self from role. Most of this increase in accuracy comes from being able to view the self across a variety of roles. And the more we know about the self, the more potential we have for avoiding roles that are unsuited to us. These patterns are not ironclad laws, they are merely tendencies that probably fit the aggregate experience of a large number of people. They are ideas about what can happen if the person is open to learning about the self and using that knowledge to inform life choices. This process need not be conscious or calculated. It may appear to "just happen."

By the time we reach middle age, we have a huge backlog of evidence about what we are like and should be like in a wide variety of roles and situations and how this self may or may not fluctuate from time to time. During the time that we are trying to separate self from role, messages from others about our selves and personalities may greatly influence what we eventually think we are or ought to be. But as time goes by, more and more people develop a firm idea of what they are like. Thus, although the self may be relatively open to outside influence during the process of self-discovery, it tends to be relatively closed to it during the process of self-maintenance.

Self-evaluation and self-esteem always go hand in hand. They are the moral and emotional reactions to an assessment of the fit between self-concept (what you are) and the ideal self (what you ought to be). The noted psychologist William James expressed the relationship as follows:

$$\text{self-esteem} = \frac{\text{success}}{\text{pretensions}}$$

which, in the language we've been using we could rewrite as:

$$\text{self-evaluation or self-esteem} = \frac{\text{self-concept}}{\text{ideal self}}$$

If this relationship is valid, then self-esteem could be raised *either* by increasing success (self-concept) or decreasing pretensions (ideal self). This theory fits the age data on the self very well.

In early adulthood, many people have low self-esteem and are unsure of themselves both in terms of what they are capable of and what they ought to be capable of. And if you are unsure, it is difficult to bring any of the elements into focus.

Over time, self-esteem increases. The self-esteem scores of older people living independently in the community are nearly double those of high school students (Cottrell and Atchley, 1969; Rosenberg, 1964). This difference probably comes about in the following way. Once a firm idea about the self-concept is reached, then the person can reevaluate how realistic the ideal self is and bring the ideal self more into line with the self-concept. Another way to say this is that self-acceptance increases with age. The person is freed to achieve this self-acceptance by the reduction in role responsibilities (mainly child rearing and employment) that usually occurs in late middle age or shortly after and by the increased potential for personalizing role relationships over time. Systems *do* bend to fit people, but it usually takes time. And people can bend to fit systems, again with time required for this to occur.

For those who experience this resolution process (the majority), the result is a solid concept of self that stands up very well to the vicissitudes of later life changes. This continuity in self couples with the continuity of personality to serve as the basis for defense against the assaults on personality and self that can occur as a result of ageism.

Defending the Personality and Self

The gerontology literature is full of assertions that ageism results in a declining self-image. But numerous studies have shown that most older people do not have negative self-images and that self-esteem tends to increase with age. This apparent contradiction occurs because the first assertion is incomplete. It should be *"In the absence of adequate defenses, exposure to ageism erodes the basis for self-esteem."* Fortunately, most people have very adequate means to defend their ideas about themselves and their personalities.

The continuity of personality and self means that how we see our-selves can involve not only an assessment of our current performance or characteristics but those from the past as well. Obviously people can differ a great deal in the weight given to the past in making their current assess-ments of self. For example, two brothers had quite different attitudes about discussing the past. Michael had had a very distinguished career as a research biologist, had seen two children become physicians, and in gen-eral was considered a respected member of the community. On the other hand, Bernard, who was two years older, had made a mess of his life. By age 35 he was an alcoholic, and by age 45 he was practically unable to hold a job. His wife left him when he was 40 and refused to let his children near their "drunken" father. It is not surprising that at age 60 Michael talked fondly of the past and looked on it as enhancing his positive self image, while at age 62 Bernard was reluctant to discuss the past and preferred instead to talk about what was going on in his life at the mo-ment.

Because the past is available and can be used in defending the self, roles a person no longer plays may provide important evidence of compe-tence and success that often is not very apparent to an outside observer. Greenwald (1980) has gone so far as to argue that people fabricate and revise their personal histories by means of a set of processes that essen-tially *guarantee* a positive evaluation. First, the past is recalled as a drama in which the self was *the* leading player. One result is a perception that one had more control of, influence on, or responsibility for results than the other actors, and one can also potentially perceive oneself as the center of the other characters' actions. This tendency could lead to a negative self-evaluation based on a previous life involving many negative results if it were not for the second process: people tend to take credit for positive results and to blame factors outside their control for negative results. This tendency may serve as an effective screen preventing poor results in the past from reaching the current self-image. Obviously, if this hypothesis is true, then as time goes by one can build a great deal of credit and very little blame. And this ability has important positive implications for the *success* element in the self-esteem equation. Finally, Greenwald points out that the self is a very conservative historian who insists that new informa-tion must *fit* and *support* the prior view of self. This theory does not imply that the self is impervious to contradictory new information but rather that, as with most ideas, the greater the amount of prior confirmation of self, the greater the amount and credibility of new information needed to change one's existing self-image. The outcome for the vast majority of older people matches what we would expect from Greenwald's theory. Most older people do have very positive self-images that are quite resistant to negative change (Atchley, 1969).

The same processes of developing personal history that lead to a posi-tive evaluation of self can also be applied in evaluating people you love. Thus, close family and friends can often be counted on to *support* one's fabricated personal history.

Not only are there tools for controlling information about our pasts, but we also have techniques we use to control information about the present. Over time, people tend to conclude that they know themselves as well as, and probably better than, anyone else does or could. This tendency can lead us to assign more weight to what *we* think about ourselves than to what others say about us. We may also feel that stereotypes about some category we might be assigned to are irrelevant to our own self-images. The gerontology literature has consistently shown that older people can both accept the stereotypes about aging and the aged *and* feel that these stereotypes have no applicability to them personally.

Continuity of self is also reinforced and defended by the fact that people tend to remain in familiar environments that allow them to exercise well-practiced skills, which in turn provides an experience of competence. Everyday tasks such as housework, driving a car, or shopping can come to be important symbols of self-sufficiency.

Continuity is also promoted by how people see themselves. When people are asked to assign *themselves* to life stages, they often assign themselves to younger age categories than the general public would. Much has been made of this tendency in the literature as evidence that no one wants to be old, presumably because "older person" is such an inferior status. But to me there is another explanation that makes more sense: they are simply making an accurate assessment of their functional life stage.

Defining oneself as old is unrelated to low self-esteem (Cottrell and Atchley, 1969); therefore it seems safe to conclude that avoidance of this label is based on something other than fear or denial. If we go back to the definitions of life stages given earlier, we can see that the label *old age* is associated with a degree of frailty that is not very common among people age 65 or older.

In one study, 3,500 retired people were asked to classify themselves on the following scale:

△ Middle-aged

△ Just past middle-age

△ Old

△ Very old

Over 70 percent classified themselves as middle-aged or just past, and almost no one said they were very old. When we looked at their characteristics in terms of health and activities, we concluded that in terms of *functional* criteria their own self-assignments to life stages were accurate and not simply a denial of aging (Cottrell and Atchley, 1969).

Relative appreciation can also help to define a condition or situation as being more positive than it might otherwise appear. For example, an older person may acknowledge that aging has reduced the amount of heavy work that he or she can do but at the same time recognize that *compared to others his or her age* the decrement has been insignificant. This process is the logical opposite to the concept of relative deprivation, in which people feel that they are less fortunate than others. Older people probably show a sizable bias toward relative appreciation rather than relative deprivation.

The preceding techniques are usually effective in insulating us from having to apply stereotypes about categories such as "college students," "professors," or "older people" to ourselves. However, when someone directs a negative evaluation at you directly, then another type of defense is needed. We can usually find something about the person who did it that we can use to *discount* what they've said. Sometimes people develop the capacity to literally *forget* such comments. We can also control negative responses from others by selective interaction—we simply interact as much as possible with people who are not so negative. People sometimes manipulate negative responses by only venturing forth on days when they are sure that their physical state will not occasion comment.

People can often restrict their interactions to those they can rely on to support a positive moral and emotional self-assessment. In this respect, the freedom from *required* involvement with people outside one's own circle that often typifies later life is a boon. The more ageist and hostile the environment, the greater the advantage to voluntary (as opposed to required) involvement.

When Defenses Fail

The foregoing picture implies that the internal and external mechanisms available to defend the self-image should be enough to protect older people most of the time in most everyday situations. And although this is indeed the case for four out of five older people, a substantial minority (20 percent) of the elderly still has low self-esteem.

To begin with, some older people never developed a solid sense of self or identity. These people have been unsure of themselves and defenseless their entire lives, and whatever we see in them now may have nothing to do with aging.

Other older people have developed the idea that rotten is the way they are *supposed* to be—that for them a bad self-image is good. For them, ageism gives them renewed opportunities to accumulate negative credit and they soak up the insults like sponges and may even seek them out. These are the masochists in our midst.

But probably the biggest category of people with lifelong low self-esteem is made up of people whose expectations for themselves far outdistanced their capacity for successes and whose moral rigidity prevented the necessary rapprochement. These are the lifelong perfectionists. For example, Miss B had been a schoolteacher for over 40 years. Although she was generally competent, she could always see things that could have been done that she did not do. Despite very positive feedback from her students and from the various principals she worked with, she continued to feel that she was not *really* doing a very good job. Instead of using her experience of herself as a basis for positive self-esteem, she used it to reinforce a negative self-image.

For all these people, the problem is not a failure to defend self-esteem but rather a failure to ever develop it. Nevertheless, there are also people who experience a loss of self-esteem in later life. The key factors that I think are responsible for this loss are (1) loss of physical capacity, (2) a vulnerable self-image, and (3) loss of control over one's physical environment.

The gradual loss of physical capacity can be incorporated gradually into the self-concept, and the ideal self can be modified gradually to take gradual declines into account. Thus, gradual changes do not necessarily result in loss of self-esteem. One crucial issue here is whether the decline simply reduces the amount or quality of an activity one can do or whether the decline prevents one from continuing at all. In other words, *physical changes that disrupt continuity of preferred activities have a much greater potential for affecting self-concept and self-esteem compared to physical changes that allow continuity at a reduced activity level.* For example, a man who sees himself as a capable carpenter who can do his own home repairs can continue to hold this image even if he is forced to slow down or to get a little help from time to time. But at the point where he wants to repair a loose doorknob and finds himself unable to hold the screwdriver tight enough to do the job, it becomes more difficult to hold the image of current capability. The value of past accomplishments would still be available as a source of self-esteem, but current accomplishment would not. If being able to do activity currently is important to the person's sense of self, then a loss of self-esteem could occur.

If such losses occur gradually, the person may anticipate them and the results for the self may not be as serious as in cases where the change is sudden and substantial. For example, people with progressive arthritis have much more time to adjust to the idea of losing activities than do people who suffer incapacitating strokes.

Some people reach later life with adequate but very vulnerable self-esteem. High vulnerability can occur in several ways, most of which relate to the basis for the ideal self. The ideal self can be based on innumerable human characteristics. Some major categories include physical ability, mental ability, appearance, roles one plays, activities one does, groups one belongs to, qualities one has (honesty and so forth), or one's relative position in a group's hierarchy of prestige or honor or wealth. Obviously, the vulnerability of our selves to the changes aging brings depends largely on the vulnerability of the specific basis for our self-images. For example, people whose appearance is an important aspect of their ideal selves are more vulnerable to aging than those whose ideal selves are based mainly on personal qualities such as warmth toward others or being trustworthy. Generally, those who base their self-images on structural aspects of life such as roles or social position are much more vulnerable compared to others because aging predictably brings role loss and a reduction in income.

As already said, most older Americans do not have low self-esteem. Thus, if the foregoing explanation is true, then most older people could be expected to value *qualities* more than positions and roles. One study of this characteristic indeed found that the top-ranking personal goals of older people were as follows: being dependable and reliable, having close family ties, and being self-reliant and self-sufficient. Thus, the emphasis was on personal qualities and on the relationships one is least likely to lose. Goals such as being prominent in the community or having an important position were ranked at the very bottom (Atchley, 1980b:74). Another study found that adults across all ages tended to stress interpersonal qualities such as honesty, being forgiving, or being helpful over instrumental qualities such as intelligence or imagination (Rokeach, 1973).

People who have a diversified basis for self-esteem are less vulnerable to aging than those whose selves depend on only two or three characteristics. For example, for some people the job is *the* basis for their ideal self, their definition of success, and their self-esteem. Such people are rare, but if they are forced to retire, either due to health or social policy, then the results could be expected to be severe. Again, the research evidence shows that most older Americans have a very diversified pattern of activities, roles, personal qualities and other characteristics that serve as the basis for self-esteem.

Loss of control over one's home or community environment can pose serious problems for maintaining self-image. So long as people remain in familiar environments, skills and knowledge developed in the past can often be used to compensate for decrements in functioning. But people who move to new environments can be confronted with changes in their ability to gather and process new information or to get about that they may not have been aware of had they not moved. And if the person has difficulty figuring out the new environment and coping with it, there can be a very unsettling lapse in the person's usual sense of competence. In addition, the person may have moved away from the group of friends or family that supported the person's use of the past as a source of self-esteem. This problem can be made even worse if the person also comes into contact at this time with service providers who think that most older people are helpless or incompetent. Nevertheless, merely changing environments does not necessarily rob people of all their defenses. They can still attach more weight to their own experiences, discount what others say to them, selectively interact with others, and selectively participate in their new social environment. In addition, relatively few older people who move to new enrivonments do not know anyone there at the time they move. Having friends already there is one of the major factors in selecting a new environment (Longino, 1981).

But entering an institution is another matter. When people enter nursing homes, they are usually at the mercy of the staff, not only for their medical and personal care needs but for their sense of self as well. They usually find themselves among people who do not know their pasts and who cannot be counted on to support this source of self-esteem. They are in an unfamiliar environment, which might pose difficulties to learn to negotiate even if they were not sick.

It is very difficult to discount or avoid negative responses from others in a nursing home. The inmate (and I use this term advisedly) is usually not in control. He or she is unable to control who will be seen, where, and when.

It is crucial for people who work in nursing homes to keep in mind consistently that people entering the facility are sick or disabled people who have usually experienced numerous physical and social assaults on their self-concepts before they entered and that, particularly during their first few days there, they are relatively defenseless.

One way to help people retain a positive sense of self during the get-acquainted period is to ask them to give lengthy personal histories. The idea here is to get people to talk about the challenges and successes they have experienced. There are at least three positive outcomes to pursue: (1) a positive self-image of the past can be remembered and reinforced; (2) staff of the facility can develop a concrete basis for treating the person as someone of value, and (3) the person may be reminded that success is most often experienced as completion, as having taken on an everyday challenge successfully.

It is also useful to be matter-of-fact about the person's infirmities (rather than sympathetic or patronizing) and to be supportive rather than punitive in terms of encouraging the person to conform to the house rules. Such attitudes help emphasize the positive aspects of being in an institution.

Summary

Direct experience of aging tells us that aging usually occurs so gradually that it can be incorporated into our self-concepts naturally and that trauma seldom results. Most people do not personally experience age as having severely limited them in any significant way until their late 70s or even later.

On the other hand, messages we receive from others are often based on erroneous stereotypes of aging or elderly people as incapable. Aging is presumed to make people unattractive, unintelligent, asexual, unemployable, and mentally incompetent. Some people then try to impose this negative image and expectations based on it on all aging or older people, regardless of whether the shoe fits. This process is called *ageism*. Fortunately, only a minority of the general public subscribes to the ageist view.

The mass media present a mixed picture of aging and the aged— sometimes positive, sometimes negative. However, in recent years, media portrayals seem to be generally moving toward a preponderance of positive portrayals.

Some programs and service providers view the aged as helpless, regardless of whether the particular clientele being served fits this image or not. As a result, capable older people must sometimes endure a climate of ageism if they are to receive services. What proportion of elderly users of services experience this problem is unknown. Nevertheless, the majority of the elderly fits the "Assist the capable" model of service delivery rather than the "Help the helpless" model.

The negative messages that people receive about aging from others, the media, and social services programs are received by a personality and self that is aging. After young adulthood, there is more continuity than discontinuity in both self and personality and both become more stable with age. This consolidation occurs as a result of a natural process of adult development in which the duration and multiplicity of relationships and environments provide the information needed to develop a consistent view of personality and self, including a customary strategy for coping with the demands and opportunities of life. Most people enter later life with a stable personality and positive self-esteem.

Coping with negative messages about aging thus becomes a matter of defending a positive self-image. Using past successes, discounting messages that do not fit our existing self-concepts, refusing to apply general beliefs about aging to ourselves, selectively interacting with others, and selectively perceiving what we are told are all ways to defend ourselves against ageism. But some people develop neither a stable personality nor a positive self-image. And there is little in the situation of older people that is conducive to doing so at that stage.

A person who loses self-esteem in later life tends to do so (1) because physical changes have become so pronounced that the person is forced to accept what he or she sees as a less desirable self-image, (2) because the person's self-esteem is precarious or vulnerable as a result of a base for self-esteem that is too dependent on positions and roles or too narrow, or (3) because the individual has lost control over his or her home or community environment to such an extent that the person is essentially defenseless. This last problem is especially likely to occur when people enter nursing homes.

Most people have the resources and defenses needed to retain or maintain self-esteem into old age. This fact is very clear from the multitude of studies showing that older people living in community settings have stable, well-defined personalities and high self-esteem and that self-esteem increases with age.

Nevertheless, there are people who have lowered self-esteem in later life. I have tried to provide you with some conceptual tools that can be used to understand better how this loss can happen. Such tools can be very useful both in developing empathy for older people with low self-esteem and in making decisions about what might be helpful in trying to improve matters.

Chapter 5

Independence and Personal Effectiveness

Feelings of independence and personal effectiveness are two main supports for self-esteem at any age. *Independence* is the capacity to rely on oneself, and *personal effectiveness* is the capacity to influence the conditions of one's life. To understand how aging affects people, we need to know how it influences independence and personal effectiveness.

Independence

Our concept of adult independence has four basic dimensions: economic, physical, mental, and social. Economic self-reliance means that the individual has the wherewithal to provide him- or herself with food, clothing, and shelter. Physical self-reliance means the ability to move about freely and the ability to take care of one's physical needs. Mental self-reliance means having an alert mind that can exercise knowledge, experience, and skills to solve problems posed by the social and physical environment. Social independence means having the social power to demand various rights without having to rely entirely on the goodwill of others.

Self-sufficiency is a matter of degree, and for each stage in adult life and for each sex an individual must attain a socially defined threshold of self-sufficiency in order to be accepted as a full-fledged, independent adult. If self-sufficiency drops below the threshold, or never gets there to begin with, then the individual is assigned to the role of dependent adult.

The concept of adult independence does not imply isolation from other people. Independence simply frees adults to develop genuinely reciprocal relationships based on mutual respect, responsibility, and trust. Becoming a self-reliant adult is a prime goal for members of American society, old and young alike. But as people grow older, they experience changes that influence their ability to continue to be self-reliant. To know how older people cope with such changes, we need to know how ideas about being self-reliant originated and developed, what changes with age occur in the meaning of self-reliance, how people react to losses of self-reliance that sometimes come with old age, and what possibilities exist for preserving self-reliance.

Becoming Self-Reliant

Babies are notoriously self-centered; at the same time, they are among the most helpless and therefore most dependent creatures on earth. They must lean on others for physical security, support, sustenance, protection, and assistance. Early in life, this need to be dependent is fully accepted. At the same time, in American society children are gradually expected to develop their own talents and resources, to make decisions, and to learn to solve problems.

Children thus learn that there are times to be dependent and times to be independent. They also learn how much independence and dependence is appropriate for people of various ages. They learn that a small child can run to mother with a skinned knee and that parents often insist on deciding about clothes, friends, bedtime, and television-watching habits. At the same time, children are rewarded for learning to go to the toilet unassisted, to put away toys without being asked, to dress themselves, and so on.

Gradually, as children grow older, approval for independent behavior increases and approval for dependent behavior diminishes. Refusing to leave home for school, seeking adult support in arguments with other children, continuous requests for reassurance from parents, and other dependent acts meet with increasing disapproval from both family and peers. Teasing, humiliation, and ostracism are strong forces that teach children that dependency is to be avoided as one gets older.

Young people also must learn to distinguish between the ability to be socially independent and the ability to develop lasting reciprocal relationships with other people. The young must learn that to rely on others, to trust them, and to get emotional support from them, and vice versa, is not to lack independence but instead to manifest independence.

As adolescents approach adulthood, both parents and peers reward them for assuming adult roles and for doing more and more things without supervision. In addition, independent adolescents are rewarded by the intrinsic satisfaction that comes from being in control of one's environment. Social expectations concerning independence are so strong that we suspect something is wrong when adolescents do *not* rebel against parental authority. We expect young people gradually to assume control over their own decisions; in fact, it is this very process that separates child from adult.

Gradually we learn to dislike the idea of being dependent. The terms we use to describe dependents reveal our orientation toward dependency itself. For example, *moocher, sponge, leech, lazy good-for-nothing,* and *bum* are all terms we frequently apply to people who cannot take care of themselves financially. We learn very early in life that any adult who must rely on others for support is inferior, relegated to a subordinate and subservient position in relation to age peers, and expected to give up many rights of self-determination in exchange for support. Usually the support required is financial, but our negativity about dependency extends to most other kinds of support as well. To the average, well-reared, adult U.S. citizen, the role of dependent is appropriate only for kids, misfits, and the disabled. Many would also relegate women to a dependent role.

On the other hand, we gradually learn to prize independence very highly. We regard it as a state to be striven for and, once gained, to be jealously guarded. Our heritage of self-reliance and individual autonomy goes back to the dawn of European civilization and even before, and is translated into norms that permeate our lives. We are expected to be financially self-sufficient, to operate autonomous households, to get around by ourselves, and to manage our own affairs. The very fact that we are free to make our own decisions expands the range of alternatives we have for solving the problems we face, and at the same time increases the problems we have making choices.

Change in the Meaning of Independence

Adults are (usually) rewarded for acts of independence by their parents, are approved of by peers, receive the satisfaction of manipulating and controlling their environments, and usually experience the mixed pleasures of having others depend on them. When such people realize that they are losing their ability to function independently, they must cope not only with society's disapproval of dependence, but also with their own fear and disapproval of the dependent role (Kalish, 1967).

The only respite from this anxiety and fear exists for those segments of the population who are allowed a little dependency. For example, housewives are allowed to depend financially on their husbands. Sick people are allowed to be more physically dependent than are healthy people. Very old people are allowed more physical dependency than are middle-aged people. Bereaved people are often encouraged to be dependent for a short time. These exceptions notwithstanding, anxiety and fear are the usual reactions of older adults who face dependency.

Apparently, the meaning of independence changes with increasing age. To the young adult, independence means a newly found freedom; to the middle-aged adult, it means the normal way of living (as continuing proof of adulthood and self-worth); and to the adult in later maturity or old age it means the same thing as in middle age, with the added feeling that independence is something to be protected. In old age, the need to maintain independence sometimes approaches desperation because of the physical problems involved. But for the majority of older adults the expectation of continued independence, particularly with regard to staying in one's own household, is realistic.

Dimensions of Independence

In order to remain fully independent, older adults must retain financial self-sufficiency, must be able to live in their own independent households, and must be able to move freely about the community. They must be mentally able to cope with day-to-day decisions and must have opportunities to give as well as receive support. They must also be in at least fair health.

Financial independence is a major prerequisite for full participation as an adult, and lack of financial resources is a frequent reason older people cite for having to rely on others. Finances are discussed in more detail in Chapter 8. Here we are primarily interested in the effect of aging on financial self-sufficiency. The vast majority of older Americans remain financially self-sufficient, but at the same time there are substantial numbers whose incomes fall below what is needed to support even bare subsistence. Older retired couples generally avoid poverty and financial dependency. In fact, the proportion of couples in poverty in later life is actually lower than the proportion of couples in poverty below age 65. But older people who live alone are three times more likely to be living in poverty compared to younger single people. Two-thirds of the older single poor are women. About 40 percent of older single individuals are living on incomes at or just above the poverty line.

Financial dependency is a major reason why older people become involved with bureaucratic officials. The U.S. General Accounting Office (1977:25) studied the degree to which older people took advantage of Supplemental Security Income (SSI), a welfare program designed to provide a "floor" of financial support for older Americans. They found that only about half of those eligible had applied for and were receiving benefits. Part of the reason for this failure was, no doubt, that some people were unaware that they are eligible, but a major part was probably due to the fact that older people often refuse to put themselves in a position of being viewed as dependent. For instance, Mrs. B was eligible for Food Stamps. However, she only drew them once. She told me that after the way she was treated by the supermarket checkout clerk, she would "never use Food Stamps again if [she had] to starve to death."

Adult independence also requires maintaining one's own household. Only 8 percent of older Americans say that they would rather live with a child or other relative than in their own homes (Shanas, 1962), and over 80 percent were living in their own households in 1970. In an individual's household, he or she has much more privacy and freedom of choice than when it is necessary to accommodate the desires of others. When an older person lives with an adult child, for example, the child often makes the decisions in the household. For an adult who is accustomed to making decisions not only for him- or herself but for others, deferring to a son or daughter can represent a significant reduction in independence. However, it should not be assumed that every older person who lives in a household with his or her adult children is dependent. Many older people are heads of households in which their adult children are the dependents. In still other cases, neither generation is dependent.

Mobility is also a vital aspect of independence, particularly in our sprawling cities. It is almost impossible to live an independent life in many cities without an automobile. Shopping facilities, service facilities such as barber shops, beauty shops, shoe repair shops, and even churches are often located far from the city's residential areas. Middle-sized U.S. cities—those with populations ranging from 50,000 to 200,000—are encountering a steady decline in the availability of public transportation.

Most older people who can no longer afford to maintain an automobile, or who are physically unable to drive, usually must depend on friends and relatives for transportation. The fact that less than half of the older population owns an automobile suggests how prevalent this kind of limitation on independence is. More research is greatly needed in this area. There are very few data on the extent to which independence in the later years is hampered by inadequacies in transportation.

Most people remain mentally self-sufficient throughout their lives. Although they usually experience decrements in memory, problem solving, information processing, and decision making, these losses seldom significantly hinder independence. Older people who are mentally dependent are usually suffering from disabling mental illness or organic brain disease. About 10 percent of the older population is mentally disabled, and the increase in mental disability with age is mainly due to an increase in organic brain disease.

The changes that occur in physical and social life as people grow older may leave them with greatly restricted opportunities to participate or to find informal support. When these changes happen, the individual is almost bound to sense a loss of independence. For example, when friends and relatives die older people may find themselves in the position of having to ask for help from people they do not know; for example, from agents of bureaucratic organizations who are not interested in what the older person may have to *give* in order to preserve self-respect. And the sense of independence can be preserved only when the person has a sense of giving as well as receiving.

Only a modest level of health is necessary for independence. As one older person put it, "I'm not looking to be a spring chicken, I just don't want to be an invalid." In fact, twice as many disabled older people live in private homes as in institutions. No doubt this situation is partly the result of financial problems, but a feared loss of independence may very well keep many people from entering institutions even when entry would be to their advantage physically.

Motivations for Remaining Independent

Clark and Anderson (1967) observed that people offered two quite different sets of reasons for wanting to remain independent in their later years. One set of reasons includes pride in autonomy and concern for the freedom of others—motivation for independence that stems from a social situation seen as essentially supportive. The pride that comes from making decisions and doing things for oneself is a major source of self-esteem in a society that values independence as highly as ours does.

Aged parents who go out of their way to avoid imposing on their children have a greater chance of having their children respect their own independence. Many older people in the United States say they wish to avoid being a burden on their families, and this desire provides strong motivation for remaining independent as long as possible. The negative evaluation of dependency also provides motivation. Being dependent not only inconveniences the person being depended on, but also lowers the dependent's status. Thus, we would expect that the stronger the desire for respect from one's children, the greater the motivation to remain independent.

A second set of motives for independence is based on a perception of one's social environment as hostile or antagonistic. Older people often seek to remain independent because they are afraid that others will attempt to use them, to manipulate them, or to impose an unacceptable situation on them. Such reactions are sometimes paranoid and sometimes realistic.

But independence to the point of isolation can be very dangerous. Research findings clearly show that isolation can be deadly for the older person. Isolation has some important side effects. It increases privacy, but in older people it also increases vulnerability to illness, accidents, malnutrition, and loneliness. In addition, isolation greatly increases the social distance between the generations.

Older people's attitudes toward dependency tend to be very negative, a tendency that is undoubtedly related to the generally high degree of motivation among older people to remain independent. The positive value of independence coupled with the negative value of not encroaching on the independence of others results in strongly negative attitudes toward the mere idea of dependency.

Apparently, the negative attitudes toward dependency and the strong positive valuation of independence can combine to make the dependent older person miserable. In their intensive sample, Clark and Anderson (1967:222) found that the primary cause of low morale among older people was dependency, either financial or physical.

Preserving Independence and Minimizing Dependency

Older people usually first attempt to solve the problem of remaining independent themselves. They cut down on how much they spend to preserve financial self-reliance. They cut down on how much they do to conserve physical energy and independence. They compensate for failing memory by taking notes. They avoid social dependency by disengaging from contacts in which they have no power. For most, personal solutions succeed. Some, however, suffer losses too great for personal solutions and must seek outside help.

The first place older people usually go for help is to their kin. Becoming dependent on their children often strains their relationship—another factor that contributes to a negative attitude about dependency. Nevertheless, most families are somehow able to transcend the conflicts, guilt, and resentment that can arise in such situations and to work out an adequate way to handle the needs of older family members. This topic is covered in more detail in a later chapter.

The dread with which most older people regard dependency is thus very realistic. Yet as age increases, so does their need for outside help. Illness, poverty, disability, declining energy, failing hearing or sight—all these roads lead to dependency. Older people avoid seeking help from community agencies because they have no way to preserve even a semblance of reciprocity in dealing with bureaucratic organizations. The rules and regulations, the forms, and the prying into clients' personal lives that often typify social service agencies are indication enough that the older person has been assigned to the dependent role. Often, services in the older person's own home might well allow him or her to retain a measure of autonomy, and in some cases such services are being provided. Visiting nurses, homemaker services, and Meals-on-Wheels are examples of community services that are available in some areas. Unfortunately, most older people do not have access to these services, and even those who do either may not know about them or may find them inadequate.

Providing specialized in-home services for older people is generally regarded as expensive and inefficient. Instead, efforts are focused on institutions—nursing homes and homes for the aged. Here the needed supports can be provided, but here also even the illusion of self-help or self-determination all too often disappears. Clark and Anderson (1967:391) found that

Some of the aged in our sample feel that, if help can be obtained only at the expense of institutionalization, if the small sphere of respectable autonomy that constitutes the aged person's shrunken life-space can be punctured like a child's balloon—then it may be best to gamble on one's own with survival. Such people will draw their curtains to avoid critical appraisals of their help-lessness; they will not get enough to eat; they will stay away from the doctor and forego even vital drugs; they will shiver with cold; they will live in filth and squalor—but pride they will relinquish only as a last resort.

Not all older people react in this extreme fashion, but there is some evidence that older people who do enter institutions are reluctant to do so because they fear loss of independence. More research is needed on the relationship between (1) the individual's social independence within the institutional setting and (2) adjustment to institutional life. The most reason-able hypothesis would appear to be that the more choices the individual is given in the institutional setting, the better he or she will like living in the institution and the better adjustment will be. This hypothesis implies that the decisions left to the individual must be as important as possible.

Personal Effectiveness

Personal effectiveness is the sense that one has the capacity to influ-ence the conditions of one's own life and the lives of others. Having this sense of effectiveness depends not only on one's personal capabilities but also on facilitating social factors such as social integration, opportunity struc-tures, and power. Aging has important potential effects on all these factors. However, age-related social limits on the exercise of personal effectiveness tend to be imposed on most people long before physical or mental aging requires or justifies such limits.

In order to be effective in a group, one must participate, and aging negatively influences the extent to which people are *recruited* by groups and *encouraged* to participate in groups they already belong to. When a job needs doing in a community group, the leadership tries to think of who in the group could do it best, would be available, and so on. In watching this process, I have been impressed with how seldom older group members *even come to mind*. For example, I was once on a local community planning committee that needed to collect some information. We spent an hour hashing over various people who might do the job. Finally, I suggested the name of a retired person in the community who had all the needed skills. "Of course! Why didn't I think of him?" exclaimed the committee chairperson. Why indeed? The tendency to exclude older people from the field of people to consider is an insidious form of ageism that is very difficult to combat because it is often unconscious. But even when older people *are* suggested, they are sometimes rejected purely on the basis of *ageism*, which is prejudice against older people. Older people who want to increase their participation in organized

groups are often frustrated by ageism. And ageism is one of the main reasons that age-segregated groups for older people have been developed.

Part of the well-known *disengagement theory* (Cumming and Henry, 1961) deals with the tendency of social institutions and the groups supporting them to exclude older people from participation in action toward the groups' goals even though older people may be the object of some of this action. Societal disengagement occurs when people are no longer encouraged to apply for positions they are qualified to serve in and when they are not encouraged to remain in positions they are functioning well in *based on age rather than ability*. Older people may not be sought out for leadership positions, their labor may no longer be desired by their employers, their unions may no longer consider their interests, or they may be "eased out" of positions in community oranizations. Societal disengagement is often an unconscious and passive process—it is a clear but subtle message to older people that they are not wanted or needed. Societal disengagement goes hand in hand with *age discrimination*, the direct and overt denial of opportunity because a person is "the wrong age." Both are based on ageism and stereotyped beliefs about aging. Thus, even if older people have the strength to ignore the sometimes not-so-subtle hints of societal disengagement that they should voluntarily withdraw, they find themselves facing the more unavoidable process of age discrimination.

However, it is important to remember that societal disengagement and age discrimination are only two factors involved in whether or not people continue to participate. For example, we tend to assume that people experience personal effectiveness in their jobs and that for this reason they want to continue in them. But the fact is that many people feel very ineffective in their jobs. Either they feel unsuited to the jobs or inept at them, or they feel that they have very little ability to influence their own working conditions. It is no accident that desire for retirement among workers in large factories or bureaucratic organizations is considerably higher than it is among the self-employed. And even those who feel effective on the job may reach the point where the worries, responsibilities, or long hours associated with the job outweigh the value of feeling effective in that situation. This situation arises particularly among people who have alternative sources of personal effectiveness. In addition, the high degree of self-determination that characterizes retirement can exert a substantial pull even for people who feel effective on the job. Retirement may actually provide *more* opportunities for personal effectiveness than employment does.

Although people tend to experience societal disengagement and age discrimination as they grow older, the problem tends to be focused mainly in organizations rather than in informal groups. Most people are well integrated into family and friendship networks that provide not only social support but also important opportunities for continued participation. It is in this sense that individual disengagement *from* society as a whole is viewed as disengagement *into* the family (Troll et al., 1979). In addition, family and friends usually can be relied on to reinforce the view of oneself as being effective. Thus, family, friends, and familiar leisure activities can serve as important buffers against the messages of implied inability that come from the society at large.

Societal disengagement is a *tendency*, not a universal. It happens more to some older people than to others. Certainly part of this disproportionate effect comes from the fact that aging has differential outcomes in terms of what it does to the functioning of individuals and at what chronological age. But a major part of society's tendency to withdraw its interest in the contributions of older people results from the effect of ageism on people's perceptions of what the aged have to offer in social exchanges of various kinds. Some people, such as semiskilled factory workers, enter later life with very few exchange resources to offer, while others, such as those in highly skilled crafts, find that their exchange resources remain more or less intact.

Exchange Theory and Age Discrimination

Exchange theory assumes that in their interactions with others, people try to maximize their rewards and minimize their costs.[1] Rewards can be

[1] Exchange theory essentially began with Homans (1961) and was later elaborated by Blau (1964), Emerson (1962, 1972), and Mulkay (1971). The major attempts to use exchange theory in social gerontology have been made by Dowd (1975, 1980).

defined in material or nonmaterial terms and include such factors as assistance, money, property, information, affection, approval, labor, skill, respect, compliance, or conformity. Costs can be defined as the loss of any of these. Because its proponents use such terms as "exchange rates" and "return on investment," exchange theory initially seems to be a rational equivalent to the well-known but more emotionally oriented pleasure-pain principle. But the exchange process involves elements that are not necessarily either rational or conscious. And as we shall see, classical exchange theory is better at helping us understand impersonal interactions in organizational settings than other types of interaction. It also works better when applied to transitory or new relationships rather than to long-standing ones.

Dowd (1975, 1980) has advanced the major argument concerning how aging affects exchange. It starts with the familiar assertions that people want to *profit* from social interaction and that profit consists of a *perception* that the rewards coming from the interchange outweigh the costs. The ability to profit from an exchange depends on the exchange resources that the actors bring to the exchange. When resources are reasonably equal, then a mutually satisfying interdependence may emerge. But if one of the actors has substantially fewer exchange resources, then his or her ability to profit from the interchange can be sharply restricted.

The *actual* exchange resources that a person has may not be as important as the resources he or she is *assumed* to have. And this is where age comes in. Along with other personal characteristics such as sex, ethnicity, and social class, age influences the resources we are *presumed* to have, particularly in terms of information, skills, and ability to do physical labor. Older people are often assumed to have less up-to-date information, obsolete skills, and inadequate physical strength or endurance.

Thus, ageism is converted into age discrimination at least partially because of its influence on our assumptions about exchange resources. And many of these assumptions have been around so long that people are not even conscious of them. Their validity is taken for granted not only by people who deal with older adults but also by older adults themselves, at least as applied to other older adults (but usually not to oneself).

The presumed reduction with age in exchange resources is acted on as if it were real, which results in a power differential that puts older people at a distinct disadvantage. And because they are at a disadvantage, the aged are relatively powerless actors who are forced into a position of compliance and dependence because they are seen as having nothing of value that they can withhold in order to get better treatment.

There is no doubt that this scenario describes quite accurately the situation that confronts many older adults who are looking for a new job, trying to become involved in community organizations, or trying to get service from a bureaucracy. But it is also of limited applicability in many situations.

Flaws in Exchange Theory Applied to Older People For one thing, age may not be as important as other attributes such as sex, race, or ethnicity in establishing presumptive limits on exchange resources. In other words, if discrimination against women, blacks, and Spanish-speaking people is more clear-cut than age discrimination, then the elderly may be better off in terms of escaping discrimination. Take employment as an example. Job discrimination increases and decreases in direct relation to the balance between the number of jobs and the number of people who want them. When jobs are relatively plentiful, then discrimination tends to be relaxed in order to get jobs filled. But when the job market tightens, discriminatory criteria come into play to allocate jobs first to the most "deserving" categories—those presumed to have the most exchange resources. The important issue is where age stands in relation to other discriminatory criteria. Is it the first used (and therefore widespread) or the last used (and therefore employed widely in only the hardest of economic times)?

Dowd (1975, 1980) argues that retirement is age discrimination and reflects a widespread and constant use of age as a discriminatory criterion. However, this position is much too simplistic. There are at least three major routes to retirement, and only mandatory retirement involves age discrimination. Parnes and Nestel (1981) examined the prevalence of various types of retirement in a national sample of over 2,000 men who retired between 1966 and 1976 and found that health-related retirement, the most common pattern, accounted for 51 percent. Voluntary retirement tended to be early—before 65—and accounted for 46 percent. Thus, only 3 percent of the retirements that occurred involved mandatory retirement of a man from a job he would have preferred to keep. In fact, less than a third of the men were even *subject* to mandatory retirement. In 1978 the legal mandatory retirement age was raised from 65 to 70 in the private sector. Thus far there is no evidence that this change has significantly altered the pattern to retire at or before 65. This finding is very persistent in the retirement literature. If the vast majority of retirements occur as a result of poor health or preference for retirement, then it can hardly be argued that retirement is evidence for age discrimination or a loss of exchange resources.

Another bit of evidence that older people may not be as powerless as they are commonly thought to be comes from the growing number of legal constraints on the use of old age as a criterion for exclusion. For example, the Age Discrimination in Employment Act (ADEA) of 1967, amended in 1978, prohibits the use of age as a criterion for hiring, firing, discriminatory treatment on the job, and referral by employment agencies. It also prohibits job advertisements reflecting age preferences, age discriminatory pressures by labor unions, and retaliation against employees who assert their rights under the act. Although employers may be inclined to discriminate against older workers, a growing number are learning that it may be expensive to do so. From 1969 to 1977, the number of complaints brought by older workers against employers rose from 1,000 to over 5,000.[2] In 1978, the U.S. Department of Labor brought suits on behalf of 4,000 older workers seeking

---

[2] The Age Discrimination in Employment Act defines an *older worker* as anyone age 45 or over.

over $14 million in lost pay and benefits. About half of these suits were successful, and another third were settled out of court. The growing volume of age discrimination suits reflects the growing awareness of older workers that they are not powerless to fight age discrimination in employment.

Effectiveness Through Organizations of Older People Part of the reason why older people have the political power to resist age discrimination relates to the existence of large national organizations of older people. The National Retired Teachers Association/American Association of Retired Persons has a membership of over 6 million people age 55 or over. The National Council of Senior Citizens has over 3 million members. The poor, women, blacks, and other minority groups are not represented by such large national organizations. In addition, many other national groups seek to influence public policy to treat the elderly favorably. The Gerontological Society of America represents about 5,000 professionals whose research, teaching, or practice involves aging or the aged. The National Council on the Aging represents over 1,000 agencies that serve the aged. Other organizations represent homes for the aged, nursing homes, state offices on aging, city offices on aging, area agencies on aging, and so forth. Still other organizations represent minority-group elders, particularly blacks, the Spanish-speaking, and Native Americans. All these organizations have banded together to form a Leadership Coalition of Aging Organizations. A large measure of the success of the so-called Gray Lobby has come from the fact that large national organizations can afford to hire professional managers who know the political system and how to get it to work for the elderly (Pratt, 1977). And the success of the Gray Lobby offers an important lesson in terms of exchange theory: *the exchange resources of an organized group can vastly exceed the sum of the exchange resources of its individual members.*

Variability in Exchange Resources Exchange theorists seem to have the idea that aging has several practically inevitable effects that serve to reduce exchange resources and that the aging individual is relatively powerless to prevent this erosion of perceived resources. However, the facts simply do not support this assumption. As we have seen, aging does not produce predictive results at the individual level. That is, although we may be able to predict that roughly 30 percent of people will eventually be disabled by aging, we are unable to predict which people will be included in that 30 percent. And the continued functioning of the nondisabled requires us to acknowledge that most older people have valuable exchange resources.

In addition, ideas about the exchange resources of older people fluctuate across cultures, over time, and across situations. In regional subcultures and in ethnic subcultures, ideas about what elders have to offer fluctuate widely. For example, in suburban Cleveland a young man may not feel that his older neighbor has much to offer him. But in rural Appalachia it may be obvious that the older farmers know a great deal about the best ways to grow tobacco. And among the Navaho it is the custom that a man is not ready even to *begin* study to be a medicine man until age 40. After decades of decline in the value placed on older factory workers, recently there has been a resurgence of appreciation of the superior dependability and reliability of older workers compared to the young.

Selective appreciation involves (1) a recognition that people offer more in some situations than they do in others and (2) an emphasis on those areas where they *do* have something to offer. For example, my mother and I used to talk a good bit about my work. Although she was an older person herself, she knew very little about the concepts people use to communicate about or do research on aging. She had relatively little to offer in that area. But she was a keen observer, and she shared with me her observation about her own life and the lives of other older people around her. These descriptions were valuable details that I could use to flesh out my general knowledge about aging. My mother had been a very successful manager of people in her work career. I found that her advice about how to handle personnel decisions at work was almost always sound. On the other hand, my mother and I disagreed substantially about religion, especially the appropriate religious upbringing for my two children. We tended not to talk about this topic because each perceived the other as being off base and there was little we could share. The point is that I saw my mother generally as having a great deal to offer me, but I also fully recognized that my appreciation for her resources did not extend to all areas of knowledge or all social situations. I selectively appreciated her.

The prevailing view of exchange and aging assumes that unequal exchange rates that disadvantage the aged become institutionalized and are accepted by old and young alike. As we have seen, the impact of age on exchange resources is variable and depends on the situation. As such, it is not very amenable to institutionalization except in bureaucratic situations. Bureaucratic ideology can deal with people in a depersonalized way as members of categories. For example, people who work in the personnel department of a large plant do not deal with the factory workers on an ongoing basis. They see them only occasionally, and then briefly. Decisions about workers made in the personnel department can be "cold and impersonal" precisely because the personnel staff have no personal information about the employees. Likewise, workers in the local Social Security office must work within the framework of a law that is quite specific about who is entitled to what and under which circumstances. There is no way they can make allowances for differences in situations or circumstances that are not already allowed for in the law.

But most situations in life, even if they occur within a bureaucratic environment, involve an element of personalization. For example, a good manager gets to know his or her employees. This knowledge creates an opportunity for the development of selective appreciation. In addition, the more we know about someone's capabilities and limitations, history, and circumstances, the more understandable that person becomes. This empathy can grow over time, and it provides us with increased opportunity for selective appreciation. Granted, some people do not appreciate anything in anyone, especially in themselves. But most people want to find value in everyone, and the longer the relationship endures and the more personalized it becomes, the greater the potential for substantial appreciation of "good" qualities and discounting of "bad." The process is akin to the one used by the self to ensure self-esteem, only in this case it assures esteem for one's associates. Again, the process is a *tendency*, not a universal, but it does serve to enhance the exchange resources of older adults because most of their relationships are of long duration.

Institutionalized exchange rates can be imposed on older people only in situations where they are essentially powerless. When older people have exchange resources, then exchange rates must be *negotiated*. In social service agencies and in nursing homes, for example, older people tend to need service far more than the service provider needs anything the older person has to offer. In these situations, the older person may be forced into conformity and compliance. Thus, those older people who are already disadvantaged by illness, disability, or poverty find themselves even further disadvantaged by the power differential they experience in their interactions with the service network. This situation may also be a primary cause of the fact that many "needy" elders who are eligible for services refuse to take advantage of them.

But when the elderly have recognized resources, be they in the form of approval, skilled work, advice, wisdom, money, property, information, affection, or conformity, older people are able to "bargain up" their exchange rate. The results of the negotiation process depend on the perceptions of the actors concerning the relative value of the rewards offered, the ability to withhold rewards, the availability of alternative sources of the desired rewards, and bargaining skill. For example, Dr. H is a man in his 70s who has a worldwide reputation for research in gerontology. He is retired and has a reliable and sufficient income independent of employment. He is also widely sought as a speaker and as a research consultant. He has a great advantage in most exchanges because he does not "need" the money attached to employment and he has quite enough achievements to satisfy himself and provide self-respect. The fact that he has scarce knowledge and skills means that he is sought after, and his financial and psychological independence mean that he has great power to pick and choose exactly what work he will do, for whom, and when.

On the other hand, Mr. N is a retired milling machine operator who receives a modest Social Security pension that barely provides enough to support him and his wife. To have a small economic cushion against emergencies, he works part-time. Because he has no exceptional skills, he works for relatively low wages doing yard work for two local churches. He knows this work is not very high status, but he is glad to have it and is careful to avoid offending his employers. How work *feels* to these two men is very different, and so is their behavior on the job. Dr. H is confident, forceful, and at home in his work; Mr. N is tentative, compliant, and slightly fearful. These differences are not simply due to variations in personality or role but reflect very basic differences in the exchange resources each can command.

Aging has no necessary effect on exchange resources. Most often differences in exchange resources in later life are merely continuations of differences that have been there throughout adulthood. That is, Dr. H and Mr. N had very different exchange resources when they were 20, 35, and 50 as well as when they were 70. Another way to put this is that age changes in exchange resources are very slight handicaps toward the finish line, while sex, social class, and race can be substantial handicaps from the beginning.

Another limitation of exchange theory as it has been applied to aging has to do with the fact that the flexibility built into age norms often allows older people to concentrate their attention on long-standing relationships with friends. In such relationships, the exchange rules have long since been established, and because changes in the people occur gradually exchange rules are adjusted gradually too.

Exchange theorists often posit that the elderly avoid intergenerational relationships because of the unfavorable exchange rates but no real evidence has been collected on this issue. Although this hypothesis may be true of some older people, others may have a different experience. For example, many middle-aged people develop mentoring relationships with younger people. And even after the mentoring function is no longer necessary, an intergenerational friendship remains that can be taken into later life. For example, when I began my career in gerontology at Miami University, Fred Cottrell was already in his 60s. For over a decade he provided me with support and sound advice, and he also used his esteemed position in gerontology to create opportunities for me that I might not have had otherwise. I succeeded him as Director of the Scripps Foundation Gerontology Center in 1974 but Fred never stopped working with me in Scripps, and until his death in 1979 I continued to rely on him for advice and perspective. He had very strong exchange resources in his relationship with me long after my need for a mentor had diminished.

One piece of evidence used to support the notion that older people avoid intergenerational contacts is the age segregation of residential areas. However, if one looks at alternative causes of age segregation, fear of crime and desire for better housing emerge as much more influential factors. In low-crime areas where low-rent housing specifically for the elderly is not available, age segregation does not occur. Such neighborhoods tend to be age integrated.

Exchange theory is least useful in illuminating relationships of older people with their adult children because the dynamics of family relationships usually transcend the rational, pleasure-pain approach to defining duty and reciprocity. Families operate under a different set of rules. For one thing, parental approval remains an important reward for most people throughout life. Adult children may not like the idea that they still want Mom and Dad's approval, but they do want it nevertheless. Likewise, most parents want to continue to do things for their children throughout their lives. In addition, the lineal transmission of property gives parents an important resource they can use to bargain with their children in exchange for compliance. Finally, many families define intergenerational reciprocity in long-range terms. Therefore the elder generation may build up exchange credit that can be cashed in later when it is needed. In these terms, *current* exchange may not be the relevant time frame. Thus painting a general picture of intergenerational exchange rates in families is a difficult task, if not impossible. In addition, concepts of duty or loyalty can override exchange as the basis for behavior, especially in families.

Summary

Independence and personal effectiveness are important foundations of adult identity. For older adults, the main issue is to avoid losing independence and personal effectiveness, to avoid having one's resources drop below the level required for self-reliance.

Economic, physical, mental, and social resources are all needed to preserve highly valued independence and to avoid dreaded dependency. Older people look on independence as a prize to be protected. In later life, financial independence is the rule rather than the exception. Nevertheless, a substantial number of older adults have incomes at or below the poverty line. Poverty is much more likely to occur among single older people than among the married. Single older women are especially likely to be poor. Fewer older people apply for income assistance than are eligible, in part because to apply for such benefits requires that people publicly acknowledge that they are dependent on public welfare.

For most older people, living in an independent household is a realistic expectation. However, it would be an even more realistic alternative if more in-home services were available.

A small proportion of elders is disabled to the point of requiring physical assistance in moving about. Very few older people lose their independence due to mental incapacity. A much larger percentage depends on others to provide transportation.

Reciprocity is an important aspect of a continued sense of independence. Older people need to feel that they are *giving* as well as *receiving* in their exchanges if they are to continue to feel self-reliant.

Older people have very negative attitudes toward dependency, which if carried to an extreme can cause social isolation and problems such as increased vulnerability to illness, accidents, and malnutrition.

Older people try very hard to maintain self-reliance by economizing, conserving energy, or dropping social relationships in which they have no power. When they do need assistance, they most often go to their kin for physical and transportation assistance. For income assistance, they are more likely to rely on government-supported programs.

Personal effectiveness is the sense that one has the capacity to control one's own destiny to an acceptable extent. This sense depends on personal attributes and also on one's level of acceptance within a group, the availability of opportunities, and the amount and kinds of power one can muster on one's own behalf. Most people encounter socially imposed limits on their personal effectiveness that are not justified by the effects of aging.

Societal disengagement is the exclusion of older people from the pool of eligibles from which people are selected for responsible positions. It also occurs when people are not encouraged to remain in positions in which they are performing effectively. Age discrimination is the conscious and overt exclusion of older people, while societal disengagement is often an unconscious process.

Elders are more likely to encounter societal disengagement and age discrimination in formal organizations than they are in informal groups. Part of the rationale for such societal withdrawal rests on the assumed effects of aging on exchange resources. Older people are assumed to have less up-to-date information, to have obsolete skills, to be less trainable, and to be less physically and mentally capable. However, many factors can reduce the effects of ageism on exchange resources. Legal restrictions on age discrimination are growing. Older people have been moderately successful in protecting themselves through the actions of large national organizations of older people. Exchange resources can also be quite variable from person to person even within the older population. And selective appreciation can result in a preservation of exchange resources even in people who have encountered some losses as a result of aging. Also, differentials in exchange resources created earlier in life are likely to persist into later adulthood.

In intergenerational relationships, older people are often able to take advantage of exchange credit accumulated earlier in the relationships between older parents and their adult children. Such advantages also apply to relationships in which the older person earlier served as a mentor.

The end result for most older people is a situation in which they can maintain their independence and personal effectiveness throughout their lives. Nevertheless, aging makes people vulnerable to changes in income, health, and social supports that can cause them to seek aid from bureaucratic organizations. In turn, seeking such aid makes them more vulnerable to societal disengagement, age discrimination, and diminished exchange resources.

Chapter 6

The Experience
of Vulnerability

Vulnerability is both a probability and a state of mind. To be vulnerable is to be continually at risk of loss or harm. For example, consider the following cases:

△ Jane has noticed that it is increasingly hard for her to climb the two flights of stairs to her apartment, especially carrying laundry or groceries.

△ Bill's younger sister just died. She was 67. Bill finds himself more aware of his own mortality than ever before.

△ Emily lives in an older part of town in a house that she and her husband bought 40 years ago. She saw a news items on television about a mugging of an older man in her neighborhood, and it made her afraid. She is considering dropping out of a church group that meets at night.

△ Fred saw in the newspaper that inflation has risen to an annual rate of 14 percent. Because a sizable part of his income comes from a private pension that does not increase with inflation, Fred is worried that before long he will not be able to make ends meet.

All these cases have in common a feeling of vulnerability. As a category, the elderly are more vulnerable than other age groups are. They are more likely to experience losses in physical capacities. They are often in a precarious financial situation. They are more likely to lose important social relationships as friends and relatives die, and are more likely to be acutely aware of their own mortality. They are more likely to lose control over their living environments. They may be less able to defend themselves against crime, exploitation, or abuse. The *feeling* that being vulnerable brings is one of insecurity—not insecurity in the sense of being uncertain of one's own worth, but insecurity in the sense of being unsafe or liable to loss or failure.

The elderly are vulnerable to loss, to exploitation, and to crime and abuse. Losses pose a threat to self-reliance and competence. Fear of exploitation, crime, or abuse produces feelings of being unsafe.

Vulnerability to Losses

The elderly are vulnerable to physical, mental, and financial losses, as well as to the loss of social resources, social roles, and housing independence.

Physical and mental precariousness comes from being on the edge of incompetence. What we mean by competence here is having a body that functions well enough to allow the person to move about freely and perform ordinary tasks of daily living, plus a mind that is alert and sensory capacities sufficient to allow normal communication with others.

Although severe limitations on mobility, mental confusion, blindness, or deafness are relatively rare among older people, as the proportion of very old people (85 and over) increases, the proportion with these difficulties will probably increase. In addition, the unpredictability of physical losses—the inability to pinpoint precisely *who* is vulnerable—leads to *fear* of physical losses that is much more widespread than the actual occurrence of physical losses. It is important to remember that being in a high-risk category can itself increase vulnerability through the fear that can be associated with it. For example, Mrs. G has high blood pressure that she controls well with medication. Otherwise she is in excellent health. Nevertheless, she lives in mortal fear of a paralytic stroke because her sister suffered one. The tension can aggravate her high blood pressure. When others in our social category begin to experience sudden and sometimes severe losses, we become more aware of the fact that it could happen to us. And even though the odds are against its happening to us, the dread remains.

Lawton (1972:133–135) developed a scale of "instrumental activities of daily living." The highest level of competence was assigned to people who were able to look up and dial telephone numbers, shop alone and return home independently, plan and prepare adequate meals independently, perform routine housekeeping unassisted, do personal laundry completely, travel independently, take correct dosages of medication at the correct times, and manage finances independently (keep track of income, write checks, go to the bank, pay bills, and so forth). This scale is a good operational definition of the minimum level of competence required to live independently. According to this definition, less than 10 percent of the elderly living in the community is incompetent on one or more of these dimensions.

Shanas (1977) studied a national sample of older people in 1975 and

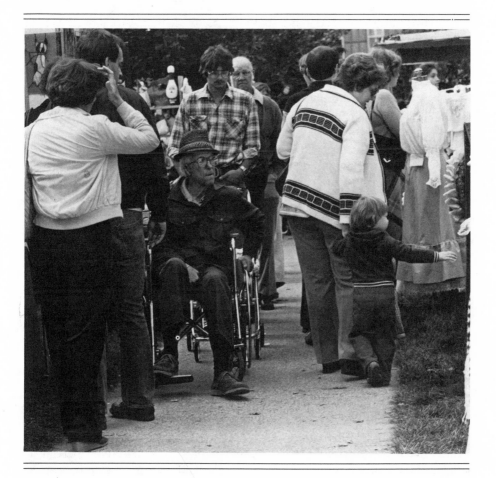

found that less than 2 to 4 percent was unable to do basic self-maintenance activities and another 4 to 5 percent had difficulty performing these tasks. I and my associates (Atchley, 1977) found that 84 percent of a general community sample of people age 55 and over in 1975 had no major activity limitations, and over 90 percent had adequate transportation. Shanas and Maddox (1976) report that about 10 percent of the elderly suffers from mental confusion.

As noted earlier, the incidence of blindness is 2.6 percent from age 65 to 74, and 8.3 percent at age 75 or older (National Center for Health Statistics, 1959:9). About 13 percent of the older population is deaf or severely hard of hearing (Corso, 1977:535). Perhaps another 10 percent of the older population has enough sight or hearing impairment to cause difficulty in either getting or giving communications. For example, poor eyesight can make it difficult to read instructions on food packages or on medication containers. Poor hearing can not only make it difficult to get messages but to send them, too. Prolonged hearing problems often lead to speech problems.

Thus, although we tend to think of the loss of mobility or mental alertness as being the common losses in old age, in fact they are relatively rare (less than 10 percent). A much higher proportion (perhaps as much as 16 percent) experiences sight or hearing losses that are sufficient to impair competence.

Thus, it is primarily *fear* of loss rather than a high probability of loss that tends to make older people quite sensitive to any hint that they may be slipping. This oversensitivity can lead to a persistent anxiety about one's health and any change in it. Sometimes the results of temporary illness are taken to be a permanent loss. It is important to realize that many older people do not see a high degree of concern for one's health as unreasonable—they see it as an important part of preserving their independence.

Precarious Finances

Aging also can increase the risk of slipping into poverty, particularly for older single people. For example, in 1975, 23 percent of older couples had incomes below a "modest but adequate" level, close to the figure for younger families. But 55 percent of older people living alone had incomes of $3,500 or less per year, which put them below the "modest but adequate" level. This situation is very clearly tied to the fact that Social Security benefits are much more adequate for couples than they are for individuals.

Minority group status also has a strong impact on the risk of being poor in later life. For example, in 1975 nearly half of older black couples and more than half of Spanish-origin older couples had inadequate incomes, compared to 20 percent of white older couples. And nearly 85 percent of single older women who were either black or of Spanish origin had inadequate incomes. Poverty among single older minority women is nearly twice as common as among single older minority men (Atchley, 1980b:137).

Financial difficulties in later life come from several directions. About 20 percent of the older population have been poor their entire lives. Poverty in later life is nothing new to them. People who lose their jobs after age 45 usually can find another job, but with an average drop of 25 percent in wages or salary (Parnes and King, 1977). The longer the period of unemployment, the greater the cut in earnings. Prolonged unemployment and lower income in the preretirement years has an obvious influence on the ability to prepare financially for retirement.

Retirement itself brings an average reduction in income of 40 percent. Nevertheless, this change is expected, and most people manage to adjust to it without serious consequence to their usual life-styles. On the other hand, widowhood or divorce can have much more severe financial consequences. Women who become widowed or divorced before they are old enough to be eligible for Social Security or other survivor benefits and who are not employed can find themselves suddenly in a desperate financial situation on top of all the emotional upheaval associated with widowhood or divorce. And even after the emotional impact fades, the financial conse-quences remain.

For instance, Mrs. S was 57 when her husband died. With two children in college and no employment, Mrs. S found herself in a desperate situation. Her husband's life insurance amounted to $25,000, which was just enough to pay off the mortgage on their house. Her children were eligible for survi-vor's benefits from Social Security so long as they remained in college, but Mrs. S had no source of income. She had had no employment experience since she was 25 and little in the way of skills that were competitive in a tight job market. Mrs. S sought help from local social service agencies, but they could do little for her. She had to live on public welfare, and her children were forced to leave college. Although we may lament her situation and tend to assign blame to a lack of foresight, Mrs. S's situation is not uncommon.

Surviving spouses who are old enough to get Social Security benefits will find that the survivor benefit is only two-thirds the amount paid to a retired worker and his or her spouse. But expenditures such as rent, taxes, transportation, and home or auto insurance and maintenance are fixed, regardless of the number of people living in the household. In addition, survivors may have to hire more services done than was the case when their spouses were living. As a result, a one-third reduction in household income can produce financial precariousness and a need to alter life-style.

In general, the older the individual, the lower the Social Security and/ or private pension. Although cost-of-living increases have been applied regularly to Social Security benefits to ease the impact of inflation, little has been done to adjust for the dramatic increase in average real income since 1935. Even with cost-of-living increases in 1970 the average annual Social Security benefit to those age 95 or over was only $1,073 compared to $1,772 for those age 65.

Thus, the older people are in later life, generally the more financially precarious they are. This precariousness tends to be translated into persis-tent worry and anxiety about financial matters. Those of us who are able to cope with inflation and the related pressures on our life-styles by working more hours, getting part-time jobs, having our spouses get jobs, or by get-ting higher-paying jobs cannot easily appreciate the frustration and worry that constant news of inflation can bring to people who have no realistic possibility of getting jobs.

Social Losses

Our social resources consist of (1) family members and friends we rely on both in meeting our daily needs and in times of emergency, and (2) the social roles that focus our opportunities to participate. The deaths of friends and relatives are thus another important type of loss that is more likely to occur in later life. Most of us can consider ourselves lucky if we have three

or four close friends or relatives in whom we can confide our innermost thoughts, feelings, hopes, fears, guilts, and joys. Then there is usually a collection of family and associates who are seen as potential but undeveloped friends. And finally there are relatives and associates with whom we have no interest in developing a more intimate relationship.

Our confidants are important resources. They give us the space to communicate important matters relatively free of fear. They give us support and acceptance, give us love and allow us to give them love. The death of such a person can be a profound loss. We get over it, but there is always a twinge of hurt and loss when we remember what he or she contributed to our lives. The elderly are much more likely than any other age group both to experience such losses and to fear them. Obviously, people who have only one confidant are much more vulnerable than those who have several. One side effect of the death of someone in our social network is the tendency to hang on tighter to those resources that remain. Mrs. A was a widow who had never had more than a few acquaintances, and really only two "true-blue" friends. When one of her close friends died, she began to press the remaining one to spend more time with her, to go more places with her, to spend more time talking with her, and so on. For a while this was all right with her friend, but soon the friend began to feel that it was interfering with other things she wanted to do. When her friend tried to reduce the amount of time that she was spending with Mrs. A, Mrs. A became very anxious that she was going to lose her last remaining close friendship. She began to press her friend too much, and as a result her one remaining friend drastically cut down the time she spent with Mrs. A. This situation was caused indirectly by the actual loss of a friend and directly by *fear* of loss.

Deaths of relatives or friends not only reduce the number of role relationships a person has, but also bring home the inevitability of one's own death. The deaths of our parents usually signify that we are now in the oldest generation. And death among our age peers makes death seem much closer and more real to us.

Roles are lost not only through death but also through energy declines, disability, ageism in organizations, and declining interest in activities outside the intimate environment of family and close friends. For example, Newell (1961) found that from age 50 to 64 about 60 percent of people were active in six or more roles, but at age 65 only 40 percent were that active, and by age 75 only 8 percent were. This reality can lead older people to fear the loss of positions in organizations, which in turn can lead to paranoid behavior even in situations where there is no attempt to oust the older person from a responsible position.

Loss of Housing Choice

The elderly also are more likely to lose control over where they live, which causes fear of loss of independence. Financial difficulties can force a move from the housing of choice to more affordable housing. Physical infirmities sometimes force a move into the household of an adult child. In 1975, about 9 percent of the elderly lived with a married child, compared to about 16 percent in 1962. This difference is due mainly to better economic circumstances for older Americans by 1975 (Shanas, 1977). Thus, we can estimate that about three-fourths live with children because of physical frailty and one-fourth for economic reasons. However, the percentage living with married children falls with age (Shanas, 1977). This decline is probably due to the increase with age in severe disability, which is less likely to be handled by living with adult children. There are two important points about the disability situation: First, because of their negative attitudes toward dependency, the elderly dread having to move in with their children, especially if they are bedridden or severely disabled and unable to contribute to the household. Second, the greater the disability, the greater the problems of trying to cope with them within the family. Shanas (1977:4–10) reported that most families tried to cope with disabled family members well past the point where severe stress was placed on the family. She also reported that the single condition most likely to lead to institutionalization of people who lived with family was incontinence—lack of control over bowels or bladder. Wells and Brink (1981) reported that among the elderly incontinence is most prevalent among the very frail and the very old (85 and over). Families can cope with a variety of infirmities in their older members, but having to deal with urine and feces is the straw that most often breaks the camel's back.

Indeed, the probability of institutionalization increases from 1.2 percent at ages 65 to 74, to 5.9 percent at ages 74–84, to 23.7 percent at age 85 and over (Kovar, 1977). Thus, as age increases, the probability of living with children decreases and the probability of institutionalization increases. Again, the probability of actually experiencing loss of control of housing choice is not high. Nevertheless, it is a potential loss that is widely feared.

No matter whether one considers physical or mental frailty, financial precariousness, role loss, or loss of control over where one lives, the elderly are more vulnerable than the rest of the population is. And as age increases, so do all the various dimensions of vulnerability.

Exploitation

Thus far we have been looking at how aging can influence one's ability to cope financially, physically, or socially. The increase in individual vulnerability with age can also lead to the elderly's being identified as easy prey.

Older people are particularly vulnerable to fraud, deception, and quackery. To begin with, older people on fixed incomes and with barely enough to live on are very susceptible to any "sure-fire" scheme to get more money or a supplementary income. Also, loneliness and isolation sometimes make older people susceptible to deception by a friendly, outgoing person who takes an apparent interest in them. Finally, hopeless illness is more frequent among older people, and many unscrupulous people have exploited the desperation that such illness can evoke. Harris (1978) reports that in two large metropolitan areas more than 90 percent of confidence scheme victims were older people. A few examples should illustrate the point.

Perhaps the most vicious of the "get more money for your money" swindles was the Maryland savings and loan scandal of 1961. From 1958 to 1961, many state-chartered savings and loan associations operating in Maryland were not federally insured. These companies advertised nationally that savings invested with them would yield as high as 8 percent, twice the interest rate of most legitimate, federally insured institutions. The appeal of increasing yields was particularly attractive to older people who were trying to make the most of a fixed amount of savings that provided them with their living. For people in this situation, such a promise was like saying, "Double your income in one easy step." Hundreds of older people transferred their life savings into these companies from all over the country.

At best these companies were ill conceived. They were able to pay such high rates of interest only by investing heavily in second, third, and even fourth mortgages—a very lucrative but also a very risky business. Following a wide-scale investigation, many officers of these companies were indicted on charges of fraud and embezzlement. Most of the companies went bankrupt, and hundreds of people lost their entire life savings.

Another example was the "investment property" business. Generally, promoters bought large tracts of cheap land—often swampy land in Florida or desert in Arizona—and carved the property up into the smallest parcels allowable. Then they printed beautiful brochures and advertised in newspapers, magazines, and so on. Stress was put on holding the land as an investment for resale later at a profit, or as a place for a retirement home. In the words of a Florida realtor,

> Lots are usually sold on installment contracts, and no deed is recorded until the contract is paid off. Most contracts stipulate that the property reverts to the seller if the buyer misses one or two payments, and the seller is not required to notify the buyer that he is delinquent.
>
> Many, but not all, contracts carry interest on the unpaid balance, usually 5 or 6 percent. Many of these lots are sold over and over again, year after year, as buyers stop their monthly payments for any number of reasons—they die, come upon hard times, come down and see the land, et cetera.
>
> Several years ago I spent almost two days, using a slow plane and a four-wheel drive, radio-equipped jeep, trying to locate a certain parcel (a Florida development) located approximately ten miles west of Daytona Beach in a dismal swamp.
>
> After two days of some of the roughest riding, we had to give up, as it was impossible to penetrate deep enough into the swamp to the point we had spotted from the air.
>
> Incidentally, this parcel was sold to a woman from Syracuse, N.Y., who had intended to use it as a homesite for a trailer home. [U.S. Senate Special Committee on Aging, 1965:34]

Many other examples could be given of "make money" or "save money" schemes that have bilked older people out of what little they have. Confidence people have preyed on older people in many ways. One of the more frequent has been the "bank examiner" gambit. A person posing as a bank examiner calls on the intended victim. He or she explains that one of the employees of the bank is suspected of embezzlement, but unfortunately the bank officials have been unable to catch the employee in the act. The "examiner" explains that if the victim will go to the bank and withdraw all his or her savings, this move will force the suspect in the bank to alter account books, and the bank will then "have the goods on the employee." If the intended victim takes the bait, and the savings are withdrawn, the "examiner" telephones, says that they have caught the suspect, thanks the victim, and then offers to send a "bank messenger" to pick up the money— "to save you the trouble of having to come all the way down here, since you have been so kind as to cooperate with us." The "messenger" then appears, takes the money, gives the victim an official-looking deposit slip, and that is usually the last the victim ever sees of his or her money. A large number of unfortunate older people have fallen for this ruse.

Many practices in the "preneed" funeral business have also been fraudulent. People have been sold "complete burial service" for $1,000 or more, and all the survivors received (if they were lucky) was a cheap casket. People have been sold crypts in mausoleums that did not exist. One ad read, "Do you qualify for these U.S. Government death benefits? U.S. Social Security, maximum $255, United Memorial's answer to the ever-increasing cost of funeral services, the United plan. The preneed plan that costs $10." For $10, the customers got a "guarantee" from United Memorial that they could have their burial service performed by whatever mortuary they chose. When the customer died, however, the relatives found that most mortuaries "endorsed" by United Memorial had no contract with them and refused to perform the service for anything even approaching a Social Security benefit price.

It has been estimated that in Colorado alone the annual sales of preneed burial service totaled $8 to $10 million (U.S. Senate Special Committee on Aging, 1965). This business thrived on the deep-seated desire of many older people to take care of burial arrangements ahead of time in order to "avoid being a burden" on their relatives. It may even be unethical for reputable businesspeople to take money from older people for prearranged funerals, because businesspeople fully realize the problems of prearranging funeral services in a society where people travel as much as they do in ours. If the person dies far from the city in which the prearrangements were made, the relatives either lose the money spent for the prearranged funeral or must pay to have the remains shipped back for burial. By encouraging prepayment, the funeral director is merely relieving the older person of his or her savings, often without paying interest on the money held.

The most frequent hazard to older people is medical swindlers and quackery. Arthritis is a good case in point. The U.S. Senate Special Committee on Aging (1965:7) found that

> Arthritis offers special opportunities to the unscrupulous. Twelve million Americans have some form of arthritis; and, as one witness testified: "If we fall for the phoney, and sooner or later most of us do, it is because the pains of arthritis are something that you just can't describe because nobody knows why it comes or how or when it goes." . . . Mrs. Bramer also made a comment often expressed by arthritis victims: "There must be an exchange list of arthritic victims because if you get on one list you receive material advertising all manner of devices, items such as vibrators, whirlpool baths, salves, uranium mitts, and things of that sort."

The committee commented on various aspects of fraud:

Worthless devices
These devices are often used by phoney practitioners to impress victims with "up-to-date" methods of "secret" treatments. One highly mobile pitchman, using and selling a machine that did little more than give colonic enemas to victims of major diseases made an estimated $2.5 million before conviction on a mail fraud charge. [1965:3]

Misleading claims

People will buy almost anything that purports to cure whatever real or imaginary ailments they have. The enforcement of fraud laws is a constant word game between those who are trying to protect the public and those who are trying to swindle it. Thus, "cures" is replaced by "aids in curing" is replaced by "is thought to aid in curing." [1965:8]

The victims

The actual extent of frauds is unknown because many victims either never suspect that they have been taken, or more likely, they are afraid to report it for fear of appearing the fool. [1965:8]

Complex technology

This gives the quack the capability of sowing the seed of doubt about the validity of accepted medical methods because most people are not able to evaluate his claims. [1965:8]

The cost of quackery in 1965 alone was estimated as follows: vitamin and health food quackery, $500 million; arthritis quackery, $250 million; ineffective drugs and devices for reducing, $100 million (U.S. Senate Special Committee on Aging, 1965).

And this review probably only scratches the surface. The true cost of fraud and quackery was summed up well by the chairman of the U.S. Senate Special Committee on Aging:

It seems to me that there are losses that go far beyond the original purchase price for the phoney treatment, the useless gadget, the inappropriate drug or pill. How can you measure the cost in terms of suffering, disappointment, and final despair? [1965:10]

One of the heaviest of these costs is surely the attitudes such practices create among older people. They become suspicious and reluctant to get involved with strangers.

Crime and Abuse

Older people fear crime much more than the general population does, even though they are less likely than the general public to be actually victimized by crime. Antunes et al. (1977) reported on a study of both reported and nonreported crime against the public, including the elderly. They found that the main crime against the elderly was robbery on the street by unarmed black youths who were acting alone and who were strangers to the older person robbed. Thus, for those older people who live in high-crime areas any strange black youth on the street represents a potential threat. In addition, although older people were less likely than the general public to experience violent crimes such as assault or rape, when they did it was most likely to occur *in their homes*. Little wonder, then, that older people in inner cities are afraid to let strangers into their homes. Older people in high-crime areas see and hear about crime all around them and see themselves as helpless to defend against it.

Although it is not common, abuse and neglect of the elderly by family members tend to be seen as common by many older people and by service providers. Hickey and Douglass (1981) classified neglect and abuse in the order of prevalence and seriousness as perceived by a sample of service providers. They found that passive neglect was seen as the most common and the least serious. Passive neglect involved leaving the older person alone, isolated, and forgotten. This situation most often happens when families are too preoccupied with their own lives to pay attention to their older members. Verbal or emotional abuse was seen as next most common. It involved situations in which older people were humiliated, frightened, insulted, threatened, or treated as children. Verbal/emotional abuse involved treating older people in a demeaning or overprotective way. Active neglect was seen as being not very common. It involved forced confinement, isolation, and withholding of food or medication. Actual physical abuse— hitting, slapping, or physical restraint—was seen as the least common type of mistreatment.

Thus, abuse and neglect is not widespread, and what clues we have indicate that the more serious types of abuse and neglect are relatively rare. Nevertheless, for those to whom it does occur such abuse is undoubtedly traumatic. It is a failure in what most people see as the safest possible environment—the family. Hickey and Douglass (1981) reported that the most common problem seen as leading to abuse and neglect was a poor initial relationship among family members compounded by sudden and severe dependency of the older person.

Cases of abuse and neglect of the elderly are highly dramatized by the media because they offend very central American values—respect and consideration for elders. They arouse the fears of the elderly because there is no way to be *positive* that it will not happen to them.

Summary

To feel vulnerable is to feel relatively defenseless against hurt or loss. It is to feel oneself at risk. It may also mean seeing oneself as on the verge of being unable to manage. Reactions to vulnerability can range from anger to apathy, from panic to depression. But scarcely anyone is pleased at the prospect.

The types of vulnerability to loss include physical, mental, financial, social, and environmental. One can also be vulnerable to harm by crime, abuse, or exploitation.

Less than 10 percent of the elderly are physically or mentally below the minimum level of functioning required for a normal later life. Perhaps another 5 or 6 percent have sight or hearing problems that make them vulnerable to social losses. About 20 to 25 percent of the elderly are living on or below the edge of poverty.

Role loss occurs for a majority of older people. About 14 percent of the elderly live in the home of a married child (9 percent) or in an institution (4 percent).

These various types of vulnerabilities are often interrelated. People with physical, mental, or sensory disabilities may make up as much as 20 percent of the older population. These same people are disproportionately likely to be poor. These vulnerabilities can lead to a change in living arrangements, which in turn accelerates the process of role loss.

Fraud, deception, and quackery are not very common, but the elderly are much more likely to be targets for this type of crime. They are less likely to be victims of other types of crimes, but when they are, the crime is more likely to occur while they are in their own homes. All this combines to make many older people quite fearful, even if they live in a relatively crime-free area.

We do not know how frequently older people are abused or neglected by family members, but indications are that the more serious forms of abuse are rare.

All the various types of vulnerability increase in prevalence with age. Thus, those over 85 very rightly feel more vulnerable than those who are 65 to 74. In addition, minority status has a strong influence on both physical and financial precariousness. Finally, older women are generally more financially vulnerable than older men are.

The probability of actual loss or harm is only loosely related to the level of fear of loss or harm among the elderly. The unpredictability of loss or harm and the severe potential consequences of loss or harm to one's sense of independence or competence or security lead to a high prevalence of fear and insecurity. Fortunately, most older people are able to cope with their fears and worries about their vulnerabilities, but some are not. And the older people get, the more difficulty they may have in putting fears aside. As we interact with older people, we should keep this difficulty in mind.

Chapter 7

Death, Dying, and Grief

My grandmother died at age 77. I was 9. I was reared until I was 7 by my elderly grandmother while my mother worked. The last two years of her life, my grandmother fought increasing illness, disability, and frailty. She had a heart condition that was later complicated by a broken hip. She spent her last year bedfast. She was hospitalized once for three days in her last year, and she died at home of heart failure. Her life simply ebbed and finally left her. I was with her when she died.

Although my father was living, I seldom saw him, and his death when I was 25 had very little reality for me. It was like the death of a distant relative who was essentially a stranger.

My most significant father figure was a man who was my mentor throughout most of my early career. When I was 40, he had a series of paralytic strokes that over a month's time reduced a vital and alert man of 75 to a shaking, disoriented, and anxious invalid. As I visited him, it gradually became clear to me that his greatest fear was that he might *not* die. While those around him talked about therapy and cures, in his lucid moments he was hoping for an end.

My mother's death was quite different. Although she was not a robust person, at 73 she was generally healthy and self-sufficient. When she first experienced severe chest pains, she called the emergency squad, called me, and then lay quietly on the couch and waited our arrival. At the hospital, the electrocardiogram results were inconclusive. She was admitted to the hospital for observation, but not in the coronary care unit. That night she was apprehensive and I held her as she talked about her fear of death. The following morning the pain had gone, and she was scheduled to be released. Her spirits were up. At 3:00 P.M. she had a cardiac arrest. When I arrived, her heart was beating again but she was unconscious and on life support systems. She died during the night without regaining consciousness.

My experience with death is very typical. I know that younger people die, but I have no direct experience with that. All the people close to me who have died have been over 70. The circumstances of each death were unique. The effect of death on me has varied depending on how close I was to the person who died, how long I had to get used to the idea of their dying, and what stage of life I was in at the time. For instance, my father's death did not affect me nearly as much as my mother's because I had not lived with him since I was an infant and I rarely saw him. My grandmother's death was easier for me than my mother's death because I was a child at the time my grandmother died and because the family had been expecting her death for some time when it finally came. I was 40 when my mother died, and part of my reaction was due to the fact that I was now the oldest generation in my family—which has a bearing on how near we see our own mortality to be. For all these reasons, my mother's death was the most difficult to get over. Nevertheless, I managed to do it within a short time—a couple of months. I still experience a twinge of psychological pain when I think of the contribution that my mother made to my life that is no longer available to me, but the strong grief reaction is no longer there.

Personal experience of death has been a rare event for me, and in this respect I am typical of those who are middle-aged or younger in the 1980s. But in earlier times, death was more commonplace and everyone was familiar with it. Infant and maternal mortality were high, and infectious diseases killed people of all ages. But in the last part of the twentieth century, death in industrial societies is concentrated among the old. Over 80 percent of those who died in the United States in 1976 were 55 or older, whereas in 1900 about a third of the deaths occurred under 5 years of age, about a third between ages 6 and 54, and about a third at age 55 or over.

The reduction in the prevalence of death and the concentration of death among older people has probably influenced what we think and how we feel about death, particularly in terms of seeing death that comes before later life as unfair or unjust. The conquering of infectious diseases has given us the illusion of control over death. The idea of death as a constant possibility has been replaced by the idea that death only happens to the old. The association of death with aging has created the illusion that death is preceded by a long period of decay. But none of this has changed the true inevitability of physical death.

People are the only beings we know of who are aware that they will eventually die. Reactions to this knowledge range from denial to resistance to acceptance depending on culture and circumstances. Through the ages, interest in death as a major part of life's drama has almost always been high, but until recently death was not a legitimate topic for open discussion. But that has changed. It is now possible, at least for some, to discuss feelings about death openly and to see death as a transition that can be accomplished better in a context of understanding and open communication than in a context of ignorance and awkward silence.

Defining Death

Death can be defined as a process of transition that starts with *dying* and ends with *being dead* (Kalish, 1976). For practical purposes, a dying person is a person identified as having a condition from which no recovery can be expected. Dying is thus the period during which the organism loses its viability. The term *dying trajectory* refers to the speed with which a person dies, the rate of decline in functioning. The word *death* can also be defined as a point at which a person *becomes physically dead*. Often when we say that someone died yesterday we are not referring to the entire dying process but instead to its final product. The moment in time when a person becomes dead was once considered an easy practical issue to resolve. Recently, however, it has become possible to stimulate artificially both breathing and heartbeat. As a result, there is currently a huge legal tangle over the issue of when a person is physically dead.

Death can also be a social process (Kastenbaum, 1969). People are socially dead when we no longer treat them as people but as unthinking, unfeeling objects. Social death has occurred when people talk *about* the dying person rather than *to* the dying person even when the dying person is capable of hearing and understanding what is being said. Thus, social death sometimes occurs *before* physical death does.

To *deny* death is to believe that people continue to be able to experience after their physical death. Physical death is undeniable. It is mental death that is deniable. Belief in an afterlife, belief in the existence of ghosts, spirits, angels, or demons, and belief in reincarnation are all ways to deny the death of the ability to experience. Denial can also mean the repression of the knowledge that one's physical death is imminent. Kalish (1976) reports that physicians often tell patients directly and clearly that they are going to die only to find out at a later meeting that their message was not heard.

The Meaning of Death

How people approach their own deaths and the deaths of others depends to some extent on what death means to them—and death can have many meanings. Some people see death as an ugly and meaningless extinction of life. Others see it as a beautiful and meaningful transition to a new and better type of life. Some see death as hateful destruction, others see it as a welcome release. Back (1971) examined the meaning of death through ratings of various metaphors about what death is like. He found little age variation in the meaning of death among respondents who were over 45. Back (1971) did find a significant sex difference in the meaning of death. Women tended to be accepting of death, to see it as a peaceful thing. They tended to see death as most like a compassionate mother and as an understanding doctor. Men tended to see death as an antagonist, as a grinning butcher, or as a hangman with bloody hands.

The most common reaction to the idea of death is *fear*. Whether fear of death is inevitable or a learned response is an unresolved issue. But whatever their cause, death fears exist. Older people do not appear to be extremely afraid of death, and older people express fewer death fears than younger people do (Kastenbaum, 1969; Kalish, 1976). There also appears to be no tendency for death fears to increase among older people with terminal conditions (Kastenbaum, 1969). Among the young, however, terminal illness increases the prevalence of death fears (Feifel and Jones, 1968).

Kalish (1976) attributes the lower prevalence of death fears in the face of a higher prevalence of death to several factors: (1) older people see their lives as having less prospects for the future and less value; (2) older people who live past the age they expected have a sense of living on "borrowed time"; and (3) dealing with the deaths of friends can help socialize older people toward acceptance of their own death.

Fear of death also depends to some extent on religiosity. Kalish (1976) reports that the most consistent finding is that people who are strongly religious show few death fears, as do affirmed atheists. Uncertain and sporadically religious people show the most death fears.

Garfield (1974) reports that people who use psychedelic drugs or who practice meditation have lower death anxiety than do others. Kalish (1976) suggests that because "altered mind states" tend to blur ego boundaries, death of the self is less threatening to people familiar with such mental states. Peck (1968) found that blurring boundaries of ego in old age served as a mechanism for transcending pain, and Kalish feels that this blurring may be related to the lower prevalence of death fears among older people.

Apparently, when people know that they are approaching death, they see little point in continuing to do things for purely social reasons. In addition, if it is widely known that the person is dying, then continued participation may be awkward, because many people do not feel comfortable around the dying.

Although death is generally accepted with little fear among the elderly, it seems reasonable to assume that some identifiable categories of older people would not react to death in this way. Less acceptance and more fear of death might be expected among older people who have dependent children, disabled spouses, career goals still to be achieved, and socially crucial positions. We know, for example, that legislators are often old. How does the prevalence of death fears among older legislators compare with that of the general older population? This and other questions along these lines need to be researched.

Dealing with Dying

Dealing with dying involves understanding what is expected of the dying, the stages dying people go through, when people should be permitted to die, and factors in the care of the dying.

The Role of the Dying Person

When a person is diagnosed as terminal, that person is assigned the social role of dying person. The content of the role depends a great deal on the age of the dying person and his or her dying trajectory. People with short dying trajectories do not spend much time in the role of dying person, regardless of age. However, age heavily determines whether or not a person is defined as terminal. For example, Sudnow (1967) found that older people were more likely than the young to be routinely defined as dead in hospital emergency rooms, with no attempt to revive them.

Among those with long dying trajectories, age is an important element in determining what is expected of them. Young people are expected to fight death, to try to finish business, to cram as much experience as possible into their time remaining. In short, we expect young people to be active and antagonistic about dying. Older people who are dying are expected to show more passive acceptance. Older people in the dying person role are less likely than the young to see a need to change their life-styles or day-to-day goals (Kalish, 1976). Older people are also less apt to be concerned about caring for dependents or about causing grief to others (Kalish, 1976).

Older people are more apt than the young to find that the role of dying person also means having less control over their own lives. All dying people find that family members and medical personnel, usually with good intentions, take away their free choices. This interference is particularly true for older people.

Finally, all people in the dying person role are expected to cope with their impending deaths, but older people are allowed less leeway than the young in expressing anger and frustration about their own deaths.

Stages of Dying

A great deal has been written about the stages people pass through in the process of dying. Kübler-Ross (1969) proposed five stages in the dying process: (1) denial, (2) anger, (3) bargaining (such as asking God to postpone death in exchange for good behavior), (4) depression and sense of loss, and (5) acceptance. The universal applicability of the Kübler-Ross model has not been determined. Kalish (1976) suggests that although denial is probably more common in the early stages of dying and acceptance is more common later on, there is considerable movement back and forth; and it is doubtful that Kübler-Ross's stages represent a regular progression. Kalish (1976) reports that many people have mistakenly treated Kübler–Ross's stages of dying as an inevitable progression. As a result, people have been chided for not progressing through their own dying on schedule, and dying people have felt guilty for not having accomplished the various tasks.

Awareness that one's death may not be far off can have substantial effects on the choices one makes. Sill (1980) found that as the perceived length of time before death decreased, activity decreased. In fact, perceived length of time remaining was a much more powerful predictor of activity level than either age or physical incapacity.

No doubt a good bit of the anxiety about death results not so much from the idea of death itself but from uncertainty about the manner in which our deaths will occur. We usually don't know what will cause our deaths, what the circumstances will be, or when or where death will occur. Although it is impossible to predict in individual cases, age is related to what one is liable to die from and under what circumstances. Beyond age 45, as age increases, the probability of dying from heart disease rather than other causes increases dramatically, and the probability of dying from cancer declines.

Permitting People to Die

As for when death occurs, the prime issue is when a person should be permitted to die. There is no clear consensus among older people about whether "heroic" measures should be used to keep them alive or whether death should be speeded in hopeless cases involving great pain. However, many older people are very aware of the burden their medical care may place on their families and may prefer to die rather than incur the expense required to keep them alive a little longer.

Kalish (1976) reports that "living wills" are being used as one means of giving patients' wishes more weight. Living wills specify the conditions under which people prefer not to be subjected to extraordinary measures to keep them alive. Kalish (1976:496) points out that although living wills are not now legally binding, some state legislatures are drafting laws to make them so. He goes on to say that

> One drawback, of course, is that the person facing imminent death may feel quite differently about his desires for heroic methods than he had anticipated when his death appeared much further removed in time, yet his condition may well preclude any opportunity to alter his living will.

Care of the Dying

In caring for the dying, it is important to remember that most dying people fear being abandoned, humiliated, and lonely at the end of their lives (Weisman, 1972). Thus, encouraging the maintenance of intimate personal relationships with others is an important aspect of the social care of dying people.

Deciding who should be told about the terminal diagnosis has a significant impact on intimate relationships. Kalish (1976) concludes that it is difficult for the patient to maintain such relationships unless the topic of death can be openly discussed. Thus, when dying people are kept in the dark about the nature of their condition, they are denied an opportunity to resolve the question of death in the company of those they love, because by the time the prognosis becomes obvious their condition may prevent any meaningful discussion. In evaluating the question of who should know, Weisman suggests that "to be informed about a diagnosis, especially a serious diagnosis, is to be fortified, not undermined" (1972:17). Yet some people do not want to be told that they are dying (Kalish, 1976). In addition, some dying people keep their own prognoses secret.

Hospices represent an innovative way to organize the efforts of health service providers and families around the goals of minimizing pain associated with terminal illness and allowing terminally ill people to die with dignity. The multidisciplinary hospice staff seeks to care not only for dying people but for their families as well.

The first well-known hospice, St. Christopher's, was started in 1967 in London. The primary goal at St. Christopher's is to make the patient free of pain and of any memory or fear of pain. Besides freedom from pain, the staff at St. Christopher's provides comfort and companionship to their patients. Families, including children, are free to visit any time (except Mondays, when there are no visiting hours and families are given a day off and do not have to feel guilty for not visiting). Families are also encouraged to help with the patient's care. Patients often go back and forth between the

hospice and home. The median length of stay at St. Christopher's is two to three weeks; about half of the patients return home to die, with dignity and without pain, after a 10-day session with the hospice staff (Saunders, 1976).

Interest in the hospice concept has grown rapidly in the United States. In 1977, there were about 50 hospices in various stages of development.

Grief

Grief is the process of getting over another person's death. The process may be finished quickly, or it may never be finished. In Lopata's (1973) study of widows, 48 percent said they were over their husband's deaths within a year, while 20 percent said they had never gotten over it and did not expect to. Individual grief takes three forms: physical, emotional, and intellectual. Some common physical reactions to grief include shortness of breath, frequent sighing, tightness in the chest, feelings of emptiness in the abdomen, loss of energy, lack of muscular strength, and stomach upset (Kalish, 1976). These reactions are particularly common in the period imme-diately following the death and generally diminish with time.

Emotional reactions include anger, guilt, depression, anxiety, and preoccupation with thoughts of the person who died (Parkes, 1972). These responses also diminish with time. A longitudinal study of widows and widowers found that those who reacted to grief by becoming depressed were more likely than others to report a disproportionately higher level of poor health a year later (Bornstein et al., 1973).

The intellectual aspect of grief consists of what Lopata (1973) calls the "purification" of the memory of the deceased. In this process, the negative characteristics of the person who died are stripped away, leaving only a positive, idealized memory. Somehow we think it wrong to speak ill of the dead. Lopata (1973) reports that even women who hated their husbands thought that the statement "My husband was an unusually good man" was true. The content of obituaries and memorial services also attests to the results of this process. The idealization of the dead has positive value in that it satisfies the survivors' need to believe that the dead person's life had meaning. But it can have serious negative consequences by interfering with the formation of new relationships (Lopata, 1973).

Glick et al. (1974) found that men and women react somewhat differently to grief. When their spouses died, men more often responded as if they had lost part of themselves, while women responded as if they had been deserted, abandoned, and left to fend for themselves. Men find it more difficult and less desirable to express grief, and they accept the reality of death somewhat more quickly than women do. On the other hand, men find it more difficult to work during bereavement than women do.

A lengthy dying trajectory not only allows the dying person to resolve the issue of dying but also allows the survivors to resolve many grief reactions in advance. In some cases, the dying process is slow enough that the final event brings more relief than grief (Kalish, 1976). This relief does not mean that the survivors are calloused people who have no regard for the person who died. It merely means that it is possible to grieve *in advance* of a person's death. To assess a person's grief reaction to another's death requires knowledge of the reaction during the entire dying process, not just at the funeral.

At least three factors help minimize grief. The first has to do with how we view death. If we can see death as natural and just, then we can more easily accept it. Also, it helps a great deal to feel that we know what happened to the person who died, what death is, and what it means in terms of afterlife.

The second factor is the degree to which our relationship to the person who died seems complete. A complete relationship is one in which there are no undelivered communications. If we can feel that we have told the person everything we needed to tell them and had recognized all of their actions we needed to and that they had done the same for us, then it is much easier to let go of the relationship. An obvious implication of this rule is the positive value of keeping relationships up to date, even if the communications are not comfortable ones to give or receive.

The third factor that eases the loss of close friends or family is the presence of surviving confidants to provide support during the grieving process. People usually do not have to go through grief alone. There are various ways in which others help the individual through bereavement. At the beginning, bereaved people are exempted from certain responsibilities. They are not expected to go to their jobs. Family and friends help with cooking and caring for dependents. Older women often find their decisions being made for them by their adult children. But social supports to the bereaved person are temporary. People are expected to reengage the social world within a few weeks at most.

Summary

Death touches the lives of older people more often than it does other age categories. The process of dying, the meaning of death, and grief are all more salient to older people than to younger people, at least in industrial societies.

Death is both an end state and a physical and social process. In a given year, about 6 percent of the older population will die. Yet more and more people are not only surviving *to* old age but *in* old age as well. Men tend to see death as an antagonist, while women tend to see death as merciful. In general, older people fear death less than do other age categories. However, more research is needed on death fears among specific categories of older people who are still highly integrated into society.

For older adults, the role of dying person demands passive acceptance of death. Older people are less apt than the young to change their life-styles when they learn that they are dying. Older people are also apt to find that being a dying person means having less independent control over one's life.

People go through various stages in dying, but there is no set sequence or necessary progression. Denial, anger, bargaining, depression and sense of loss, and acceptance are all common reactions to dying. Acceptance of death does not mean a wish to die. It is merely an acknowledgment of an inevitability.

Where and when a person dies is a matter of values. Most people prefer to die at home. However, just when in the process a person should be allowed to die is still a subject of controversy. Two crucial aspects of care for the dying are maintaining personal relationships and reassuring the dying person that he or she will not be abandoned or humiliated.

A lengthy dying trajectory allows the survivors to grieve in advance and often softens the final blow. Bereavement is the process of dealing with someone's death. It usually encompasses symptoms of physical, psychological, and emotional stress. In addition, bereavement usually results in a sanctification of the memory of the person who died. People usually receive social support during bereavement, but only for a short time.

Part Three

The Environment
in Which
Aging Occurs

Aging does not occur in a vacuum. It occurs in a context that includes the individuals' needs and resources, their patterns of activities, their relationships with others, and their attachments to their surroundings. Aging interacts with all these aspects of the physical and social environment. This is the subject of Part Three.

Chapter 8

Instrumental Needs
and Resources

A great deal of what we experience in life is shaped by our circumstances. How much money we have affects what we are able to do, the kinds of clothing we have, where we live, whether we have cars and what kind, what kinds of food we eat, and even whether we are able to afford needed medical care. The quality of homes we have and where they are located affect both our comfort and enjoyment and also the degree of security and safety we feel. Preventive and remedial health care affect our physical capacities and morale. Physical health in turn has a strong influence on what activities are possible and in what amounts. Transportation is an important necessity if we are to take full advantage of the range of activities in most communities. Finally, the kinds, number, and location of community facilities and services also affect the kinds of activities and assistance that are available. Because income, housing, health care, transportation, and community facilities and services are factors that *enable* people to participate, we call them *instrumental*. They are the means that people use to pursue an incredible variety of goals. They also greatly influence our sense of independence, as we saw in Chapter 5.

Accordingly, to fully understand aging requires that we know how aging affects both our instrumental needs and the resources available to meet them. As with physical and mental aging, people vary widely in instrumental needs and resources, and aging has neither a uniform nor an individually predictable influence. In general, aging does not alter instrumental needs or resources enough to change life-styles appreciably. However, certain categories of older people are more likely to encounter problems. For each of the instrumental areas, we will look at what the needs and resources are; what the typical problems are; which older people are most likely to have problems; what individuals, families, or communities can do about them at present; and changes that could be made in our social system to reduce the number of older people who have problems.

Income

Because very few of us grow all our own food, make our own clothes, construct and maintain our own homes and so forth, access to disposable income is essential. To understand the income issue, we need to know something about how aging influences both income needs and income sources.

Income Needs

Aging affects income needs in several ways. On the one hand, retirement reduces the amount of money needed for transportation, special clothing, meals away from home, and so on—expenses connected with employment. Launching children into adulthood reduces day-to-day expenses such as allowances, food, clothing, entertainment, vacation expenses, and so on. On the other hand, increased physical frailty increases the need to buy services that formerly could have been done for oneself or by one's spouse. For example, hanging drapes, washing windows, house painting, and yard work are all unlikely to be done by people over 80. Estimates of the average income needs of people of various ages generally assume that the elderly need slightly less income than people under 65 in order to maintain comparable life-styles. This differential is entirely based on the assumption that older people need slightly less food (Atchley, 1980b:135).

The U.S. Bureau of Labor Statistics (BLS) estimated the income needs of the elderly in 1980 as follows:

	Married Couple	Unmarried Individual
High budget	$11,890	$6,510
Intermediate budget	8,650	4,750
Low budget	5,730	3,150

The high budget reflected a modest middle-class level of living, the intermediate level was a working-class level, and the low budget was a survival-only level. These estimates were developed by estimating the costs of housing, household maintenance (e.g., utilities, repairs), household furnishings, food, clothing, transportation, medical and dental care, personal care (e.g., laundry, cleaning, grooming supplies), entertainment or recreation, insurance, taxes, and miscellaneous expenses. The survival-only budget assumed almost no replacement clothing or home furnishings; very little household maintenance, recreation, entertainment, or insurance; and a subsistence level for food and medical and dental care. The high budget allowed for such items as replacing one's winter coat or one's television set every five years, modest amounts for vacation travel, entertainment, eating out, insurance, and personal care. However, the biggest contrasts were in food and housing, where the high budget allowed two to three times the amounts provided in the low budget.

The BLS budgets are based on an absolute approach to income needs. However, most people judge the adequacy of their incomes in relation to what they think they need. The elderly generally tend to think that their incomes are adequate even when their incomes are well below what others might think they would need. For example, in an unpublished community study of older adults, I found in 1979 that only 10 percent of the men and 20 percent of the women thought that their incomes were inadequate, even though many more of them had incomes that were below the BLS intermediate budget.

In 1980 about 60 percent of elderly couples had incomes at the modest middle-class level or higher, while only about 25 percent of unmarried older individuals did. About 21 percent of older couples and 55 percent of older unmarried people had incomes at or below the survival-only level. These data clearly show that most older couples have incomes that can support comfortable lives, while most unmarried older people are in financial trouble.

Income Sources

Aging changes the sources of income that are available. Older people have access to retirement income and services and facilities with economic value that are specifically reserved for the elderly. Aging also very strongly affects the ability to secure income through employment.

Direct income sources include earnings, pensions, income from assets, and public assistance. About 20 percent of men and 8 percent of women age 65 or over have earnings, and the proportion decreases for those of older ages. Incomes of older people with earnings are about double the incomes of those whose incomes come mainly from pensions. About half of those who are employed need earnings to supplement inadequate pensions.

Retirement pensions come in two basic varieties—Social Security benefits and job-related pensions. Social Security benefits can be retirement benefits paid to workers covered by the system or survivor benefits paid to surviving spouses of covered workers. Social Security retirement benefits are available to those who have worked on covered jobs for a specified minimum period of time (usually 10 years) and have reached age 62. Social Security retirement benefits also carry a spouse benefit that provides retired couples with 150 percent of the pension entitlement amount of the covered worker.

The normal retirement age under Social Security is 65. Those who retire earlier than 65 receive a benefit that is reduced by an amount that roughly compensates for the increased amount of time over which benefits will be drawn. But those who retire later than age 65 do not receive an increased

**TABLE 8-1. Percentage of Older Households
Having Income from Selected Sources, by Age
and Household Type (United States 1978)**

	Ages 62–64		Age 65 and Over	
Source	Couples	Single Persons	Couples	Single Persons
Earnings	77	50	41	15
Social Security	46	58	91	89
Public Pension	13	9	16	12
Private Pension	19	13	31	14
Public Assistance	2	10	5	14

Source: Social Security Administration (1981:9).

benefit to compensate for the decreased amount of time that benefits must
be paid. The increment for late retirement is only about half what it should
be in order to fairly compensate the worker for late retirement.

About 90 percent of retired Americans draw Social Security, and over
half of them draw reduced benefits as a result of having retired prior to
age 65. In 1980, average Social Security retirement benefits were $4,097 per
year for retired individuals and $6,060 for retired couples. The average
Social Security benefit to surviving spouses was $3,697 annually. These
very modest average benefits replace about 55 percent of earnings in the
last year of employment for couples and only about 37 percent of earnings
for single individuals. These benefits represent an increase of over 60 percent in the purchasing power of Social Security pensions since 1965
(Atchley, 1980b:138). Increases in Social Security payroll taxes since 1977
have gone to eliminate poverty, not to provide lavish pensions.

About 60 percent of men and 40 percent of women who retired in 1970
were entitled to a job-related pension on top of Social Security. These people
tend to have had high earnings and thus to qualify for the highest Social
Security benefits. The result is a growing disparity between the incomes of
those who have multiple pensions and the incomes of those who are only
entitled to Social Security, with dual pensioners averaging incomes twice as
high as those with Social Security alone (Atchley, 1980b:143).

Assets such as income-generating property, savings, or investments
are often presumed to be a major source of income for the aged, but this is
true only for the small proportion of very well-to-do elderly people. In fact,
few people find themselves actually able to put away substantial amounts of
savings or investments to support their later years. Most retired people have
liquid assets of less than $2,000—hardly enough to generate much income.
Although about 60 percent of older couples and 30 percent of older single
people own their homes free and clear, home ownership is worth only about

$500 per year in savings if the expenses of home ownership are taken into account.

Supplemental Security Income (SSI) is a federal program of public assistance to the elderly. In 1982, SSI guaranteed every older American $264 per month regardless of prior work history ($397 for older couples). Here is how it works. Suppose an older man draws a Social Security retirement pension of $160 per month and has no other source of income. To determine his SSI income, $20 of his Social Security benefit is excluded, giving him an income for SSI purposes of $140 per month. This $140 would be subtracted from the guarantee of $264 to yield an SSI benefit of $124 per month. Over 2 million older people were drawing benefits averaging about $100 per month from this program in 1982. In addition, 25 states provide a state supplement over and above SSI. All SSI applicants must demonstrate that their incomes from other sources fall below the prescribed minimum in order to qualify for SSI. This is called a *means* test.

Indirect income sources include many public and private programs that directly serve older people and also indirectly help to supplement inadequate incomes. Federal programs that indirectly give financial aid to older people include low-rent public housing and rent subsidy programs, Medicare, Medicaid, the food stamp program, and meals programs for the elderly.[1] Many states give property tax exemptions to people over 65. In addition, senior centers and transportation programs often provide services free or at reduced prices.

Indirect income sources increase the real incomes of older Americans, but research into the magnitude of this factor is sparse because of the difficulties involved in getting comparable information on various sources of indirect income. It is probably safe to say that, as a result of their eligibility criteria, most indirect income sources help the poor rather than the middle class. Indirect income sources are also much more available to the urban elderly than to those who live in rural areas.

Contrasting case histories may be useful to illustrate the wide variety that exists among the elderly in sources of income. Mr. B worked for an insurance company as an actuary—someone who computes the life expectancy of insurance applicants in order to determine the premiums the company must charge. He was employed by the same company for 45 years, and he retired at age 65. Mr. B was in very sound financial shape for retirement. He had earned a high salary during his working life, and he paid the maximum Social Security taxes. He thus qualified for a monthly Social Security retirement benefit of $757 for himself plus an additional $378 for his wife. In addition, Mr. B drew a private pension from his employer of $690 per month, and he had income from an annuity of $150 per month. His income from all of these sources totaled $1,975 per month or $23,700 per year, which represented 65.8 percent of Mr. B's income in the year preceding his retirement. And of his retirement income, only a little over $10,000 was taxable compared to $36,000 for his preretirement income. Mr. and Mrs.

---

[1] These programs are discussed in detail later in this chapter.

B both reported that retirement had not affected their capacity to afford the life-style they had led prior to retirement.

In contrast, Mr. J had not been so fortunate in his work life. He had worked for various employers, mostly small businesses, doing unskilled work in shipping or stocking. His last job had been as a "stock boy" in a liquor store. He worked six days a week unloading cases of liquor, wine, and beer and shelving them. He did not earn the minimum wage. Throughout his working life, Mr. J had been unemployed many times, but never for an extended period. Mr. J's Social Security benefit was only $182 per month, despite the fact that he had worked nearly 50 years. His wife received $122 per month from her own Social Security pension. They had no income from other sources. They applied for and received $93 per month in SSI. They also moved into rent-subsidized housing for the elderly, where their rent was fixed at 25 percent of their monthly income ($99 per month). This housing saved them $38 per month over what they had paid in their previous apartment and left them with $3,576 per year for all their other expenses. Combined, these benefits replaced only 38 percent of their earnings in the year before they retired. Both reported that they were having a lot of trouble making ends meet.

Who Has Income Problems?

Retirees, widows, and the lifelong poor are most likely to have income difficulties in later life. Among retirees, those who have worked for large employers are quite likely to have private pensions in addition to ample Social Security benefits. They are most likely also to have fringe benefits such as medical and dental insurance coverage that continue into retirement. On the other hand, those who worked for small businesses are least likely to have private pensions. They are also likely to have earned less for the same work, with correspondingly lower Social Security benefits, compared to those with the same job in a large company. They are also not likely to have substantial fringe benefits either before or after retirement.

Women are more likely than men to have worked sporadically, to have worked part-time, to have worked for small businesses that do not have private pensions, and to have worked in jobs not covered by union bargaining for pensions and fringe benefits. For all these reasons, women are more likely than men to be poor in retirement, because in our system retirement income is closely tied to the level of earnings over a lengthy working life.

Among retired people, the very old are also likely to find their incomes inadequate because although there have been cost-of-living increases in Social Security benefits, private pensions usually do not increase with inflation, and those workers who are very old today earned their Social Security pension entitlement with average wages much lower than today's wages, even when adjusted for inflation.

Finally, retired minority group members are likely to have inadequate incomes for many of the same reasons that women's incomes are too low—

working for employers who do not provide private pensions, high rates of unemployment over the working life, lower average wages even for the same work, and so on.

Widows are more likely than the married to encounter income problems in later life. First, many women find that they are too young to collect survivor benefits at the time they become widows. About 13 percent of women in their 50s are widows, yet widows do not qualify for survivor benefits under Social Security until they are age 60. Second, even if they qualify for survivor benefits, their Social Security incomes will go down by one-third. As we saw earlier, fixed expenses such as rent and automobile payments do not go down when the household size changes from two to one. If their husbands' Social Security was already marginal, then widowhood can bring on financial disaster. Finally, some unfortunate women find out too late that their husbands selected a "no survivor benefit" option in order to have a higher pension.

For example, Mrs. D was married to a man who had worked for a large office equipment manufacturer. When he retired, he was given two pension options. Under the first, he would have drawn $550 per month. If he died, his wife would continue to receive $550 per month as a survivor benefit. Under the second, he would receive $822 per month with no survivor benefit to his wife. The reason for the drastic difference in amount of pension with and without survivor benefits is based on seven years difference in the expected duration of the pension given the longer average length of life for women and the fact that Mrs. D was three years younger than her husband. Without telling Mrs. D, Mr. D selected the "no survivor benefit" option to get the pension of $822 per month.

The first inkling Mrs. D had that something might be wrong was when the pension check failed to come in the mail at the first of the month after her husband died. She called the plant and finally reached a benefits clerk. The poor benefits clerk got the job of having to tell Mrs. D that there would be no more pension checks. Her next shock was that instead of the $990 per month that she and Mr. D had received from Social Security, she would now be receiving only $660. Thus, the household income dropped from $1,812 per month to $660! All this on top of the grief she had to deal with having lost her husband of over 50 years.

A final category of people who are likely to have income problems in later life is the lifelong poor. The poor are very unlikely to have access to private pensions. Their low average wages do not generate much above the minimum Social Security benefits ($122 per month in 1982), even for those who have managed to be employed nearly all of their adult lives. However, unlike the case of Mrs. D just cited, many poor people do not encounter so drastic a change in their level of living. In fact, with SSI, Food Stamps, and low-rent housing for the elderly, some lifelong poor find that their situations in old age actually improve. Nevertheless, it is hardly a standard that many would choose. Even Mrs. D is better off in absolute terms with her $660 per month.

What Can Be Done?

When older people encounter income problems, they can take only a few courses of action. They can get jobs. They can apply for SSI, provided their incomes are low enough. They can take advantage of programs such as low-rent housing or Food Stamps, again providing that their incomes are low enough. And they can ask their families for financial support.

The prospects for getting a job in later life are not good, especially for those who are in the categories most likely to have inadequate retirement incomes. Many older people with income problems have difficulty sustaining their former middle-class life-styles, but their incomes are far above the level that would qualify them for income assistance programs. Most older people do not believe that it is their children's responsibility to provide them with an adequate income. They see this as a government responsibility (Harris and Associates, 1975). As a result, older people are very reluctant to ask their children for money. The end result is that for thousands of older Americans, there is essentially nothing they can do if they feel that their incomes are inadequate.

What Needs to Be Done?

In 1981, the President's Commission on Pension Policy reported that

△   A minimum universal pension system should be created to ensure that *all* workers are covered by job-related pensions in addition to Social Security. This system would be financed through payroll taxes on all employers. Such a system would provide minimum pensions to those who are unlikely to be covered by private pensions now.

△   Postretirement survivor protection should be mandatory. This would prevent situtations such as Mrs. D's from happening.

△   Social Security benefits for divorced people should reflect a share of their former spouses' earnings.

△   SSI benefits should be no lower than poverty level. As it now stands, SSI provides slightly lower than poverty-level benefits.

If enacted, these four changes would go a long way toward preventing income problems in later life.

Housing

Housing is an important source of continuity in the lives of most middle-aged and older people. After age 35, Americans do not change residence often. Part of the reason for this is home ownership. But a larger part

is the feeling of comfort and ease that comes with living in a familiar environment. As we saw earlier, one way that people cope with changes in their physical and mental capacities with age is to concentrate their time and attention on long-standing patterns of activity. And a large measure of this continuity comes through having lived in the same dwelling for a long time. Sixty-six percent of the elderly living in cities and 90 percent of those in rural areas own their homes. Their homes tend to be more than 40 years old, have a relatively low value compared to the homes of younger people, and are more likely to be dilapidated. The majority of older Americans have lived in their present dwellings for more than 20 years.

Housing is more than a place to live. It can be a symbol of independence, a focal point for family gatherings, a source of pleasant memories, and a link to the neighborhood and surrounding community. Remaining in one's customary abode can become more important as people get older because one's home is a major symbol of standing in the community. Its appearance can be a source of self-esteem and also a source of meaningful goals. In the community where I live, for example, the homes of the retired are generally more well-kept, with attractive decorations and immaculate landscaping, compared to the homes of the middle-aged.

Aging can bring a need for special modifications to housing. Disability is more common in later life than in any other life stage. Accordingly, the elderly are more likely than the young to need ramps, widened doorways to accommodate wheelchairs, or sturdy hand-support fixtures in the bath. But as we saw earlier, the elderly are not usually in the position to be able to afford to renovate their homes.

Disability can also bring the need for more in-home services. Almost half of the elderly who live alone need help with tasks of daily living (Better Housing League of Cincinnati, 1978). Shanas (1977) found that about 80 percent of the in-home services to the elderly were being provided by family. But about 15 percent, especially housework and meal preparation, were being done by paid helpers. Only about 2 percent were being provided by social services agencies. Obviously, the availability of in-home services is related to the income of the older person. The low percentage of in-home aid provided by social services agencies is a reflection of the sparse availability of home aid. In communities that have home aid programs, utilization is usually high. For example, Home Aid Service of Cincinnati provided regular in-home services to over 1,500 older people in 1978, and they had a substantial waiting list. Until these services are widely available, there is little way to estimate the true level of demand for them.

Disability can reach the point where some sort of specialized housing is necessary. For instance, Mrs. M was a 72-year-old widow with no children or other family living in the area. She lived alone in an older apartment building. Her neighbors noticed that she was increasingly disoriented. She often did not recognize her neighbors or remember their names even though they had known one another for several years. The situation came to a head when Mrs. M forgot a pot on her stove, which resulted in a lot of smoke (but fortunately no fire) and which "smelled up" the building. A protective services caseworker[2] was called in to investigate the situation. Mrs. M was moderately mentally impaired. After a thorough medical checkup, it was determined that she was probably suffering from chronic organic brain disease. She was not able to continue to live unassisted.

Mrs. M had an income of $284 per month. She had a small Social Security pension plus SSI. There were several choices available to the caseworker. Adult Foster Care could monitor Mrs. M while she continued to live in her apartment. She could move to a private boarding home or nursing home. Or she could move to the County Home for the indigent elderly. None of these solutions was ideal. Mrs. M was too mentally impaired for Adult Foster Care. With her meager income, the private boarding and nursing homes that would take her were not appealing. And the County Home had a waiting list. Eventually it was decided to monitor Mrs. M at home until she could get into the County Home. This solution placed a heavy burden on the Adult Foster Care program, but it worked.

Table 8-2 shows the continuum of housing alternatives of the disabled elderly. About 5 percent of the elderly live in group housing of all types, but as age increases so does the probability of living in group housing. At age 85 or over about 25 percent of the population lives in group housing.

The share-a-home concept may offer a viable alternative among those who need semi-independent housing. Begun in Orlando, Florida, share-a-home puts older people in touch with each other who want to establish a "family," purchase a home, and operate it together. The realities of semi-

[2] Protective services are discussed later in this chapter.

TABLE 8-2. Levels of Housing by Degree of Independence

Housing Type	Significant Criteria
Independent	
Fully independent	Self-contained, self-sufficient household; residents do 90 percent or more of the cooking and household chores.
Semi-independent	Self-contained but not entirely self-sufficient; may require some assistance with cooking and household chores. Example would be independent household augmented by Meals-on-Wheels, Homemaker Services, or Adult Foster Care.
Group housing	
Congregate housing	Can still be self-contained, but is less self-sufficient; cooking and household tasks are often incorporated into the housing unit. Most common is the retirement hotel.
Personal care home	Neither self-contained nor self-sufficient; help given in getting about, personal care, grooming, and so forth, in addition to cooking and household tasks. Most common type is the retirement home.
Nursing home	Neither self-contained nor self-sufficient; total care, including health, personal, and household functions.

independence are built right into the concept. Each "family" hires a cook and a housekeeper, thus avoiding problems of having to divide housekeeping among people of varying physical capacity. This alternative is attractive for some older people, but in many areas zoning and housing restrictions are major obstacles to starting a share-a-home. Streib and Streib (1975) point out that local bureaucratic zeal will have to be relaxed quite a bit if home sharing is to become a widespread alternative for older people to meet their housing needs.

Retirement Housing

Retirement can bring an opportunity for people to move from housing or a community that they did not prefer but were tied to by employment, to housing or a community more in tune with their ideals. Some choose to move to planned retirement communities. Others move to communities that were not planned as retirement communities but simply attract large numbers of retirees.[3]

[3] Retired people can be referred to as *retirers* or *retirees*. Since most people retire on their own initiative, *retirer* is probably more appropriate but harder to say than *retiree*.

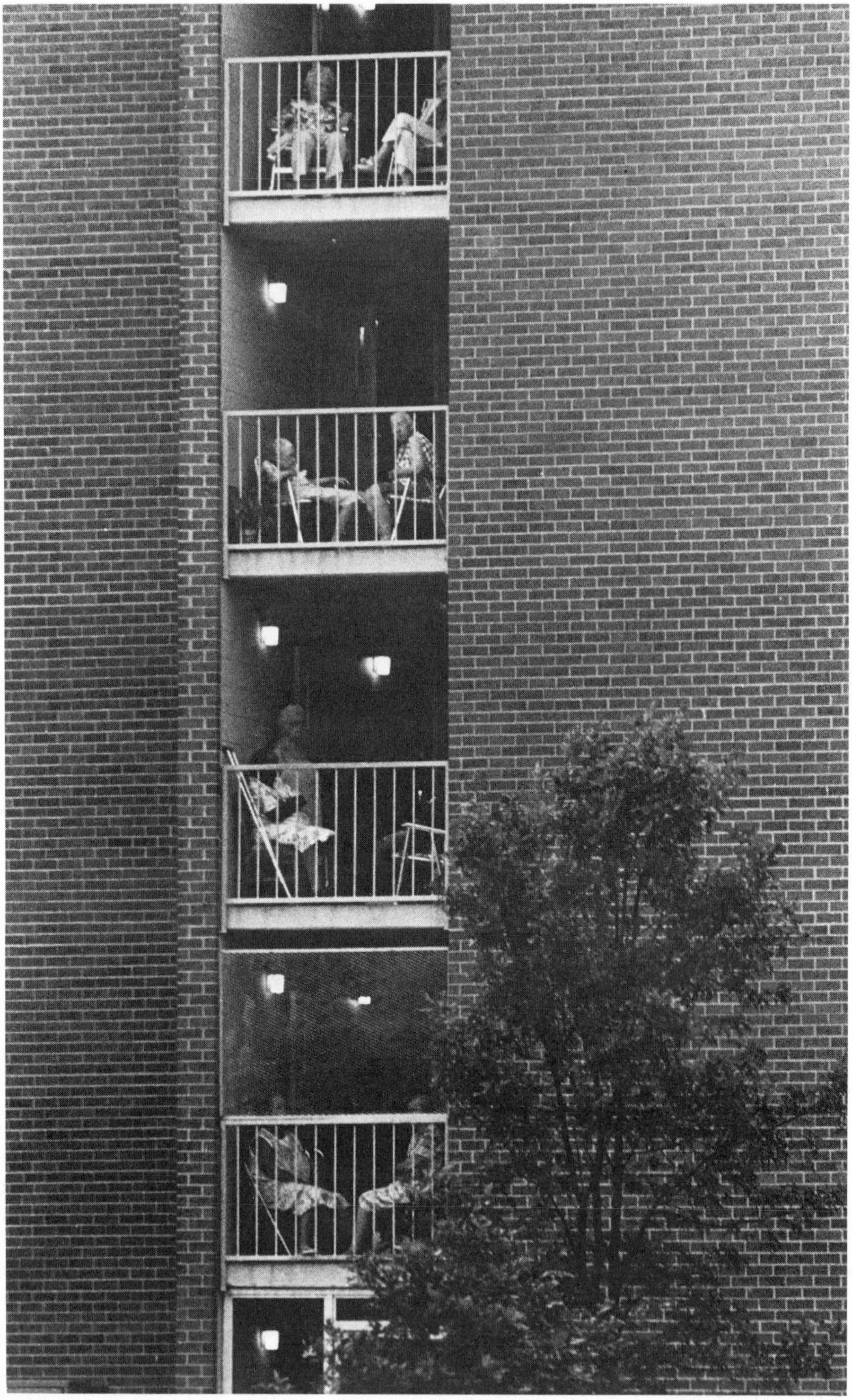

Retirement communities tend to be homogeneous with respect to social class, racial, and ethnic backgrounds of the residents. And there are retirement communities for people at most points on the social spectrum. However, the majority of retirement communities draw residents from the more affluent social classes (Bultena and Wood, 1969a).

Movement to retirement communities seems to self-select those older people who are amenable to life in age-homogeneous settings. As a result, morale in retirement communities is quite high. Conversely, there are indications that many older people who remain in age-integrated communities would not be at all happy in a retirement community (Bultena and Wood, 1969a).

The homogeneity of retirement communities fosters greater social interaction and formation of new friendships. Because retirement communities draw heavily from former managers and professionals, their members are often quite accustomed to moving and have the skills needed for making new friends. For the vast majority of people in retirement communities, the move did not bring increased isolation from their children (Bultena and Wood, 1969a). Although living in planned retirement communities may not be for everyone, there is no evidence that it is detrimental for those who do choose it.

The working-class equivalent to the more affluent retirement community is the mobile home park for older adults. Basing her analysis on the situation in California in the mid-1960s, Johnson (1971) concluded that the mobile home park is a mixed blessing for retired residents. Most older people who live in mobile parks want to live in a controlled environment without having to pay a high price for it.

> Slightly authoritarian in outlook, justifiably fearful of urban violence, and anxious to maintain all the visible outward signs appropriate to "decent people," the retired working-class mobile home resident wants to live in a park that is neat, attractive, quiet, safe, all-white, and friendly. [Johnson, 1971:174]

These people are willing to pay a park owner to control the neighborhood, but they complain bitterly if these controls infringe too much on *them*. All too often, the cost of living in a mobile home park also includes considerable economic exploitation by park owners (Johnson, 1971). Nevertheless, the popularity of such parks in many areas of the country attests to the felt need for living areas that provide a safe, secure environment for a community made up largely of older adults.

Longino (1981) reported on a study of three types of retirement housing: planned full-service retirement communities,[4] planned public housing for the elderly (nearly all of whom are retired), and *de facto* retirement communities that result from large-scale migration of retired people to small towns in certain regions of the country.

Those who moved to planned, full-service retirement communities tended to be older (mean age 76), affluent individuals who were oriented

---

[4] Full-service retirement communities offer a continuum of independent and semi-independent living plus nursing home care. They also offer a wide range of programs and services such as recreation, transportation, or education.

around the availability of housekeeping, meals, and nursing service. Those who moved to *de facto* retirement communities tended to be younger (mean age 68), affluent couples who were oriented toward independence and enjoyment of nature. Movers to public housing tended to be older (mean age 78), black women from the local area who wanted out of an unsafe neighborhood and to take advantage of the financial relief provided by subsidized housing. Longino's study supported the idea that older people select housing that meets their needs. He predicted that those who moved to planned communities probably would not move again because they had selected housing suitable to the needs of the old. However, he predicted that those who lived in *de facto* retirement communities would resemble people on an extended vacation who, when needs for assistance increased substantially, could be expected to return to their area of origin in order to be nearer to family.

Types of Housing Problems

Many older people cannot find housing both that is suitable for them and that they can afford. There is a shortage of subsidized low-rent housing for the elderly, particularly outside the major metropolitan areas. The Better Housing League of Cincinnati (1978) found that the demand in Cincinnati for low-rent housing for the elderly exceeded the supply by at least 25 percent. For the middle class, the situation is not much better. For instance, John and Ethel wanted to sell their home and move into an apartment. They could not find a buyer because interest rates were too high. In addition, the available apartments in the community were either very expensive or cheap and shabby. There was virtually nothing in the middle. John and Ethel decided to stay in their home, at least for now, even though it is much more space than they need or want to take care of.

As mentioned earlier, many older people need assistance if they are to remain in independent housing. Most of the services they need consist of personal care such as help in moving about, dressing, or bathing, and housekeeping care such as housework and meal preparation. About 12 percent of the elderly who live in independent households and are 75 or older receive such care. Although the percentage is not large, every community has older people who need in-home services and who either (1) do not have families that can assist them or (2) cannot afford to pay someone. Many if not most communities do not have programs to provide in-home services to the indigent elderly.

The majority of older people probably do not want to move, nor do they need in-home services—yet. However, they do need to maintain their homes. Because their homes tend to be older and more dilapidated than the housing of the young, more maintenance is required. This problem in turn translates into a need for funds to provide for maintenance and people to do it. In 1979, the State of Ohio began offering home maintenance and repair services to the rural elderly as part of its public employment training program (CETA). In those counties where such programs were instituted, the demand for services was nearly four times the capacity. This statistic indicates that a main reason that older people do not maintain their homes is that they cannot afford to. Another important factor involved sponsorship. The building "industry," especially in renovation and repair, is mostly small-scale entrepreneurs, and companies often have not been in business long. In addition, various confidence rackets involving home improvements have been widely publicized. As a result, the elderly are not sure with whom to deal and whom to trust. When government-sponsored programs came along, they were more willing to allow workers in their homes.

Who Has Housing Problems?

Older people who are most likely to have housing problems include the frail elderly, the disabled, the rural elderly, and those with low incomes. The frail elderly and the disabled are apt to find that they can get neither the in-home services they need to remain independent nor suitable group housing that can meet their needs for assistance within their capacity to pay. The low-income elderly find that there is a shortage of low-rent housing for the elderly. At the root of all three of these problems is financing. We simply do not have an adequate system for financing the nonmedical care of the frail elderly and the disabled. We also are not willing to divert the resources necessary to ensure that the elderly poor have adequate low-rent housing available. This latter problem is part of a larger picture of housing shortage in the U.S. The government has attempted to keep inflation under control by increasing the cost of borrowing money. The results have been interest rates above 20 percent. Under these conditions, builders simply cannot build housing that can be sold or rented at prices people can afford, and the elderly are the least likely to be able to afford expensive housing.

Health Care

As noted earlier, health is a major factor that enables people to enjoy life. Aging changes the health care people need if they are to maintain good health or avoid worsening health. Preventive health care can reduce the probability of chronic disease and disability, treatment can often reverse the negative effects of chronic disease, and rehabilitation can help people not only to restore lost functions but to compensate for functions that cannot be restored. As a group of people gets older, they need more treatment and rehabilitation compared to preventive health, although right now few age groups in the U.S. get adequate preventive health care.

Treatment

Treatment includes self-treatment with home remedies or over-the-counter medications, visiting a doctor, going to an outpatient clinic, short-term care in a hospital, and long-term care of chronic diseases at home or in a nursing home.

About 40 percent of acute conditions, such as common colds or flu, are self-treated. Most drugstores carry numerous preparations for the self-treatment of colds, allergies, constipation, indigestion, skin rashes and itching, and so on. Indeed, many minor chronic ailments such as eczema can be effectively treated by using over-the-counter drugs.

But as age increases, so does the severity of both chronic and acute illnesses. As a result, older people are likely to go to a physician. Compared to adults under 45, older adults make 50 percent more visits to doctors' offices. Those elderly with incomes over $10,000 per year are even more likely to make numerous visits to the doctor. In 1975, over 80 percent of the elderly saw a doctor at least once (Kovar, 1977).

In-home health care is not common. House calls by physicians fell from 23 percent of all doctor visits in 1959 to less than 5 percent in 1975. About 80 percent of home health care is provided by family living in the household, usually the spouse. In 75 percent of the cases, home care has been done for one year or longer. Thirty percent of home care involves constant care. Fortunately, only a very small proportion of the elderly need such care—12.5 percent at age 75 or older (Wilder, 1972).

Older people are not very much more likely than other age groups to go to a short-stay hospital. About 13 percent of the elderly was hospitalized at least once in 1976, compared to about 11 percent for the general population. However, those elderly who have serious illnesses account for an enormous number of stays in the hospital. As a result, the elderly have hospitalization rates that are three times higher than those for people under 17, and the average duration of stay is nearly three times as long.

At any one time, only about 4 percent of the elderly is in personal care homes, nursing homes, or intermediate care facilities.[5] However, as age goes up, so does the percentage who need constant care. Palmore (1976) found that 25 percent of the elderly in a 20-year longitudinal study experienced institutionalization at some time before they died.

Types of Health Problems

The elderly are likely to find that the kind of care they need is not available. The kind of care they are offered may be inappropriate. There may be no one willing to manage the long-term treatment of multiple chronic conditions. They may be plagued by problems resulting from interactions among multiple medications used to treat multiple chronic conditions. And last but not least, most older people find that the system we have for financing health care is not adequate.

Mrs. C's case illustrates the problem of needed health care being unavailable. She was 76 and lived alone. She was in good health generally, but

[5] Personal care homes provide meals, housekeeping services, and assistance with tasks such as dressing and bathing. Nursing homes provide personal care plus minimal medical care. People who require hospital-quality care over a long period are cared for in intermediate care facilities.

she came down with the flu. She tried to manage on her own but reached the point where she could not get out of bed to fix meals or go to the bathroom. She called her doctor and instead got his receptionist. The receptionist insisted that Mrs. C would have to come into the doctor's office. Mrs. C replied that she could not get out of bed, much less come to the office. The receptionist instructed Mrs. C to call the emergency squad and go to the hospital emergency room because "That's what emergency rooms are for." Mrs. C did as instructed. She was more than slightly embarrassed about being carried out of her building on a stretcher "all on account of the measly flu." At the hospital she was seen after a two-hour wait by the emergency room physician, a complete stranger who knew nothing of her medical history, which included two chronic conditions and five regular medications. He told her she had flu and should go home and stay in bed! Almost in tears, she told him of her problem of not being able to care for herself at home. He said that there was nothing to be done about it because she was not sick enough to require hospitalization, and Medicare would not pay for it.[6] She could not afford to pay $140 per day to finance her own hospital stay, yet she needed around-the-clock care for a few days. What Mrs. C needed was personal care for a short time, but nursing homes usually do not admit short-term residents. In addition, the health care financing system makes no provision for personal care. In desperation, Mrs. C called her sister, who lived over 200 miles away. The sister came for a few days, and Mrs. C recovered. But what would have happened if Mrs. C had not had family?

Mrs. C's problem was caused partially by the way care is financed, but more important perhaps is the underlying philosophy about what illness is and how it should be treated that pervades our entire health care system. The "medical model" basically assumes that there are only two kinds of people to be treated, those who are seriously ill and need hospitalization and those who are up and about and can go to a doctor's office or clinic. Obviously, incapacity is a matter of degree, and our system for treatment needs to recognize this fact.

Brody (1973) also pointed out that when health is viewed as a positive good to be pursued rather than merely as an affliction to be eliminated, the range of services required for adequate health care expands. He argued strongly against viewing personal services such as bathing and dressing, support services such as recreational therapy, maintenance services such as housekeeping, and coordination services such as counseling or referral as "ancillary" services—as somehow not quite as essential as direct medical care to the maintenance of good health. Brody further pointed out the uneven availability of nonmedical health services. For example, Medicare and third-party medical insurance will pay for such services in a short-stay hospital or extended care facility, but not in the patient's home. Although home health service is technically available under Medicare, it is seldom used

---

[6] Medicare is a public system for financing health care. It is discussed in detail later in this chapter.

because the patient must be virtually housebound but still able to make do with only intermittent care.

As noted earlier, many middle-aged and older people have more than one chronic condition that requires long-term treatment. *Long-term care* used to mean care provided by an institution, but today the term has a broader meaning and includes the long-term management of illness and disability (Koff, 1982). Long-term care is thus possible in both community and institutional settings. However, the specialization of medicine discourages the coordination required to manage multiple chronic conditions effectively in the community. As a result, an older person may be going to two or three doctors for several different conditions, and there is often no communication among the doctors. Effective long-term care in the community requires *case management*, a process that involves looking at all the person's needs and resources and developing a coordinated treatment plan. Unfortunately, very few communities have case management services.

Drugs are a major component in the treatment of most acute and chronic conditions common among older people. What drugs to use and in what amounts depend on several factors: how much of the drug is *absorbed* how fast from the site of administration, how efficiently the drug is *distributed*, how quickly and completely the drug is *metabolized*, and how quickly the drug or its by-products are *eliminated* from the body (Kayne, 1976). Aging changes all these factors, "often resulting in greater concentrations of the drug at its site of activity or a longer persistence of drug activity" in older people compared to other adults (Kayne, 1976:437). For example, because kidney functioning declines sharply with age, drugs that are eliminated by the kidneys must be given in lower dosages to older people in order to avoid accumulation of the drug to the point where it produces adverse effects. Moreover, many older peole have multiple chronic conditions for which they are taking several drugs.

Establishing proper dosages and avoiding adverse drug reactions or adverse interactions among drugs require initial metabolic information, history, and monitoring that is beyond the capacity of medicine as it is currently organized. In many cases, the physician does not know how age effects appropriate dosage. Sometimes such information is simply not available. As a result, establishing proper dosages is a trial and error process in which a great many errors are made and only sometimes detected.

About 5 percent of all hospitalizations occur as a result of adverse drug reactions, and this percentage is higher for people over 60. In addition, 10 to 30 percent of those who are hospitalized have adverse drug reactions in the hospital, and such reactions occur more often in older patients than in others (Kayne, 1976:436–437). And these data probably reflect only a small portion of the actual medical problems that result from the use of inappropriate drugs, incorrect drugs, or drug interactions. In addition, mental problems such as depression or confusion are common results of adverse drug reactions. Unfortunately, these symptoms are all too often attributed to "senility" in older patients.

Problems with Financing Medical Care

Medicare is a program of health insurance for older Americans that is administered by the Social Security Administration. It consists of two parts: hospital insurance and medical insurance. Nearly all older Americans are eligible for hospital coverage. Here is how it worked in 1979. After a $160 deductible paid by the patient, hospital insurance covered the full cost of up to 60 days of hospitalization for any spell of illness. From 61 days to 90 days, the patient paid $40 per day. In addition, a "lifetime reserve" of 60 days could be used for illness that required hospitalization for longer than 90 days. However, the patient had to pay $80 per day during coverage under the lifetime reserve. Hospital insurance also covered up to 100 days in an approved intermediate care facility. The first 20 days were covered in full, and after that the patient paid $20 per day. Hospital insurance is financed through payroll deductions and employer contributions to a Medicare trust fund that is separate from the Social Security trust fund.

Supplementary medical insurance is a voluntary program administered under Medicare that requires a monthly premium from the older person. The premium is matched by the federal government out of general tax revenues. In 1979, after a yearly deductible of $60, medical insurance paid 80 percent of the allowable costs of doctors' services and outpatient physical therapy. It did not pay for medical checkups, prescription drugs, eyeglasses, dentures, or hearing aids.[7]

Medicare has covered almost all people age 65 or over since July 1, 1966 (West, 1971). Initially the in-hospital services rose, along with all supporting medical services, with the introduction of the program, and continued to increase, but at a declining rate. However, the average length of each hospital stay has actually dropped slightly. The use of ambulatory physician services has remained fairly stable throughout the period since 1966, and there has been very little use of posthospital alternatives—extended care facilities and home health services. Per capita expenditures under Medicare have more than doubled since the program began, mainly because of increases in charges to the program for covered services. A large proportion of the funds are spent on the behalf of a relatively small number of people with serious illnesses. About 20 percent of the insured population uses no covered service in a given year. Another 20 percent is hospitalized. Among the 20 percent that is hospitalized, one-fourth are hospitalized more than once in the year, and the bulk of the physician costs arise from hospitalized illness.

Medicaid is a comprehensive health care program designed to provide health care to the poor, regardless of age. It is administered by local welfare departments using federal and state funds. Medicaid pays for everything that Medicare does, as well as for many other services, including drugs, eyeglasses, and long-term care in licensed nursing homes.

---

[7] Because Medicare regulations are constantly changing, it is not possible to include much detail about the program. This situation represents a minor headache to authors writing books in gerontology and a major headache to older people, who are never quite sure what is covered or for how long.

About 55 percent of older Americans carry private health insurance to fill the major gaps in Medicare coverage. However, at present none of the available policies provide complete medical care coverage. Thus, out-of-pocket expenses for medical services remain a major expense item for older Americans.

Who Has Health Care Problems?

Virtually everyone who has a chronic condition in the United States has some sort of problem finding appropriate and effective care or paying for it. Nevertheless, certain subgroups of the older population are more likely than others to have problems. The very old (80 and over) are especially likely to be frail. Often the adult children who could care for them are themselves older people with limited physical and financial resources. The very old tend to have multiple serious conditions, and they are much more likely to be disabled by them. Older members of some minority groups are also more likely to have health problems. Particularly among blacks and Native Americans, disabling chronic illness tends to occur earlier than among whites.

What Needs to Be Done?

It is literally true that an ounce of prevention is worth a pound of cure, especially in the area of health care. Yet our approach to the provision and financing of care does not reflect this. At the very least we need much more effort to educate the public about the value of prevention, to educate health care professionals about the most effective measures, and to perform the research needed to advance our knowledge about effective prevention.

But we must also acknowledge that the major problem in prevention is not financing or lack of knowledge or lack of prevention services—it is a lack of motivation. I am sure that a majority of the American population knows that it is unhealthy to smoke, to be overweight, to drink too much alcohol, and not to exercise. Yet cigarette sales have increased every year since the Surgeon General reported over 20 years ago that smoking was linked to lung cancer and heart disease. The average weight of the American people has gone up steadily and so has the proportion that is obese, despite widespread publicity linking overweight to heart disease. Despite the popularity of exercise right now, hundreds of thousands of adults get none.

Somehow we must create awareness and willingness for the American people to assume responsibility for their own health. Underlying the current apathy, in my opinion, is a tendency to assign responsibility for health to the medical profession. This tendency is a mistake. It puts the responsibility for our health in the hands of people who have no direct experience of our physical or mental states. It also fosters the illusion that we do not have to worry about our own health. Ultimately, the only way that people in general will begin to take charge of their own health-related habits is if they carefully observe the effects of those habits on how they feel. This goal requires that they be trained to do so.

In the area of rehabilitation,[8] we should disconnect the financing of rehabilitation from the prospects for employment. Just because someone is retired is no reason to deny him or her needed rehabilitation services! We also need to do a better job of training family members to aid in the rehabilitative process, because they are the ones most likely to provide care at home.

In the area of treatment, we pointed earlier to the need for a continuum of services. In-home services, outpatient clinics, residential care, and long-term care are all in short supply right now. Our system is also spotty with respect to a continuum of mental health services. Although an estimated 15 percent of the elderly need mental health services, they represent only 2 to 4 percent of the clients of psychiatric clinics, community mental health centers, or private practitioners. These figures suggest that moving older mental patients from state-run mental hospitals into "the community" may have been ill advised. Beginning in the 1960s, there was a wholesale transfer of geriatric mental patients out of mental hospitals. This transfer has been partially responsible for the dramatic rise in nursing home residents since 1960. Such policies may look good on paper, but in actuality people are being sent out into communities that are not prepared to monitor their progress. In many cases there is not even provision for continuing necessary drug therapy (Butler and Lewis, 1973).

We also need to fill the gaps in our current systems for financing health care. For example, right now Medicare does not pay for eyeglasses, dentures, or hearing aids. It should. Medicare also does not recognize the fact that long-term care can indeed be long-term. As the system is now, older people, including couples in which only one member needs long-term care, are forced to become paupers in order to qualify for the only system that provides truly long-term care—Medicaid.

Health Care Needs and Growth of the Older Population

In the 30 years from 1970 to 2000, the growth of the older population and the aging of the older population will produce significant increases in demand for all kinds of health services. At the 1970 rates of utilization, the population explosion of older Americans will increase the annual demand for space in acute care hospitals from 79 million bed-days in 1970 to 125 million in the year 2000. Demand for physician visits will increase from 117 million to 188 million annually. Nursing home residents will increase from 720 thousand to over 1.3 million. Nursing home residents over 85 years of age will increase from 262 thousand to 584 thousand.

The implications of these increases in demand are frightening. Physicians and adequate nursing homes are in short supply now. What will happen when the demand nearly doubles? The mental health needs of the

[8] Rehabilitation is discussed further in Chapter 13.

older population are 85 percent unmet now. What will happen when the over-85 population more than doubles? Health insurance cannot pay for services needed now. How can it cope with both inflation and the population explosion of older adults? These are apt to be some of our most serious policy questions over the next two decades.

Transportation

Aging changes our needs and resources in the area of transportation in several ways. For some, declining sight impairs ability to drive a private automobile. Declines in income force still others to give up their cars or use them sparingly. The increase in the proportion of physically impaired people with age also increases the proportion who need specialized transportation.

In this country, we have been experiencing a long-term trend away from public transportation. Its use is declining in all but our largest cities. No longer a paying proposition, and usually requiring tax subsidy, public transportation is most used for travel to and from work. The needs of the elderly are not considered in most decisions about public transportation.

Older people fall into two categories with regard to transportation: those who can use present facilities and those who cannot. Those with no transportation problems tend to be the ones who can afford to own and operate their own cars—about 46 percent of those 65 and older. For these people, public transportation is something to be used when it snows or for long trips.

Who Has Transportation Problems?

The elderly with transportation problems fall into three groups: (1) those who could use existing public transportation but cannot afford it; (2) those who for one reason or another need to be picked up and returned directly to their homes; and (3) those who live in areas where there is no public transportation.

Cost is an important factor. In this country roughly 10 million older people are hampered by the cost of transportation, often because they cannot afford a car; because bus fares of 50¢ or higher are beyond their means; or because they cannot pay cab fares of $2.50 or more. For these people, lack of adequate, inexpensive transportation is one of the most important limitations on their independence and activities.

Among older people with transportation problems, most are still able to get to the doctor, dentist, and grocery store. But many do not get out to see their friends and relatives or go to church or recreation facilities. Although they still manage to keep alive, they are unable to do the things that give meaning to life. And when they can get out, it is usually at someone else's convenience. Pride and a sense of dignity often prevent older people from relying on friends and relatives to transport them. What they need is a dependable transportation system at prices they can afford.

What Is Needed?

The ideal transportation plan for older people would consist of four elements. First, older people need fare reductions or discounts on all public transportation, including interstate transport. Second, public subsidies are needed for adequate scheduling and routing of existing public transportation. Third, taxi fares for the disabled or infirm should be reduced. Fourth, funds should be allocated to senior centers to purchase and equip vehicles for use in transporting older people, particularly in rural areas with no public transportation.

Increasingly, the federal government has been willing to provide funds for transportation as a necessary element of service delivery in programs for older people. However, federal cutbacks now threaten the gains that were made in the 1970s.

Community Facilities and Services

Communities, or subcommunities in larger areas, are important focal points in the lives of most people. People are born, reared, educated, married, housed, fed, healed, mourned, and buried in local communities. The effort devoted to work, play, love, politics, fellowship, or self-discovery most often is expended in the context of local communities. Thus, the picture of society people gain is substantially influenced by the extent to which the cities or neighborhoods they live in are unified communities. Because older people are usually long-term community residents, they are especially likely to see the community as the locus of life's most salient moments. Thus, how services to the elderly are organized within communities is extremely important.

The Older Americans Comprehensive Service Amendments of 1973 created a new community organization, the *Area Agency on Aging* (AAAs). Along with significant increases in federal funds to local programs for older Americans, the Comprehensive Service Amendments (through the AAA) brought new priorities on coordination of services and on *planning*. There are currently just under 400 AAAs, each of which is charged with developing plans for a comprehensive and coordinated network of services to older people and with offering facilitating services in the areas of information and referral, escort, transportation, and outreach. The concept of the Area Agency on Aging emphasizes flexibility in uniting particular sets of local organizations to meet the needs of local older people, and thus allows for local and regional variations in resources and service needs. At the same time, the AAA concept seeks to make a minimum set of services available to

all older people. Since the AAAs were created in 1974, services to the elderly have improved dramatically in most parts of the nation.

Facilities That Serve the Elderly

Facilities in a community are organized service centers such as stores, banks, churches, doctors' offices, hospitals, and so forth. There is usually a mixture of public and private facilities in any given community. Taietz (1975) made an intensive study of community facilities serving the aged in 144 New York communities. He found that specialized facilities tended to be present in communities that had a high degree of complexity and specialization. Only the most rudimentary facilities were available in a majority of the 144 communities surveyed, and facilities were particularly lacking in rural areas.

Because most Americans live in urban areas, it is easy to forget that the majority of communities are in rural areas. In 1974, 86 percent of the land area of the United States was rural, nonmetropolitan land. The impact of this fact on the prevalence of facilities is a topic very worthy of study.

Services

Social services consist of a broad range of often unrelated programs that revolve around a general goal of helping people get the things they want. The range includes family services, senior centers, the Foster Grandparent program, Talking Books, meals programs, employment services, and protective services. Communities vary widely with regard to the number and range of such programs, and program titles vary widely. Therefore, instead of trying to describe the typical community, it is probably more useful to examine general types of programs that are commonly found in communities. I will deal here only with services *to* older people. Services *by* older people are covered in Chapter 9.

Services to Older People Services that provide *meals* either take food to people or bring people to food. "Meals-on-Wheels" programs deliver hot meals to older people in their own homes. Congregate meals programs bring older people to a central site for meals. In recent years, the congregate meals approach has been gaining favor because it provides fellowship as well as more opportunities to tie in with other social service programs at the congregate meal sites.

Services providing *information and referral* serve as a bridge between people with needs and appropriate service agencies. Area Agencies on Aging are responsible for these programs in most areas. Many areas have directories of services for older people.

Some programs offer *visitor* contact between older shut-ins and the outside world. Visitor programs often serve institutionalized older people as well as older people living in their own homes. The programs are usually staffed by volunteers, and older people often work as visitors.

Programs involving *outreach* services seek out older people in the community who need services. Older people who need services often become known to the program via relatives or neighbors. Outreach workers contact the older person and refer him or her to the appropriate agency. Sometimes outreach workers make agency contacts on behalf of older people.

Programs offering *telephone reassurance* give isolated older people a point of contact and a sense of continuity. In the ideal reassurance program, the people working on the phones are well trained in referral and yet also know the older person through regular telephone visits. Regular calls from the program assure older people that someone cares about them and will be checking on their welfare regularly. Volunteers are often used for telephone reassurance.

Certain *employment* services seek to place older workers in jobs. Sometimes such services maintain a file of retired people from various occupations who are available for short-term or part-time employment.

Various *homemaker* services provide household support services to semi-independent older people living in their own homes. In addition to the usual housekeeping chores such as cleaning, shopping, and laundry, some programs also offer home maintenance and food preparation services. Berg et al. (1974) stress the need for a continuum of service that can be suited to the older person's level of impairment. Highly impaired people need a variety of housekeeping services on a daily basis, while others may only need occasional specialized services.

Services that offer *income counseling* help people get maximum use of their income resources by making sure they are aware of all possible sources of income and by helping them make the transition from a pre- to a post-retirement budget. Income counseling often includes such things as how to buy consumer goods at the lowest prices, how to take advantage of seasonal sales, the cost of credit buying, how to form consumer cooperatives, how to save on rent or get into low-rent public housing, ways to save on auto insurance, ways to save on building, repairs, and so on. Although this type of assistance is highly valued by older people, very few communities offer it.

Most large communities have *senior centers*, which usually take the form of private nonprofit corporations, often underwritten with United Way money. The several thousand senior centers in the United States often constitute the sole community attempt to offer recreational and educational programs for older people. The small percentage of older people who use them (usually 1 to 5 percent) would seem to indicate that senior centers do not constitute a focal point for recreation and education among the overwhelming majority of older people. Of course, many older people who might otherwise use a senior center's facilities are prevented from doing so by difficulties of access—poor transportation service, disability, health, and so on. Yet even in communities where concerted efforts have been made to give older people access to senior centers, only a small minority have taken advantage of them.

The average multipurpose senior center tends to adopt a flexible program—one that involves informal companionship, community services, self-government within the center, and a wide variety of other possible features. Membership in senior centers tends to be drawn from a wide area rather than from a single neighborhood. Initial membership is often related to a major life change such as retirement or widowhood, and joiners tend to be healthy and able to get around. Members of senior centers do not seem to be very different from other older people. However, Tissue (1971) indicates that centers cannot easily accommodate members from different social classes.

Some programs offer *protective services*, taking responsibility for older people who are no longer capable of being responsible for themselves. Everyone has heard of aging, confused hermits who have outlived their families and who are starving because they have hidden their Social Security checks and cannot recall where they put them. For example, Mr. M had been complaining to a variety of agencies about Mrs. S, an 88-year-old woman whose house was adjacent to his—and he finally reached the Senior Information Center. Mrs. S was a recluse who had harassed the M's by making loud noises through their bedroom window, banging her porch door, calling vile and obscene things to their children playing in the yard. Her house was run down, weeds and bushes had overgrown the garden, and neighbors photographed her feeding rats in her backyard. They described her as resembling the witch of fairytales—with flowing gray hair and long, dirty skirts, living in seclusion in a silent house. Her only relative was a niece, who for the last several years had refused to be involved. Her income was only $72 a month from Social Security.

A home call confirmed the grim picture. Mrs. S, suspicious at first, refused to let the caseworker into the house, but came out on the porch to talk. She tried to hide a dirty, stained slip, and there was a strong odor of urine about her. She denied having any problems other than those caused by the "gangsters" next door, and there was a paranoid trend in her thinking. As she talked she became almost friendly, joked about getting a miniskirt, and assured the caseworker that there was nothing to worry about in her situation.

Later, a city sanitation inspector went through the house, saw one rat and evidence of rats' presence throughout the house. The odor of urine and feces was strong. The inspector also found about 50 wine bottles, which added to the frightening picture.

Finally, Mr. M in his anger over the continued harassment, nailed shut the back door of her house. Fortunately, another neighbor, realizing the danger in case of fire, removed the nails (adapted from Ross, 1968:50).

Protective services are used by the community when it becomes clear from the behavior of older people that they are mentally incapable of caring for themselves and their interests. It is estimated that something on the order of 1 in every 20 older people needs some form of protective service. In addition, this proportion can be expected to increase as the proportion of older people over age 75 increases.

The typical response to someone like Mrs. S is to put her in an institution, but this solution is coming under increased scrutiny. Many older people now in institutions could be left at home with a minimum of help in securing the support services that are already available to them.

The most difficult problem is often to find someone to initiate action. In many states, the law assumes the proceedings will be initiated by a relative. In the absence of a relative, no one is willing to take the responsibility. Laws need to be changed in such a way that responsibility is pinpointed.

Ultimately, protective services are casework, outreach services rather than deskbound ones. Legal intervention is usually a last resort, used only when all other alternatives have been exhausted. Agencies must often seek out people who may not want the service at all. It is obvious that protective services must be a part of any community service program for older people, but assigning responsibility for such services is a difficult task.

Summary

Availability of resources to meet instrumental needs varies widely among the elderly. Most older Americans have adequate incomes, housing, health care, transportation, and access to facilities and services. It's a good thing, too. If the nation had to finance special services to more than a very small proportion of its older citizens, the costs would be astronomical indeed.

But within this generally favorable situation, many categories of older people have great difficulty in meeting their instrumental needs. Financial difficulties are far more prevalent among single older women, older blacks or Hispanic Americans, rural residents, and the very old than in the general older population. The fact that private pensions are least likely to be available in the lowest-paying jobs is creating an increasing gap between the haves and the have-nots with regard to retirement income. The cutbacks in both direct and indirect income support to the poor that began in October 1981 as part of the Reagan Administration's economic program are bound to widen this gap further.

Although Social Security needs various adjustments to account for economic trends and population change, none of these adjustments are drastic and the system can easily remain solvent. Short-run problems can be solved with interfund borrowing, and long-run financing will require gradually raising the retirement age. Beginning around the year 2010, the minimum retirement age can be raised gradually from 62 to 65 and the normal retirement age from 65 to 68. Those who will be affected by this change will have plenty of time to plan for it. However, if the retirement age is raised, provision will need to be made for those who have health problems that require retirement earlier than at 65.

Most older people live in independent households and want it that way. Nevertheless, as the number of very old people increases, there will be a growing need for in-home assistance. Indications are that the need for such services is not being met now, and this situation probably will get worse. Middle-income older Americans are often frustrated by the unavailability of housing options they can afford. There is also a shortage of subsidized housing for the elderly poor. Retirement community living comes in several varieties, and older people seem to select the variety that best meets their needs. But retirement community options are scarce in many areas of the country.

Health care problems encountered by the elderly include lack of resources for preventive health care, gaps in coverage by Medicare, lack of facilities or services to care for older people with short-term disabling acute conditions such as flu, poor availability of mental health services, and poor availability of health care facilities and services in rural areas. In addition, the growing older population will place a severe strain on facilities and services and many may not be able to meet their needs at all unless we plan now to increase the availability of health practitioners and facilities.

Dramatic increases in the over-80 population will compound the current problems of transportation. The proportion who cannot or should not drive personal automobiles is going to increase rapidly. We need to plan for this eventuality.

Older people are served by a large and complex network of public and private organizations. As federal funds earmarked for some services to the elderly disappear into block grants to the states, the elderly who need services will be put in direct competition for resources at the local level. What this competition will mean in terms of quality of services remains to be seen, but most practitioners are not optimistic. At the very least, much energy that could have gone into providing service will now have to go into the political activity needed to secure funds.

More attention needs to be paid to older people as *providers* of services. Retired people represent a large pool of potential community resources that could be used to serve older people who need assistance.

The overall picture is that several categories of older people encounter problems and that the problems they are likely to have vary. Women, minorities, and the very old are more likely to have income problems. Middle-class elders who do not qualify for subsidized housing, and older rural people are more likely to have housing problems. Preventive health care is a problem for everyone. The elderly poor are often able to get more types of services paid for, but they have more trouble finding someone to provide such services. Transportation problems are more likely among older women and the very old. Therefore, of course, no single policy will meet these various needs.

Chapter 9

Activities

People like rhythm in their lives, and the ebb and flow of activity provide it. Each of us has a familiar routine for approaching the day. Our routines can also vary on holidays, on weekends, in the summer months, and on special occasions. These routines give a comfortable predictability to life, especially if they are satisfying ones. Our routines can be highly structured or not, but they are constructed of expected and/or preferred activities.

Aging changes activities in many ways. Role changes in later life, such as retirement or launching one's children into adulthood, change the amount of time that must be given to the job and to child rearing. Changes in physical functioning can impose limits on what we are able to do physically and may eventually become serious enough to restrict our activities to an institutional environment. Age discrimination can also limit the quality and quantity of activities available to us. Thus, age-related role changes may free us to concentrate our efforts on activities of our own choosing, while declining physical capacity or financial resources and age discrimination may constrict our choices. The balance between freedom and constriction that an individual experiences is greatly influenced by his or her position in the social hierarchy. People who are well-to-do and powerful are not likely to find their activities seriously limited because they are likely to remain in good health and to have the economic resources necessary to enjoy the freedom of retirement. However, for those at the lower end of the social ladder, inadequate incomes and serious health limitations are more likely, and so is age discrimination.

When aging becomes obvious, the gradual attrition of activities can be quite distressing. The case of Mrs. A is not necessarily typical in its particulars, but it illustrates the process. Mrs. A was first interviewed at age 70. At that time she lived alone in a comfortable apartment. Her daily round of activities was not a complex one. She spent a good deal of time keeping her apartment and herself comfortably neat and clean. She took frequent walks to nearby stores to pass the time of day as well as to make purchases. She spent an hour or more per day just talking with friends. On Thursdays, she usually drove to a nearby city to attend the program at a senior center. Afterward she would often visit with friends. Her major pastimes were reading, watching television, talking with friends, and housekeeping.

However, Mrs. A's most meaningful activities involved visiting and talking with her daughter and her grandchildren. Although these contacts were not always smooth ones, because of generational differences in values, the level of mutual affection and respect was an absolutely essential element of Mrs. A's life. Although Mrs. A had several close friends, they were not able to provide for her a feeling of belonging. Whatever her pattern of activities, Mrs. A needed enough interaction with her family to maintain this sense of belonging.

At age 74, Mrs. A's situation had changed remarkably. She had increasingly found the stairs to her apartment difficult to negotiate, especially with packages, laundry, or groceries. As a result, she had moved to a first-floor apartment in another neighborhood. This move relieved the problem of the stairs, but it cost Mrs. A her contacts with neighbors and shopkeepers in the area she had left. These contacts were no longer a convenient by-product of everyday living. To see these people became a special project. About this same time she had begun to have difficulty driving at night and had to give up her visits to the senior center and to her friends in the nearby city. She still talked frequently with friends, but such contact was more likely to be by phone now rather than face to face. Mrs. A had had to curtail her reading because of eye trouble. She could still read, but not as much. Her eye specialist said nothing could be done about the problem. She seemed to feel that she was watching about all the television she could stand. To add to her distress, Mrs. A was finding it more difficult to care for herself and her apartment. She resented the fact that she could not vacuum under her furniture without being "out of commission" for two days afterward. She seemed particularly angry at having had to give up tub baths in favor of showers because she could no longer easily get up and down in the tub. Thus, Mrs. A had not only had to relinquish activities, but had had to substitute less preferred options for several of those she retained.

The big gap in Mrs. A's activity pattern was contact with people and with the outside world. She lost the contacts in her old neighborhood, at the senior center, and in the nearby city. She compensated somewhat by talking to old friends on the phone and by making new friends in her new neighborhood. But her decreased physical capacity made it difficult for her to get out into the community. She turned to her daughter for more interaction and for assistance in getting out and about, especially when Mrs. A was feeling bad. So far these increased demands have been met, but Mrs. A is fearful lest she jeopardize the most meaningful relationships in her life.

As Mrs. A's case illustrates, changes in activity patterns as a result of

aging are not simply a matter of dropping activities and sometimes substituting others. Lifelong preferences, emotional reactions, and social relationships are usually involved. This area is not an easy one to research, especially if the research adequately follows people through time. Nevertheless, such research is essential if we are to have an authentic understanding of the dynamics of aging.

In this chapter, we look first at some general factors that influence the mix of activities going into middle age and later life. Then we look at some changes often connected with aging and at how they influence activities. Finally, we look at some of the age-related factors that influence activities in particular environments such as the workplace, at home, or in the community. The goal is to provide an overview of the forces that influence activities and the context in which activities are performed. This understanding is vital if you are to be able to understand how older people relate to their activities.

Factors Influencing Activities in Middle Adulthood

The range of activities that occupy human time and attention is practically infinite. Nevertheless, we can predict with some assurance that most middle-aged adults will have jobs, will spend time at home, will be involved in community activities to some extent, and will do things with their families. Within these general areas or spheres of participation, the factors that influence the choice of *particular* activities include the meanings attached to activities and how these meanings relate to the personal goals of the individual, to the person's sense of competence for various activities, and to sex, social class, and ethnic norms about the desirability of various activities.

The Meaning of Activity

The same activity can mean quite different things to different people. The following is an incomplete list of some of the meanings activities can have:

△ A source of personal identity—I am what I do

△ A way to make money

△ A way to be with people

△ A way to get the "vital juices" flowing

△ A source of personal development

△ A way to focus creativity

△ A source of sensory experience

△ A source of prestige or status

△ A source of new experience

△ A way to be of service to others

△ A way of passing time

△ Something to look forward to

△ A way to exercise competence

△ A source of peace and quiet

△ A means of escape

△ A source of joy and fun

△ A source of feelings of accomplishment

Any activity could be rated as to how much these various meanings are attached to that activity for a given individual. For example, writing this book is for me a source of personal development, a way to focus creativity, a source of prestige or status, a way to be of service to others, a way to exercise competence, a source of feelings of accomplishment, and a way to make money—not necessarily in that order.

The point is that any activity can have many meanings for an individual. In order to understand how an activity fits into an individual's life, we must know the meaning of that activity for that person *and* how that activity (given its meaning) fits into the person's life goals. For example, writing this book has a different meaning and fits into my life goals in a very different way from the first book I wrote some 12 years ago. At that time, career success was a major objective for me, and I must confess that the book I wrote was mainly aimed at making a name for myself and getting me promoted. Now success is no longer a high-priority issue because I have the highest possible academic rank and I am well recognized within my field. As a result, this book is primarily an attempt to exercise my skills, focus my creativity, serve you, and make a little money. We cannot assume that we know the meaning of an activity for a particular person—we have to find out. For example, earlier I cited a case in which I ran into trouble by assuming that jobs are a crucial source of identity for people, when in fact jobs have many meanings.

Activity Competence

Although there are plentiful opportunities to enjoy a wide variety of activities in adulthood, people need *skills* and *knowledge* to take advantage of them. For example, older people—particularly the less educated—are reluctant to engage in activities such as art, music, handiwork, or writing. And this reluctance is at least partly caused by the older person's feelings of incompetence in such activities.

Critics of education have attacked this apparent deficiency in our orientation toward education. Contemporary education, it is said, devotes anywhere from 80 to 90 percent of the students' time for 12 to 19 years to teaching them how to fill jobs, but makes little effort to prepare them for life outside the job. As the noted publisher Norman Cousins (1968:20) put it, "I contend that science tends to lengthen life, and education tends to shorten it; that science has the effect of freeing man for leisure, and that education has the effect of deflecting him from the enjoyment of living." The point is that to open up the full range of possible activities requires some training.

Research on exposure to "high culture" in American society has shown that college-educated people are no more likely to enjoy a wide range of activities than are semiskilled workers (Wilensky, 1964; Marquis Academic Media, 1978). Television, which often requires little competence, is the major leisure activity in American society. One could conclude that our education and communication systems do little to develop the potential for the creative use of free time.

There is some evidence that the learning necessary to take advantage of available opportunities must begin early. The decline in learning speed that occurs with age, the reluctance most older people show toward attempting anything entirely new, and the extreme stability that activity patterns show lead to the conclusion that activity competence created early in life can be maintained into later life. Oliver (1971) found little change with age in the types of activities among his healthy, financially solvent respondents. But if activity competence is not learned by middle age, it may never be. Lambing (1972) found, for example, that lack of skills and literacy seriously limited the leisure activities available to older lower-class blacks in Florida, a situation that Lambing's respondents recognized and wished to correct. The individual should probably begin to develop activity competence as soon a possible. An active and creative use of free time in one's youth is the surest way to guarantee a similar pattern in old age, because older people tend to retain patterns and preferences developed in the past.

Sex, Social Class, and Ethnic Differences

Although many choices of activities are purely based on individual preferences, many others are constrained by what is considered "normal" for a person of a given sex, social class, or ethnic group.

Sex roles have received increased attention over the past decade. Many activity differences between men and women are not the result of "natural" differences in preferences but instead are the result of differences in the cultural conditioning that boys and girls receive. Thus, right now middle-aged men are much more likely than women to be involved in vigorous sports, crafts such as woodworking or metal work, or repair work involving machinery. Women, on the other hand, are much more likely than men to be involved in needlework, cooking, and child care.

Substantial social class differences also exist in preferences for activities. For example, while upper-middle-class people may watch television about as much as others do, they tend to watch different programs. A large portion of the audience of the Public Broadcasting System (PBS) is made up of the upper middle class, while the audience for all-sports networks tends to be mainly working class. Havighurst (1973) found that voluntary associations, sports, reading, and gardening were much more common among the upper middle class, the middle-middle class was more inclined toward crafts and television, and members of the working class were more likely to spend their time visiting with neighbors and kin. Social class also has obvious economic effects on the range of possible activities. Traveling, entertaining, going to concerts or plays, playing golf or tennis, and dining out require much more money than watching television, talking with neighbors, or puttering around in the yard. Thus, some social class differences in activities are the result of differences in what people are taught to prefer, and part is due to differences in financial capacity.

We do not know very much about ethnic differences in activity patterns, but certainly they exist. For example, blacks participate in church activities more than whites do. People of Italian or Mexican descent are more likely to spend time with their families compared to people of English or Scandinavian descent.

Thus, meanings, skills, and values all influence the activity patterns that adults develop. And age changes in activities occur in the context of these various influences. We now turn to some of the changes that commonly occur with age and how they influence activities.

Aging and Changes in Activities

The life course exerts significant pressure to make choices about jobs and family. Most remaining choices of activities result from *preferences* that have been learned by trying the alternatives in vogue at the time of one's early adulthood. Once adult activity patterns are established, they tend to persist. Yet aging or changes associated with it cause activity patterns to change—if not in the type of activity, at least in the amount of it. The common factors that could potentially affect activities include the completion of child rearing, retirement, physical aging, a move to congregate housing, and institutionalization.

Completion of Child Rearing

Having launched the children does not seem to require a large emotional adjustment for most people. However, it probably does mean some adjustments in the use of time. In the middle class, lost interaction with children tends to be replaced by increased interaction with one's spouse. Reduced demand for service work in the household is offset by employment for many women. Social circles that brought parents together as a by-product of having to do things for their children, such as parent-teacher organizations and car pools, are likely to disappear. Leisure activities probably do not change very much after the empty nest. This area is much in need of research.

Retirement

Retirement is usually total, and most retired people go from full-time employment to no employment quite abruptly. But for most people, this anticipated change produces little feeling of discontinuity. Cottrell and Atchley (1969) found that 80 percent of their retired respondents saw their friends either as often or more often than they did before retirement. Three-fourths of the respondents reported the same or more involvement in organizations following retirement. Their findings generally showed that social participation was not adversely affected by retirement.

Simpson et al. (1966a) found that many activity patterns that were supported by the job persist into retirement. Factors such as having a higher-status job and an orderly work career were as important in predicting a high level of activity with friends, organizations, and interests after retirement as they were before retirement. These researchers found that if social participation was not developed prior to retirement, it was not likely to be. They also concluded that having had irregular work histories was responsible for the low levels of social participation among retired semiskilled workers and that retirement was not a factor.

When people retire, they increase the amount of time they spend doing both obligatory and leisure activities. Many find that properly taking care of financial and social affairs occupies much more time than they were able or willing to devote to such activities prior to retirement (Atchley, 1976). As one woman put it, "Now that I'm retired, I feel guilty if I put off answering letters. I sometimes spend a whole morning on one letter!"

About 25 percent of those who retire experience an overall decrease in activity. But this decrease is sometimes welcome. For some, it is a relief not to have to keep up the pace of the preretirement period. This is particularly true for people who retire for health reasons.

Apart from the impact of retirement on activity *level*, there is the question of retirement's effect on the *meaning* of activity. According to one school, leisure activities cannot be done full-time by adults in Western societies without provoking an identity crisis. The thesis is that the job identity mediates all other activities and that without it other activities cannot provide the person with an identity (Miller, 1965). This view was very prevalent in the 1950s, and it received modest support from research being done at that time. However, more recent research shows that job identity carries over into retirement (Cottrell and Atchley, 1969) and that an increase in leisure activities in retirement is viewed by society as an earned privilege and opportunity (Atchley, 1971a; Thompson, 1973). The fact that only a small proportion of people take up entirely new activities following retirement does not appear to be the result of an identity crisis.

Retirement also tends to reduce financial resources, which in turn tends to reduce activity level. Simpson et al. (1966a) stress the role of financial security in providing support for participation in various activities. Atchley (1976) points out that poverty creates a barrier to getting involved in new activities in the general community, especially for those who formerly had middle-class incomes.

Physical Aging

Physical change has two types of influences on activities. The first is a series of changes that move individuals from more active pursuits toward more sedentary ones. The second is the constraining effects of serious illness and disability. Gradually, as it ages, the human body becomes less capable of high rates of physical output and recovery from strenuous activity takes longer. This decline probably accounts for some movement away from strenuous activities in middle age. However, people who have remained in peak physical condition can probably continue these activities into later maturity. Perhaps more important influences on strenuous activity come from life course factors and age norms. Middle-aged people who are highly involved in job, family, and community responsibilities may find it difficult to allot time to stay at a level of physical conditioning that allows strenuous activities without discomfort. In addition, there is a general expectation (age norm) that after about age 35 people should be exempt from pressures to involve themselves in strenuous activities. It will be interesting to see what effect the current exercise craze will have on attitudes about strenuous activities in middle age and later maturity.

The relatively sedentary activity patterns of most middle-aged Americans are well within the physical capabilities of later maturity. Only when symptoms of disabling illness or old age appear must there be a change in activity patterns. How disability and aging change activities is a highly individualized matter. It depends on the mix of activities prior to physical change, the specific physical changes that occur, and the individual's capacity to adapt to them. Generally, the narrower the range of activities in middle age, the more vulnerable the individual is to physical change.

A Move to Congregate Housing

Moves to congregate housing generally increase opportunities for activity and activity levels usually increase for movers. This increase is not simply a short-term flurry of activity in response to a new environment, but instead is a genuine change that is maintained over time. In a well-done longitudinal study of this subject, Carp (1978–1979) found that compared to older people who did not choose to move to an activity-rich congregate housing environment, people who did move reported increased activity levels. Increases in activity took place both in "regular responsibility" activities such as lobby receptionist, senior center responsibilities, or church work, and in pastimes such as club meetings, table games, and visiting. Over the eight-year period of the study, movers maintained their increased activity levels even though they averaged 72 years of age when the study began. On the other hand, comparison respondents in the community showed a decline in activity over this same period. People who move to congregate housing with extensive activity programs are self-selected, and certainly it would be incorrect to assume that high levels of activity are good for everyone. Perhaps more important is the degree of fit between the person's desire for activity and the opportunities present in that person's living environment. Carp's findings show that, for people who want a high activity level, congregate housing that offers plentiful opportunities for activity can successfully meet this need.

Institutionalization

Institutionalization by its very nature could be expected to reduce activity. It cuts people off from their daily contacts in the community. And it is usually the result of disability that curtails activity. Yet little research has been done on before and after changes in activity resulting from institutionalization. We don't know for a comparable disability if the activity reductions due to disability occur more frequently in institutions than in the community. We don't know how institutionalization influences the person's desire for activity or how discontinuity between wants and possibilities for activity in the institution influences adjustment to the institution. Whether the disability that led to institutionalization is mental or physical undoubtedly influences activity. All these topics deserve further research.

Spheres of Activity

Thus, all the common life changes that accompany aging can potentially influence activity patterns. In addition, age discrimination and societal disengagement do not operate with the same force in all areas of life. Accordingly, we now examine how aging influences activity within various domains: on the job, in the community, and at home.

On the Job

Aging affects employment from several standpoints. Aging can cause job-related disabilities, it can cause people to be denied the opportunity to work even when they are able-bodied, and it can increase the motivation to leave the workforce in favor of the freedom of retirement. Before we examine each of these factors in turn, we need first to look at overall patterns of employment and how they change with age.

The *labor force* consists of people who are employed plus those who are unemployed but are looking for work. *Labor force participation rates* are the proportion of the population of an age category that is in the labor force. By age 25, 93 percent of men were in the labor force in 1970. The proportion in the labor force remained at 90 to 95 percent through age 50, when it began to decline (see Table 9-1).

TABLE 9-1. Labor Force Participation
Rates by Age and Sex

Age	Male	Female
45	93.3	50.3
46	95.0	50.8
47	93.2	55.4
48	91.6	56.1
49	93.4	50.3
50	91.7	53.6
51	93.5	52.0
52	90.5	52.0
53	90.2	53.5
54	88.8	48.5
55	89.8	49.0
56	88.8	49.7
57	85.7	49.5
58	82.7	43.5
59	82.1	46.6
60	81.1	41.7
61	79.6	36.0
62	71.8	33.2
63	69.6	33.1
64	64.0	28.6
65	44.4	21.4
66	41.5	18.6
67	35.7	14.7
68	33.0	14.8
69	33.5	13.7
70	25.7	11.5

Source: 15% Public Use Sample of Basic Records, 1970 United States Census.

For women, labor force participation peaks at age 20 to 24, then declines as women drop out of the labor force for child rearing. The proportion
who drop out for child rearing has been greatly exaggerated. Most women
who enter the labor force stay in the labor force continuously throughout
adulthood, although they are more likely than men to work part time (Jaffe
and Ridley, 1976; Mallan, 1974). From age 35 to age 50, there is only slight
fluctuation in women's labor force participation rates.

For both men and women, labor force participation declines beginning
in the early 50s. As Table 9-1 shows, labor force participation of men declined steadily but gradually after age 50. Nevertheless the labor force participation of 61-year-old men was 13.9 percent lower than the level for
51-year-old men. Note also the significant drop at age 62, when men become
eligible for reduced Social Security benefits, and the sharp drop at age 65,

when men become eligible for full Social Security benefits. There is also another significant drop at age 70.

For women, the pattern is not so clear-cut. There is a 16 percent drop from age 51 to age 61, but there is no significant drop at 62, nor is there a sharp drop at 65. This more gradual pattern may result from a tendency of women to tie their retirements to their husbands' ages rather than to their own ages.

These various patterns of involvement in the labor force are the result of different sets of social forces. Withdrawal from the labor force before age 62 is mainly due to three factors: labor market problems of older workers, increasing rates of disability, and opportunities for early retirement. Withdrawals after age 62 are nearly all related to retirement, though employment problems and disability exert pressures to retire.

Employment Problems of Older Workers To the U.S. Department of Labor, a "mature worker" is any employee age 45 or over. Mature workers are less likely to become unemployed, but if they do, they encounter difficulty getting another job. Thus, unemployment *rates* may be lower for mature workers, but on the other hand unemployment has more serious *consequences* for them. For example, in 1974, men 65 or over were only 1.2 percent of the total unemployed, but they were 3.5 percent of those unemployed 27 weeks or more. Mature workers are much more likely to be unemployed long enough to exhaust their unemployment benefits (Sheppard, 1976).

Several factors are responsible for employment problems among middle-aged and older workers. Changes in the labor market can result from plant closings, company reorganizations, or mass layoffs. Sheppard (1976) reports that over half of the companies involved in a mass layoff of over 190,000 workers from 1963 to 1965 went out of business or moved their business elsewhere. Seniority is often little protection if one's job is abolished. And if experience, technical competence, and education are held constant, older workers tend to be laid off first (Sheppard, 1976; Parnes and King, 1977). Those who are laid off or who lose their jobs tend to work in trade or manufacturing jobs, to work for small business, to have no pension coverage, and to work for nonunionized firms (Parnes and King, 1977).

Displaced homemakers can also experience employment problems in middle age. These women chose homemaking as a full-time job and, either through widowhood or divorce, find themselves in need of jobs. Women who choose to be full-time homemakers generally assume that their economic support, health insurance, and retirement benefits will come as a result of their marriages to employed men. However, women who become widowed or divorced in middle age can be thrust suddenly into the job market. They often lack marketable job skills. Because homemaking is not looked on as employment, they lack work histories and are ineligible for Social Security or SSI, but they are old enough to encounter age discrimination in the job market (Sommers and Shields, 1979). That displaced homemakers have severe employment problems was recognized by the U.S. Congress in 1978 when displaced homemakers were designated as a hard-to-employ category under the Comprehensive Employment Training Act (CETA).

Once unemployed, mature workers face stiff age discrimination. The Age Discrimination in Employment Act of 1967 (ADEA) protects workers 45 or over from denial of employment strictly because of age. In 1978, over $14.5 million was found due to over 4,000 workers as a result of violations of the ADEA. There is reason to believe that these cases represent merely the tip of the iceberg regarding age discrimination. To begin with, compliance officers are able to check only a small percentage of the 1 million establishments covered by ADEA. In addition, ADEA does not apply to small businesses with fewer than 20 employees, and these employers are most likely to lay off mature workers.

Parnes and King (1977) found that displaced middle-aged workers eventually found other employment, but at lower-status jobs with lower earnings. Displaced workers, compared to others, moved down the occupational ladder, particularly out of professional and managerial positions. As a result, from 1966 to 1971, 20 percent of displaced workers suffered a decline in earnings, while those who remained employed averaged a 25 percent increase in earnings. The larger the period of unemployment, the greater the drop in occupational level and earnings.

Age discrimination in employment is based on the unfounded prejudice that mature workers are usually less capable than younger ones. However, employment studies show that mature workers have superior attendance records, that they are less likely to change jobs, and that their output is equal to that of younger workers. Although it is true that some older workers are slow to learn, the range of individual differences is quite large, and many older people are still quite capable of learning new skills. Age discrimination in employment thus deprives the economy of human resources and creates hardships for mature workers. The small number of mature workers in job retraining programs probably reflects cynicism about finding jobs rather than unwillingness to be retrained. In addition, the record of various state employment services in placing mature workers is dismal.

The *Foster Grandparent program* employs low-income older people to help provide personal, individual care to children who live in institutions. In a series of studies, the Foster Grandparent program has been shown to be a great benefit to both the older people involved and the children they served. After exposure to the program, children have been observed to be more outgoing and to have improved relationships with both their peers and institutional authorities. Children have shown increased self-confidence, decreased insecurity and fear, and improved language skills.

Older people also receive a great deal from the program. To begin with, older people are able to augment their incomes, and for many older people this addition is quite a help. Many older people who are involved have reported feelings of increased vigor and youthfulness, of an increased sense of personal worth, of a renewed sense of purpose and direction to life, and of pleasure in renewed personal growth and development.

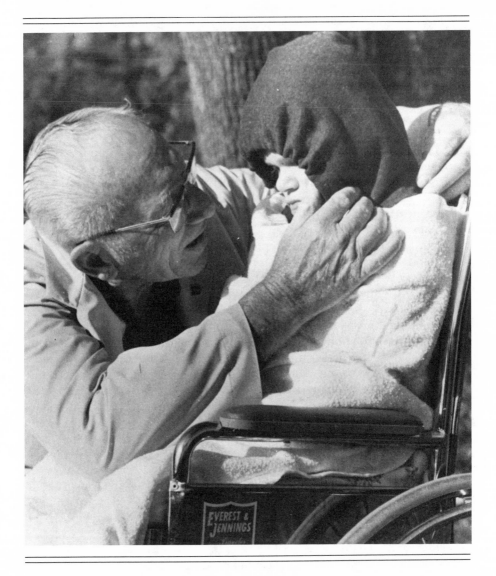

    Administrators have been pleased with the way older people seem to
adapt to the various tasks—many of them involving new skills that the older
people had to learn. Special assignments in day care, physical therapy,
speech therapy, and as teacher's aides have been made possible by the
willingness and ability some of the older people have shown. Several inferences can be drawn from the experience of the Foster Grandparent program.
For one thing, low-income older people will work for modest but reasonable
pay if the job proves satisfying to them, and thus they offer a vast pool of
relatively inexpensive labor that can be used to do needed work within the
community. The role that older people might play in day care alone is
enough to stagger one's imagination. It has also shown that older people are

interested in continued participation in community affairs, particularly in useful and dignified participation.

Disability As age increases, so do rates of disability. For example, in 1974 only 1.4 percent of men under 45 were physically unable to work compared to 9.4 percent of those 45 to 64 (Wilder, 1977:14). Another 10.5 percent of those 45 to 64 were physically limited in the amount or kind of jobs they could do.

Some of this disability is due to premature symptoms of aging, which occur most often in physically demanding jobs and in jobs with poor working conditions. However, a large proportion is the result of an accumulation of job-related injuries. For example, in 1977 over 11 million people were injured on the job seriously enough to require medical attention or more than one day of restricted activity (Howie and Drury, 1978). Although older workers are less likely to be injured, they are exposed to greater risk that injuries will eventually produce disability. More than half of those who apply for disability under Social Security are over age 50.

Early Retirement Retirement is discussed in considerable detail in Chapter 11. For now, I will consider only some of the factors related to early retirement. The common notion is that most people who retire early do so because they want to and can afford to. And this notion is undoubtedly true in many cases. However, other factors exert pressure for early retirement. Employment problems and poor health are the two main pressures for "involuntary" early retirement. As was pointed out earlier, unemployment is tough for mature workers, and no doubt some retire early rather than brave continued unemployment and age discrimination. There are also many mature workers whose health is poor, but not poor enough to qualify them for disability benefits. Early retirement with a reduced pension is their only out.

How withdrawal from the labor force in middle age is distributed among various causes—unemployment, disability, early forced retirement, and early voluntary retirement—is unknown. This would be an excellent topic for research.

In the Community

Most of the things we do take place in a community, but here we are concerned mainly with involvement in the activities of community organizations. Community organizations are groups that develop around a collective desire to achieve some purpose or pursue some interest. Most communities have churches, political parties, labor unions, veterans' groups, fraternal organizations, community service groups such as Kiwanis or Rotary, professional associations, and parent-teacher organizations. Most communities also have hobby and garden groups, groups related to sports, and other special-purpose groups.

In this section we look first at how aging affects participation in com-

TABLE 9-2. Percent Belonging to Various Types of
Associations by Age and Sex

Type of Association	Age				
	35–44	45–54	55–64	65–74	75+
Men					
Church-related	42	42	41	38	53
Sports-related	30	26	16	9	8
Fraternal	20	22	19	23	30
Labor unions	28	33	36	20	13
Veterans'	13	24	22	9	19
Professional	25	18	11	7	5
Service	14	16	10	9	12
Women					
Church-affiliated	49	48	56	57	52
School service	40	22	8	5	0
Sports-related	17	14	9	6	3
Professional	11	8	9	11	5
Hobby or garden	11	8	14	10	11
Discussion or study	8	11	9	12	10

Source: Adapted from Cutler (1976:464).

munity organizations in general, and then we look at participation in churches, political groups, and in volunteer work.

Participation in General Cutler (1975) reported that if the effects of socioeconomic status differences in participation were controlled, then age produced little or no change in organizational participation from middle age into later life. He found that young adults tended to have low levels of participation, middle-aged people had higher levels, and the participation levels for older adults were at the middle-age level or higher.

Cutler (1976) also examined age and sex patterns in membership in various types of organizations (see Table 9-2). For both men and women, affiliation with church-related groups was by far the most common, with women being slightly more involved than men. This pattern persisted across the entire age range. For men, involvement with sports-related, labor, and professional organizations peaked in middle age and was lower for older age categories. Involvement with fraternal, veterans', and service groups was generally consistent across the age categories. For women, school service groups were a major choice. But by age 55, when presumably their children were less likely to be in school, women's involvement in school service groups dropped sharply. Involvement in sports-related groups diminished across the age categories, while involvement with professional, hobby or garden, and discussion or study groups remained relatively stable. Note that although women were less involved than men in professional groups in middle age, their involvement paralleled that of men after age 55. Except for church-related and school service groups, participation in voluntary associations was less common among women than among men.

Factors Affecting Participation in Later Life Changes such as residential mobility, retirement, or widowhood have no predictable, consistent impact on participation in community organizations. For example, retirement has been found to increase, decrease, or produce no change in participation, depending on the situation (Cottrell and Atchley, 1969). In a longitudinal study, Cutler (1977) found that people with either increased or stable participation far outnumbered those whose participation declined. However, poor health or dwindling financial resources—factors that are particularly prevalent among the working class—have a predictable dampening effect on participation. The impact of declining health is direct and obvious. Eroded financial resources have a subtler impact. Because community groups are almost always nonprofit, they must be subsidized, usually by members' contributions. Older people on tight budgets can be forced out of participation by the embarrassment of being unable to contribute.

For those who do continue to participate, community organizations take up a great deal of time. Yet many experience a decline with age in the satisfaction they report from participation as they see groups "letting in a different sort of people" or "having changed so much." Others are self-conscious of their age and would rather "leave it to the youngsters." Still others have done every job in the organization two or three times and see little opportunity for continued growth in further participation. Thus, voluntary associations often subtly "squeeze out" older members.

Transportation problems can limit participation, particularly in small towns and rural areas that lack public transportation. Cutler (1974) found that older people who did not drive or who did not have a car had much lower levels of participation than did those who had access to a car. He also found that this effect increased with distance between residence and meeting sites, particularly with respect to frequency of attendance at meetings.

Thus, we see that aging in and of itself has no predictable effect on overall participation in community organizations. Changes that do occur are most likely to be declines in participation associated with poor health, inadequate income, and transportation problems. We will now look at some specific types of organizations, beginning with churches.

Churches Churches are the most common community organization membership for older people. Membership in churches also tends to be higher at the older ages, especially after 75. Leadership positions in churches also tend to be concentrated among older people, and participation in religious organizations declines among older people at a much slower rate than does participation in other types of organizations.

About half of the general population attends church regularly (twice a month or more). Catholics are much more likely to attend regularly than Protestants or Jews, although this tendency is diminishing. A higher proportion of women than men attend frequently. Also, church attendance is positively related to income, education, and length of residence in the community. Age is thus only one of many factors that influence church attendance. If we look at age patterns in church attendance at a given point in time, there is a steady increase from the late teens until attendance peaks in the late 50s to early 60s at about 60 percent. After that, the curve shows a consistent but very slight decline, almost certainly the result of the increasing prevalence of ill health, disability, and transportation difficulties. Among older people, there is also an increase in percentage never attending.

What about older people's place in the church? Most ministers, priests, or rabbis assume that worship services are as available to older people as they are to others. It is usually through contacts with shut-ins, hospitalized older people, and older people in nursing homes that local congregation pastors first confront the problem of older members of the congregation. Only gradually do they come to recognize that many of their ambulatory older members also have problems. Longino and Kitson (1976) found that although there was some ageism among American Baptist clergy in the form of preference for working with youth, the majority did not have an aversion to ministering to the elderly.

Older people can come to feel neglected by churches in a number of ways. Moberg (1972) notes that many churches tend to emphasize programs for adolescents and young families, lack outreach programs for older people, and tend to push older people out of positions of responsibility within the church. These tendencies are important mechanisms that encourage older adults to disengage from organized religion. In research on church attendance, for example, it would be useful to relate feelings of neglect by organized religion to church attendance by age. What many consider to be personal disengagement might turn out to be socially induced.

Some churches set up senior centers or clubs for older people; others allow their facilities to be used by such groups. The churches are also becoming interested in housing programs, particularly retirement homes for middle-income older people. They are beginning to see housing programs as a legitimate service, and not merely as an act of charity. Because the proportion of older people in the average congregation is about the same as the proportion in the total population, it is not too surprising that the churches have begun to feel some pressure from their older members concerning housing problems.

At this point, however, church programs for older people are few and far between. Although 80 percent of the Presbyterian churches, for example, report special social groups for older people (including age-segregated Sunday school classes), only two-thirds report any type of educational program specifically for older people, and very few have employment, homemaker, or health services.

Thus while it appears that most churches are quite willing to *passively accept* the participation of older people in church affairs, few are willing or

able to *actively solicit* the participation of ill, handicapped, or isolated older people.

    Political Participation There is a significant increase with age in political activities such as working for the party in a local vote, signing petitions, and belonging to political groups. Older people represent the same percentage in party organizations that they do in the general population. In addition, older party members have more clout at nominating conventions compared to their younger counterparts (Kapnick et al., 1968), which gives them a great deal of influence over the selection of party-supported candidates for political office.

    One reason why older members of political parties are influential is the weight that tenure carries in politics compared to other types of groups. In politics, the older person can play the role of sage. In fact, the word *politic* means "wise" or "shrewd." Political prowess is still something one learns mainly from experience rather than from a book or in a professional school.

    Glenn and Grimes (1968) suggested that as people grow older, politics becomes more a source of personal fulfillment and less a means to a concrete end. This notion is supported by studies showing that as they grow older people maintain and perhaps even increase their involvement in politics, while simultaneously feeling that their individual political action neither does nor can have an impact on the political process (Schmidhauser, 1968). In short, older people enjoy political participation, but at the same time are cynical about its concrete results.

Volunteer Work Older people participate in a variety of types of volunteer work in communities. The Older Americans Act has increased opportunities for this by providing administrative support and transportation services.

The *Retired Senior Volunteer Program* (RSVP) offers people over age 60 the opportunity of doing volunteer service to meet community needs. RSVP agencies place volunteers in schools, hospitals, libraries, courts, day care centers, nursing homes, and a host of other organizations. RSVP programs provide transportation to and from the place of service.

The *Service Corps of Retired Executives* (SCORE) offers retired businessmen and businesswomen an opportunity to help owners of small businesses and managers of community organizations who are having management problems. Since 1965, over 175,000 businesses have received help from SCORE. Volunteers receive no pay but are reimbursed for out-of-pocket expenses.

The *Senior Companion Program*, modeled after Foster Grandparents, offers a small stipend to older people who help adults with special needs, such as the handicapped and the disabled.

A program called *Green Thumb*, sponsored by the National Farmers Union in 24 states, provides part-time employment in conservation, beautification, and community improvement in rural areas or in existing community service agencies.

The U.S. Department of Labor has three programs that offer part-time employment to older people who serve as aides in a variety of community agencies including child care centers, vocational training programs, building security, clerical service, and homemaker services. The *Senior Aides* program is administered by the National Council of Senior Citizens; *Senior Community Service Aides* is sponsored by the National Council on the Aging, and *Senior Community Aides* is sponsored by the National Retired Teachers Association/ American Association of Retired Persons.

The success of these programs illustrates that older people can be quite effective in both volunteer and paid positions. For the time being, however, we can expect volunteer opportunities to outnumber opportunities for part-time employment. A major obstacle to the effective use of older volunteers has been an unwillingness to assign them to responsible, meaningful positions on an ongoing basis. The result is a vicious circle. Because volunteers are assigned to menial tasks, they get bored or frustrated and quit. Because they quit, administrators are reluctant to put volunteers in anything other than nonessential jobs.

Studies have shown that older volunteers can be counted on to perform well on an ongoing basis (Babic, 1972; Sainer and Zander, 1971), particularly if the agency placing volunteers adheres to the following guidelines. First, agencies must be flexible in matching the volunteer's background to assigned tasks. If the agency takes a broad perspective, useful work can be found for almost anyone. Second, volunteers must be trained. All too often agency personnel place unprepared volunteers in an unfamiliar setting. Then the volunteer's difficulty confirms the myth that you cannot expect good work from volunteers. Third, a variety of placement options

TABLE 9-3. Types of At-Home Activity

Type	Examples
1. Work	Housework, home maintenance, household chores
2. Relaxation	Resting, sleeping, meditating
3. Diversion	Television watching, listening to music, reading
4. Personal development	Studying, learning, practicing, inquiring, personal care, worshiping
5. Creativity and problem solving	Crafts, cooking, planning, handiwork, arts
6. Sensory gratification	Sexual activity, eating, drinking, smoking
7. Socializing	Discussing, arguing, entertaining, gossiping
8. Appreciation of nature	Walking, gardening, bird watching

Source: Adapted and modified from Gordon et al. (1976).

should be offered to the volunteer. Some volunteers prefer to do familiar things; others want to do anything but familiar things. Fourth, training of volunteers should not make them feel that they are being tested. This point is particularly sensitive among working-class volunteers. Fifth, volunteers should get personal attention from the placement agency. There should be people (perhaps volunteers) who follow up on absences and who are willing to listen to the compliments, complaints, or experiences of the volunteers. Public recognition from the community is an important reward for voluntary service. Finally, transportation to and from the placement should be provided (Sainer and Zander, 1971).

At Home

The tendency to view activities in terms of roles has led to an artificial separation of the study of activities. Work, home, community, and other environments are viewed separately and studied by different researchers with different concepts and research agendas. Even those who look at activities at home tend to study specific types of activities rather than the entire array of at-home activities.

Table 9-3 shows a classification of at-home activities with examples. The examples are not iron-clad in the sense that particular activities could fit into different categories, depending on their meaning to the individual. For example, if a person gardens mainly to supplement the family food budget and does not enjoy it very much, then gardening would be mainly a household chore rather than an appreciation of or contact with nature. Cooking can be either a chore or a creative act. The examples have been placed in the categories that fit the meaning of the activity to most middle-aged or older adults most of the time.

The amount of activity centered around the home depends on the amount of time spent there. Even before retirement, the amount of time spent at home tends to increase with age past age 50. Part of this increase is due to a loss of roles in environments outside the household and part is due to a growing preference for in-home activities. Physical limits restrict activities to the home for only a small proportion of adults, including those over 75.

The distribution of in-home activities was reported by one sample of older people as follows: sleep, 37.5 percent; work (meals, housework, personal care, shopping, caring for others), 27.9 percent; diversion (television watching, reading), 14.5 percent; socializing, 8.8 percent; crafts and gardening, 5 percent; other, 6.3 percent (Riley and Foner, 1968:513). Thus, the majority of what people do at home is to sleep and to perform various tasks. Leisure or "free-time" activities account for only about a third of the time spent at home.

What Activities Are Desirable for Older People?

Middle-class professionals often judge the activities of older adults in terms of their appropriateness for middle-aged, middle-class people. Thus, the literature often implies that work is better than other kinds of activity and that group-centered activities are "better" for people than solitary activities are. From the viewpoints of older people, this evaluation may not be justified. Because activity patterns established in early adulthood tend to persist and because what is fashionable in the way of activities varies from time to time and between social groups, it seems safe to assume that no single standard can be used to determine the "adequacy" of activity patterns among mature adults.

The tendency to assume that only leisure activities or employment can provide meaning to life has caused many researchers to overlook the potential importance of mundane activities such as personal care, housekeeping, cooking, shopping, tinkering, and puttering (Lawton, 1978). In later life, these activities reflect one's continued ability to be independent in the face of age whereas earlier the ability to do them is taken for granted.

Likewise, there is a common conception that inactivity is detrimental. In massive doses, this idea is undoubtedly true, but the general statement overlooks the benefits that contemplation can have. It is important to find out what is happening inside the person during physically inactive but wakeful time rather than simply to assume that the result is negative.

Summary

Activities provide a very basic structure to our lives and, for many people, satisfaction with life depends on having what to them is a satisfying and meaningful round of activities.

Activities can be categorized in a vast number of ways. Some important dimensions are the intensity of the activity, the frequency with which it recurs in a person's life, the number of different environments in which the activity occurs, the skills and the knowledge required to do the activity, the extent to which the activity is obligatory, the capacity of the activity to provide a sense of leisure, the meaning(s) of the activity for a particular individual and for people in general, whether the activity can be solitary or requires others, and how expensive the activity is.

The knowledge and skills necessary for a varied set of activities are generally developed in early or middle adulthood and maintained into later life. If people want to develop new activities in later life, they can sometimes get assistance from organizations such as senior centers, continuing education institutions, or voluntary organizations. But most older people find that they are on their own if they want to take up new activities.

It is important not to impose notions of which activities "ought to be" satisfying to older people. For example, mundane activities around the house are meaningful to many older people—much more so than many people who work with the elderly would expect.

Activities generally show a great deal of stability in later life, even with the substantial environmental changes that can occur as a result of child launching or retirement. People tend to cope with lost activities by increasing their involvement in those activities that remain. Most people have a wide variety of activities that can absorb even important losses. However, some people have a very limited set of alternatives or place a very high value on the lost activity and are distressed by changes in activities.

As a prevalent activity, employment begins to fade in importance in the early 50s, but much of the decline prior to age 65 is related to employment problems such as ill health or unemployment rather than personal choice. At age 65 and later, the overwhelming majority of retirements are voluntary.

Participation in community organizations tends to be high in middle and later life. Transportation problems, poor health, and lack of money are the major factors that hamper participation for older people. Religious groups are the most common voluntary associations with which middle-aged or older people are involved. Churches generally welcome the participation of older people but do little to actively promote it. Apart from churches, no other type of voluntary organization involves participation by as much as a third of the middle-aged or older population. Older people who have been involved in local politics for many years usually find that their skills and experience give them a good deal of political influence. Volunteer work by older people has expanded dramatically in the past decade. However, at this point we do not know how prevalent this activity is among older people.

Activity patterns are highly individualized and show a high degree of stability across the life course. Nevertheless, options are sometimes limited in later life by physical, financial, or transportation factors. Personality, family, and social class values can narrow the range of options even further. It is probably fortunate that as they age people tend to gravitate from obligatory activities toward discretionary activities, from activities outside the home toward at-home activities, and from social activities toward solitary activities. This general movement can create flexibility and freedom for the individual provided it is what he or she wants, and in most cases it is.

Chapter 10

Relating to Others and to the Environment

People do not cope with aging in isolation. They do it in the company of others who provide social and emotional support and in surroundings that provide a sense of connectedness and belonging. In this chapter we look at how aging influences, and is influenced by, relationships such as spouse or mate, parent, child, sibling, relative, friend, and neighbor. We also look at the importance of attachments in the lives of middle-aged and older people. But first we need to understand what relationships and attachments are.

Relationships are reciprocal connections between people. There are three basic types of bonds: interdependence, intimacy or affection, and belonging. Interdependence brings people together in order to satisfy their needs better than they could as individuals acting alone. For example, the division of labor reduces the number of things each person must do or know how to do. Interdependence can also increase available resources. We can pool our knowledge, financial resources, insights, or encouragement.

Bonds of intimacy or affection allow for the exchange of love, trust, and confidences. Some intimate relationships also allow us to meet our needs for sexual expression. Our confidants' opinions of us and our past histories are important sources of self-respect.

Relationships can also be based on a need for belonging—the sense of being more than an isolated individual. Such relationships can be the source of companionship, socializing, identity, and safety or security.

These three types of bonds—interdependence, intimacy, and belonging—can exist in combination or in isolation. Given the many possible combinations among these dimensions, it should be clear that relationships

This chapter draws heavily on Troll et al. (1979), Atchley and Miller (1980), and Atchley (1980b) for documentation and sources.

can vary a great deal in quality and purpose. In addition, the quality and purpose of relationships are influenced by factors such as sex, social class, and ethnicity to ensure that relationships *do* vary a great deal, even within a given social role such as that of spouse.

Relationships emerge when people interact with one another, usually in the process of playing their various social roles. Interdependence is built into many role relationships, but whether intimacy and/or belonging develop depends more on the nature of the interaction, which is in turn influenced by such factors as equality, self-disclosure, similarity, acceptance, agreement, trust, and cooperation.

Relationships can also be destroyed or diminished. All kinds of relationships can be diminished by permanent geographic separation—a move apart with no likelihood of return. Interdependence bonds can be weakened if one or both of the participants become less effective. Belonging bonds can be weakened by growing feelings of superiority or inferiority or difference in one or both of the participants. And intimacy bonds can be weakened by selfishness, breaks in trust, or withdrawal by one or both participants.

Attachments are one-way bonds that reflect only the perceiver's view of his or her affectional ties with people, environments, or objects. There is no necessary reciprocity. I may be quite attached to my favorite pipe, for example, and obviously the pipe does not reciprocate. Plants and animals may show some appearance of reciprocity, but essentially the attention and affection is one-way. One big advantage to attachments to objects, plants, or animals is that we can give fully of ourselves and without concern about getting a return. It is more difficult to be merely attached to people—we also want relationships with them.

In this chapter we look at aging in the context of relationships such as spouse or mate, parent, child, sibling, relative, friend, and neighbor. We also look at aging's influence on the importance of attachments.

With a Spouse or Partner

In the United States, more than 70 percent of older men and 36 percent of older women—more than half of the older population—are married and live with their spouses in independent households. At younger ages, the proportion married is even higher. For example, half of women age 65 to 69 are married. In addition to married couples, both heterosexual and homosexual couples live together as mates without being married. As male death rates go down in the future, couples will be even more common in middle and later life than they are now.

Most middle-aged and older couples have been together since early adulthood, but marriage in later life is becoming more common. For example, in 1976 there were nearly 400,000 brides and grooms age 45 or over. Of these, 48,000 were age 65 or over. Only 5 percent were first-time mar-

riages. Remarriage in middle age or later is much more available to men than to women for two reasons: women vastly outnumber men of their own or older ages, and men tend to marry women younger than themselves. Grooms 65 or over outnumber brides in that age category by 2 to 1, and the median age of the grooms of women 65 or over is 67.4, whereas the median age of brides of men 65 or over is 57.6. Even if people married only others their age, there would be no potential mates available for 50 percent of the unmarried women.

Couples are thus very prevalent even among older people. The couple relationship tends to be a focal point in people's lives, especially when the departure of children and retirement have increased the amount of contact between spouses and perhaps reduced the number of alternative relationships. As the average length of life increases, so does the average number of years a couple can expect to live together after the children leave home.

Whether the increased focus on the couple is a bane or a blessing depends of course on the quality of the relationship. A happy and satisfied relationship is a blessing. The couple relationship is a source of great comfort and support as well as the focal point of everyday life, and satisfied couples usually grow closer as the years go by. Such couples often show a high degree of interdependence, particularly in terms of caring for one another at times of illness. The husbands in strong couple relationships are particularly likely to see their wives as indispensable pillars of strength. They tend to share many activities, and happy couples tend to be characterized by greater equality between the partners than is true for unhappy couples. This equality results from a gradual loss of sex role boundaries and a decreasing sexual definition of household division of labor. Happy couples tend to remain sexually active into later life (Clark and Anderson, 1967:237–41).

Although most couples are generally happy and satisfied, a small proportion are not. Some people feel that their spouses are the cause of all their troubles, and they often wish that they could somehow terminate their marriages. People remain in unhappy marriages for a variety of reasons. For some it is a matter of religious orthodoxy. Some stay rather than confront negative community opinions about divorce. Others remain because they do not see any other way to economically sustain their life-styles. Others stay "for the sake of the kids." Some remain because they need poor relationships to continue in their role as martyrs. The list could go on and on. Sometimes the strains are too much, and people divorce in middle age or later life. In 1976, 168,000 divorces were granted to people age 45 and over in the 29 states that register divorces. Of these, 12,000 were granted to people 65 or over.

What happens to marital satisfaction over the life span? From various studies, a consistent picture emerges of high marital satisfaction in early adulthood, a gradual decline in satisfaction through middle age, and a steady increase in marital satisfaction in the period after child rearing. This curvilinear pattern has not been found in all studies, but it has been found often enough that it is probably correct. What appears to happen is that the stresses of marriage become progressively greater from young adulthood and peak in middle age, when often there are teenagers at home, high job demands, and high community demands on one's time and energy. People may also have to care for aging parents during this stage. Logically, the rise in satisfaction after middle age could be due to the breakup of unhappy marriages in middle age, but the data on age at the time of divorce do not support this notion. Of women who divorce, 65 percent do so before age 30, and only 11 percent become divorced after age 40 (U.S. Bureau of the Census, 1977). This proportion is not enough to account for more than a small fraction of the age difference in marital satisfaction between middle-aged and older adults that has been observed in many studies.

Thus, marital satisfaction appears to be higher in later life than earlier. Part of the reason is a shift in the focus of marital expectations. Thurnher (1975) found that among middle-aged respondents, the husbands' expectations centered on the wives' performance as housekeepers and mothers while the wives' expectations centered on the husbands' role as family providers. In the preretirement stage (mean age of 60), both husbands and wives showed greater interest in their spouses' personalities, and their descriptions involved more emotional qualities. Another aspect relates to goal conflict within some wives. Livson (1976) found that traditional wives tended to be satisfied both in middle age and later, but that women who wanted involvement outside the household felt unhappy and constrained by their roles as wives and mothers. Thurnher (1975) found that unhappiness with their spouses was mainly concentrated among middle-aged women and that there was little difference between middle-aged and preretired men in satisfaction with their spouses. More than 80 percent of both husbands and wives stated positive feelings about their spouses in the preretirement stage.

For married people, marital satisfaction is a central factor in their over-all satisfaction with life. For example, Lee (1978) found that among older married men, only health was a more powerful predictor of their overall life satisfaction than was marital satisfaction. For older married women, marital satisfaction was by far the strongest predictor of overall life satisfaction. For both men and women, marital satisfaction was more important than age, education, retirement, or standard of living in predicting life satisfaction. Thus, high marital satisfaction is extremely important to the overall well-being of older couples.

Marital satisfaction does not occur in a vacuum. It is very much tied to other happenings, especially in relation to careers and child rearing. The following scenario shows how various life course factors may interact—but keep in mind that life course factors can vary considerably across social classes and ethnic groups.

Americans typically marry young. The median age at first marriage in 1976 was 21 for women and 23 for men. Early in the marriage, both spouses are likely to be employed. By their late 20s, most couples have completed childbearing. Even though a majority of women are now remaining in the labor force during their children's preschool years, about 40 percent leave their jobs and remain out of the labor force through middle age. Once children come, the roles of the spouses change. The men tend to concentrate on their jobs and economic providing, and women tend to concentrate on housekeeping and child rearing even if they have jobs. They may have little energy and pay little attention to each other or to their relationship, and this situation may persist for 10 to 15 years. The result is what Cuber and Harroff (1965:45–47) called the "devitalized" relationship:

> The key to the devitalized (relationship) is the clear discrepancy between middle-aged reality and the earlier years. These people usually characterized themselves as having been "deeply in love" during the early years, as having spent a great deal of time together, having enjoyed sex, and most important of all, having had a close identification with one another. The (middle-age) picture, with some variation from case to case, is in clear contrast—little time is spent together, sexual relationships are far less satisfying qualitatively or quantitatively, and interests and activities are not shared, at least not in the deeper and meaningful way they once were. Most of their time together now is "duty time"—entertaining together, planning and sharing activities with children, and participating in various kinds of required community responsibilities.

But whereas jobs and child rearing absorb the couple's energies and attentions to the best possible detriment of the marital relationships in early and middle adulthood, changes in these dimensions play an important part in bringing undivorced couples back together. In middle age, men's careers tend to reach plateaus. The job no longer offers prospects for explosive personal growth, advancement, or financial success. Instead, men settle into a more routine process of continuing to function in a familiar job with only minor increments in status or economic rewards. Maintaining careers can also take less time than making them. The launching of children into adulthood leaves women with greatly reduced workloads and responsibilities at home. Women may devote more time to their careers and may see this as their time to show what they can do. This shift is made easier if their husbands are in career plateaus that allow them to begin to share more of the workload at home. The fact that there are no children to evoke different sex roles facilitates a return to the more egalitarian relationship that typified the early years of marriage. Retirement frees the couple even further from external constraints that can interfere with the process of merging the individuals into a single unit. Thus, in later life, many couples rediscover one another, to their delight and growing satisfaction. They tend to become what Cuber and Harroff (1965:55) call a "vital" couple:

> The vital pair can easily be overlooked. . . . They do the same things, publicly at least; and when talking for public consumption say the same things—they are proud of their homes, love their children, gripe about their jobs, while being proud of their career accomplishments. But when the close, intimate, confidential, empathic look is taken, the essence of the vital relationship becomes clear: the mates are intensely bound together psychologically in important life matters. Their sharing and togetherness [are] genuine. [This relationship] provides the life essence for both man and woman.

Cuber and Harroff (1965) describe two other types of couples that probably persist into later life: conflict habituated and passive-congenial. The major focus of the conflict-habituated relationship is on controlling the ever-present potential for overt hostility. Quarreling and nagging are the major communications exchanged. It is as though the validation of each partner were provided by the existence of his or her clear opposite in the relationship.

Passive-congenial relationships are marriages of convenience. The relationship provides little excitement or emotional support. It does get the work done in a "comfortably adequate" fashion, and it provides companionship. Vinick's (1979) description of late-life remarriages suggests that many are passive-congenial and that the spouses expect little more.

When we look at couples in the period after child rearing, the tremendous range of functions the couple can have for its members is striking. I have organized them for discussion in terms of intimacy, interdependence, and belonging.

Intimacy in the Couple

Intimacy involves mutual affection, regard, and trust. It also involves sexual intimacy in most couples. Men's wives are often their only confidants. Lowenthal et al. (1975) found a prevailing lack of mutuality and intimacy in relationships among men, a fact that men in midlife regretted. In their review of the literature on intimacy, Lowenthal and Robinson (1976) found substantial evidence that men have difficulty establishing close relationships with anyone but their wives. And Glick et al. (1974) found that the most common reaction to widowhood among men was a feeling of having lost a part of themselves.

Farrell and Rosenberg (1981) found that wives played a crucial role in validating middle-aged husbands' images of themselves as beloved family patriarchs. According to Farrell and Rosenberg, a major problem in most men's lives is the need to be in control at home and at the same time be loved there. In actuality, the wife more often controls the home situation and, often in collusion with the children, protects the husband by avoiding confrontations that might undermine his belief that he is in charge and has the family's support and respect. Part of the decline in marital satisfaction that occurs in middle age may be thus a by-product of the strains involved in supporting what is increasingly a myth of patriarchy. And the upturn in satisfaction after child launching may be related to the fact that when the children leave, control over them is no longer a power issue that can divide the couple and interfere with intimacy.

Sexual Intimacy

Sex is an integral part of the couple's relationship. In counseling older couples and older people in general, the sexual component of human interaction must be taken into account. Sexuality in middle and later life reflects physical capacity, emotional needs, and social norms. Unfortunately, the simultaneous influence of these various factors has seldom been studied.

For older females, Masters and Johnson (1966) found that five major factors served to limit sexual response: (1) steroid starvation, which makes coitus painful; (2) lack of opportunity for a regular sexual outlet; (3) the lingering Victorian concept that women should have no innate interest in sexual activity; (4) physical infirmities of the desired partner; and (5) the fact that many older women never learned to respond to sexual desire and use menopause as an excuse for total abstinence. They also found, however, that with therapy to eliminate the pain associated with coitus and with the uterine contractions that often accompany orgasm, no time limit was imposed on female sexuality by advancing years.

Among older men, sexual performance does wane with age. Levels of sexual tension, ability to establish coital connection, ability to ejaculate, and masturbation or nocturnal emission all decline as age increases. Yet older men who have established a high sexual output, by whatever means, in their middle years, show a much less significant decline.

Masters and Johnson tied the increase with age in sexual inadequacy to several factors, the least of which is physical. The Victorian myth that older men have no sexuality was identified by Masters and Johnson as a major force leading to self-doubts and in turn to impotence among older men. Research indicates that many older men who suffer impotence as a result of psychological factors can be trained to overcome it by adequate counseling.

Masters and Johnson stated that once a high sexual output was established in the middle years, it was usually possible to maintain it physically into the 80s, provided health was maintained. They went on to say that six factors reduced this possibility: (1) boredom with one's partner, (2) preoccupation with career or economic pursuits (this factor would affect only a tiny proportion of older men), (3) mental or physical fatigue, (4) overindulgence in food or drink, (5) physical and mental infirmities, and (6) fear of poor performance. Masters and Johnson further stated, "There is no way to overemphasize the importance that the factor 'fear of failure' plays in the aging male's withdrawal from sexual performance" (1966:269).

Wives sometimes lack insight into the "fear of failure" problem and are very likely to feel personally rejected by their husbands' apparent disinterest in sexual activity. Thus, the older couple may face some serious sexual problems that do not usually confront younger couples. Very often the older couple is not aware of the exact nature of these problems. To solve them, the couple must understand what conditions are necessary to maintain sexual functioning and what can be done to create these conditions.

Aging can also bring some advantages in sexual expression. Starr and Weiner (1981) studied 800 people between 60 and 91 and found that 36 percent said that sex was better for them now than when they were younger. Only 25 percent said it had gotten worse. Most felt that sex should play a large part in an older couple's life. About 80 percent were sexually active, and a majority had intercourse at least once a week. Most had experienced an increase in the spontaneity of sexual expression as a result of the empty nest and retirement. Being able to spend a long time making love whenever they wanted was seen as being a major advantage to older couples. In a survey that I did, "being free to make love in the morning" was mentioned by several people as an advantage of retirement (Atchley, 1975c).

The prevailing myth is that older people are not interested in sex. When Starr and Weiner (1981) approached senior center personnel for permission to distribute questionnaires to center participants, they encountered resistance based on the assumption that older people would be offended by questions about sex and would be embarrassed about their lack of sexuality. In fact, however, older people responded to the questionnaire in substantially higher percentages than had been achieved in other studies of sex among middle-aged adults.

Sex has much the same meaning to older people that it does for others. To the question "What is a good sexual experience?" one of Starr and Weiner's (1981:5) older respondents replied, "To be really horny with a partner who is just as horny. To take plenty of time and when you can't stand it another minute, make it!" I suspect that this definition would get a lot of agreement from adults of any age! Starr and Weiner's respondents liked lots of things about sex: a sense of contribution to the other; feelings of desirability, zest, completion, and relaxation; feeling loved and loving; the comfort of touching and cuddling; and even transcendence. The vast majority of their sex lives were satisfying.

Sex is fortunately an important area where older people generally refuse to do what society at large expects of them. Yet undoubtedly some people withdraw from sexual activity because they feel such withdrawal is expected or "normal." It is for such people that the myths and stereotypes about aging and sexuality are most harmful. But even the sexually active may feel the need to hide the fact for fear of disapproval. This situation is not healthy. Sex is a powerful expression of intimacy, and its continuation into later life should be celebrated.

Interdependence in Older Couples

Interdependence involves instrumental sharing of housework, income, and other resources. In terms of housework, the picture is not very clear. Some studies have shown that even employed wives bear a disproportionate share of the household chores (Bahr, 1973; Ballweg, 1967). Other studies have shown that with greater employment of wives, the empty nest, and retirement, couples tend to share housework (Gordon et al., 1976; Lipman, 1961, 1962; Kerckhoff, 1966a, 1966b). Changing attitudes about "men's work versus women's work" around the house may make getting a clear picture even more difficult. In addition, trends may vary by types of work. Most people, especially men and better-educated women, tend to dislike routine work such as housecleaning. Men may try to fall back on traditional sex roles to avoid it, while working women may lobby for hiring a maid. In both cases, the idea is to avoid housework. Right now, older people seem to enjoy housework more than younger people do. Whether this tendency will change over time remains to be seen.

Over time, men apparently increase their involvement in more expressive or creative types of housework such as cooking and home decorating (Gordon et al., 1976), and husbands and wives are more equal in these areas in later life compared to middle age. Men tend to be expected to do heavy work and mechanical repairs throughout the life course. Both husbands and wives tend to increase their involvement with gardening in later life. However, apart from grocery shopping wives show an unfortunate and persistent lack of knowledge or interest in household financial management.

Income sharing is a major dimension of interdependence for most couples. Income adequacy—the income the couple has relative to what they feel they need—fluctuates across the life span. Of particular importance is the financial pinch as a result of children. Working-class couples often recover from this pinch by early middle age, but for middle-class couples the financial pinch can be worst when their children are in college. The need to financially support older parents may arise at the same time that children need financial assistance in getting launched into adulthood. The result is not just a pinch, it is a squeeze. And because the partners usually share income in middle age, conflicts can result from this income squeeze. Although retirement usually reduces available income, it normally does not produce a feeling of financial pressure comparable to the strains felt at midlife. Indeed, many couples find themselves more financially comfortable in retirement than at any other time in their married lives. This factor may also contribute to a rise in marital satisfaction later in life.

Taking care of one another in time of illness is an interdependence that grows drastically in importance with increasing age. Shanas (1977) found that among older people who need assistance in such household matters as personal care, meal preparation, housework, or shopping, spouses were *the* major providers of such help. Although assistance is an essential element of continuing to live in an independent household, it can be a severe strain on the spouse, particularly if he or she is also having health problems. Lopata (1973) found that 46 percent of the widows in her study had cared for their husbands at home during their final illnesses, and nearly 20 percent had done so for over a year. Not only do such health problems severely curtail many kinds of marital interactions, they also reduce the spouse's freedom of action.

A major problem can occur when caregiving shifts from interdependence to dependence—when one spouse can no longer reciprocate. The more able spouse may feel resentment at the one-sided flow of attention and energy, and the reduction of equality between spouses may reduce the intimacy between them as well. Most spouses do what is needed if they can, and most could use more emotional support, aid, and counseling than they get.

The Sense of Belonging for Older Couples

Belonging involves identification with the group, sharing of values and perspectives, a routine source of comfortable interaction and socializing, and a sense of safety and security. Identification with the group means that one sees oneself as a group member and that group membership says a lot about the individual. For example, traditionally oriented women are likely to answer the question "Who am I?" primarily in terms of membership in a couple—"I am the wife of _____ and the mother of _____ and _____." In middle age the couple tends to be less a source of identity than it is in the postparental period.

A sense of belonging based on shared values or perspectives thrives on *agreement*. A major determinant of agreement is potential for conflict. In middle age, most couples have a high potential for conflict over jobs, money, sex, and children. Child launching, career plateaus (and the withdrawal of personal stakes that usually goes with such plateaus), and greater financial security—all changes common to couples in late middle age—reduce the potential for conflict and increase the fund of agreement that supports a sense of belonging. The rediscovery of one's spouse can reduce sexual conflicts, and retirement can reduce disagreements over the provider function.

The reduced size of the household after child launching usually means / more socializing and companionship between spouses, which also increases the sense of mutual participation and belonging. Atchley et al. (1979) found that married older women interacted much less with friends and relatives outside their households compared to widowed or never-married women.

Finally, the availability of a spouse to provide caregiving when needed enhances most older people's sense of safety and security. Thus, caregiving supports ties of belonging as well as ties of interdependence.

From the foregoing, it should be absolutely clear that the increase in marital satisfaction that typifies the transition from middle age to later maturity is no accident. It is the result of many forces, the vast majority of which are pulling the couple together toward a greater and greater appreciation and acceptance of one another. The empty nest and retirement increase opportunity for companionship and decrease potential conflicts, especially for those couples who remain physically healthy.

Remarriage

As mentioned earlier, a substantial number of older couples are formed in later life. Only two studies have looked at this phenomenon in depth (McKain, 1969; Vinick, 1979).

In a study of 100 older couples who married in later maturity, McKain (1969) found that the desire for companionship was by far the most frequently given reason. Previous experience with marriage also predisposed older people to remarry. Few of the couples believed in romantic love, but they were interested in companionship, lasting affection, and regard. As McKain (1969:30) states,

> The role of sex in the lives of these older people extended far beyond lovemaking and coitus; a woman's gentle touch, the perfume on her hair, a word of endearment—all these and many more reminders that he is married help to satisfy a man's urge for the opposite sex. The same is true for the older wife.

A few older people remarried to allay their anxiety about poor health, and some remarried to avoid having to depend on their children.

Many older people tended to select mates who reminded them of a previous spouse. Also, older couples followed the same pattern of homogamy, the tendency for people of similar backgrounds to marry, that is found among younger couples.

Using such unobtrusive measures as displays of affection, respect and consideration, obvious enjoyment of each other's company, lack of complaints about each other, and pride in their marriage as indicators of successful marriage, McKain found that successful "retirement marriage" was related to several factors. Couples who had known each other well over a period of years before their marriage were likely to be successfully married. A surprisingly large number of couples McKain studied were related to each other through previous marriages. Probably the prime reason that long friendship was so strongly related to a successful marriage in later life is that intimate knowledge of the other allowed better matching of interests and favorite activities. Marriages in which interests were not alike were less successful.

Approval of the marriage by children and friends is also important for the success of marriage in later life. Apparently, considerable social pressure is exerted against marriage in later life, probably growing partly out of a misguided notion that older people do not *need* to be married and partly out of concern over what will happen to their estates. Older people are very sensitive to this pressure, and encouragement from children and from friends is important in overcoming it. Also, a marriage that alienates older people from their families or friends is not likely to be successful.

Financial factors were also related to successful marriage in later life. If both partners owned homes, success was more likely than if one or neither did. The importance of dual homeownership was probably symbolic, indicating that each partner brought something equally concrete to the marriage. If both partners had sufficient incomes prior to marriage, they usually had a successful marriage. The arrangements for pooling property or giving it to children were important for predicting marital success because they indicated the priority one partner held in the eyes of the other. It was important for the marriage partner to have first priority on resources, if the marriage was to be successful.

Vinick (1979) found many of the same factors operating in the 24 couples she studied. She also found that time before remarriage was easier for older women than it was for older men. Despite their greater financial difficulties, women had more social support than men during their time alone, especially from family. Women also found it easier than men did to ease loneliness by keeping busy. Thus, for these reasons men were much more highly motivated to remarry, and the large number of widows in later life made it a much more realistic prospect for them.

Courtship did not last long, perhaps because the partners were already familiar with marriage and had a sense of what they were getting into. Family were more likely to approve of the remarriage than friends were, at least initially. After remarriage, interaction with children and friends declined as partners used one another as their primary source of interaction. Most people were quite satisfied with their remarriages.

With Adult Children

For most older people, particularly those who are single, their most important relationships are with their adult children. There are many myths about how older people and their adult children relate in American society.

It is erroneously thought that older people are abandoned by their children, that they seldom see them, that older people in nursing homes have been rejected by their families or have no family, and that older people are mainly takers rather than givers of aid. This section is designed to give you an overview of the facts about how older people and their adult children tend to relate. It can help you identify important dimensions of these relationships and to get an idea of what is typical, so that you can put your own observations into context.

About 80 percent of the older American population has living children. About 10 percent of older Americans have adult children who are 65 or over. Most older Americans are not isolated from their children. In fact, older people and their adult children have a wide variety of types of relationships. The aspects of the relationships older people have with their adult children that have been studied include residential proximity, frequency of interaction, mutual aid, feelings of affection, and sense of filial duty or obligation.

Residential Proximity

Troll (1971) found more than 25 studies of residential proximity between older parents and their adult children. Older people prefer to live *near* their children, near being defined functionally in terms of travel time rather than geographic distance. Shanas (1977) found that 84 percent of older people who had children lived less than an hour away from one of their children. This proximity is probably more likely as older parents reached very advanced age. There may be a period in the life course—when parents are middle-aged and children are beginning their own households and occupational careers—when the two generations are more geographically distant. For example, Adams (1968) found that only 33 percent of young adults live near their parents. When older parents retire, if they move, they tend to move near their children (Bultena and Wood, 1969a). There is also some evidence that people in their middle years return to the geographic areas where they grew up (Lee, 1974). In addition, some adult children migrate to be closer to an ill or disabled parent (Sussman and Burchinal, 1962). Thus, the tentative picture that emerges is residential convergence as adult children "settle down" and as older parents grow older. This possibility needs to be more carefully examined.

Interaction Frequency

Interaction frequency tends to be high among older parents and their adult children. Shanas (1977) found that 52 percent of her respondents had seen one of their children in the past 24 hours. Harris and Associates (1975) found that 55 percent of their older sample had seen one of their children within the last 24 hours and 85 percent within the last week or two. These data from various sources all show that older people generally have frequent contact with their children.

However, this general trend masks variations among older people. For example, married older women interact less with their children compared to those who are widowed or divorced. In urban areas, intergenerational visiting occurs more often among women than among men. But in rural areas older men may interact with their children more than older women do.

There also remains the issue of the *nature* of the contacts. Although frequent, intergenerational contacts are often brief encounters to "pass the time of day." If older parents are ill or disabled, the contacts are a way to check to see that all is well, and this sort of monitoring probably increases with the age of the parents. These frequent contacts probably mean that adult children are apt to learn quickly if their parents need something or have a problem, but this guess needs to be studied.

Mutual Aid

Mutual aid is seen as the crucial intergenerational dimension by many researchers (Troll et al., 1979). Aid flows in both directions and may consist of services such as babysitting or housework, of information and advice, of moral support for various decisions, or of money or gifts. About a dozen studies have looked at this dimension.

Bracey (1966) found that less than 15 percent of the older people in his Louisiana sample got *regular* help with everyday household tasks from their sons or daughters. The most frequent services they received were shopping and housework, followed by cooking and advice about financial and maintenance matters. No more than 9 percent of the older people received regular financial help from a son or daughter, and an additional 4 percent said they received occasional money gifts. Atchley (1976) found even less help; about 3 percent of retired couples reported cash gifts from family and friends. However, Bracey found no evidence of real neglect of old people by their children where there was obvious need. Thus, helping was specific, not generalized.

Riley and Foner (1968:551–52) state,

> Contrary to the often-held theory of a one-way flow of contributions to old people, the flow of support between aged parents and their adult offspring appears to be two-directional, from parent to child or from child to parent as need and opportunity dictate. Altogether, the proportions of old people who give help to their children tends to exceed the proportions who receive help from their children.

However, Hill (1965) concluded that the grandparents he studied generally gave less often than they received for most categories of mutual aid. The differences in these results probably stem from social class differences in the samples studied. In the middle class, considerable aid continues to flow from older parents to middle-aged children even into old age, but in the working class more help goes to old parents from middle-aged children. A key factor in patterns of mutual aid seems to be the financial and physical capacity of older parents to offer aid.

Seelbach (1977) found that the more vulnerable older people were, the more aid they expected and got from their adult children. Older respondents who were widowed or divorced women, who had low incomes, and who were in poor health expected and received more aid. This situation held true for both blacks and whites.

As a general rule, parents seem to give to their children one way or another for as long as they are able. A shift from this pattern may therefore coincide with a deterioration in the financial or health condition of the parents.

> In illness, from a third to two-fifths rely for help with housework, meals and shopping upon husbands and wives and a similar proportion upon children or other relatives. . . . Between eight and nine in every ten of the bedfast at home depend primarily on members of their families for meals, housework, personal aid, and so on. [Shanas et al., 1968:428–29]

Whether or not older parents are satisfied with the frequency of interaction and mutual aid patterns with their adult children seems to depend on what they expect. Kerckhoff (1966b) found that older people fell into three types of orientation toward family relationships. Older parents with an extended family orientation (20 percent) expected to live near their children and enjoy considerable mutual aid and affection. Those with a nuclear family orientation (20 percent) expected neither to live near their children nor to be aided by them. And those with a modified extended family orientation (60 percent) believed in mutual aid and affection but took a middle-of-the-road position with regard to interaction frequency and extent of aid and affection. In actual experience, most of Kerckhoff's respondents had relationships that fit the modified extended family orientation. Not surprisingly, older parents with an extended family orientation tended to be disappointed, the middle-of-the-roaders were getting what they expected and were satisfied, and those with a nuclear family orientation were pleasantly surprised at the amount of interaction, aid, and affection between generations.

Affection and Regard

Proximity, interaction frequency, and mutual aid are important indices of adult parent-child relationships. However, *qualitative* aspects such as degree of closeness or strength of feelings (affection or dislike), may be even more revealing. Investigators have only recently started to explore these more intangible aspects of kin relationships.

It is commonly assumed that closeness is synonymous with liking or loving and that distance indicates negative feelings—that we love those relatives we feel close to and hate those we feel distant from. But feelings that run high are rarely only positive or only negative. Where love can be found, so can hate. Probably most family relationships ebb and flow (Troll et al., 1979).

Most parents and children report positive feelings for each other. For example, most middle-aged parents studied by Lowenthal et al. (1975) felt good about their children. About half had only positive things to say about them, and only about 10 percent of the middle-aged and none of those in their 60s had any strong negative comments. For older ages, Bengston and Black (1973) found high levels of regard reported by both older parents and their middle-aged children.

Parents remain important to their children throughout the life of the children. When adults of all ages were asked to describe a person, they tended spontaneously to refer to their parents more frequently than to any other person (Troll, 1972). The oldest members of Troll's sample, in their 70s and 80s, were still using parents as reference persons.

Johnson and Bursk (1977) found that ratings of their relationship provided both by older parents and by one of their adult children were highly congruent. Occasionally, the parents rated their relationship higher than their child had. Both generations felt better about each other when the parents were in good health and able to be financially independent.

Harris and Associates (1975) found that as age increased, so did the percentage of older people who said they felt close enough to their children to talk to them about "things that really bothered them." At age 55 to 65, only 25 percent felt close enough, but at age 80 or over, 43 percent felt this way. In fact, many people cannot find substitutes for the ties they have with their children (Cumming and Henry, 1961; Rosow, 1967). Older people do not tend to disengage from their children regardless of the amount of affection present in the relationship (Brown, 1974; Ingraham, 1974).

Duty

Feelings of obligation or a sense of duty often underlie frequent visiting and aid. Some interactions may be motivated either by shame that others would consider one delinquent in expected duties or by a more internalized guilt (Troll et al., 1979). Because dependency on the part of older parents introduces a high potential for conflict, it is surprising that nearly all adult children carry out their responsibilities (Blenkner, 1965). There is no evidence that any but a tiny minority of adult children neglect their older parents (Troll et al., 1979). But this general finding may have socioeconomic or ethnic exceptions. For example, Brown (1960) found that about 40 percent of lower-class older black parents felt neglected by their children.

Other Factors

The findings on various dimensions of relationships between adult children and older parents present a generally positive picture of physical nearness, frequent visiting, aid as needed, high mutual regard, and dutiful adult children. However, there are major sex, social class, and probably ethnic variations. Older women tend to have more intergenerational relationships than older men do. Some researchers contend that older women are more family oriented and thus have more contact and receive more aid, while others find little sex difference. This area needs more study.

Social class seems to have its greatest impact on the flow of mutual aid. Affluent older people tend to continue to aid middle-aged children, while blue-collar older people are more likely to be on the receiving end. However, more research is needed on class differences in family interaction patterns.

Ethnicity is a prominent influence on family life for many Americans, yet little of the research on older Americans and their families has taken this influence into account. Woehrer's (1978) excellent literature review found that nearly all the research on ethnicity and family was focused on households headed by middle-aged people. However, those studies had many implications for older family members. To begin with, compared to older whites, older blacks are much more likely to live in multigeneration households and to live with extended kin. Also, in many ethnic groups, women's roles are confined to the household, which results in strong bonds with children and perhaps a higher likelihood that older women of Italian, Puerto Rican, Mexican, or Polish descent will move in with their children if they become widowed. In addition, compared to Anglo families, family members from Jewish, Italian, or Polish traditions tended to visit older parents more frequently and to see more ties between generations. In terms of mutual aid, the picture is less clear. It does appear that black families are involved in more mutual aid at all stages of the life course. Finally, some ethnic groups view the family as the locus of social life, and others do not. For example, people of Polish and Italian descent tend to be family centered, while those of Scandinavian descent do not. Blacks and those of Irish descent tend to be somewhere in between. Woehrer's observations provide a rich source of ideas from which further research on the impact of ethnicity could proceed.

Geographic mobility is presumed to be prevalent in American society and to lead to the breakup of extended families. Both these presumptions are ill founded. There have been a number of interesting studies of migration effects on kinship, and when the findings are pooled, disruptive effects of migration on kinship ties appear to be at most only temporary. As Litwak (1960) suggested, kin ties in the modified extended family may even assist a nuclear unit's geographic venture for occupational advancement. Furthermore, Britton and Britton (1967) found that older people in a rural area in Pennsylvania, although they missed their distant children, reported increased morale and pride at their success. There is a tendency after a period of time for some older parents, past retirement, to move near their now-settled middle-aged children—that is, if these middle-aged children have not already moved back near their parents. Eventually, more kin may be available to those who have moved to the new area than to those who stayed behind.

Little is known about the extent to which middle-aged people experience being squeezed between the dependency needs of both their children and their parents. Data on typical childbearing patterns and data on the typical age of onset of physical or financial dependency lead to the conclusion that the average family should not experience such a squeeze. By the time older parents begin to need assistance, the children should be out of the middle generation's household.

Retirement of older parents frees them for more visiting with geographically distant children but it generally reduces their economic resources for doing so. Widowhood tends to increase interaction with children (Atchley et al., 1979).

We do not know how divorce or separation affects relationships between adult children and older parents. There are a good many aspects that could be studied. Do the children of divorced parents keep in touch with both parents? Is the frequency of contact affected by divorce? Are divorced parents as likely as widowed parents to receive aid from their children? Do older divorced mothers become financially dependent on their children more frequently than widows do? What effect does the timing of the divorce in the adult child's life have on the effect of divorce on parent-child relations? Does divorce affect parent-child relationships for mothers more than for fathers? Many other questions that need study could be added to this list.

The evidence indicates that most older parents understand and comply with the norms for relationships between older parents and adult children. The demands on the older parent are to recognize that the adult children have a right to lead their own lives, to not be too demanding and thus alienate oneself from one's adult children, and above all, to not interfere with their normal pursuits. At the same time, the adult child is expected to leave behind the rebellion and emancipation of adolescence and young adulthood, and to turn again to the parent, "no longer as a child, but as a mature adult with a new role and different love, seeing him for the first time as an individual with his own rights, needs, limitations, and a life history that, to a large extent, made him the person he is long before his child existed" (Blenkner, 1965:58).

This type of relationship requires that both the older parent and the adult child be mature and secure. Therefore mental, physical, and financial resources on both sides improve the chances of developing a satisfactory relationship.

It may be worthwhile to mention that a growing number of the children of older people are themselves older people. About one out of ten older people has a child who is over 65. In these cases, an even greater strain is usually put on both parties by the financial squeeze in which they find themselves and by the greater incidence of disabling illness among the very old.

With Other Kin

Older people interact with a variety of other kin. Grandchildren and siblings tend to be particularly important.

Grandchildren

Of older people, 75 percent are *grandparents,* and about 5 percent of households headed by older people contain grandchildren. Yet the research evidence suggests that the grandparent role does not usually bring continu-

ing interaction into the lives of the grandparents. Older people who are
separated from their children by the need for autonomy and independence
are separated even farther from their grandchildren. Moreover, the strong
peer orientation of adolescents in American society sometimes leaves little
room in their lives for older people.

The satisfying period of grandparenthood is usually when the grandchildren are small, but with the trend toward early marriage and early parenthood, most people become grandparents in their mid or late 40s. Few have
very young grandchildren after age 65. Because teen-age grandchildren usually shy away from their grandparents, the grandparent role is basically an
inactive one for most older people. As time goes on, the decline in marriage
age since World War II should make this trend even more prevalent.

Grandmothers appear to have a somewhat better chance of developing
a relationship with their granddaughters than grandfathers have in developing one with their grandsons. The key to this trend is the relative stability of
the housewife role in comparison with the occupational roles of men. The
grandmothers simply have more to offer their granddaughters that is perti-

nent to the lives they will lead. Sewing, cooking, and child rearing are but a few of the subjects that granddaughters often want to learn about. In contrast, the grandfathers very often find their skills unwanted, not only by industry but by their grandsons as well. As women's roles in society change, however, the grandmothers' knowledge may be less pertinent to their granddaughters' aspirations.

Visiting patterns are also important in the middle and upper social classes in developing ties of affection between grandparents and grandchildren (Boyd, 1969). Troll (1971) concluded that the "valued grandparent" is an achieved role based on the personal qualities of the grandparent and is not automatically ascribed to all grandparents.

Siblings

About 80 percent of older people have living brothers and/or sisters. With the advent of old age, many older people seek to pick up old family loyalties and renew old sibling relationships. More effort is made to visit siblings, even at great distance, in old age than in middle age. The narrower the older person's social world, the more likely he or she is spontaneously to mention a sibling as a source of aid in time of trouble or need. Next to adult children, siblings are the best prospects for providing older people with a permanent home. Except where long-term family feuds exist, siblings offer a logical source of primary relationships, particularly for older people whose primary bonds have been reduced by a spouse's death or the children's marriages. Shanas and her associates (1968:166) report that siblings are particularly important in the lives of older people who never married. The death of a sibling, particularly when the relationship was a close one, may shock an older person more than the death of any other kin. Such a loss apparently brings home one's own mortality with greater immediacy.

Other kin, such as cousins, aunts, and nieces, also serve as a reservoir of potential relationships, but here the ties are probably more often based on individual characteristics than on the closeness of kinship. One's "favorite" niece or nephew may be a family member with whom to have a "special" relationship. Relationships with extended family are usually activated by special occasions: weddings, funerals, holidays, or reunions.

With Friends and Neighbors

Friends and neighbors are important sources of relationships in later life. They also provide help and contact with the outside world, although they are less important in this regard than children or other relatives.

How do older people define friendship? Quite a variety of relationships are lumped together under this label. They range from close, intense, and continuous interaction marked by mutual understanding and concern, all the way to cursory contacts over the years with people whose names one happens to know (Clark and Anderson, 1967:303–10). Probably the best way to divide such contacts is to call the former *friends* and the latter *associates*.

Clark and Anderson (1967:305) observed that older women seemed to have an abundance of friends, while older men had an abundance of associates. In comparison to men, women appeared to speak more about their friendships and to place more value on them. They also tended to depend more on them. Men were much more passive about their friendships, and Clark and Anderson attribute this passivity to the fact that many more of the men were married and thus had less need for friends as a source of primary bonds. Yet men seemed to feel the implied stigma that being old and friendless brings. In addition, men were apparently less willing to continue friendships via correspondence or telephone, which may have shut them off from potential contacts.

Friendships tend to be retained into later life from middle age, and the higher socioeconomic status of the individual, the more likely this tendency is. Older people tend to pick their friends from among people with similar characteristics (including age). As a result, the longer the person lives in a given neighborhood, the more extensive his or her ties are apt to be (Riley and Foner, 1968:561).

Most people report a decline in their number of friendships over the years. However, a small minority of older people report that they have *more* friends than ever before. Many friendships among older people are related to a high socioeconomic status, good health, high density of older people in the neighborhood, long-term neighborhood residence, and residence in a small town rather than a large city (Riley and Foner, 1968:562–71).

Older people are fairly restrictive in terms of *who* they will accept as friends. Age peers seem to have priority as potential friends. Also, friends tend to be selected from among those of the same sex, marital status, and socioeconomic class (Riley and Foner, 1968:571–73).

Many factors influence the age structure of friendships, including how long one has lived in the same community, the age structure of one's fellow employees, the age structure of one's neighborhood, and how age-related one's main interests are. People who live out their lives in one community are likely to have friendships they developed in childhood that persist into later life. People who in adulthood settle in an area distant from where they grew up may find that their friends were selected from among their neighbors, their fellow employees, and members of various organizations they belong to. How age-integrated these various environments are obviously influences the age range of a person's friends.

But even in age-integrated environments, one's own stage in the life cycle has a great bearing on the possible age range of one's friends. People at the early ages of entry into an environment can only have friends who are their age or older. People at the middle ages have the widest latitude to range on either side of their own age in selecting friends. Those who are older can only have friends about their age or younger. People who select a wide age range of friends are generally less vulnerable to loss, because their younger friends are less likely to die before they do, while those who select friends who are mostly older than they are are most vulnerable.

As Hess (1972) pointed out, people's friends are selected from among other people they consider their social equals. The same experiences—growing up, living in the same neighborhood, having a similar occupation, having children the same age, having similar interests, being the same general age, and being the same sex—are all used by people at various times to define who is eligible to be considered as a friend. Just how age similarity compares to these other factors is unknown. Undoubtedly its influence fluctuates over historical time and depends on the age mix in the social environment. The effects of age similarity would be an excellent topic for further research.

Older people can hang onto the role of friend indefinitely. Long after the roles of worker, organization member, or even spouse have been lost, the role of friend remains. The demands of the friend role are flexible and can be adjusted to fit the individual's capability in terms of health and energy. It is the greatest source of companionship next to that of spouse.

Most older people recognize that the loss of friends is an inevitable accompaniment to growing older, and most also believe that replacing lost friends is very difficult. Older people cite difficulties in transportation, geographic moves, lowered economic status, and a life-style limited by illness or disability as significant obstacles to the replacement of lost friends.

Confidants are important, especially to older people, and most older people can identify at least one confidant—a person with whom they have a close, intimate relationship. Lowenthal and Havens (1968) found that presence of a confidant served as an important buffer against trauma in adjusting to social losses such as widowhood.

Support Systems

Thus far, I have discussed various kinds of relationships separately, but obviously this is not the way most people view them. Instead, people tend to look at their close relatives and friends as constituting a whole that serves their needs, even if each person is not in contact with every other person in that whole. The term *support system* was developed to refer to those relationships that involve the giving and receiving of assistance, that are viewed by both the giver and receiver as playing a significant part in maintaining the psychological, social, and physical integrity of the receiver (Lopata, 1975; Cantor, 1980). The assistance can be ongoing or sporadic. Cantor (1980) lists three major needs that support systems help meet: socializing, carrying out the tasks of daily living, and personal assistance during times of crisis.

Support systems fall into two main categories: informal and formal. Informal supports are those family and friends who provide assistance. Formal supports consist, first, of various functionaries such as postal workers,

building superintendents, or shopkeepers who may provide occasional assistance such as being aware when an older person may be ill. Second, some
social services agencies provide direct services to the elderly. Finally, planning and coordinating agencies and legislative agencies establish the need
for services, plan for their provision, and enact legislation to provide the
necessary funds.

Shanas (1977) found that among older people who got assistance, 80
percent got assistance from family members, some from friends (5 percent),
about 20 percent from paid household staff, and only 2 to 3 percent received
assistance from social services agencies. Thus, the informal support systems
were crucial in maintaining older people at home.

In industrial societies, the beginning of a division of responsibilities
increasingly has developed between families and social services agencies.
Kamerman (1976) examined services to older people in eight countries and
found cross-national uniformity in assigning responsibility for financing income and health programs for the elderly through national government
programs. The picture with regard to other social services was much less
consistent.

The helping professions customarily view the rise of social services to
the older population as a response to a weakened family system. However,
this interpretation is misguided. The fact that social service organizations
provide services to older people does not warrant the assumption that families do not. Shanas (1979) did a representative study for the United States in
1975 and found that families were very much involved in providing help
(especially in time of illness), exchanging services, and visiting with their
older members. Very few older people lived *with* their adult children, but
this situation simply reflects the preferences of both generations. Shanas
(1979:169) pointed out that the emotional bond between older parents and
their adult children is of prime importance. And although income and
health programs for the elderly are funded by both federal and state governments, many families provide health care and income assistance to their
older members (Shanas, 1979).

Shanas and Sussman (1977:216) pointed out that

> The family in its everyday socializing can provide the elderly person with
> necessary succor, nurture, and information, and can be especially influential in
> decision making regarding the older person's relationships with bureaucratic
> organizations. It can also provide an immediate and quick response to crisis
> situations (involving) older persons; be a buffer for elderly persons in the
> latter's dealings with bureaucracies; examine the service options provided by
> organizations; effect entry of the elderly person into the program of bureau-
> cratic organizations and facilitate the continuity of the relationship of the aged
> member with the bureaucracy.

Bureaucratic agencies, on the other hand, are poorly equipped to
handle the humanistic needs of older people. They usually lack the life
history perspective needed to understand the *context* of the older person's
concerns. Bureaucratic service agencies are much better equipped to deal
with repetitive and relatively uniform tasks such as medical treatment,

home-delivered meals, financial support, homemaker services, transportation, or home maintenance and repairs. And certainly there is a need for agencies that provide recreation, education, housing, and so forth for the independent elderly.

The goal of assisting families to function effectively is more in tune with general public preferences than is the goal of social agencies taking over family functions. Service providers need to be sensitized to look at the client's family as part of the client's total support system. If this were done, more *families* rather than individuals would be assisted by agencies. In addition, families could benefit from education about the resources available to them through the social service network. However, at this point such notions are more often idealistic than practical because the structure imposed on public social services by the legislation that created them assumes that services go to individuals directly and that families are not to be involved.

Attachments

As noted earlier, an attachment is a one-way relationship, usually with an animal, plant, or object. There have been very few studies of attachments and the place they occupy in the lives of middle-aged or older people, but those studies that have been done suggest that attachments can play a significant role.

Brickel (1980) reviewed the literature on pets. Apart from their utilitarian functions as protectors, seeing-eyes, or controllers of pests, many studies have found that pets meet various psychological needs. Pets can provide companionship, entertainment, and a sense of purpose. They can also be unquestioning sources of comfort and affection (Brickel, 1980:120). The dependency of the pet on its master can provide a sense of responsibility and self-esteem. Pets often serve as topics of conversation. Brickel (1980) cites several exploratory studies showing that pets were effective in helping treat patients with mental problems and in improving adjustment of nursing home residents. Dogs, cats, and birds are all apparently capable of providing the benefits of pet ownership. This topic needs much more research.

No one has studied attachment to plants among the elderly, yet it is clear from the data on gardening that working with plants is a favorite activity among today's older people. Whether they become attached to their plants is another matter.

Sherman and Newman (1977–1978) looked at the meaning of cherished personal possessions among the elderly. They found that more than 80 percent of their sample could name a cherished personal possession. The possessions named ranged from small items such as jewelry or photographs to houses. Having a cherished personal possession was very important to the person's overall sense of well-being.

Millard and Smith (1981) found that when older people in nursing homes were allowed to have personal belongings such as photographs or

plants in their surroundings, medical students had more positive attitudes
toward them compared to patients in bare surroundings. Nevertheless, Millard and Smith encountered stiff resistance when they tried to get policies
against personal possessions changed.

This smattering of research indicates that attachments can indeed be
important to older people and that they also serve as cues to society at large
that the person is still engaged with the world.

Summary

Relationships connect us to one another through our needs for interdependence, affection, and/or belonging. Relationships emerge when people interact with one another, usually in their various social roles. By personalizing role performance, long-term relationships articulate the personalities, resources, and needs of the people involved into a whole that is often greater than the sum of its parts. In this sense, the group is stronger and more capable than any of the individuals acting alone would be.

Relationships based on interdependence arise from the fact that ours is a complex, technologically advanced society in which it is virtually impossible to be completely self-sufficient. Our need for interdependence is the foundation on which intimacy and belonging are built through communication, agreement, self-disclosure, trust, similarity, and acceptance. Relationships can be weakened by disagreement, disability, selfishness, betrayal, or withdrawal. How well relationships resist negative forces can depend greatly on duration. The major long-term relationships for most adults are spouse or partner, parent, relative, friend, associate, and neighbor.

Most middle-aged and older people are part of couples. For those who have children, marital satisfaction tends to reach a low point when the children are in their teens and to improve steadily after the children leave home. Retirement also improves many marriages. A major part of the rise in marital satisfaction in later life is probably related to a reduced potential for conflict over jobs and children.

There are many types of couples, and the couple relationship can serve many possible purposes for its members. Nevertheless, satisfied couples in later life tend to be egalitarian in their approach to household work, flexible in terms of traditional sex roles, deeply involved with one another psychologically, and sexually active. The availability of a spouse for caregiving if needed meets not only the need for someone to depend on but also the need to feel safe and secure. Being part of a couple is the major social resource for the vast majority of middle-aged and older adults.

Unfortunately, by age 70 half of older women are widows, and although they get social support from family and friends, they still must make major adaptations. Whether they succeed or not usually depends on their economic resources and community supports. Older men become widowed too, but most of them remarry. Remarriage is a much more possible option for men because they are greatly outnumbered by unmarried women of their own age and they also may marry women younger than they are. Most people remarry for companionship and affection.

Contrary to the popular myth, older people are not isolated from their adult children or neglected by them, especially when older parents need assistance. The flow of interaction, aid, and affection tends to go in both directions, with older parents giving as much as they are able. When parents are in later maturity, there is a great deal of independence among generations, with visits spaced weekly or less frequently and focused around social-izing. When parents enter old age, they tend to need more assistance and support. Visits or contacts tend to be daily, particularly if the older parent has a serious chronic illness or disability, and there is much more "doing for" at this stage—housework, shopping, and transportation. The older parents are, the more likely they are to see their adult children as confidants.

Relationships with adult children are greatly influenced by the sex of the parent, social class, and ethnicity. Older women tend to interact more with their adult children than older men do. Obviously, middle-class adult children have more economic resources that could be used to aid older parents. Working-class older parents are more likely to assume responsibil-ity for rearing their grandchildren. Black families tend to be involved in more mutual aid compared to other ethnic groups. Relationships between older parents and adult children are not generally disrupted by migration. However, we do not know how they are affected by such factors as divorce.

Relationships with grandchildren, siblings, or other types of kin tend to be more voluntary and have a less predictable meaning than spouse or parent relationships. The valued grandparent must earn that position, and one's favorite grandchildren, siblings, or cousins are selected by the same processes we use to select friends. Relationships with extended kin that were developed earlier in life and then neglected for a period may be picked up again later in life. This renewal is a major resource for replacing relation-ships lost through death.

Friendships tend to be formed in middle adulthood and retained into later life particularly among the middle class. We select our friends from among people we consider to be our social equals. Developing new friends is a skill that most people do not have to maintain, because they already have a circle of friends. But aging usually means that some members of this circle will die. The older the individual, the more likely this is to be true. Making new friends is made difficult by rusty social skills, and because of the great amount of time and energy required to develop a new friendship. Therefore, new friends are more apt to be selected from among already existing acquaintances. Women tend to have more friends and to get more from friendship than men do. Men tend to have associates—people to do things with—but not confidants.

Support systems are the totality of family and friends that people de-pend on to meet their social, psychological, and physical needs. Support systems are of vital importance in helping older people adjust to changes such as widowhood or disability. Fortunately, most older people have an informal support system that complements the services available through formal service agencies.

Attachments are one-way bonds—relationships to animals, plants, or personal possessions. Pets have been found to provide companionship, enter-tainment, and a sense of purpose that can sometimes improve the adjustment of older people. Having cherished personal possessions is associated with high life satisfaction. We need more research on the importance of attachments in people's lives and how this factor may change over the life course.

Part Four

Aging Produces Changes and Challenges

Throughout the book, we have seen that aging produces changes and challenges. In this final part of the book, we look at some of the major transitions that occur for most people in later life and the effects they have. We also look at the various strategies people use in attempting to cope with the changes and challenges that aging can bring. Finally, we look at some of the problems of aging that stem from the way our society deals with aging and the aged.

Chapter 11

Major Transitions
in Later Life

In an earlier chapter, we discussed the life course as an ideal pattern of sequential changes in a person's life. Changes such as retirement are based on social expectations and usually involve elements of planning and choice. Others such as widowhood or physical dependency are essentially unplanned (except as a contingency) and usually unwanted. The same event can be variously defined as a positive event or negative, substantial or trivial, as something to look forward to and to plan for or as something to deny, depending on the individual's perspective or circumstances.

"Stressful life events" are commonly assumed to have a negative effect on both mental and physical health. Midlife career change, child launching, retirement, widowhood, physical aging, financial dependency, and a host of other changes are touted as causes of various "crises" that, unless successfully coped with, will surely leave its victim broken in body and spirit. Fortunately, once the polemics are set aside, it appears that few of these changes cause health problems for any but a small minority of those who experience them. Indeed, Sheehy (1976) contended that the word *crisis* was too strong; she preferred the word *passages* as a more neutral term for the transitions that occur in adult life.

Some changes of later life involve a great deal of change, and others do not. What requires substantial change for some may require little for others. Holmes and Masuda (1974) found considerable agreement in various U.S. samples and in a Japanese sample on the *relative* degree of perceived life readjustment required by various life events (see Table 11-1). Marriage was the base point from which people were to rate the average amount of restructuring that they expected would be required. All the more important changes (above 50) were those that were most likely to be seen as both negative and *unanticipated*.

Table 11–1 Readjustment Rating for Various Life Events

Life Events	Readjustment Rating %
Widowhood	100
Divorce	73
Marital separation	65
Jail term	63
Death of close family member	63
Personal injury or illness	53
Marriage	50
Being fired at work	47
Retirement	45
Change in financial state	38
Death of close friend	37
Changing careers	36
Son or daughter leaving home	29
Change in work hours	20
Change in residence	20
Vacation	13

Source: Adapted from Holmes and Masuda (1974:52).

Studies of the impact of life changes generally support the rankings in Table 11-1. Although most widowed people weather the loss of a spouse without serious effects on their health, widowhood does significantly increase the probability of both illness and death. Retirement is more ambiguous. Studies that have controlled for health at the time of retirement have generally found little influence of retirement on either physical or mental health. The empty nest and retirement migration appear to have no impact on health.

This chapter considers several transitions that occur in middle age and later life and that are considered to be at least potentially stressful or disruptive: launching one's children, midlife career change, retirement, widowhood, dependency, disability, and institutionalization. For each type of change, we will look at the prevalence of the change, when it is most likely to occur, the common assumptions made about the effects of the change, and what research evidence shows the effects to be. The goal is to give you a solid foundation in fact for understanding what typically happens as a result of various life events associated with later life.

Launching the Children

The launching of one's children into adulthood generally occurs early in middle age. For example, partners who married in 1955 and had children could expect on the average to see their last child leave home in 1980, at which time the average husband would be just over age 47 and the average wife would be about 45 (Troll et al., 1979:14).

The rhetoric of American society has proclaimed parenting to be mainly reserved for women and to be the major focus of their lives' meaning. Following this supposition to its logical conclusion, it was presumed that "the empty nest" would result in a meaningless existence for most mothers. However, researchers who have put this conventional wisdom to the test have found quite a few surprises.

To begin with, the term "empty nest" is somewhat misleading. It carries the connotation that newly matured people, like newly matured birds, leave the nest once and for all. But Ryder (1968) found that many newly-weds visited and telephoned their parents often and still used their parents' charge accounts, cars, and so on. As delayed marriages become more common, *getting* the children to leave home sometimes can be a bigger problem than *having* them leave.

Lowenthal and Chiriboga (1975) found that the period after the launching of the last child was not stressful. Indeed, middle-aged women whose children were not yet launched reported much less positive self-concepts, particularly their interpersonal skills, than did those who had already launched their children (Chiriboga and Thurnher, 1975:75). This deficit is probably related to the high potential for parent-child conflict when the child is a young adult living at home. Dealing with adolescent or young adult children may be the most difficult task a person can attempt. The youngsters' inconsistent yearnings and capacities for independence sometimes yield awesome unpredictability. Parents feel the need both to let their children experiment with assuming responsibility for their own decisions and behavior and to supervise them closely enough that potentially drastic errors can be avoided. This internal conflict makes parents somewhat unpredictable, too. These various conflicting postures make for an uneasy situation on both sides and help explain why so few parents feel that they are "a success" at this stage.

Mothers generally look forward to having their children launched. They see it as a chance for greater freedom and opportunity (Neugarten, 1968). This attitude is less true if motherhood has been the focal point in their lives and if they have few other interests (Spence and Lonner, 1971; Bart, 1971). The fathers' viewpoint has not been researched. Farrell and Rosenberg (1981) studied fathers' reactions to the launching stage and found many conflicts, but their research did not extend to the period after launching.

Thus, it would appear that having all one's children launched into adulthood is not as complete or abrupt as folklore would have it. In addition, it is a change that women generally look forward to, prepare for, and do not find especially stressful. This is not to say that there is no tension or conflict associated with launching the children. In fact, the tensions of the launching phase may play a signficant role in the tendency for parents to look forward to having the children launched. In addition, no doubt a small minority find letting go of the children very stressful.

Part of the controversy over the effect of the empty nest no doubt results from the fact that researchers have sometimes falsely attributed results to the empty nest that are in fact caused by other factors. For example, the absence of children may unmask an empty marriage, but it is the quality of the marriage that causes divorce, not the empty nest. There is no evidence that solid marital relationships are harmed by having launched the children. Studies are needed that examine the empty nest as a *transition* and that look at men and women both before and after the last child is launched.

Midlife Career Changes

The popular press carries frequent accounts and case studies of persons who begin new careers in middle age. However, statistics on how common this change is are scarce. Troll (1975) suggests that many employed middle-aged women attend school part-time in order to qualify for new careers. Military personnel often "retire" in middle age in order to take up a new career. Sarason (1977) reports widespread interest in programs designed to train middle-aged people for new careers.

A good bit of the presumed interest in midlife career change is no doubt based on an idealization of self-improvement. Recently there has been an increased emphasis on self-improvement, "self-actualization," and autonomy. In popular opinion, happiness is often tied to being able to change oneself and/or one's circumstances. A certain amount of romanticism is obvious in this approach, and some people believe that if one is unhappy with one's job, spouse, ego, car, stereo, or whatever, then *the* way to deal with it is to ring out the old and ring in the new. No doubt some job changes are related to this more general cultural factor.

Nevertheless, at this point it is difficult to say how prevalent midlife career change is, what preparations precede such changes, and what consequences they have. Certainly many job changes occur, but how these relate to the person's own projections about his or her occupational career is unclear. Obviously, even the idea of careers may apply to only a small portion of the labor force.

Blue-collar workers change jobs in middle age primarily as a result of poor health or being laid off (Parnes et al., 1975). For middle-class workers, the situation is more complex. Thomas (1977) studied 73 middle-class men who left managerial and professional careers between the ages of 34 and 54. He found four paths to midlife career change among these men. About 34 percent of his sample were men who had little internal motivation to change careers but were forced into it by external circumstances such as being fired or having their jobs terminated as a result of office reorganization and being in a field with an oversupply of workers. Another 26 percent were faced with external pressures to change *and* had high internal motivation to change as well. In the sample, 23 percent had neither high desire to change nor high external pressures. Only 17 percent changed purely because of their own desire to do so. External factors associated with the job career were thus the prime force in these midlife career changes. Career changes were not related to rejection of the work ethic, desire for more money or job security, or family factors. There was some indication that a desire for meaningful work was important for most of these men. Thomas's study is noteworthy in that it carefully screened out those who merely changed jobs and concentrated on those who had genuinely changed careers.

Retirement

Retirement is a socially accepted means of withdrawing from one's occupation or business in later life in order to cope with health problems or problems in finding a job or in order to enjoy more leisure or freedom. Entitlement to retirement is based on having held a job for a number of years, and the amount of retirement pension a person receives is generally tied closely to the number of years of service and income during those years. Latitude is usually given to allow the individual to choose the age at which he or she retires, sometimes as early as 50 and often as late as 70.

For our purposes, an individual is retired if he or she is employed at a paying job less than full-time, year-round (whatever that may mean in a particular job) *and* if his or her income comes at least in part from a retirement pension earned through prior years of employment. Both these conditions must be met for an individual to be retired. For example, many former military personnel draw retirement pensions but are employed full-time, year-round. Housewives often are not employed, but neither are they eligible for a retirement pension.[1]

Sometimes couples as well as individuals may be considered retired. A couple is retired if neither person is employed full-time, year-round and if most of the couple's income is from one or more retirement pensions. The extent of retirement can be measured by the number of weeks *not* employed (over and above usual vacation periods) for individuals who are drawing retirement pensions (Palmore, 1971). These definitions are somewhat arbitrary, but they illustrate two important dimensions of retirement; namely, (1) that retirement is an *earned* reward and (2) that its main effects concern separation from a job and a shift in the source, and usually the amount, of individual or family income.

The process of retirement involves withdrawing from a job and taking up the role of retired person. In studying individual aspects of retirement, we are interested in the preparations people make both for withdrawing from the job and for taking up the retirement role, in the decision to retire, in the retirement event, in the consequences of retirement for the individual, and in how individuals adjust to the changes retirement brings.

Preludes to Retirement

The retirement process begins when individuals recognize that some day they will retire. Most adults expect to retire (less than 10 percent do not), and most expect to retire early (Harris, 1965).

How younger people view the prospect of retirement has a bearing on

---

[1]There is increasing recognition that housewives make an enormous contribution to society through maintaining households and rearing children. Perhaps one day this recognition will be appropriately translated into the right to a general public retirement pension, but this will probably not happen in the near future.

how they assess their retired friends and, more importantly, perhaps, on how they themselves fare when retirement comes. In general, people's ideas about retirement are favorable. In a study of adults ranging in age from 45 up, Atchley (1974) found that attitudes toward retirement were very positive, regardless of the age or sex of the respondent. The only variation from this very positive view of retirement occurred among retired people who would have liked to have continued on the job, and even they had generally positive attitudes—just not as positive as others' attitudes. Generally, the individual's attitude toward retirement is closely allied to his or her financial situation. The higher the expected retirement income, the more favorable the attitude. About two-thirds of employed adults envision no financial troubles in retirement, although most expect retirement to reduce their incomes by up to 50 percent from their preretirement levels.

There is a complex relationship between high income, education, and occupational status on the one hand and attitudes toward retirement on the other. People with high incomes realistically expect to be financially secure in retirement, although they tend to estimate their income requirements at a level substantially below their present incomes. People with a college education are more likely than others to plan an early retirement (Morgan, 1962). Those at higher occupation levels, with the exception of professionals, executives, and government officials, tend to see retirement more favorably than do people in lower occupational groups (Thompson, 1956). Workers at the higher occupation and education levels not only have higher earnings and more favorable attitudes toward retirement, but they also find their jobs more interesting and in actual practice are less prone to retire (Riley and Foner, 1968:445).

People at lower occupational levels have less income and anticipate more financial insecurity in retirement. These people favor retirement, but dread poverty. Here, the question is money. Apparently, few people at the lower occupational levels continue to work because they love their jobs. At the middle occupational level, positive orientation toward retirement is at its peak. These people anticipate sufficient retirement income and at the same time have no lasting commitment toward the job.

Retirement Preparation

Because almost everyone expects to retire, it is useful to examine the planning and preparation that precede retirement. Very few people make specific or detailed plans for retirement, and very few are exposed to retirement preparation programs. But most people manage to adjust quite well to retirement even though they have had little formal preparation for it, and the main effects of retirement preparation programs are to reinforce preexisting positive orientation toward retirement and to facilitate concrete financial planning (Green et al., 1969; Atchley et al., 1978).

The most important facet of any retirement preparation program is a very early exposure to the facts of life concerning retirement income. This is the only area where a majority of employees see a need for information (Atchley et al., 1978). Some employers or unions can point with pride to programs providing a retirement income high enough to meet the individual's needs. Others may have to spell out the shortcomings of their programs and the steps individual employees can take to guarantee their own financial security in retirement. Professional associations can also make it a point to provide realistic retirement information to their members, particularly to those just entering the profession.

It is imperative for employees to know as soon as possible precisely where they stand with regard to retirement income. For example, many younger employees will receive only Social Security on retirement. Most experts agree that Social Security is basically on a sound footing, and this message needs to be a part of retirement planning programs. Then a direct comparison between (1) the average salary of a mature employee in a given occupation and (2) the Social Security benefits he or she would receive should be given to illustrate the need for additional individual financial planning. And this information should be offered before it is too late for the individual to do anything about planning. The retirement income picture has improved in recent years, but at present the most important element of retirement preparation still is teaching people how to assure their own financial security, if indeed that is possible. In addition to the usual ways of trying to provide increased income, programs can also point out ways to minimize expenditures.

Retaining good health, keeping active, and finding part-time employment are other topics that interest people facing retirement (Atchley et al., 1978). In addition, retirement preparation programs often include topics such as retirement communities or legal affairs that are not spontaneously mentioned by employees.

Gradually increasing the time spent in roles other than the job and gradually decreasing the time spent on the job can be particularly useful in preparing for retirement. This tapering off can be accomplished by gradually increasing the length of the annual vacation, but perhaps a method more in tune with the physical decline in energy is gradually reducing the length of the work day. This proposal would only apply if the transition were to begin after age 60. Before that, the declines in energy are probably not great enough to matter. Right now, most people retire suddenly. There is seldom an opportunity to "rehearse" retirement by gradually reducing the amount of employment.

Retirement preparation programs are on the increase. Almost all are offered by companies whose workers are covered by a private pension and by government agencies. These retirement preparation programs fall into two categories. The *limited* programs do little more than explain the pension plan, the retirement timing options, and the level of benefits under various options. The *comprehensive* programs attempt to go beyond financial planning and deal with such topics as physical and mental health, housing, leisure activities, and legal aspects of retirement. About 30 percent of the programs surveyed by Green and his associates (1969) were comprehensive.

However, retirement preparation programs cover, at most, only about 10 percent of the labor force (Schulz, 1973). In addition to covering far more people, most programs should begin sooner, especially if they are to successfully encourage the development of activities, interests, and adequate financial planning. Thus far, the need for retirement preparation is not being met for the vast majority of people. In addition, retirement preparation programs need to be more adequately evaluated. Kasschau (1974) concluded that group information programs were more in line with the retirement preparation needs of most jobholders than were individual counseling programs.

The Retirement Decision

Both attitudes toward retirement and planning or preparation for it affect the decision to retire. Other important factors include the hiring and retirement policies of employers and the health of the individual.

First, an individual may decide to retire because he or she cannot find a job. *Hiring policies*, particularly in manufacturing, tend to discriminate against hiring older workers. A case illustration may make clear just how this kind of hiring discrimination can influence decisions to retire. In December 1956, a large printing company that published several widely circulated magazines ceased operations and closed down its nine-story plant. Over 2,500 workers were left jobless.

Among those affected was John Hilary, age 59, a master printer with 42 years experience. Hilary was put in a real bind by the shutdown. He could have secured employment elsewhere, but it would have meant a move of over 1,000 miles for himself and his family. Hilary was reluctant to leave his hometown. He had been born there, and many of his relatives and all his friends were there. He was active in his church and in local politics. In short, his ties to the community were too strong to make it worth his while to uproot himself completely in order to continue his chosen trade.

Instead, Hilary tried to find employment outside his profession. His age prevented him from being hired by any of the many local manufacturing concerns, even though his skills were easily adaptable to any situation requiring skill in running or repairing machinery. Even though he was willing to work for less than he had made as a printer, he was unable to get a job. He finally decided to retire from the labor force.

At 73, Hilary still supplemented his union and Social Security retirement incomes by doing carpentry work for relatives and neighbors. He said bluntly that he was not really sorry he was forced to retire, but that if he could have found a job he would have continued to work for another 5 to 10 years. He was bitter that in order to get any kind of job that would allow him to maintain his self-respect, he would have had to leave everything else that had any meaning to him. Hilary's decision to retire clearly was precipitated prematurely by the fact that employer hiring policies prevented him from gaining employment.

On the other side of the coin are employer policies that allow employees to generate entitlement to *early retirement*. Early retirement plans usually allow employees to retire before they become eligible for a Social Security retirement pension by providing supplemental pension payments to keep pensions at an adequate level until the retired person becomes eligible to collect Social Security. For example, in 1970 the United Auto Workers negotiated a contract with General Motors that allowed employees with 30 years service to retire at age 56 on a pension of $500 per month. At age 65, the private pension would drop to cover the difference between the employees' Social Security retirement pension and $500 per month.

Early retirement is favored by dissatisfied factory workers who want to retire as soon as economically feasible (Barfield and Morgan, 1969, 1978) and by employers who see early retirement as an effective way to deal with technological change, mergers, plant closings, and production cutbacks.

Mandatory retirement policies require retirement at a specific chronological age. Reno (1972) found that 36 percent of the men and 23 percent of the women who retired in the last half of 1969 reported a compulsory retirement age on their most recent job. The most common age was 65 (68 percent of the cases) followed by 70 (20 percent of the cases). Compulsory retirement fluctuated a great deal by occupation. For example, 56 percent of men with professional and technical jobs were subject to mandatory retirement compared to only 23 percent among service workers.

Schulz (1974) estimated that in a cohort of retired male workers only about 7 percent were retired unwillingly at a mandatory retirement age *and* unable to find new employment. Parnes and Nestel (1981) found that only 4 percent of over 2,000 retirements they studied fit this category.

Nevertheless, mandatory retirement has not been popular. Harris and Associates (1975) found that 86 percent of both the older population and the general public felt that people should not be forced to retire purely because of age if they wanted to continue and were still able to do the job. Accordingly, in 1978, Congress amended the Age Discrimination in Employment Act to abolish mandatory retirement in the Federal Civil Service and generally to raise the mandatory retirement age to 70. Several states had earlier abolished mandatory retirement for state civil servants. Because the proportion of people affected adversely by mandatory retirement is small (around 5 percent), the overall impact of this change has been minimal.

Unfortunately, the debate over mandatory retirement obscured a more important policy issue—the gradual decline of the *minimum retirement age.* All sorts of evidence indicates that most workers retire as soon as financially feasible (Barfield and Morgan, 1969; Bixby, 1976). Thus, policies governing the *minimum* age for retirement have a much more direct effect on the level of retirement (proportion retired in the population) than mandatory retirement policies do. This effect is amply illustrated by the fact that as soon as Social Security retirement benefits became available to men at age 62 rather than 65, the "typical" age of retirement under Social Security quickly went from 65 to 63, even though early retirement meant reduced benefits.

How health influences retirement is unclear. On the one hand, both disability data and survey data on reasons for retirement indicate that there is a substantial health component to the decision to retire (Lando, 1976; Reno, 1971). However, among those who retire before age 60 health seems to be declining in importance (Pollman, 1971). In addition, people sometimes cite health as the reason they retired because they see it as more socially acceptable than simply a desire for retirement (Schulz, 1976). In their longitudinal study, Parnes and Nestel (1981) found that 38 percent of white men and 47 percent of black men who retired had reported job-related health problems prior to retirement. No doubt variations in working conditions over the life course are important determinants of the extent to which poor health is an actual factor in early retirement. Research is needed on this topic.

An individual's decision to retire is also influenced by the informal norms of the work situation. For example, most professionals are probably discouraged from retiring by the attitudes of their colleagues. Because retirement tends to be viewed negatively among professionals, to retire is to buck the system. On the other hand, assembly-line workers generally favor retirement and indeed show a growing tendency to retire early (Barfield and Morgan, 1969). It would be absurd to assume that two individuals anxious to retire face the same decision in these two quite different occupational areas.

Attitudes of friends and family may also probably play a role in the retirement decision. One man's children may want him to retire, another's may not. One woman's husband may want her to retire, another's may not. One man may live in a neighborhood where retirement is sneered at, while another may live in a leisure community where retirement is the rule rather than the exception. If we retire, then the characteristics our friends and family impute to retired people will be imputed to us. All these factors may encourage or discourage retirement (Atchley, 1976).

Employers sometimes exert informal pressures on employees to retire. They may do so by suggestion or by job transfers or job reclassifications that substantially alter the employees working conditions. There are countless ways that employers can apply pressure to retire, but as yet we have no basis for estimating what proportion of older workers experience such pressures. However, three-fourths of the complaints of age discrimination in employment concern conditions of employment other than hiring or firing (U.S. Department of Labor, 1979).

These various factors combine to produce a situation in which most people want to retire and to do it while they are still physically able to enjoy life. The small proportion that does not want to retire can expect to find it increasingly easier to stay on as long as they can still do the job.

The decision to retire is thus more a question of *when* to retire than *whether* to retire or not. The timing of retirement appears to be influenced primarily by the minimum age of eligibility for *socially adequate* retirement income. The generally high level of desire for retirement and poor health both exert pressures that cause most retirements to occur shortly after the minimum age.

Retirement as a Role

After the event, be it formalized or not, the individual is expected to assume the role of "retired person." Gerontologists have had a lengthy debate over the nature of the retirement role, and, in fact, over whether such a role even exists. Most people agree that there is a position, *retired person*, that individuals enter when they retire. The disagreement comes when an attempt is made to specify the *role* associated with that position.

The rights of a retired person include the right to economic support without holding a job (but at the same time without the stigma of being regarded as dependent on society, as in the case of the unemployed). They also include autonomy concerning the management of time and other resources. And often more specific rights are associated with the former job, such as the right to retain library privileges or to use employer health facilities.

The retirement role also involves duties—things that are expected of retired people. Foremost is the expectation that retired people will avoid full-time employment. This expectation is backed up by the Social Security provision of a financial penalty for retired people with annual earnings from employment that exceed the allowable amount. For example, in 1979, workers who retired at age 62 could earn $3,480 annually and still draw their full retirement benefit, but for every $2 they earned over $3,480, $1 in Social Security benefits was withheld. This sort of "retirement test" exists in four-fifths of the nations that have general public retirement systems (Social Security Administration, 1975).

Retired people are also expected to carry over into retirement their skills, experience, knowledge, and identity with the jobs they had. They are sometimes expected to provide free services to community projects or organizations. For instance, a retired bookkeeper may find that he is expected to "do the books" for his church or lodge without pay. A retired carpenter may find that he is solicited to donate maintenance work. A retired dietitian may be asked to donate her expertise to a Meals-on-Wheels project. As one retired accountant put it, "If I responded to all of the appeals to donate my time to this or that organization, I would be working more hours than when I was employed! Some of these people act insulted when you tell them no."

In addition, retired people are expected to assume responsibility for managing their own lives. For a great many people, retirement means a great deal of added decision-making responsibility. This responsibility, added to the responsibilities of parenthood, friendship, and so forth that continue after retirement, means that much of the retired person's time is not available for leisure.

Retired people are also expected to live within their incomes. Certainly many people cannot meet this expectation, usually through no fault of their own, but the expectation is there, nevertheless. Retired people are expected to avoid becoming dependent either on their families or on the community (Atchley, 1976).

As a *relationship*, the retirement role connects retired people to those who are still employed, either in a particular profession or in a particular organization. The crux of the relationship is the fact that both the retired person and the person still on the job tend to identify themselves in terms of the same occupation or work organization. In this sense, the position of retired person is similar to the position of alumnus or alumna.

Although retirement *does* represent a role, this role is usually flexibly defined, allowing the individual a certain amount of latitude in adjusting to his or her less consistent physical capabilities. This flexibility is also related to a major attraction of retirement—freedom and autonomy. The United States is a very individualistic nation, and individual freedom and autonomy are cherished American values. It is apparent that a large proportion of older workers are quite willing to sacrifice a certain amount of income and social status in order to get the freedom that retirement represents.

The Retirement Event

When retirement occurs abruptly, it may be seen as an occasion for ceremony. We don't know very much about retirement ceremonies or the role they play in the transition from employment to retirement. Certainly, the stereotyped "gold watch" ceremony was never part of the retirement experience of most workers, and as retirement has become more and more desired and commonplace, the austerity and mock honor of the stereotype seem even further out of place.

The most notable characteristic of retirement events is their complete lack of standardization. They range from highly personalized, informal affairs involving current coworkers only to all-day tributes and speeches involving colleagues from around the country. Sometimes the occasion is a dinner party involving family members as well as coworkers. Others are afternoon events at the workplace. Most are arranged by the employer but some are done by friends at work. Some are mass ceremonies honoring several people who were approaching retirement; others are for a particular individual. People whose job performance was highly respected tend to be singled out, whereas ordinary performers tended to be honored as part of a group.

When speeches are made, they tend to focus on acknowledgment for past contributions, with much less emphasis on the transition or on the "new career" as a retired person. However, informal conversations usually provide plentiful expressions of envy and good wishes. The atmosphere is seldom negative.

We do not know how common retirement ceremonies are, but it is probably safe to say that they are most likely to occur for those people whose upcoming retirement is known well in advance. Those who retire suddenly, who retire due to ill health or unemployment, who retire as a result of adverse circumstances, or who retire gradually would seem less likely to experience a ceremony.

Reactions to Retirement

The person's route to retirement has a significant bearing on what life is like immediately after retirement and, in turn, on how the person reacts. The four main routes to retirement are (1) planned and desired retirement, (2) being forced out by the employer, (3) being forced out by ill health, and (4) gradual retirement by choice or prolonged unemployment. People who plan their retirement well in advance may go through a "honeymoon" phase in which they travel a lot and are quite active, or they may go through an "R and R" phase of recuperating from the stresses and strains of employment. But by the end of six months most people who planned their retirement have settled into a routine of activities that is satisfying and long lasting. Parnes and Nestel (1981) found these people to be slightly more satisfied with various aspects of life than their nonretired age mates.

Not many people are forced to retire by their employers, but the potential stress in their situation is often high. Parnes and Nestel (1981) found that these people were more dissatisfied than those who retired voluntarily. But those who retired due to ill health were by far the most likely to be dissatisfied with life in retirement, and not just about their poor health. Those with health-related retirements also tended to be much less satisfied with their housing, standard of living, and leisure activities.

Those who retire gradually either by choice or after lengthy unemployment probably experience very little sudden change in their lives as a result of retirement, and their reactions could be expected to be muted accordingly. However, this guess needs to be researched.

In the Scripps Foundation's longitudinal study of retirement (Atchley, 1982), we found that activity levels did go down substantially after retirement, which means that a lot of people fit the "R and R" model, because nearly all had planned to retire. But by three years after retirement activity levels tended to return to the level of the preretirement period.

Retirement and Health

Retirement is widely thought to have an adverse effect on health. Everyone seems to know people who carefully planned for retirement only to get sick and die shortly after leaving their jobs. However, the crucial question is whether people retire because they are sick or whether they become sick because they retire. If people retire because they are sick, then it should not be surprising that some remain sick or die. The decisive test is the state of health following retirement, as compared to just preceding retirement. Using their data from a large longitudinal study of people both before and after retirement, Streib and Schneider (1971) concluded that health declines are associated with age, *but not with retirement*. That is, retired people were no more likely to be sick than people of the same age who were still on the job. In fact, unskilled workers showed a slight *improvement* in health following retirement. Haynes et al. (1978) studied nearly 4,000 workers in the rubber tire industry before and after retirement and found that *preretirement* health status was the only significant predictor of mortality within five years after retirement.

A good deal of research has been devoted to the impact of retirement on mental health, but no definite impact has yet been found (Nadelson, 1969). Lowenthal (1964) found that mental illness tended to cause social isolation, not the reverse. Likewise, it is quite probable that mental illness causes retirement, rather than the other way around. It is true that several studies point to a higher incidence of mental impairment among retired people (Nadelson, 1969:10). However, Lowenthal and Berkman (1967:76) found that the association between retirement and mental illness was mainly a function of poor health, low social activity, and unsatisfactory living arrangements rather than of retirement in itself.

Retirement and Social Adjustment

Much research on the personal consequences of retirement concerns the impact of retirement on social adjustment. The broad category of social adjustment includes such factors as life satisfaction, morale, and self-esteem. It has been generally assumed that retirement has a negative impact on social adjustment, but research has disproved this assumption.

Morale and life satisfaction are two concepts that have been used to assess overall emotional reaction to one's life at a given point in time. For example, Simpson et al. (1966b) found that morale was generally unconnected to work or retirement. They concluded that morale was influenced as much or more by health, family situations, and other personal factors as by work or retirement. George and Maddox (1977) found a great deal of longitudinal consistency in morale during the retirement transition. Streib and Schneider (1971) found that retirement produced no significant change in life satisfaction. Nearly half of their respondents did not expect retirement to reduce life satisfaction, but even so a sizable proportion overestimated the adverse effect of retirement on life satisfaction.

Another area of interest concerns the *self*. Several aspects of the impact of retirement on self have been studied. Back and Guptill (1966) identified three dimensions of the self-concept: involvement, optimism, and autonomy. They found that retired people were considerably less likely to see themselves as involved compared to people in preretirement, regardless of socioeconomic characteristics. However, retirement had very little effect on the optimism or autonomy dimensions. Back and Guptill concluded that the decline in perception of self as involved resulted almost entirely from loss of the job. Their findings indicated that an individual who was healthy, had a middle- or upper-stratum occupation, and had a high number of personal interests, would feel a minimal loss of sense of involvement brought on by retirement. Nevertheless, they also concluded that even these people did not completely fill the gap left by the loss of their jobs.

Cottrell and Atchley (1969) studied the impact of retirement on the self-esteem of older adults. Using Rosenberg's (1964) scale of self-esteem, they found that self-esteem in retirement tended to be quite high, much higher than among the high school students studied by Rosenberg. They also found that retirement produced no difference in self-esteem scores.

Apparently, no matter how the subjective reactions to the retirement life situation are measured, retirement makes little difference. The proportion with a high degree of satisfaction in retirement depends more on factors such as family situation, job history, and other personal factors such as health than on retirement itself.

Retirement and Social Participation

Social participation is assumed to be tied to support from a job role; loss of the job role presumably hinders participation. However, only in a relatively small minority of cases does retirement produce a decrease in participation and consequent loneliness and isolation. And if the effects of widowhood are controlled, the proportion in this category is substantially reduced. Rosenberg's (1970) data suggest, however, that retirement is more likely to produce social isolation among the working class.

Simpson et al. (1966a) found that many patterns of community and organizational involvement supported by jobs persist into retirement. They found that having a higher-status occupation and an orderly work career were as crucial for involvement in retirement as at earlier ages. They also found that if social involvement was not developed prior to retirement, it was unlikely to be initiated after retirement. Finally, they found that retirement itself is not responsible for the lack of involvement among semiskilled retired people and some middle-status workers; rather, *work histories* involving frequent job changes had not allowed these people to become integrated into the community. Simpson and her coworkers particularly stressed the role of financial security in providing support for participation in society.

In retirement, most people continue to do the same *kinds* of things they did when they were working. About a third increase their level of role activities not related to jobs to fill the gap left by retirement. About a fifth of the retired population experiences a decrease in activities. However, gains or losses in activity are relative. For someone who was uninvolved prior to retirement, leaving the job can result in an increase in activities and still leave gaps of unfilled, unsatisfying time. On the other hand, for an overinvolved professional retirement may reduce the net amount of activity, but at the same time bring the level down to a point more suitable to the person's capabilities and desires.

A great deal of attention has been paid to the impact of retirement on *leisure participation*. According to one school of thought, leisure cannot legitimately be engaged in full-time by adults in Western societies without resulting in an identity crisis for the individual and social stigma of implied inability to perform (Miller, 1965). At one time, and in some cultures more than others, this set of assumptions may have been widely applicable. In fact, much of the retirement research done in the United States in the early 1950s supports such a view. However, growing evidence shows that in recent years the leisure of retirement (to the extent that retirement brings leisure rather than a new set of obligations) is viewed both by retired people and by society at large as an earned privilege and opportunity (Atchley, 1971c; Thompson, 1973).

Adjustment to Retirement

Some people have difficulty adjusting to retirement; others do not. In a sample of retired teachers and telephone company employees, Cottrell and Atchley (1969:20) found that nearly 30 percent felt they would never get used to retirement. This percentage was higher among retired teachers.

About a third of those who retired in 1965 encountered difficulty adjusting to it, broken down as follows. Thirteen percent had income difficulties. Another 13 percent had difficulties with factors such as declining health or death of a spouse—factors not directly related to retirement. And 7 percent missed their jobs (Harris, 1965).

Some people avoid the problems of adjustment to retirement by going back to a paying job. In their longitudinal study of retirement, Streib and Schneider (1971:145–58) observed a number of people (about 10 percent) who returned to jobs after having retired. Those who returned were characterized by having a negative attitude toward retirement, by attaching a positive value to the satisfaction of work, by having been forced to retire, and by having a high degree of *felt* economic deprivation. Of these factors, low income provided the greatest incentive to reject retirement and seek a job. Factors that *allowed* people to return to a job were good health and an upper-status occupation. Motley (1978) surveyed a sample of workers who retired in 1969 and found that no more than 12 percent of these recent retirers were interested in returning to employment and were physically able to do so.

On the positive side, Cottrell and Atchley found that 49 percent of their sample adjusted to retirement in three months or less. Surprisingly, women were less likely than men to adjust to retirement quickly (Cottrell and Atchley, 1969; Streib and Schneider, 1971). Quick adjustment to retirement was related to having an adequate income and having had a semi-skilled job.

Heidbreder (1972) examined white-collar and blue-collar differences in adjustment to early retirement. Although she found that an overwhelming majority of the people were satisfied with retirement, she also found that adjustment problems were concentrated among former blue-collar workers who had low incomes, poor health, and little education.

Adjustment to retirement is greatly enhanced by sufficient income, the ability to give up one's job gracefully, and good health. In addition, adjustment seems to be smoothest when situational changes other than job loss are at a minimum. In other words, assuming that one's plans concerning the retirement role are realistic, factors that upset retired people's ability to live out their retirement ambitions hinder smooth adjustment to retirement.

Most people seem able to make the retirement transition smoothly. A major influence on this ability is the generally held image of the retired person. The fact that both the retired person and the people with whom he or she interacts and negotiates share at least to some extent a common idea of the nature of the retirement role gives everyone a place to begin the interaction. Very quickly, however, the individual retired person learns how to personalize this interaction. Thus, the vagueness of the retirement role allows retired individuals to negotiate definitions of this role that fit their particular situations and are consistent with their own personal goals.

Widowhood

Widowhood is another role change that is common among older people. In 1975, more than 50 percent of the women and 14 percent of the men 65 or over were widows or widowers (U.S. Bureau of the Census, 1976).

By age 70, a majority of older women are widows, but a majority of men do not become widowers until after age 85. As noted earlier, this trend results from lower female mortality rates and the tendency for men to marry women younger than themselves. Most women have to adjust to widowhood sooner or later, but the increasing trend is for widowhood to come later.

Widowhood can bring several kinds of changes. For many people, widowhood allows no fulfillment of sexual needs. It also diminishes the possibility of gaining identity through the accomplishments or positions of one's spouse. Widowhood also marks the loss of an important type of intimate interaction based on mutual interests. For example, the widow often replaces one intimate, extensive, and interdependent relationship with her husband by adding several transitory and interdependent relationships with other widows. The case of Mrs. Willoughby illustrates what can happen:

> Mrs. Willoughby is having problems adjusting to widowhood and compensating for restrictions in her social, as well as physical life space after three decades of marriage and joint employment with her husband. Together, they managed an apartment building. She has no children. Today, her most regular contacts are with a younger sister, but there is little comfort in the relationship, for the sister is condescending toward Mrs. Willoughby and her abilities. Mrs. Willoughby feels she thinks too much about herself: "I just think about sitting here and vegetating. I didn't used to have time to think of myself before. I had my husband and we were busy taking care of the apartment house we managed." With the loss of her husband, Mrs. Willoughby's financial situation as well as her health began to deteriorate. She could not continue to manage the apartment building without her husband, and so she is now living on her savings and some Social Security benefits. She would like to work and try to find companionship, perhaps with a man, but her sister has persuaded her she could probably not succeed at either endeavor. She does have misgivings about her sister's wisdom in these things, but not enough self-confidence to act on her own initiative, for she is used to depending on the judgments of others. "I had to do everything my husband said because he was the boss, although I did resent it deeply." In near desperation, she seems to feel there *must* be a way for her to get some of the most pressing needs met; that somewhere close at hand, there must be a new way of life—if only she could discover it. She would like to make a grasp at it: "I want to do something, but I don't know just what it is or how to go about it." She constantly chides herself for minutes spent in late-morning sleep when she could be doing other things, but she admits frankly she does not know what those things might be. [Clark and Anderson, 1967:408]

The Role of Widow

Part of Mrs. Willoughby's dilemma is caused by the nature of the role of widow. This role is a long-term role primarily for older women. Young widows can play the widow role for only short time, after which they are considered single rather than widowed (Lopata, 1973). Because they are so much in the minority, younger widows feel stigmatized by widowhood, but older widows see widowhood as more normal because even as young as age 65, 36 percent of women are widows. The prevalence of widowhood in later life combines with low rates of remarriage to produce for women a more definite social position for the older widow.

Yet the role of older widow is vague. Ties with the husband's family are usually drastically reduced by widowhood. The position of older widow serves primarily to label a woman as a member of a social category that has certain salient characteristics. Older widows are supposed to be interested in keeping the memory of their husbands alive, and they are not supposed to be interested in men. They are supposed to do things with other widows or with their children. Thus, being an older widow says more about the appropriate social environment for activity rather than the activity itself.

Effects of Widowhood on Identity

Being a widow changes the basis of self-identity for many women. In addition to loss of a central role, widowhood often also causes the loss of the person best able to support the woman's concept of her personal qualities. If a woman's husband knows her better than anyone else and is her best friend and confidant, his opinions may be very important in supporting her view of her self as a good person. I have encountered older widows who, after more than 10 years of widowhood, still "consulted" their dead husbands about whether they were "doing the right thing" by referring to the husband's values.

Although widowhood carries great potential for creating an identity crisis, that potential remains unrealized far more than might be imagined. The reason is that an older woman can maintain her self-concept as Mrs. John Doe, and her memories can preserve a continued identity. In addition, her continued identity as Mrs. John Doe is supported by family and friends.

However, women vary a great deal in the extent to which the role of wife is central to their identity. For many women, the role of mother supersedes the role of wife, and after the children grow up and leave the role of wife is an empty prospect. Other women have resented the traditional role of wife because of its subordinate status. Others have never developed close, intimate relationships with their husbands. For any one or all of these reasons, some widows do not wish to preserve their identities as wives. These widows must then negotiate with family and friends to gain acceptance in their own right rather than as someone's wife. This renegotiation of social identity is a particularly necessary prelude to remarriage. Thus, for some widows, the identity problems brought on by widowhood are more external and social than they are internal and psychological.

Loneliness in Widowhood

Loneliness is generally thought to be a particularly prevalent problem among widows. Widows most often miss their husbands as people and as partners in activities (Lopata, 1973). Although no doubt much loneliness is caused by the absence of a long-standing and important relationship, some results from economic factors. Widowhood means poverty for most working-class women, and this poverty is translated into lower social participation outside the home (Atchley, 1975a). The influence of economic factors on loneliness in widowhood deserves more research attention than it has received thus far. But not all studies show that loneliness is a problem in widowhood. Kunkel (1979) reported that in her small-town sample of widows only a quarter often felt lonely. This finding suggests that there may be important differences in reactions to widowhood between those who live in large urban areas and those who live in small towns. Lopata (1973) and Blau (1961) found high levels of loneliness among urban widows, while Atchley (1975a) and Kunkel (1979) found low levels in medium-sized cities and small towns. Both Atchley (1975a) and Morgan (1976) suggested that there is an economic component to loneliness in widowhood, and Kunkel (1979) points out that economic conditions for widows have greatly improved in recent years. This change may also play a part in the lower prevalence of loneliness in more recent studies.

Many widows quickly grow accustomed to living alone, and more than half continue to live alone. And as they become more involved with friendship groups of older widows, they tend less to miss a partner in activities. In residential areas with a high concentration of older widows, loneliness is much less prevalent.

Widowhood's Effects on Relationships

Widowhood has an immediate impact on family relationships. When older women become widows, they usually lose their contacts with their in-laws, especially if their children are grown. Contacts with children usually increase for a time, but those widows who move in with their children do so as a last resort (Lopata, 1973). There are two basic reasons why widows seem to prefer "intimacy at a distance." First, they do not wish to become embroiled in conflict over managing the flow of household activity, and after being in charge it is hard for widows to accept a subordinate position in another woman's house, especially a daughter-in-law's. Second, they do not want to be involved in the dilemmas of rearing children. They feel that they have done their work, raised their children, and deserve a rest (Lopata, 1973).

Patterns of mutual aid between children and parents are altered by widowhood. Older widows often grow closer to their daughters through patterns of mutual assistance (Adams, 1968). Widows sometimes grow more distant from their sons. Because adult sons often feel responsible for their mother's welfare and because older widows often want to be responsible for themselves, there is great potential for conflict and guilt in the older widow-son relationship.

Relationships with the extended family (brothers, sisters, aunts, uncles, cousins, and so on) increase immediately following the spouse's death. But within a short time, widows generally retain only sparse contact with extended kin (Lopata, 1973).

The impact of widowhood on friendship largely depends on the proportion of the widow's friends who are also widows. If she is one of the first among her friends to become widowed, she may find that her friends feel awkward talking about death and grief—they do not want to face what probably is their own future. If friendship groups consisted mainly of couples, then the widow may be included for a time, but she will probably feel out of place. The widow may also encounter jealousy on the part of still-married friends.

On the other hand, if the widow is one of the last to become widowed among her friends, then she may find great comfort among friends who identify very well with the problems of grief and widowhood. As a group of women friends grows older, the still-married sometimes feel "left out," because their friends do many things as a group that they do not feel free to leave their husbands in order to do. For such people, widowhood brings the compensation of being among old friends again.

Thus, the age at which widowhood occurs is important. The younger the widow, the more problems she faces. The older the widow, the more "normal" widowhood is considered to be and the more supports are available from the family, friends, and the community to help women cope with widowhood. Older widows appear to adjust better than younger widows (Blau, 1961).

The impact of widowhood also varies considerably, depending on the widow's social class. Middle-class women tend to have balanced their roles between being wives and companions to their husbands and being mothers. The loss of this comradeship triggers considerable trauma at their spouses' death. As a result, middle-class women tend to have difficulty dealing with grief. However, middle-class women also tend to be broadly engaged. They have a number of friends and belong to various organizations. They have many personal resources for dealing with life as widows. And they usually have secure incomes, are well-educated, and often have job skills and careers. On the other hand, working-class women tend to emphasize the mother role more than the wife role. Consequently, they may experience less trauma associated with grief. But working-class women have fewer friends, fewer associations, less money, and fewer of the personal resources that make for an adequate long-term adjustment to widowhood. Working-class widows are thus much more likely to be isolated and lonely than are middle-class widows.

There are also considerable ethnic differences in the impact of widowhood. Foreign-born widows are much more likely than others to have had traditional marriages, which can cause greater identity problems with widowhood. In addition, the impact of widowhood on family relations has more potential for conflict among the foreign born. Many foreign-born older women were reared in cultural traditions that offer widows more involvement with extended kin. To the extent that such kin do not share this orientation, a greater gap may appear between what the older foreign-born widow expects from her family and what she gets. A similar pattern prevails among older widows reared in an Appalachian tradition.

The Older Widower Role

The impact of widowhood on older men has received little attention. The literature on this subject is long on speculation and short on systematic research. Nevertheless, it is important to outline both what we do and what we need to know about being a widower, as a stimulus for further research.

The role of widower is probably even more vague than that of widow. Because widowers are not very common in the community until after age 75, the status of widower does not solidify groups of older men as it does groups of older women. But older widowers are expected to preserve the memories of their wives, and they are not expected to show an interest in women. Indications are that many widowers adhere to the former and ignore the latter.

Because the male role traditionally emphasizes other roles in addition to the role of husband, widowers are probably not as apt as widows to encounter identity crises caused by loss of the husband *role*. But men are more likely than women to see their spouses as important parts of *themselves* (Glick et al., 1974). In addition, older men are less likely than women to have confidants other than their spouses (Powers et al., 1975). Thus, both sexes are likely to have problems with the loss of a significant other.

How older men cope with widowhood's impact on their identity also probably depends, as older women's reactions do, on how the lost relationships fit into the men's goals. Despite current stereotypes concerning men's overinvolvement with their jobs, there is little evidence that widowhood is any less devastating for men than for women. In fact, widowhood is very likely to wreck a man's concept of life in retirement completely. Likewise, there is little basis for assuming that marriage is less important to older men than it is to older women.

Older widows and widowers apparently do not differ in the extent to which they experience loneliness (Atchley, 1975c). However, this finding may be caused by the higher average age of widowers. When the factor of age is controlled in research, we may find that older widowers are less lonely than older widows.

Thus far, the impact of widowhood on men's roles outside the household has hardly been studied. Widowers do have more difficulty with work during the grief period (Glick et al., 1974). It also appears that widowers are more cut off from their families than widows are (Troll, 1971). Widowhood tends to increase contacts with friends among middle-class widowers and decrease them among lower-class widowers (Atchley, 1975c). The large surplus of widows probably inhibits community participation by widowers. Particularly at senior centers, widowers tend to be embarrassed by the competition among the widows for their attention. They also feel pressured by widows who constantly try to "do" for them.

Very little has been written about social class or ethnic variations in the impact of widowhood on older men. However, some of the variations noted for widows no doubt apply to men as well. This area is greatly in need of research.

Dependency

Perhaps one of the most dreaded role changes accompanying old age involves dependency, the shift from the role of independent adult to that of dependent adult. Older people, both in the community and in institutions, fear becoming dependent, whether physically or financially—either way, it is a difficult position for most adults to accept. This fear is easy to understand. We are taught from birth that becoming independent and self-sufficient is a primary goal. This value is deeply ingrained for most people, so it is not surprising that they are hostile to the idea of giving up autonomy and becoming dependent on others.

Dependency is all the more difficult to accept because of the changes it brings in other roles. For example, older people are sometimes forced by necessity to rely on their children. This need strains the parent-child relationship for a number of reasons. Parents sometimes resist and often resent having to depend on their children. They may become angry and frustrated by the changes in interaction brought on by the reversal of positions. They may feel guilty because they feel that they should not be dependent. Their children, now adults, may also resent having to provide for both their own children and their parents, yet they may feel guilty for having this resentment. And finally, the spouses of the adult children may not willingly accept the diversion of family resources to aged parents.

What makes the position of "dependent" especially difficult is the set of expectations attached to it. Dependent people in our society are supposed to defer to their benefactors, to be eternally grateful for what they receive, and to give up their rights to lead their own lives. We demand this behavior of our children, the poor, or any other dependent group. Is it any wonder, then, that older people, often having spent as many as 50 years as independent adults, rebel at the idea of assuming a dependent position? Interestingly, although many older Americans find themselves having to ask their children for some kind of help at one point or another, on balance older people tend to give as much help as they receive.

Disability and Sickness

Disability is another new role that older people are likely to experience. There are varying degrees of disability, and extreme disability usually turns into dependency. But even for the many older people whose disabilities have not reached that stage, disability restricts the number of roles they can play and changes other people's reactions to them. Over a third of the older U.S. population has some disability serious enough to limit ability to work, keep house, or engage in other major activities (Wilder, 1973).

Sickness is similar to disability in that its influence is felt mainly through a limitation of role playing. Good health, or absence of sickness or disability, operates alongside age and sex as a major criterion for eligibility for various positions. Most positions outside one's circle of family and friends require activity that is impossible for severely sick or disabled people.

Our society has long recognized that sick people occupy a unique position. They are not expected to hold jobs, go to school, or otherwise meet the obligations of other positions, and they often depend on others for care.

If they play the sick role long enough, they may be permanently excluded from some of their other positions, such as their jobs, offices in voluntary associations, or positions as family breadwinners. Sick people are usually exempt from social responsibilities, are not expected to care for themselves, and are expected to need medical help. The more serious the prognosis, the more likely they are to find themselves being treated as dependents.

Whether people are defined as sick partly depends on the seriousness and certainty of the prognosis. Even if they have a functional or physical impairment, individuals are less likely to be allowed to play the sick role if the prognosis is known not to be serious. Yet sick people are often expected to want to get well, and actually to do so, *regardless of the prognosis* (Gordon, 1966).

The importance of aging to sickness and disability is of course the fact that as age increases, the probability of disease, illness, or disability becomes greater. For example, people age 65 and over are twice as likely to suffer limitations of activity due to chronic conditions compared to people at age 45 to 64 (Wilder, 1973).

The Role of the Institutional Resident

When illness and disability become a serious handicap, many older people take up residence in nursing homes and homes for the aged. Those who enter an institution usually encounter important role changes. In the institutional setting, opportunities for useful activity, leisure activities, contacts with the outside world, and privacy are all less frequent than they are outside. Coupled with the extremely negative attitude of most older people toward living in an institution, these changes create significant obstacles to role continuity.

In 1976, there were over 18,000 nursing homes and homes for the aged in the United States (U.S. Bureau of the Census, 1978). These homes repre- sented 77 percent of all long-term care institutions, and they housed 97 percent of the elderly who lived in institutions. The median age of the nearly a million elderly who lived in institutions was 80. Just over 4 percent of the elderly were institutionalized, but as age increased, so did the per- centage. For example, 24 percent of those 85 years old or over lived in institutions (Kovar, 1977). Kastenbaum and Candy (1973) found that 20 per- cent of the deaths of older people in Detroit in a given year occurred in nursing or personal care homes. Palmore (1976) found that 25 percent of people in a 20-year longitudinal study experienced institutionalization some- time before they died. These findings imply that while only 4 percent of older people are in institutions at any one time, the percentage that will *eventually* experience life in a nursing home is much larger.

Most older people regard nursing homes very negatively. These views result partly from a desire to remain in familiar surroundings and near relatives, but they are also partly influenced by the concept of the poor- house, which has survived from another era. In fact, the nursing home is about the *last* place most older people would prefer to go, although many recognize that this living arrangement may be the best for people who can no longer take care of themselves. Most of the fear that leads older people to reject the idea of living in a nursing home is related to a perceived loss of independence, a perception that the nursing home represents formal proof that death is near, and a fear of rejection by their children. Older people who live with their spouses or children, or in an owned home, are the most resistant to the idea of living in an institution. But these negative attitudes do not prevent older people from moving into nursing homes.

The facts of life in long-term care facilities sometimes justify the nega- tive view most older people have of them. Many lack adequate physical facilities, staff, and provision for activities. Many facilities have overly re- strictive institutional rules and often do not offer any useful occupations and leisure activities. Many nursing homes are cut off from the community and make little or no use of community resources to benefit their residents. Finally, most nursing homes usually offer far less privacy than the residents would like. Such conditions are most likely to be encountered by the poor who are not seriously ill, because their care must be financed within the meager SSI benefits available.

Adjusting to an Institution

New residents in an institution often face several simultaneous changes than can make it hard for them to adjust to their new circum- stances. Illness, dependency, widowhood, and loneliness are the changes most frequently encountered.

Illness can bring important changes for two reasons. First, illness forces the individual to become dependent. Second, it creates internal states within the individual that make it difficult to maintain a reasonable perspective on the outside world. When people are in pain, or under medication, or just plain fatigued from fighting illness, they find it much easier to allow themselves to become irritable and depressed. For some people, a long-term illness can produce profound personality changes.

In addition to the unfamiliar surroundings, the shock of moving, and often the depressing influence of illness, new institutional residents may also find that they have lost their independence. They have lost personal control over many of the simplest everyday functions. When to get up, when to go to sleep, when and what to eat, whom to associate with, whether the television set will be turned on or off, whether the windows will be open or closed, whether to use a heavy or a light blanket—these and a host of other *seemingly* trivial decisions are often now out of people's hands. They have also lost their ability to control the images others have of them.

Kahana (1973) found that humane treatment in institutions was not necessarily related to the degree of professionalism of the staff or to having modern facilities. Humane treatment seemed to be more related to the value attached to showing respect for the *person* of the aged resident.

Kleemeier (1961) proposed three dimensions along which institutions differ and that could be expected to influence the response of the older person to the institution: (1) degree of segregation of the residents from the outside world, (2) congregate as opposed to individual orientation, and (3) the degree to which the institution controls the daily life of the individual. Kahana (1973) cites research showing that the more segregated the residents are from the outside world, the greater the depersonalizing effects of the institution. The staff of institutions for the aged often develop an informal staff subculture that emphasizes congregate orientation and high institutional control as the easiest and most effective way to "master" the residents. Yet the morale and well-being of residents depends on the congruence between their perceived needs and the orientation of the institution. Flexible procedures would allow residents to choose the degree of segregation, of congregate programs, and of structured control over daily life that will be imposed on them. Kahana (1973) sees this flexibility as the keystone of humane treatment in institutions.

Summary

Many transitions occur in adulthood. The individual's response to these transitions depends largely on his or her personality and circumstances. Most people cope successfully with the transitions of middle and later life in the sense that they continue to function well throughout.

Launching the children and retirement are transitions that are expected and can be anticipated. Both tend to be positive transitions for the majority of people who experience them. Child launching frees parents from day-to-day responsibilities that can be maddeningly ambiguous, creates opportunities for growth, and reduces potential sources of conflict for couples. On the other hand, single parents may feel the empty nest as a transition to aloneness that can represent a substantial and difficult change. Launching the children may also remove focuses of interaction, attention, and concern. For the vast majority, however, the advantages outweigh the liabilities.

Most people today have a very positive view of retirement—they look forward to it. Retirement's major attraction is freedom and autonomy. Its major liabilities are reduced financial resources and social status. Only a small proportion of people receive any formal preparation for retirement. Nevertheless, a majority accomplish the transition with ease.

Early retirement tends to result from either health problems, financial entitlement to early retirement, or employment problems. Health problems are the most common cause of the decision to retire before age 65, but desire for retirement is very nearly as common. Employment problems such as layoffs, unemployment, or plant closings account for a much smaller proportion of early retirement.

Most people who retire at 65 do so because that is the customary retirement age, the age at which they are entitled to maximum retirement benefits, and, therefore, the age at which they had planned to retire. Only a very small proportion of people retire as a result of mandatory retirement age policies.

How a person retires has a profound bearing on his or her reaction to retirement. People who retire due to ill health sometimes find that their health improves, but most find that their life in retirement is not very satisfying. Their housing, activities, and standard of living, not to mention their outlook on life, are negatively influenced by their illness or disability. People who are forced to retire but who are in good health are not as satisfied as those who retire voluntarily, but they are much more satisfied than those who retire for health reasons. Those who retire voluntarily and are in good health represent the majority, and they make a good adjustment to retirement. By the end of the six months in retirement, the vast majority have established a satisfying life routine, but those who are disabled are still markedly less satisfied—not a surprising finding.

Retirement has little effect on physical or mental health, morale, life satisfaction, or self-esteem. It has an unpredictable effect on social participation, marriage, and leisure activities.

Widowhood is an undesired and often unanticipated change. It has immediate negative physical and emotional effects on the surviving spouse. Yet most people adapt successfully to widowhood. The older the person, the more likely that widowhood will be a permanent status. Older widows in particular have many age peers who are also widows and who can be turned to for social support. Loneliness is the most pervasive problem widowed people have, and there may be an economic component to this problem, particularly for women. However, recent studies suggest that loneliness in widowhood may be less prevalent now than it was earlier. Sex, social class, and ethnicity all can influence the impact of widowhood.

Dependency and institutionalization also tend to be unwanted changes that can occur in later life. Nevertheless, probably not more than 40 percent of older people ever experience substantial physical or social dependency or disability, and only about 20 to 25 percent ever become long-term residents of institutions. For those who do, the loss of autonomy and independence can be very vexing and frustrating. Continued respect for the person is the key to high-quality assistance to these people.

Thus, the major adult transitions vary considerably. The most common—retirement and child launching—are not predictably either positive or negative, although both are positive transitions for the vast majority. Widowhood is a negative change that usually, but not always, has a positive outcome. Disability and institutionalization are negative changes that can, but often do not, have positive outcomes.

Most people encounter more than one of these transitions, and the order and number can be important. For example, entering retirement as a disabled widower is vastly different from entering retirement as a healthy husband of a healthy wife.

Positive adjustments to these various accumulated changes outnumber negative ones by at least two to one.

Chapter 12

How People Cope
with Aging

As shown in previous chapters, aging can result in many types of changes. This chapter discusses how people adapt to these changes to achieve the generally positive adjustment that most older people have. The discussion begins with a definition of adaptation, some general approaches to adaptation, and the general goals of adaptation. Then the chapter considers some specific ways to adapt to specific changes associated with aging. Finally, the chapter focuses on some ways people try to avoid adaptation, and finishes with a discussion of successful aging.

What Is Adaptation?

Adaptation is the process of adjusting oneself to fit a situation or environment. It is actually several processes we use to deal with constant changes we encounter in our everyday lives. Changes that require adaptation can occur either in ourselves or in our situations or environments. Early in our lives we develop basic routine approaches to dealing with change. Each of us has a threshold of change that can be taken in nearly automatically, without special effort. For example, Mr. Z was employed in an office that developed planning reports for a large city. One day his boss came into his office and told him to drop what he was doing and concentrate on a new project aimed at evaluating the city's need for water. Mr. Z adjusted to this change without batting an eye. Why? Because such shifts were frequent in his job, and he had long since learned to deal with them effortlessly.

Just as changes that require adaptation can be internal or external, so can the means for adapting. *Assimilation* is an internal process of adaptation

in which new experience is modified in the process of perception so that it fits with already existing ideas. It adjusts the outer "reality" to fit the inner. Thus, an older person who is insulted by a youngster may simply alter his or her perception of the younger person's behavior to deny the insult. *Accommodation* is a process of altering one's behavior to more nearly conform to external demands. An example might be an older mother who stops visiting with her friends at a local tavern because her daughter said that she is too old for this activity. Both these processes of adaptation can be either conscious or unconscious.

Three General Ways to Adapt

Habituation, continuity, and conflict management are three general means of adaptation. When we are exposed to the same experience over and over, we gradually pay less and less attention to it. This process is called *habituation*.[1] It is learning *not* to pay attention. Habituation is vital in early childhood because it allows us to ignore most environmental stimuli and to concentrate our attention. This process is an important prerequisite for

[1] For a more detailed discussion of habituation, see Kastenbaum (1980–1981).

learning. The speed with which individuals habituate varies considerably; once learned, habituation tends to be a widely applied skill. Habituation is a way of ignoring millions of small changes that occur in both self and environment. Kastenbaum (1980–1981) has suggested that psychological symptoms of aging may in fact be the result of overhabituation. The person has become so habituated that he or she is aware of very little new information and as a result may seem psychologically stagnant. To the extent that people live in familiar environments and experience only very gradual changes in themselves, habituation may mean that they perceive very little need to adapt. Optimal habituation is somewhere between being so overhabituated that no adjustment seems needed and being so underhabituated that every small change seems to require attention. Habituation generally lowers the perceived need for attention and adjustment, and may increase with age. This latter possibility needs to be studied.

Like adaptation in general, *continuity* can be both internal and external. The term *internal continuity* refers to the persistence of a personal structure of ideas based on memory. The term *external continuity* refers to living in familiar environments and interacting with familiar people. Continuity does not mean that nothing changes. Rather, it means that new life experiences occur against a solid backdrop of familiar and relatively persistent attributes and processes for both the self and the environment. One of the most frequent findings in gerontology is that continuity overshadows change for most people in midlife and after. This finding is true for internal aspects such as personality and self as well as for external aspects such as relationships, housing, community residence, activities, and life-styles. *Continuity is an adaptive response to both internal and external pressures.*

Internal pressures toward continuity come from our basic need for stable viewpoints concerning ourselves and the world we live in that we can use as a basis for anticipating what will happen and deciding how to respond to what does happen. Epstein (1980) has pointed out that these constructs are often preconscious and that the individual may not be aware of them as viewpoints or be able to describe them. Once developed, these viewpoints exert pressure toward continuity because of the nature of assimilation. Assimilation requires that new information be reconciled with the old; therefore, the more experience that is contained in memory, the less effect new information could be expected to have. As mentioned in Chapter 3, this is why new information does not have the same weight for older people that it does for youngsters and also why it reinforces the appearance of conservatism in the aged. The greater the weight of previous evidence, the greater the pressure toward continuity. Thus, the more experienced the person (and usually the older), the higher the likelihood that new information will be interpreted as continuity and thus not requiring adaptation. The focus of internal continuity is a unique past history; therefore, what seems to be continuity for one person may not to another.

We defend our personal viewpoints, once they are developed, because we define them as necessary for our security and survival. And *the more vulnerable the person sees him- or herself to be, the stronger the internal motivation for continuity.* This is why older people in institutions so often think and talk about the past. Their present offers them little opportunity to reinforce their images of themselves as capable and self-reliant people, so they concentrate their attention in such a way that they can maintain ties to their pasts. Older people who are involved in current activities in the community are not nearly so likely to focus on the past.

External pressures for continuity come from environmental reinforcement and from the demands of the roles we occupy. Environments condition us to fit them, and to the extent that environmental demands remain relatively constant, there is pressure for continuity in our responses. For example, I have a garage door that often does not close completely, and I have gradually become conditioned to the need to check it. So long as the door remains the way it is, I will continue to check it. My dryer has a timer that is supposed to buzz when the dryer stops, but it doesn't always work. I have been conditioned to set the timer on my stove as a backup so I don't end up with a load of wrinkled clothes. I could give hundreds of examples of things that I do over and over again because I have been conditioned to do so by my environment, and so could you. To the extent that older people live in familiar environments, conditioning exerts pressure for continuity.

The people we interact with in the roles we play expect us to remain the same from time to time. They want us to be predictable, which of course involves maintaining continuity in our actions, appearance, mannerisms, and thoughts. But lest we think that this expectation overly constrains our freedom, remember that we also have internal motives for wanting the same thing. In addition, the constraints of continuity provide us with useful guidelines for deciding how to adapt to change. Obviously, *the more relationships a person is involved in, the greater the potential for external pressures for continuity.*

Conflict management involves placing experiences in a context that changes our perceptions of the conflict from "negative" to "positive" or at least neutral. We can use various mechanisms to accomplish this shift, and Vaillant (1977) found that some were more effective than others.

The most effective mechanisms of conflict management included altruism, humor, sublimation, anticipation, and suppression (Vaillant, 1977:80). *Altruism* is a type of unselfishness that allows people to see their own needs in a context that includes the needs of others. *Humor* allows people to defuse the anger associated with conflict by focusing on its comical elements. *Sublimation* directs the energies produced by conflict into constructive and socially acceptable channels. *Anticipation* is the capacity to perceive future conflicts clearly, and as a result minimize their effects. *Suppression* is the ability to cope with conflict by putting it out of one's consciousness temporarily. All these very effective strategies are skills or habits of mind. They all involve learning how to adapt to life without persistently denying or severely distorting one's own nature or the situation within which one is trying to adapt.

People can also react to conflict in less adaptive ways. People who wanted sexual freedom in their youth but were afraid to go for it become staunch puritans with regard to their children's sexuality. People may permanently repress their internal conflicts over care of an aged parent, only to have them resurface later as seemingly irrational fears that they themselves will not be cared for when the need arises. People who experience conflict in their relationships with others may respond by adopting overly rigid approaches to people. People who make mountains out of molehills are often trying to shift their emotional attention away from what to them are real mountains (Vaillant, 1977:139). Some people cope with conflict by becoming too "sick" to deal with it. People sometimes turn anger on themselves in an attempt to preserve important social relationships that nevertheless are in conflict.

The habitual pattern of coping with conflict people learned in the process of growing up and the amount of conflict both affect the selection of mechanisms of conflict reduction. Through a combination of disposition, guidance, and luck, most people develop the ability to adapt effectively when conflict is at its "normal," or usual, level. However, *as the amount of conflict increases above its usual level, the probability increases that a less effective mechanism may be activated.* The usual level of conflict fluctuates widely from person to person. Some people thrive on large amounts of conflict (Lieberman, 1975), and others try to avoid conflict at all costs. Most people operate somewhere in between.

Goals of Adaptation

As shown earlier, aging brings new opportunities for freedom and autonomy. But it also can bring physical and social constraints on what people are able or allowed to do. It often brings losses of relationships and activities. And it changes instrumental needs and resources.

In adapting to these changes, individuals seek first to preserve continuity, for the reasons given earlier. But this motivation for continuity is also in part based on the perception that continuity is the best way to achieve certain ends. First, continuity of life-style and residence is seen as a way of preserving one's ability to meet instrumental needs for food, clothing, shelter, and transportation. Second, continuity of roles and activities is seen as an effective way to maintain one's capacity to meet socioemotional needs for interaction and support. Third, continuity of independence and personal effectiveness is seen as the best way to maintain one's self-esteem.

A second major focus of adaptation in later life is to allow a gradual shift in life purpose. As people grow older, many find that achievement, social position, and acquisition of wealth or property are no longer their most important life goals. Instead they want to concentrate their attention on personal qualities such as being dependable and reliable, being self-reliant, or having good relationships with their families.

Specific Adaptations

In this section we look at how older people typically adapt to specific changes. We consider how people adjust to reduced financial resources, increased physical dependency, lost roles and activities, declining independence and personal effectiveness, and new life goals.

Adapting to Less Income

The major way that older people adapt to reduced financial resources is learning to make do with less. Certainly a large part of the adjustment to reduced income in retirement is made easier by the fact that employment expenses such as transportation or special clothing are no longer required. However, much economizing is still necessary if most retired couples are to make ends meet, which the vast majority do. Single retired people often face a very difficult financial situation, because (see Chapter 8) retirement income for single individuals averages only about 40 percent of preretirement income.

Relatively little research has been done on how people cope specifically with reduced incomes. Douglass (1982) studied the impact of the rapid rise in fuel costs for home heating on the elderly living in Michigan. He found that 40 percent cut down on their expenditures for food and another 16 percent did without needed medical care in order to pay their fuel bills. The elderly often have no frills in their budgets that can be cut out in order to deal with unanticipated expenses, so they must dip into the most flexible items in their budget—food and medical care.

Many of us live well above what we actually need in order to enjoy satisfying lives. In this respect, retired people can offer the rest of us an example of how to get by on less without sacrificing the enjoyment of living. We need more research on the *processes* people go through in making this adaptation.

Adapting to Increased Dependency

Coping with increased physical infirmity and disability cannot be an easy matter for adults who have not only been responsible for themselves but for others as well. A major task is to learn how to accept assistance from others without losing one's self-respect. We know that many older people are able to learn to do so, but very little study has been made of *how* they learn to do so. Lieberman (1975) suggested that people who are able to adjust well to increased dependency need two things. They need sufficient physical and mental resources to mobilize energy that can be used to adapt, and they need to be tough-minded and stubborn about their own worth. For example, the "nice" older people who moved into institutions did not fare nearly so well as those who were aggressive, irritating, narcissistic, and demanding (Lieberman, 1975). In other words, it may take a big ego to accept assistance effectively. Certainly it must take a sturdy one. Fortunately, as noted earlier, most older people have high self-esteem.

Adapting to Lost Roles or Activities

Gerontologists have paid more attention to the problem of adapting to the loss of roles and activities than they have to the preceding topics. When people lose activities or roles, they can react in three possible ways. They can replace the losses with new roles or activities, they can concentrate their energies on the roles and activities that remain, or they can withdraw. These approaches are called *substitution, consolidation,* and *disengagement,* respectively.

Substitution

When people lose certain roles or the capacity to perform certain activities, an obvious way to adapt is to find a substitute (Friedmann and Havighurst, 1954; Havighurst, 1963).[2] How feasible this avenue is depends on a number of factors. First, substitutes must be available. Second, the person must have the physical and mental capacity to perform a substitute role or activity effectively. Finally, the person must *want* a substitute.

Substitutes are often not readily available. Retired people often cannot easily find new jobs; widows cannot easily find new mates. If roles or activities are lost through income decline or physical decline, then substitution is not a very available strategy. And to the extent that the person has been too active, he or she may not want to look for a replacement for lost activity. Thus, although substitution may be a feasible and attractive way to cope with loss early in life, with age it becomes increasingly more difficult to put into practice. Nevertheless, activity levels remain quite high as long as the elderly do not become disabled.

Consolidation

Consolidation of commitments and redistribution of available energy is another way to cope with lost roles, activities, or capacities. People who are involved in several roles and a variety of activities may not need to find a substitute for lost roles. They may find it easier simply to redistribute their time and energies among their remaining roles and activities. The general level of activity that results from this redistribution may be on a par with the preloss level, or may be somewhat reduced.

For example, retirement is a very common role loss that involves consolidation for most people. When Mr. A retired, the time he spent on the job became available for other activities. He now sleeps about an hour longer

---

[2] This approach is often called "activity theory" because it implies that older people want to maintain high levels of activity.

than he did when he was employed. He spends more time than he used to reading the morning paper. In good weather, he spends the rest of his morning puttering around in his yard. He fixes his lunch—usually a sandwich and a beer, and then straightens up the house. Around 3 P.M. he walks to a nearby cafe where he has coffee and talks with some of his friends, some of whom are retired and some not. Around 4:30, Mr. A goes home and starts supper. He has always liked cooking, and since he retired he has more or less taken over the job of preparing evening meals for himself and his wife, who still works. Nothing in Mr. A's day is new to him. What has changed is the distribution of time and energy he devotes to activities he has done most of his adult life. As a result, Mr. A's home is in the best condition ever, Mrs. A is delighted to have less housework to do, and Mr. A is proud of the good adjustment he has made to retirement.

The consolidation approach is available to most people. However, some people have so few roles or activities that when they lose some of them, the ones remaining are not able to absorb the energies freed by the loss. Unless they can find a substitute, these people are forced to disengage. Consolidation also may not be a satisfactory solution if the lost activity was extremely important to the person and if the remaining activities, though perhaps plentiful, are not able to serve as the basis for a meaningful life.

Disengagement

Disengagement occurs when people withdraw from roles or activities and reduce their activity level or sense of involvement. Based on their work in Kansas City in the 1950s, Cumming and Henry (1961) theorized that the turning inward typical of aging people produced a natural and normal withdrawal from social roles and activities, an increasing preoccupation with self, and decreasing involvement with others. Individual disengagement was conceived as primarily a psychological process involving withdrawal of interest and commitment. Social withdrawal was a consequence of individual disengagement, coupled with society's withdrawal of opportunities and interest in older people's contributions (societal disengagement).

The disengagement theory caused a flurry of research because, in positing the "normality" of withdrawal, it challenged the conventional wisdom that keeping active was the best way to deal with aging. After 20 years of research, it is clear that disengagement is neither natural nor inevitable and that most cases of disengagement occur as a result of a lack of opportunities for continued involvement (Atchley, 1971b: Roman and Taietz, 1967; Carp, 1968).

Streib and Schneider (1971) suggested that *differential disengagement* was more likely than total disengagement. That is, people withdraw from some activities but increase or maintain their involvement in others. This approach is similar to the consolidation approach mentioned earlier. Troll (1971) supported this notion when she talked of disengagement *into* the family, which meant that older people coped with lost roles by increasing their involvement with their families.

Disengagement theory went astray at many points (Hochschild, 1975). Because it was based on observations of older people in the 1950s, it dealt with people who were trying to adapt to a much more adverse situation than the situation since 1965, particularly in terms of retirement income and public attitudes toward the aged. Perhaps more people did disengage in those days, but it is certain that they do not do so now. However, in my opinion the results that Cumming and Henry (1961) attributed to a voluntary process of psychological disengagement were probably the unconscious results of habituation and continuity. Remember, if someone is habituated then he or she pays relatively little attention. This inattentiveness could look like disengagement. Also, when people are threatened, their motivation for continuity increases, which in turn means that they restrict their activities to those areas where habituation is likely to be the highest. The fact that relatively few people appear disengaged today compared to the 1950s may thus be the result of the improved living conditions and attitudes toward the elderly, which in turn may have reduced the degree of threat perceived by the elderly. If this hypothesis is true, then whenever living conditions for the elderly worsen, we would expect a larger percentage of them to appear to be withdrawn and stagnant.

Implications

None of the preceding approaches to coping with lost roles and activities is a successful model by itself. People can be found who fit each of them. The real question is "What proportion of people fit which model?" Right now the consolidation approach seems to be the most inclusive, partly because it allows the greatest flexibility.

The balance among the three outcomes that role or activity loss can have depends partly on social conditions. Opportunities to replace lost roles and activities determine the availability of substitution. Norms about what is acceptable or proper for older people affect what friends and relatives advise in coping with role loss. Consolidation may be the most common outcome because it preserves continuity both for the individual and for those around him or her. Clark and Anderson (1967) refer to it as the "path of least resistance." Disengagement may depend very much on how threatened by their environment older people feel.

Finally, the balance among consolidation, substitution, and disengagement depends very heavily on health. Good health is a prerequisite for the consolidation and substitution approaches to coping with role and activity losses. People in poor health are much more likely to be forced into disengagement.

Coping with Threats to Self-Concept and Self-Esteem

Declining independence and increasing vulnerability threaten older people's self-concepts. The major ways that they can cope with these threats are by using the defense mechanisms covered in Chapter 3, developing an acceptance of themselves as aging people, and emphasizing their maintained competence.

Older people can use the past to sustain an image of themselves as worthwhile. This is easier to do in a group of friends or in a community of long-time residents because people one interacts with tend to share the older person's view of the past and may well have participated with the older person in creating his or her personal history. When we interact with older people whom we do not know, we must keep in mind that their talking about their past is their way of telling us the basis for their self-esteem.

People who are becoming less independent are most likely to use the past in this way, and they are also most likely to have to deal with service providers who are essentially strangers. This fact no doubt has added to the stereotype that "older people live in the past." I once interviewed the superintendent of a county home for the aged who had included this statement in the brochure for the home. His experience with older people coming into an institution for older people who were financially but not physically dependent had convinced him that the stereotype was true of all older people.

Relative appreciation can allow people to minimize the importance of their dependencies by comparing themselves with other older people who are worse off. Selective interaction and selective perception allow people to concentrate their attention on people and messages that support their own view of themselves and to avoid those that do not.

But note that these defenses gradually lose their power as the person becomes more and more dependent. At the point where the person becomes bedfast either at home or in an institution, he or she loses the control necessary to use defenses such as selective interaction. And the shift in power that accompanies severe dependency means that the older person can no longer influence people to accept relative appreciation or past accomplishments as valid bases for his or her self-concepts. This shift explains why the behavior of older people in institutions often appears stange. They are among strangers in a situation in which their self-concepts are severely threatened and in which they have few resources with which to defend them. As a result they may be combative, apprehensive, untrusting, and anxious.

Many young people do not understand why some older people show anger when younger people try to help them. This anger is based on their perception that their image of self-sufficiency is being threatened. Older people hold self-reliance as one of their most important values. As a result, they try to do things for themselves as long as possible and to resist letting anyone know that there may be times when they cannot do it. This tendency is a major reason why many older people gradually let their homes deteriorate. They know that their homes are not in the condition that they would wish, but they do not want to have people coming in who may realize how helpless they are at times. The problem can reach pathetic extremes, as in the case of Mrs. D, who had lived alone for many years, had become a hermit in her own home, and had recently refused to let anyone in. Finally, neighbors complained of rats in the area, and a health department worker was sent to investigate. He had to obtain a court order and be accompanied by police before Mrs. D would let him in. When they entered, the sights and smells were overpowering. Trash lay everywhere, with narrow paths between pieces of furniture that Mrs. D used. The house smelled strongly of urine. There was evidence of rats, and the house was completely infested with roaches. Most people on hearing this story would conclude that Mrs. D was not of sound mind, but she was. Her story graphically illustrates the lengths to which people will sometimes go to avoid dependency.

It is most important that older people have some way to maintain a sense of competence. We need to work with them to see how they would like to accomplish this goal, and we should be as flexible as possible in accommodating their preferences. Their views can be somewhat unrealistic so long as behavior that endangers themselves or others is not the result.

Nevertheless, learning to accept a definition of competence appropriate for an aging individual is also useful. At some point it is adaptive for the older person to acknowledge that some activities can no longer be done as successfully as when he or she was younger. This recognition is an important prerequisite for the person's conservation of energy. It is also important for the elderly to recognize that social norms impose very real limits on what one is allowed to do as an older person. One need not *like* these limits, only accept their reality. Clark and Anderson (1967) found that people tended to try to deny aging and its effects in two ways. The first was by trying to avoid the appearance of aging by the use of cosmetics, hair dyes, figure control devices, and so on. A second way that people sought to deny aging was by attributing limitations to sickness rather than to aging.

Some people seek to deny aging by refusing to go along with rules that exclude them from participation and by fighting the system. In itself, this strategy is not bad if the person is indeed still capable. However, it is maladaptive when the individual's level of functioning means that continuation is not a real possibility. For example, Mr. G had played in the Thursday afternoon men's golf league at a local golf course for over 20 years, and at age 68 he was very proud that he was still capable of playing. But by age 70 Mr. G was no longer able to keep up with the other players in the league. When the league secretary asked him to drop out and allow a substitute to play for him, Mr. G refused. He spoke heatedly with individual members of the league about the unfairness of the request but got little support, because most of the players agreed with the league secretary. By refusing to withdraw, Mr. G forced the league to exclude him formally. In the process, Mr. G probably became more depressed than if he had made the decision himself.

In addition to accepting changes in one's concept of activities and roles that are part of the self, it is also useful to accept changes in the criteria that are used to evaluate the self and that serve as the basis for self-esteem. Regardless of one's personal capacities to continue as an older person in positions of leadership and to further one's achievements, societal disengagement and age discrimination combine to make continuation an unrealistic goal for many older people. Moving toward less emphasis on position and achievement as personal goals is typical of older people, and thus most people seem to accomplish this adaptive change.

But there is probably no easy way to help those older people who resist being realistic about either their capacities or their opportunities. A certain amount of realism is necessary for adaptation, and almost the only thing one can do is to tell the truth in as kind a way as possible. It is also essential to be sure that the limits one is trying to get an older person to accept are indeed genuine and not based on one's own age biases.

Most people can adapt to changes without losing their self-esteem because most never become so disabled that they lose their sense of continuity. Even among people in institutions a sizable proportion are able to maintain a sense of integrity with their pasts. But people—both in the community and in institutions—who perceive that changes in themselves or in their social situations have produced a negative discontinuity are likely to feel bad about themselves and to be depressed. Some try to escape their situation through isolation, alcohol, drugs, and even suicide.

Escape Rather Than Adaptation

Why do some people confront and resolve the conflicts posed by aging while others choose various forms of escape? Based on bits and pieces of information on various forms of escape, a picture begins to emerge of a process that leads people to seek escape. People who encounter many losses are prone to seek escape. Although social supports from the community, family, and friends often can lead the person out of escapism, some people perceive their losses as too great to be coped with. Others see the available "solutions" to their problems as involving intolerable compromises. For these people, escape is a preferred alternative.

We should not assume that escape is always an irrational choice. For some people, it is the most viable alternative given their values. Some people are able to gain the degree of escape they need by withdrawal, alcohol, tranquilizers, or some combination of the three. For others, the pain is too great, and they eventually choose suicide.

Isolation

Bennett (1980) reviewed 20 years of research on social isolation in the elderly and found that isolation in later life was connected to the past. Many aged isolates had been isolates their entire adult lives. Others had been outgoing earlier and had only become isolates in later life. Some were voluntary isolates, and others became isolates as a result of changing circumstances such as widowhood.

Those who use isolation as an adaptive strategy tend to be free to withdraw from interactions and roles that they define as unsatisfactory. Retirement, widowhood, and divorce are examples of changes that can free people to choose isolation. Lowenthal and Berkman (1967) found that mental illness tended to lead to social isolation. Thus, we could expect that people who have difficulty in getting along with others (one symptom of mental illness) would be more likely to withdraw in later life, particularly in reaction to conflicts over their own self-concepts.

Bennett (1980) found that social isolation prior to moving to an institution was associated with difficulty in adjusting to the institution. She concluded that this difficulty was the result of "desocialization" in which the individuals forgot what they had learned earlier in life about conformity to norms and how to get on with others. However, another possible interpretation is that people who choose isolation are already having difficulty conforming and getting along with others and that is why they choose isolation.

In the Scripps Foundation longitudinal study of adaptation (Atchley, 1982), I and my colleagues found that less than 1 percent of our older respondents were voluntary isolates who had chosen low levels of social activity. This finding suggests that isolation is a seldom-used adaptive strategy.

Alcohol

Zimberg (1974) reviewed the literature on alcohol use in later life and concluded that about 15 percent of the elderly have serious alcohol problems and that the proportion is as high as 40 percent in some urban neighborhoods. Mishara and Kastenbaum (1980) put the figure somewhat lower, 8 percent for older men and only about 1 percent for older women. The elderly are less likely to have alcohol problems than are younger age categories. For example, the incidence of problem drinking is twice as high among men age 21 to 39 as among those 60 and over.

Zimberg (1974) found that there were two types of older alcoholics— long-term alcoholics who had grown older and people who had become alcoholics in later life. As yet no reliable estimates exist of what proportion of older people have turned to alcohol in later life, although we know that some do. People who become problem drinkers in later life are usually responding to depression and boredom, which are often associated with life changes such as widowhood or physical decline (Butler and Lewis, 1973).

Drugs

Anxiety sometimes accompanies the changes that aging brings, physicians often prescribe tranquilizers to alleviate these anxieties, and tranquilizers sometimes become a permanent way to cope with aging. In one study, tranquilizers accounted for 35 to 40 percent of the medication prescribed for older Medicaid patients in Illinois, Ohio, and New Jersey (Butler and Lewis, 1973:249). Of the top 20 drugs commonly prescribed for older adults, 12 are tranquilizers. Tranquilizers such as Librium can become addictive, in that emotional dependence develops and physical withdrawal symptoms can occur if the drug is withheld.

Suicide

Suicide is a disturbing and fascinating subject for most of us. We have a deep-seated drive to learn why suicides occur, why some people purposefully reject what most of us value highest—life itself. Suicide is related to age for men, but not for women.[3] Suicide rates increase steadily from age 15 to age 85 for men, with around 60 suicides per 100,000 men at age 85 and over (Atchley, 1980a). Most of the literature on the subject starts by assuming that suicide is more common among the elderly and then proceeds to speculate about why age is related to suicide. Bereavement, social isolation, failing health, depression, sexual frustrations, and retirement have all been suggested as causes of suicide in the elderly. However, these factors are usually more common among women than among men. Therefore we cannot use

[3]Age is correlated with suicide for men in all countries for which the cause of death statistics are reliable, but for women the picture is mixed. For example, in German-speaking countries, women's suicide rates tend to be highly correlated with age, but in English-speaking countries they are not (Atchley, 1980a).

them to explain suicides, because male suicide rates at the older ages are seven times higher than those of women. Many of the proposed explanations look good on the surface but do not stand up under close examination. For example, it is widely held that suicide is related to retirement. However, if we look at the suicide data we find that from age 55 to 70—the prime years for retirement to occur—there is relatively little change in the suicide rate and that after age 70 the suicide rate increases sharply. Although some people no doubt commit suicide as a result of retirement, if retirement-related suicide were a systematic trend, such a trend would appear in the suicide data.

Menninger (1938) proposed a classification of suicide motives into the wish to kill, the wish to be killed, and the wish to die. Analysis of suicide notes indicates that the elderly are much more likely than other age groups to see suicide as a release. Their motive is simply to be dead. The individual reasons for this choice are many, and no single or simple explanation can encompass the wide variety of situations that lead to suicide. Nevertheless, certain groups of the elderly are at high risk. For example, very old men who have recently been widowed, who have recently been given a terminal diagnosis by a physician, or who have experienced rapid physical deterioration are all at high risk. Older people in institutions are high risks for suicide, especially if they receive no visitors. Older people who are severely depressed are at higher risk. Miller (1978) reported that in many cases older people gave clear clues that they were intending to kill themselves, but these clues were ignored. Generally, when older people suggest that they might kill themselves, they mean it. And when older people attempt suicide, they usually succeed. To stop elderly suicides, we have to prevent the attempt.

In addition to overt suicides, some older people die because they have given up. Failing to continue treatment for illnesses such as heart disease or diabetes, engaging in detrimental or dangerous activities, or neglecting one's health are all indirect ways to kill oneself. No one knows how many older people die as a result of such actions.

Successful Adaptation

But what of those people who do manage to cope with aging? How do we know that a person has successfully coped with aging? Whereas earlier we were concerned with the various means of adapting, here we are concerned with the *outcome* of the adaptive process. The internal adaptive process is successful if the person has a high degree of life satisfaction and if the person is able to remain relatively autonomous at least psychologically and able to maintain his or her sense of continuity. External adaptation is successful if the individual continues to receive rewards for participation.

If older people are satisfied with their present and past lives, they have adapted to aging. Havighurst et al. (1963) identified five components of life satisfaction:

1. *Zest*—showing vitality in several areas of life, being enthusiastic.

2. *Resolution and fortitude*—not giving up, taking the good with the bad and making the most of it, accepting responsibility for one's own personal life.

3. *Completion*—a feeling of having accomplished what one wanted to.

4. *Self-esteem*—thinking of oneself as a person of worth.

5. *Outlook*—being optimistic, having hope.

They developed a scale to measure these components of life satisfaction that has been used in hundreds of studies. The results indicate that a majority of the elderly have high life satisfaction, which means of course that on this very general criterion a majority has successfully adapted to aging. Harris and Associates (1975:161) found that when income was controlled, life satisfaction of the elderly was equal to or greater than that of younger age categories.

Autonomy is the perception that one is responsible for one's own life satisfaction. Continuity is the persistence of one's view of self and environment. These topics have been researched less than has life satisfaction. Williams and Wirths (1965) reported that 65 percent of their sample had successfully adapted to aging. In the Scripps Foundation longitudinal study of adaptation (Atchley, 1982), I and my colleagues found that about 55 percent of the elderly saw themselves as highly autonomous, and nearly 90 percent saw their lives as extensions of their pasts. These were relatively healthy older people who lived in a community setting. Lieberman (1975) reported that failure to preserve a sense of continuity occurred in about half of their subjects who moved into institutions. Thus, those who remain in community settings are much more likely to adapt successfully, compared to those who enter institutions.

External adaptation involves adjusting to aging so as to maintain participation in social life and to continue to receive the rewards it brings. Most older people adapt well in terms of maintaining informal social ties, but are generally unsuccessful in retaining formal ties, as a result of age discrimination.

Thus, given sufficient instrumental resources, the vast majority of the elderly cope well with aging both internally and in their informal relationships. At this point, let us look at a case of successful adaptation to aging.

A Case of Successful Adaptation to Aging

Clark and Anderson (1967) cite the following interesting case history of a person who had aged successfully.

> We first saw Mr. Ed Hart when he was ninety years old. He was born in 1870, the only child of middle-aged parents. He started working and contributing significantly to the household budget at a very early age; while still in his teens, he turned over his considerable savings to his parents, enabling them to purchase a home. Still in his youth, he assumed a "parental" role toward his parents, being obliged to do so because much of his father's time was spent taking care of the then invalid mother. Mr. Hart attended school, learned cabinet making from his father, and devoted himself to caring for his parents.
>
> Mr. Hart idolized his father throughout his life. Cabinet work was always dear to him because it had been taught him by his father. He regarded his father's guidance as invaluable; it was he who kept his son away from the alcohol which he dearly loved, and it was also from his father that he acquired a sincere love for people. The relationship was a very harmonious one, each gladly accommodating himself to the wishes of the other. Although Mr. Hart married at the age of twenty-four, he and his wife continued to live with his parents until their death in 1912. Mr. Hart was closely attached to his wife, but his father had always remained the most important figure in his life.
>
> He was content with cabinet work until the age of thirty-five, at which time he bought a ranch, deciding to become a financial success for the sake of his children. He describes himself during this period as over-ambitious and given to excessive chronic worry. His preoccupation with making a fortune from this ranching endeavor led to a nervous breakdown and confinement in a sanitarium for two months. This experience, when he was about forty, proved to be the turning point of his life. He emerged with a highly integrated personality and a satisfying personal philosophy. He had formerly been a zealous member of the Methodist Church, but following his hospitalization, he eschewed all organized religions, feeling he needed no one to dictate to him how

he should serve God. Nonetheless, Mr. Hart expresses a profound belief in divinity, a love of his fellow man, a full acceptance of everything life has to offer, and an adamant refusal to be unhappy.

Following this hospitalization, Mr. Hart sold his ranch and worked as a vocational teacher for the following six years. Again, he found deep satisfaction in his work and was loved by students and fellow teachers alike. He showed great understanding and evidently displayed remarkable skill in nurturing the talents of his students, adapting his teaching to the individual child's potential. His dislike for the regimentation practiced in the school led him to resign and to return to his former vocation of cabinet making, work he pursued up to the age of fifty-five. An injury to his arm, however, finally made him give up this successful occupation (some of his work had been exhibited at the 1939 San Francisco International Exposition). For the next twenty years, he was employed in the hotel business, work that he found congenial because of his interest in people. Retirement did not find him idle. Up to the age of ninety, he did cabinet work as a hobby, manufacturing various items to present to his numerous friends.

Mr. Hart looks back on sixty-four years of harmonious and contented married life. His first wife died suddenly after twenty-five years of marriage when he was forty-nine years old. After living alone with his children for two years, he remarried at the age of fifty-one. Thirty years later, he lost his second wife, and it was upon her "last request" that he again married. His third wife had been a widowed friend they had both known for almost thirty years. This final marriage lasted for nine years. During the last two years of her lfe, the third wife was severely ill, and Mr. Hart nursed her through to the end. She died in 1960. Even during his last wife's terminal illness, Mr. Hart showed the same serenity and the same positive acceptance of life he expressed in all of our interviews with him. He does not differentiate among his wives: he describes them all as "dear, loyal women."

Mr. Hart finds it somewhat "humiliating" that he has outlived three wives and both of his sons. He took pains to raise his children as best he could and was anxious to let them develop their own individual ways. Rather than seeing himself as the provider of an estate, a role he had once thought so important, he finally perceived his parental role as that of the provider of good example and wise guidance. His close relationship with his sons changed when they married, and Mr. Hart believes that it is only right that this should be so: "With marriage the offspring form independent units of their own, and parents should release their hold upon them." Mr. Hart was never possessive in his life. The persons closest to him at present are his daughter and stepdaughter, who are equally dear. He mentions with pride that both have invited him to come and live with them, but he will not take this step until it is absolutely necessary. He does not wish to inconvenience them, but unlike many other of our subjects, he does not harp on the prospect of "becoming a burden" to somebody else.

From his middle years onward, Mr. Hart suffered a number of major illnesses: in 1926 he was operated on for a bilateral hernia; and in 1949, for a perforated ulcer; finally, a prostatectomy and colostomy in 1953 (he was eighty-three years old at the time) resulted in a complete loss of control over his bladder, requiring him to wear a urinal twenty-four hours a day. When he was ninety, his physical condition no longer permitted him to indulge in his hobby of woodworking, and, at ninety-three his failing eyesight ruled out television and limited his reading to one hour a a day. Yet he takes his declining physical functions in stride, not finding it irksome to make necessary adjustments. His mental faculties have remained remarkably intact. He is keenly aware that few men his age are as mentally alert as he is, or have aged as gracefully. He is proud of this fact and attributes it to the philosophical orientation he has worked out for himself and incorporated into his life.

Although Mr. Hart has been obliged to curtail many of his social activities, he still corresponds with numerous friends and receives almost daily visits from solicitous neighbors. He gives much of himself and is warmly appreciated by others; he appears to bring out the best in others, which may be one of the reasons he claims he has never been disappointed by a friend. Mr. Hart has led a full, creative, and serene existence. It is perhaps because his life has been one of fulfillment that he is ready to surrender it at any moment; he still finds life quite enjoyable, but he is as willing to die as he is to continue living.

This man has made a profound impression on all our interviewers. They found him alert, intelligent, serene, and wise. His self-acceptance is complete. He found it difficult to answer our self-image questions or to describe himself in terms of the list of various personality traits we submitted to him; he simply stated, more appropriately, "I'm Ed Hart and I don't want be anyone else—I will be the same ten years from now, if I'm alive."

According to American middle-class standards, Mr. Hart has not been a particularly successful man. Looking at his life in one way, he has no particular reason not to be disappointed with his past and depressed with his present. He failed in his one great effort to become wealthy. After a nervous breakdown, he gave up on this venture altogether. He quit a second time when he dropped out of the teaching profession because he disagreed with established policy. One might expect him to be bitter about this, or terribly lonely, since he has outlived nearly all his friends and relatives—but he is neither. Crippled with disease, forced to wear a urinal at all times, and nearly blind, Mr. Hart gave one of our interviewers his philosophy of life: 'I have an original motto which I follow: 'All things respond to the call of rejoicing; all things gather where life is a song.'''

It is clear that Mr. Hart has adapted to aging. He has admitted to and accepted physical limitations, first giving up the demanding manual labor of cabinet making, and later retiring without regret from hotel work.

Mr. Hart has no problems in controlling his life space—he does not over-extend himself: "As long as I don't strain myself, I'm okay. I take it easy. The other day I declined an invitation to go on board a ship, since I knew there would be stairs there."

All his life, Mr. Hart has successfully practiced substitution, so this adaptation has been natural for him. He enjoyed married life and never remained a widower for long. He was capable of substituting one vocation for another, as necessity required, developing a deep interest and satisfaction in each. Even after his retirement from hotel work, his last job, he continued to be interested and active in union affairs. "That's my pork chop, so to speak," he says.

In personal philosophy, Mr. Hart has no problems at all. His standards for self-evaluation are not predicated on mutable factors such as productivity, wealth, or social status. He is first, last, and always himself: "I'm Ed Hart and I don't want to be anyone else." This is a standard not likely to totter with age.

However, his discovery of adaptive values and life goals was hard-won: at forty, he early found himself unable to cope with the instrumental and achievement-oriented values of his society. He suffered a severe emotional upheaval at that time, was hospitalized for a period, and emerged with a warm humanistic philosophy which has carried him not only through middle-age, but through old age as well. [Clark and Anderson, 1967:415–419, reprinted by permission]

Summary

Adaptation is both an internal and an external process. Internally, it involves the assimilation of new information about changes in the self and in the environment. Externally, it involves the modification of behavior to accommodate changing demands of the social world. Obviously, these internal and external aspects of adaptation interact.

Habituation, continuity, and conflict management are three general means of adaptation. Habituation involves learning not to pay attention to nonessential aspects of the environment. Optimum habituation occurs when the individual has the skill to ignore trivial changes but to pay attention to changes that require conscious action in order to adapt. The lack of attention to the environment that occurs in some older people may be overhabituation rather than disengagement.

Maintaining continuity of personal viewpoints and familiar associations and environments is an adaptive response to both internal and external pressures. Internal pressures for continuity come from the need to make new information consistent with the old. The older the individual, the greater the backlog of information with which new information must be reconciled, and the greater the likelihood of continuity. Individuals who feel threatened by change feel more pressure to stick with tried and true ways of doing things than others do.

External pressures for continuity are exerted by the conditioning we receive from our environments and by the demands of the roles we play. The more consistent the individual's environments and the greater the number and familiarity of the person's relationships with others, the greater the external pressures for continuity.

Aging can bring a greater perception of threat, usually brings a large backlog of experience, and increases the duration of residence in a given environment and participation in a given set of relationships. Therefore aging very greatly increases the pressures for continuity as an adaptive strategy.

Continuity is also a means for maintaining the capacity to meet instrumental needs, needs for interaction and support, and needs for sources of self-esteem.

Conflict management involves transforming negative energy associated with conflict into a more positive form. Altruism, humor, sublimation, anticipation, and suppression are adaptive mechanisms that can be used to manage conflict. Less effective means include repression, rigidity, overreaction, and self-hatred. People usually develop a habitual pattern of coping with what for them is a normal amount of conflict. Aging can increase the amount of conflict. As the amount of conflict increases above the "normal" level for the individual, the probability also increases that less effective means will be used to handle it.

Specific adaptations to aging include learning to live on a lower income, learning to accept help from others without losing one's self-respect, coping with lost roles and activities, and coping with threats to self-esteem.

We don't know very much about how people adjust to lowered incomes. As long as the reduction is less than 50 percent, most people seem to be able to adjust somehow. But when the reduction is greater, financial dependency is likely to result. Older people cope with unexpected demands on their incomes by cutting down on food and needed medical care.

Physical energy and solid self-concepts help people adjust to needing assistance from others. Most older people have both. Nevertheless, because of the high value most people place on self-reliance, there is great potential for both internal and external conflict for older people who must rely on others for financial or physical assistance.

Most older people cope with role losses by redirecting their time and attention within the roles and activities that remain. Those who are younger, healthier, and more financially secure are more likely to be able to substitute for lost roles and activities. Disengagement, which is not very common, is usually imposed by age discrimination or ill health rather than being a voluntary choice.

Threats to self-esteem are dealt with through selective interaction, selective perception, use of the past, and relative appreciation. Sometimes they are dealt with by increasing isolation. To maintain a sense of competence in later life, it is also useful to develop a self-concept as an aging person that incorporates real changes in both capacities and opportunities. By revising the ideal self, people can maintain self-esteem.

Most older people are able to maintain a sense of continuity and meaning throughout later life. But a few experience changes so great that, rather than try to adapt, they try to escape through isolation, drugs, alcohol, and suicide.

Less than 1 percent of the elderly apparently become isolates in an attempt to escape from the realities of their situation. Many more turn to alcohol. As much as 10 percent of the elderly have drinking problems, although we do not know what percentage have turned to alcohol only in later life and how many for whom alcohol abuse represents the continuation of a lifelong pattern. Perhaps 10 percent of the elderly are also taking tranquilizers routinely and are essentially addicted to them. Many of these people also have problems with alcohol abuse.

Suicide is not very common, but men over age 70 are much more likely to commit suicide than any other age and sex category in the United States. Factors that expose older people to high suicide risk include severe depression, recent bereavement, terminal diagnosis for a physical ailment, rapid physical deterioration, and living in an institution and having no visitors.

Other factors such as retirement are occasionally associated with suicide, but not often enough to represent a trend.

Family and community supports are often successful in helping older people to abandon escapism. But in the case of clues to an impending suicide, it is important to act quickly. When older people mention suicide, they are often serious, and if they attempt suicide they usually succeed on the first try.

Success of one's adaptation to aging can be judged from the subjective level by life satisfaction and a sense of autonomy and continuity. Well over half of the elderly (about 60 percent) have adapted to aging quite well by these criteria, and perhaps another 25 percent could be said to have adapted adequately. The overall adaptation of the elderly is not much lower than the level for people under 55. Older people also adapt well in terms of maintaining their participation in social life. Only age discrimination and disability seem to thwart the adaptive attempts of a majority of those who experience them.

Given sufficient health and instrumental resources, the elderly are quite able to adapt to aging. The "problems" they encounter are more often social in origin than simply due to personal aging. These social problems are discussed in the next (the last) chapter.

Chapter 13

Aging as a Social Problem

This chapter briefly reviews what we have learned thus far about aging individuals and where in their lives problems are most likely to arise. It then examines age discrimination, social inequality, and disability as social problems that seriously interfere with the ability of many older people to adapt optimally to aging. The chapter then looks at some solutions that might help and finally considers aging and the future.

Individual Aging

Throughout this book, several themes occur repeatedly. First, the physical, psychological, and social effects of aging on an individual are not very predictable. Very few changes occur in all aging individuals, and there is considerable variation in when changes begin and the rate at which they occur.

Most people experience some physical and psychological decrements in functioning, beginning in middle age, but these changes seldom limit the individual seriously. Social continuity minimizes these effects of aging by allowing people to function in familiar environments and to use practiced skills. Compensation and practice minimize sensory and psychomotor changes and also help to maintain intellectual functioning.

Most adults have stable personalities and high self-esteem which are maintained in later life by social continuity and by various defenses such as selective perception or selective interaction. Aging usually occurs so gradually that it does not produce a "crisis" in terms of personality or self-concept.

About three-fourths of Americans currently are living out their lives without experiencing severe losses connected with aging. The changes associated with aging are usually well within the individual's physical, psychological, and social coping capacities. Thus the elderly are usually capable people who continue to function adequately in their various adult roles.

Physical vulnerability increases with age, but not markedly so until age 75 to 80. Social vulnerability due to age discrimination begins much earlier— at age 45 to 50. People who are most likely to encounter difficulties as a result of aging are (1) the very old, (age 80 or older); (2) people of lower socioeconomic status; (3) women; (4) members of minority groups; and (5) residents of inner cities and rural areas. Losing control over one's activities, relationships, and environments is the change most likely to produce serious physical and psychological distress. This change is in turn most likely to occur as a result of disability, which is not very prevalent until age 75 to 80.

Most older people have adequate incomes, but about 30 percent do not. Those who do not tend to be single, female, black or Hispanic, rural residents, or very old. Social Security, Supplemental Security Income, and improved private pensions have dramatically improved the incomes of older Americans since 1965. Moreover, the structure of Social Security is essentially sound. Its current and long-range funding problems can be solved with relatively minor adjustments, provided we do not encounter a major economic depression.

Most older people have one or more chronic ailments, but these do not seriously limit activity in most cases. Medicare and Medicaid have greatly improved the general medical care of the elderly, but the cost of these programs is growing faster than revenues. Moreover, they do not adequately address the growing need for long-term care. Unless we begin now to expand health care facilities and services and develop a viable system to contain the growing cost of care, health care for the elderly will decline in quality.

Most older people live in independent households and want it that way. Federal subsidies for housing for the elderly and improved incomes of older people have greatly increased the proportion of older people living in independent households since 1962. Rapidly rising housing costs and federal cutbacks in subsidized housing will probably somewhat erode this improvement.

Transportation services connected with Older American Act programs have greatly improved access to transportation for older people unable to drive their own cars. Federal cutbacks will erode this improvement, too.

Thus, most older Americans have satisfactory incomes, housing, and transportation as a result of major advances in federal programs since 1965. The 1982 federal cutbacks threaten the elderly in all three of these very important areas.

Activities show a great deal of stability in middle age and later life. Most people are quite active throughout. Poor health is the major cause of low activity, followed by lower socioeconomic status. As people grow older, their activities tend to shift away from organized group activities outside the home toward at-home activities done alone or with a small group of friends.

This shift may or may not be a response to age discrimination, but it offers flexibility in dealing with ups and downs in health.

Most older people have satisfying relationships with their families and friends. More and more are going into retirement and later life as members of a couple. Most are not abandoned, neglected, or abused by their adult children. Intergenerational visiting and aid patterns are based on need and capacity rather than on some abstract notion of duty. Friendships tend to be maintained throughout adulthood. Lapsed relationships with family and friends may be revived in later life to compensate for losses that occur as friends and relatives die. Support systems made up of family and friends are available to over 80 percent of the very old.

Service needs of the elderly vary considerably across various service areas (e.g., mental health, physical health, rehabilitation, income mainte- nance, transportation, housing, housekeeping, long-term care, nutrition, rec- reation, or information and referral). Needs also vary from community to community. As a result, no single policy about services will meet the needs of the elderly. Nevertheless, federal guidelines covering a network of ser- vices to the elderly have greatly increased the availability of services in most areas of the Unites States since 1972.

Hence, the overall picture we get is that the physical and psychological changes associated with aging are within the coping capacities of the vast majority of older people. Retirement, the empty nest, and even widowhood are generally adapted to within a year's time.

Thus, for the vast majority today, the experience of aging is more postive than negative. But what about those for whom aging is mostly negative? How does this situation arise, and can anything be done about it?

Sometimes a negative impact of aging results from purely personal problems. For example, no matter how much money one has or how careful one has been, physical health can deteriorate or disability can occur. Income can be lost due to bad luck or mismanagement by trusted agents. People can encounter problems because they lacked the foresight or motivation to avoid them. For example, people are sometimes isolated because they never learned to get along with others.

But the most common vulnerabilities of older Americans result from flaws built into American society and its operation. The major social prob- lems that affect large numbers of older people are (1) age discrimination, (2) the continuation into later life of our system of social inequality, and (3) the obstacles that confront disabled people who want to participate in commu- nity life.

Age Discrimination

Age prejudice, or ageism, is a dislike of aging and older people based on the belief that aging makes people unattractive, unintelligent, asexual, unemployable, and senile (Comfort, 1976). It may be that only a quarter or less of the general public endorses this extreme and inaccurate view (McTavish, 1971), but most Americans probably subscribe to some erroneous beliefs about aging and have at least a mild degree of prejudice against aging and the aged. This notion is borne out by the research reviewed so far in this book.

If people kept their prejudices to themselves, no harm would result. But people act on their prejudices. *Age discrimination* is the treatment of people in some unjustly negative manner because of their chronological age and for no other reason. Age discrimination occurs when human beings are avoided or excluded in everyday activities because they are "the wrong age." Older people sometimes must *intrude* into various spheres of daily life in order to make people aware that they have something to offer. For example, 72-year-old Mrs. C was interested in community mental health programs for the elderly. She felt that her experience as a former member of the city council would be a useful addition to the local mental health association, and she volunteered to serve on the board. She was essentially told, 'Don't call us, we'll call you." Fortunately, Mrs. C had a few friends from "the old days" who put up a fuss, and Mrs. C was eventually allowed to serve on the mental health association board. She later served as its president and was quite involved until her death at age 81. Most older people are not willing to fight for this recognition, and a great deal of age segregation results in activities and interactions. Only in their families do older people usually escape this sort of informal age discrimination.

Equally important is the impact of age discrimination on opportunities for beginning or continuing participation in various organizations. As noted earlier, job discrimination makes it more difficult for older workers to continue in the labor force and if unemployed, to find jobs, The stigma of implied inability and the resulting discrimination sometimes extend past paying jobs and into volunteer jobs and other types of participation as well. Organizations especially designed for older adults offer an alternative to those who have been rejected by organizations in the "main stream," but at the cost of age segregation. Although many older adults prefer associating mainly with their age peers, those who do not often find themselves without choices. Research on age discrimination in nonjob organizational settings is greatly needed.

Age discrimination can also take the form of unequal treatment by public agencies. The U.S. Commission on Civil Rights (1977) found that age discrimination was present in many federally funded programs—community mental health centers, legal services, vocational rehabilitation, social services to low-income individuals and families, employment and training services, the food stamp program, Medicaid, and vocational education. And this problem existed in all regions of the country.

As their age increases, the more likely older people are to experience discrimination from public agencies. In addition, age discrimination was often compounded by discrimination on the basis of race, sex, national origin, or handicap status. The U.S. Commission on Civil Rights concluded that much of this discrimination stems from a narrow interpretation of legislative goals. For example, community health centers generally interpret "preventive health care" as applying only to children and adolescents. Directors of employment programs see their most appropriate clients to be males aged 22 to 44. Even age 22 is too old as far as some job *training* programs are concerned. The commission also found that state legislatures sometimes convert federal programs designed to serve all Americans into categorical programs aimed at specific age groups. For example, the state of Missouri passed a strong child abuse and neglect law—a worthy goal. But the state provided no funds to carry it out. Instead, federal funds for social services to everyone were earmarked to support the child abuse program, and as a result most Missouri cities discontinued their adult protective services programs. In many cases where states or local governments are responsible for defining the population eligible for federal programs, age discrimination results. For example, several states excluded older people from vocational rehabilition programs because they were not of "employable age." Age discrimination sometimes occurs when services are provided under contract with agencies that limit the ages of people they will serve. For example, a general social services contract with a child welfare agency is unlikely to result in social services to older adults. The commission also found that outreach efforts are often aimed at specific age groups, which lessens the probability that other age groups will find out about programs for which they are eligible.

The commission also concluded that general age discrimination in the public and private job market was an important underlying factor in age discrimination in employment, training, and vocational rehabilitation programs. As long as older people are denied jobs, agencies see little value in preparing them for jobs.[1]

Continuation of Social Inequalities

The continuation into later life of the social inequalities built into our social system represents a second major social problem affecting the lives of the elderly. In this section, we look at social class, race, ethnicity, and gender as major components of inequality. We also look at how these components can interact to produce even more drastic inequities than when they operate alone.

Social Class Inequalities

A *social class* is a body of people who are thought to have certain social, economic, educational, occupational, or cultural characteristics in common. Furthermore, social classes are arranged in a *hierarchy* of relative social desirability. Social classes are not organized. Instead, they are categories of

---

[1]For a more complete discussion of age discrimination, see Atchley (1981).

people who recognize one another generally as social peers and who are recognized as such by others.

The study of social class in American society is made difficult by a number of factors. To begin with, ours is an open-class system in which people may move up or down. Although most people live their entire lives in the social class into which they were born, there is enough upward and downward mobility to complicate the study of social class in life course or intergenerational perspectives. Second, the criteria used to cateorize people relative to oneself vary between social classes. For example, family history may confer little status in the working class but may be of crucial importance in selecting peers among the rich. Criteria also vary by size of community. In large urban areas, "objective" characteristics such as occupation, education, income, or residence generally carry a great deal of weight. "Appearances" are also important factors influencing secondary social relationships with service personnel, bureaucrats, shopkeepers, and the like. This reliance on attributes is an obvious outgrowth of the relative anonymity of large cities. In medium-size cities or small communities criteria for class assignment tend to focus on behavior as well as attributes. Thus, in long-standing neighborhoods and small communities, a person's or family's past history of performance is usually an important dimension of social class assignment by the community at large. There are also regional differences in class criteria. Finally, certain class criteria are specific to certain life course stages. For example, one class of retired people in the U.S. defines peers by their affirmation of leisure as the focus of their life-styles and by having the necessary financial resources.

No clearly defined points separate various social classes in American society. The terms *upper, middle,* or *lower class* refer to stereotyped composites of life-styles, educational backgrounds, family values, occupations, housing, and so forth. In fact, the attributes and behavior used to rate others in relation to oneself form a continuous distribution over which very many distinctions can be made. Yet it is possible to discuss general categories if we keep in mind that in every individual case the boundaries of the categories are very fuzzy.

The upper class is typified by wealth, and distinctions within the upper class center around family history and values. Upper-class children are educated in private schools with other upper-class children. They attend the "best" private universities. Their occupational careers prepare them for their "proper" place as leaders of the nation's corporate, military, financial, political, and legal institutions. Upper-class people lead very private lives in circles largely unknown to the general public.

Upper-class people have access to wealth and power. U.S. tax structure allows Americans to amass great fortunes and to pass them on from generation to generation (Streib, 1976). The fortunes of upper-class people do not depend on their having jobs, and upper-class people carry their fortunes into later life. In fact, most very rich people (centimillionaires) are over 65 (Louis, 1968). As a result, older upper-class family members have wealth and the power that comes with wealth. This privileged position means continuity of power within the family, generally better health and vigor, and much less likelihood of dependency in old age. Nevertheless, no amount of money can forestall aging. It can only delay it. Eventually even upper-class people experience declines in physical functioning and erosion of the social environment as their friends and associates die. Because the upper class tends to insulate itself rather severely from others, developing new relationships may be more difficult. In addition, physical aging among the upper class may produce much greater change in life-style than in the middle class. These topics deserve much more research.

The American middle class is a large and heterogeneous category. Jobs and educational attainment are the measures most often used for sorting out various subcategories in the middle class. At the top are college-educated people with professional and managerial jobs. The middle level consists of well-educated white-collar workers who push the nation's paper and market its goods. The lower middle class consist of skilled blue-collar and service workers who may or may not be well educated and whose jobs involve "dirty" work, but whose incomes are often more than sufficient to allow them a middle-class life-style. Middle-class life-styles emphasize "getting ahead" in educational and occupational spheres and diverse activity patterns that often center around the family. Middle-class jobs and values usually result in good health and adequate financial resources in retirement. And family values in the middle class usually ensure prompt response to dependency needs of older family members.

The working class is made up of people whose livelihood is or was generated from semiskilled and unskilled blue-collar and service jobs. Working-class people often did not finish high school, and their jobs are more physically demanding and precarious than middle-class jobs. Working-class life-styles emphasize avoiding slipping downward more than getting ahead, and activity patterns tend to separate men and women. Working-class jobs carry more health and disability hazards and are less likely to produce adequate retirement benefits, compared to middle-class jobs. Family values of the working class support the idea of caring for older family members, but the financial capabilities to do so are limited. Working-class people often find it necessary to rely on public assistance to supplement inadequate retirement incomes.

The working poor live on incomes from the least desirable types of jobs—dishwasher, busboy, presser in a cleaning shop, farm laborer, private household worker. Many poor people never have much success at getting or holding a good job. They have neither the education nor the family upbringing necessary to get steady jobs. Life-styles emphasize survival, and older family members' old age benefits are sometimes a crucial source of family income. In fact, the availability of SSI and all sorts of indirect income assistance can mean a substantial *improvement* in level of living for those poor people who survive to become eligible for them. Yet even though aging may improve their financial situation, the aged poor are apt to find themselves physically less able to take advantage of these opportunities than are their working-class counterparts.

Social class has often been used as a variable in gerontological research. Studies of retirement, widowhood, adaptation to aging, and many other topics have found that social class makes a difference. For example, compared to the working class and the poor, the middle class enters later life with better health, more financial resources, more activities, better housing, and fewer worries. Accordingly, middle-class people seem to cope better with just about every life course change in later life, particularly in the long run. Consequently, middle-class people have good marriages that tend to get better as a result of child launching and retirement. This situation is less often true for the working class and poor. Institutionalization and loss of independence are both less likely for middle-class people compared to the working class and the poor. Thus, to a great extent the optimistic picture of aging presented in this book results from the fact that most Americans are middle class. But for those who are not, the picture is much less rosy. A lifetime of poverty translates into poor health and poor living conditions in later life. Poor working conditions earlier in life translate into greater rates of disability in later life. Semiskilled and unskilled jobs provide meager financial resources not only during one's working life but in retirement as well. To the extent that adequate income and good health are prerequisites for a satisfying life in the later years, the working class and the poor are at a distinct disadvantage. Their jobs are unlikely to entitle them to adequate retirement income and expose them to a greater risk of premature physical aging or disability.

Social class position tends to persist across generations. Therefore, lower-class older people's physical, financial, and social resources for coping with life are less than those of their middle-class age mates. Moreover, the adult children of lower-class older people are also substantially less likely to have financial resources that can be used to aid their older parents.

Racial Inequalities

Racism is a complex of attitudes and discriminatory behavior patterns based on the notion that one racial category is inherently superior to another. In American society, the dominant white majority behaves generally as if it were superior to several other racial categories, particularly to black Americans, Asian Americans, and Native Americans.

Aging Blacks

In 1970, the 1.6 million older black Americans represented 8 percent of the older population and were by far the largest racial minority. The visibility of the black population is heightened by its concentration in central cities as a result of residential segregation. Racial discrimination has also concentrated the black population in blue-collar jobs and in the less desirable jobs within the blue-collar category. For example, among black men age 55 to 59 in 1970, 44 percent were laborers, janitors, and other menial service workers, compared to 9 percent among white males of the same age. Among black women

55 to 59 years old, 69 percent were in menial jobs, compared to 21 percent of white women the same age. In addition, unemployment rates of blacks are much higher than those for whites. And although the occupational situation for blacks has improved substantially since 1964, this improvement is little help to middle-aged or older blacks who are much less likely to have benefited from expanded occupational opportunities compared to younger blacks.

A main effect of racism toward blacks has been to restrict the number who could get jobs that support a middle-class life-style. For example, in the 1920s college-educated blacks had to settle for jobs as porters on the nation's trains (Drake and Cayton, 1962). Yet many black families adapted in ways that allowed them to retain middle-class values. It is common to assume that stifling of opportunities gradually erodes values, but this certainly has not been the case for blacks. Even in the face of job discrimination and low incomes, many black families have raised their children to value education in itself and to live by the middle-class values of thrift, hard work, sacrifice, and getting ahead. Liebow (1967) found these values to be alive and well even among the black working poor. Although a smaller proportion of blacks are middle class compared to whites, there has been a black middle class for decades (DuBois, 1915), and many black Americans were well prepared to take advantage of new opportunities that grew out of the Civil Rights Act of 1965 (Kronus, 1971). As a result, future cohorts of older blacks will be more like older whites not only in terms of values but also in terms of education, health, and financial resources.

Sterne et al. (1974) studied the aged poor in Model Cities areas of Rochester, New York. They found that older blacks were disadvantaged even in relation to the white elderly poor. The white elderly poor had better jobs, had higher retirement incomes, and were better educated. Older blacks in poverty were poorer and had little education. These differences reinforced the already negative view that the elderly white poor had about blacks. As a result, the white elderly poor resisted the idea of integrated clubs, employment, or advocacy. These findings may or may not be typical of racial differences and relations among the urban elderly, but these conditions are probably common enough to present a problem for the elderly black poor. Older whites deal with differences they see, not with the causes of what they see. Older whites have little awareness of, much less compassion for, the effects of racial segregation in the South on the educational level, life-styles, speech, or values of those blacks who moved to the cities. And residential discrimination has often perpetuated these differences, and sometimes expanded them, in the nation's cities. These differences are largely a creation of the racism built into various social institutions, yet many Americans, particularly older Americans, continue to see these differences as the result of skin color.

Older black Americans also suffer the effects of many inaccurate stereotypes. It is commonly assumed that the black population is homogeneously lower class, that most black families are headed by women, that older blacks die substantially earlier than older whites, and that older blacks are mostly dependent on welfare. However, a substantial portion of older blacks are indeed middle class.

In 1976, older blacks had incomes that averaged about 70 percent of those for older whites (Hill, 1978). This situation represented a substantial improvement over the mid-1960s and was mainly the result of the advent of SSI as a supplement to Social Security. The poor occupational histories of older blacks due to racial job discrimination was reflected in the fact that much smaller proportions got private pensions compared to older whites. Hill (1978) reported that Social Security, earnings, and SSI were the major income sources for older blacks, and that for older whites the major sources were Social Security, pensions (not SSI), and earnings. Because 90 percent of older blacks draw Social Security retirement benefits and only 25 percent draw SSI, it seems safe to conclude that the stereotype of older blacks as mainly dependent on welfare is degradingly inaccurate.

Racial segregation in housing has resulted in a much higher percentage of older blacks than of older whites in substandard housing. In 1977, 70 percent of all black families headed by an older person lived in an owned home, while nearly 60 percent of older blacks living alone were in rented housing. About a third of elderly blacks lived alone (Hill, 1978). This pattern was similar to that for whites. However, the housing of older blacks tends to be older and of lower value than that of older whites. Housing of older blacks is especially poor in rural areas of the South. Atchley and Miller (1975) found that more than half the older blacks living in rural southern areas were living in housing that lacked one or more basic features such as plumbing, kitchen facilities, central heating, or sewage disposal, compared to the national rural average of only 13 percent.

In summary, the racial discrimination that has typified the treatment of black Americans for many decades has concentrated older blacks in low-paying jobs and in substandard housing. These conditions continue into later life in the form of lower Social Security benefits, fewer private pensions, and more prevalent health problems. There is evidence that the situation of black Americans is improving, which should mean less disadvantage for upcoming cohorts when they reach later life. However, parity with older whites is still nowhere in sight.

Aging Asian Americans

In 1970, over 100,000 older Asian Americans—primarily Japanese, Chinese, and Filipino—lived in the United States. Although the white majority tends to see these various categories of Asian Americans as similar, they differ considerably in language, customs, background of involvement in American life, and social class structure. In most cases, on the eve of retirement Asian American workers are considerably better off than black Americans are. Incomes of older Japanese Americans are much closer to those of whites than are the incomes of other Asian races, and all Asian races are better off than older blacks. Yet the wide variations *within* the group mean that many Asian Americans are both financially comfortable and financially poor.

The situation of the older Asian American poor was highlighted by a special concerns session at the 1971 White House Conference on Aging. Older Asian Americans have unique language, dietary, and cultural problems that make the current mix of services for the elderly more difficult for them to use. For example, congregate meal programs are not geared to people who do not eat red meat. And older Asian Americans have much higher proportions of men than the general population does because past immigration laws that allowed men to enter as laborers did not allow entry of women and children. In addition, because of the ebb and flow of "yellow peril" feeling in America older Asian Americans are reluctant to use public programs and services.

Aging Native Americans

The situation of Native Americans (American Indians) in the United States is clouded by many issues, not the least of which is difficulty in gathering information about those who do not live on reservations. According to the U.S. Bureau of the Census, nearly 44,000 older Native Americans were living in the United States in 1970, of which about 28 percent lived on reservations. Incomes of older Native Americans were the worst for any minority elderly.

Older Native Americans on reservations face conditions that are substantially different from those of the older population in general. They lead an agricultural life-style that has changed more slowly than has society as a whole. The federal government views Native Americans not as independent citizens but as unfortunates to be protected. Accordingly, many services to older American Indians on reservations are overly paternalistic compared to services to older Americans in general. In addition, Native Americans share in the general unavailability of federal programs for the elderly in rural areas. Housing and sanitation on the reservations are the most substandard in America. Tuberculosis, cirrhosis of the liver, diabetes, and alcoholism are all more common among Native Americans than in the general population (Benedict, 1972).

The older Native American poor in cities suffer disadvantages similar to those experienced by poor blacks. They have had poor jobs, little education, and little preparation for life in the urban United States. And, like Asian Americans, they often have language problems.

The problems of older Native Americans are likely to persist. Younger generations of Native Americans are not making the strides found in other minorities. Only if U.S. society is opened to full participation by the continent's first settlers can elderly Native Americans solve their problems in the same ways other older Americans do.

Ethnic Inequalities

In 1970, about 2 percent of the older U.S. population was of Spanish heritage—mainly Mexican, Puerto Rican, and Cuban. Black Americans have experienced discrimination against their skin color; Hispanic Americans have experienced discrimination against their language. Obviously, succeeding generations may adopt the language of the dominant white majority, but adopting its skin color is another matter. As a result, older Hispanic Americans are much better off than older blacks are. They have occupational histories and incomes that are generally better than those of blacks. Yet Hispanic Americans still have a considerable distance to go before they will be on a par with whites. Unemployment is particularly prevalent among Hispanic Americans just before retirement.

In addition, like "older Asian Americans," "the Hispanic elderly" is a diverse category. The Hispanic elderly poor share with other minority poor problems of little education, high illiteracy rates, high incidence of disability, language barriers to participation in society, and cynicism with regard to the effectiveness of government programs. However, many Hispanic American older people have the resources to live middle-class life-styles in retirement. In addition, Mexican Americans in the Southwest, Puerto Ricans in the Northeast, and Cubans in Florida differ greatly by culture of origin and by their economic and social situations in their areas of settlement in the United States. Generally, Cuban Americans are more advantaged than Mexican Americans, who in turn are better off than Puerto Ricans.

Gender Inequalities

Only recently has the United States become aware that women constitute its most oppressed minority. Sexism—the idea that women are generally less capable than men and fit only for certain jobs—has resulted in a unique position for women in relaion to jobs. To many, a woman's place is in the home. Many older women have been nonemployed housewives, and although the percentage of employed women may be increasing, many will be nonemployed housewives throughout their adult lives. Such women depend completely on their husbands' lifetime earnings and the retirement income those earnings can generate. They are *quite* vulnerable to the effects of divorce and widowhood. If they divorce after age 40, they will find it difficult to work long enough to get adequate Social Security.

Many women like having the option of caring for house, husband, and children rather than participating in the job market. But if they select this option, they are taking a big gamble that the marriage will stay intact long enough to give them financial security in their later years.

Women who do seek employment find themselves channeled into "women's work." In 1970, the 10 most common jobs of middle-aged women were precisely those that fit the stereotype of "women's work"—secretary, clerk, teacher, nurse, bookkeeper, and so forth. These stereotyped women's jobs account for the *majority* of women's employment, and this situation has changed very little since 1940 (Baxandall et al., 1976). Even if a move toward sexual equality should take place in the job market, it is unlikely to affect the position of middle-aged and mature woman for some time to come.

Of the top 10 "women's jobs," only the teachers and nurses have a high probability of getting a private pension in addition to Social Security. In addition, women's earnings average only about 60 percent as high as men's earnings at the same occupational and educational levels. These various factors mean that retirement incomes of women average only about 55 percent as high as those enjoyed by men. And for minority women the situation is especially dismal.

Interacting Dimensions of Inequality

Thus far we have been concerned primarily with how various types of social inequality, taken separately, affect aging. But many older Americans are simultaneously members of several disadvantaged groups. For example, compare the pictures in your mind of an upper-class white older man and a lower-class black older woman. Imagine their lives as they experience growing older. Beyond these obvious extremes, however, it is difficult to get a good picture of just how various minority characteristics interact.

One way to examine the issue is to look at how education (which is related to social class), race and ethnicity, and sex simultaneously affect earnings *within* various occupations. Within most occupational categories, lower education and being black are decided disadvantages, but the greatest disadvantage is being female.

Palmore and Manton (1973) examined inequality on a number of dimensions. They addressed themselves to three important questions: How do ageism, racism, and sexism compare on observable inequality? Are their effects cumulative? How have these various types of inequality changed in recent years? They found substantial inequalities of all three types. Income and occupational inequalities were greatest with regard to gender, and educational inequality was greatest with regard to age. Palmore and Manton also reported that in weeks worked, age inequality was highest. No one form of inequality was consistently greatest on all dimensions.

Age inequality in income was much greater among men than among women and was somewhat greater among nonwhites than among whites. It is particularly noteworthy that almost none of the older black women were earning as much as the lowest-paid young white men. This is the reality of triple jeopardy! Palmore and Manton found that from 1950 to 1970, racial inequality decreased, sexual inequality stayed about the same, and age inequality increased substantially.

The quality of life in later years depends heavily on health and financial resources. In U.S. society, both resources are closely tied to jobs. For this reason, we must conclude that although social inequalities may have a bearing on the availability of housing and services, the primary impact of social inequalities on aging is through their impact on jobs and on the opportunities those jobs allow or the limitations they impose.

Obstacles Confronting the Disabled

A *disability* is a long-term functional incapacity (Nagi, 1965). Although 46 percent of the elderly are somewhat limited, only about 14 percent of all elderly have severe functional limitations (Atchley, 1980 :113). But at age 85 and over, 31 percent have serious limitations. Among those 75 or over, 16 percent use canes and 5 percent use walkers. Among those 85 or older, nearly 20 percent need some assistance in dressing and bathing. About 5 percent of the elderly in independent households cannot go outdoors without assistance (Miller, 1982).

Disabled people can participate in U.S. society only with a great deal of help. Special transportation, motorized wheelchairs, ramps, sidewalk cuts, paid assistance at home, and physical rehabilitation services are just some of what must be available if disabled people are to move about the community with some semblance of the freedoms and opportunities enjoyed by the nondisabled. In recent years, we have made significant strides toward making these items available to disabled people who are young or middle-aged adults. They are still relatively unavailable for the elderly.

The problem is that rehabilitation services such as physical therapy to handicapped people tend to be tied to the prospect of employment. Because most disabled Americans are retired, they are judged ineligible for most services. We cannot even be sure of the numbers who are not being served, because research on disability conducted by the Social Security Administration stops at age 64.

Because ageism occurs in services to the handicapped, elderly handicapped people have even less access to U.S. society than do handicapped people in general. So far very little has been done even to draw attention to this problem, much less solve it.

Solutions

Solving these social problems is outside the capacities of any individual and requires concerted social action. Such action can include steps to eliminate age prejudice, age discrimination, the invidious effects of social class, and the limits disability imposes on participation. We can see action taking place at every level in society, but a continued national effort is particularly important.

Changing Age Prejudice

Attitudes and beliefs about aging have probably always been ambivalent. Most people accept the idea that the scope of experience that comes with age may be a prerequisite for wisdom, and that having made one's fame and fortune can free people to be more supportive of those coming along. But at the same time, most people also do not see these positive changes as always happening. And they still retain strong reservations that biological aging has inevitable physical and mental effects that offset the advantages of wisdom and warmth. These negative reservations, groundless as they may be, underlie age prejudice and discrimination.

It is somewhat puzzling that the vast majority of the public's *stated* attitudes and beliefs about aging can be positive, and yet those *acted on* tend to be negative. Part of the answer to this anomaly may lie in the perceived threat that aging represents to American values. Rokeach (1973) found that family security, personal freedom, and contentment were major values for Americans, and all these values could possibly be affected by one's own aging, the aging of family members, or the aging of sociey as a whole. In addition, the negative stereotypes of aging are seen as particularly threatening to high productivity and efficiency—keystone values that serve as guiding principles for formal organizations.

Yet the choice may not be in deciding whether older people as a category are unable to work. Instead, the choice may be whether, in a society with a glut of labor, it is worth trying to identify those older people who are able to work. The issue involves the proportion of older people who are capable of working. If the common view is that most older people are incapable, then obviously it may not be worth trying to find those few old workers who are capable and to continue to employ them. (This picture is as seen from the vantage point of the public good rather than that of what may be good for individuals.) If, on the other hand, the vast majority of older people are seen as capable, then there is no reason to exclude them wholesale from the labor force.

The public dialogue surrounding the evolution of programs to serve the aged has had an unfortunate side effect of reinforcing negative stereotypes of the aged as dependent, incapable, and needy. At the same time, ordinary, capable older people have remained relatively invisible, of no interest to the media, to human service agencies, or to legislators. Over 70 percent of the elderly are ambulatory, physically independent people who live in ordinary communities. We do not see them, precisely because they cannot easily be distinguished from other adults. In order to change the image of aging, the public must come to recognize that incapable older people are a small minority. The public must come to see that the active, interested, involved older person is the rule rather than the exception.

There are signs that this attitude change is happening. As noted in Chapter 3, the media are broadcasting increasingly frequent messages that most older people are not frail or incapable and that older people are quite able to make positive contributions to society. There is a growing recognition that the quality and fiber of a person says more about his or her potential contribution than does age. As the older population becomes more affluent and well-educated, we can expect the volume of these messages to increase. And presumably at some point there will be a turnaround in public acceptance of the negative stereotypes of aging.

Organizations of older people also sometimes make concerted efforts to combat ageism. The Gray Panthers are an example. Although relatively small in membership compared to other organizations of older people, the leaders of the Gray Panthers have very effectively raised national consciousness about ageism. Such efforts usually emphasize the desire and capacity of large numbers of older people to remain involved and productive participants in society.

Combatting Age Discrimination

Age discrimination is being fought primarily through legislation and the courts. So far, the Age Discrimination Act of 1975 and Age Discrimination in Employment Act of 1967 are the major legislative efforts to reduce age discrimination.

The Age Discrimination Act (ADA) of 1975, amended in 1978, is a civil rights-type statute that prohibits age discrimination in any program that receives federal funds. As cited earlier, the U.S. Commission on Civil Rights found age discrimination in all 10 largest federal aid programs. Thus, the need for such legislation is clear, and potentially it could have wide-ranging effects.

The Age Discrimination in Employment Act (ADEA) of 1967 is designed to promote employment of older people based on their ability rather than their age and to prohibit "arbitrary" age discrimination in employment. Specifically, ADEA prohibits ageist refusal to hire, discharge, discriminatory treatment during employment, advertisements reflecting age preference, refusal of employment agencies to refer clients because of their age, discriminatory treatment by labor unions, and retaliation against employees who assert their rights under the act.

The only exception to ADEA is cases in which age is a "bona fide occupational qualification." In court tests of this exception, a policy of not hiring bus drivers over age 35 was upheld by an appeals court, presumably to protect the public, and the U.S. Supreme Court upheld the forced retirement of a highway patrol officer on grounds that law enforcement duties require physical capacities beyond those of a 50-year-old man. These court decisions are not supported by any scientific evidence, and they graphically illustrate the fact that courts often operate to justify common prejudices and the resulting discrimination. In the case of the bus company, no evidence was offered that bus drivers trained after age 35 were less safe than those trained at an earlier age. The court merely accepted the company's assertion that this was true. The U.S. Supreme Court upheld the dismissal of a highway patrolman who had just been pronounced physically fit for duty by the highway patrol's own physician. Following the intent of ADEA, it seems imperative that courts require concrete evidence of age-related changes that interfere with job performance before certifying age-based employment policies as "bona fide." In addition, the burden of proof should be on the employer to provide such evidence. In other words, age categories of people should be presumed able until proven otherwise.

Combatting age discrimination in public programs has also been a priority of the largest organizations of older people—the National Council of Senior Citizens (3 million members) and the National Retired Teachers Association/American Association of Retired Persons (6 million combined membership, jointly administered). These organizations employ skilled lobbyists to ensure that the U.S. Congress and the administration set aside appropriate program funds for older people. The National Council on Aging, a group made up primarily of agencies and practitioners serving older people, pursues similar goals.

Organized advocates of older people have been very successful in getting federal program dollars earmarked for these people, at least compared with the attention being paid to other disadvantaged groups. For example, during the 1970s federal program dollars aimed at the poor and at minorities decreased substantially, while dollars going to the programs for older people showed a sizable increase. This change suggests that because aging cuts across social lines it has a high level of legitimacy among the public, legislators, and administrators. This legitimacy can be exploited by advocates of the elderly. However, there are certain limits to how much the public is willing to do for older people, and we may become more aware of those limits in the 1980s.

Implications of Continued Social Inequality

Social class, ethnicity, and race are very stable individual characteristics that arrange people in a hierarchy of desirability and access to rewards and opportunities, and problems of inequality require unequal solutions. The upper class needs nothing in the way of assistance. Rather, it represents a pool of potential leadership for the elderly, and our policy should be to *actively* recruit able upper class people for such positions.

The main problem for the middle class is economic support for the widowed and divorced. Otherwise, most middle-class Americans enter later life with sufficient economic, emotional, intellectual, and physical resources. The working class needs better access to private pensions and health insurance. The poor need better access to jobs in early adulthood, especially for those who are members of minorities. All these policy implications are focused on the middle years or earlier because they set the stage for entry into later life. If we can reduce somewhat the inequalities among the middle-aged, we will prevent many "problems of the aged."

In addition, social class in old age has various impacts. The middle-class elderly are often limited in opportunity because they are not affluent enough to attract the attention of entrepreneurs, and are too well off to qualify for public programs. For this reason, proposed cutbacks in services to the middle-class aged may have more serious economic consequences than anyone now expects.

The working class and the poor need services in later life both because services such as subsidized housing and nutrition programs can ease a drastic economic situation and because their families are less able financially to pick up the slack. It is also important to remember that a large number of the poor live in rural areas where services may not be available.

Our policies should provide more incentives (such as subsidies or tax relief) for private business to become concerned with middle-class elderly as consumers so that appropriate goods and services will be available. We need to mobilize upper-class people to champion the cause of the elderly before philanthropic organizations in order to bolster and preserve services to the elderly poor.

In addition, we need to recognize that our society's political, economic, and legal structure produces a class of peole known as "the poor" in order that those who are not poor can enjoy a higher standard of living. Those who enjoy the fruits of this system incur an obligation to provide the poor with enough resources to live like human beings. Therefore public programs for the elderly poor *must* receive continued support.

Federal programs developed since 1965 have made tremendous strides in minimizing the effects of inequality for the elderly. Social Security improvements and SSI have raised more than 30 percent of the elderly out of poverty. Low-rent public housing and federal rent subsidies have made decent housing available to thousands of older Americans. Medicare and Medicaid have made at least a modest amount of health care available to all older Americans. Older Americans Act programs have created a network of nutrition, transportation, information and referral, and other services to the elderly in virtually every area of the United States. All this has happened as a result of 20 years of sustained and cumulative federal effort to guide the nation toward better programs for the elderly.

We can and should do even more. For most of the elderly, employment is not a feasible way to ensure themselves adequate incomes, housing, and health care. In this respect, the elderly are a very special category. Despite its recent slump, the American economy produces a vast economic surplus—income over and above that required for subsistence. We and our policymakers must remain committed to the policy that a share of that surplus must be used to ensure that *all* older Americans have access to adequate income, housing, and health care.

At the 1981 White House Conference on Aging, the Leadership Coalition of Aging Organizations[2] advanced a modest agenda called "8 for the 80s." The petitions circulated among the delegates were as follows:

8 for 80s

Eight Policy Positions for the 1981 White House Conference on Aging

The undersigned delegates and observers to the 1981 White House Conference on Aging endorse the following policy position as a basis for actions on behalf of older Americans in the coming decade. We reaffirm the special role of the federal government in achieving these goals—a role already endangered and impaired by wholesale federal budgetary and program cutbacks. The federal government must, in particular, assure basic health and income security for the elderly, and must lead the fight against ageism in America.

1. Safeguard current eligibility conditions, retirement ages and benefit levels in Social Security.
2. Broaden opportunities for older workers to remain active voluntarily in the labor force.
3. Older persons should be assured an income sufficient to maintain a minimum level of dignity and comfort.
4. Enact a comprehensive national health plan for all Americans.
5. Interim steps must be taken to improve health care for older persons.
6. No fewer than 200,000 units of publicly financed housing for the elderly should be made available each year during the decade.
7. Comprehensive service delivery systems for older people at the community level must be completed in the 1980s.
8. Strengthen the federal commitment to gerontological research, education and training.

From this, you can see that the major priorities were income, housing, health care, eliminating age discrimination in employment, availability of comprehensive services at the local level, and the education, training, and

---

[2] The Leadership Coalition of Aging Organizations is a group made up of leaders from the major membership organizations of older people, organizations of practitioners and agencies serving the elderly, organizations of researchers and educators in gerontology, and organizations of state and local offices on aging.

research necessary to ensure high-quality programs. The majority of delegates endorsed this petition.

Where will the money for such programs come from? This question was asked repeatedly by White House Conference delegates appointed by the Reagan Administration. Let's take the issue of service delivery programs at the local level. The primary federal effort here has been the responsibility of the Administration of Aging (AoA). In 1978, the federal government spent $700 million for all AoA programs, including research, training, planning, and administration in addition to direct services. To put this expenditure in perspective, note that an equal amount was spent in 1978 to advertise toiletries and toilet goods. Maybe we should decide to give up watching Mr. Whipple squeeze the Charmin! In 1978, the federal government excused corporations from paying over $700 million in taxes because of debts they couldn't collect. In 1978, the federal government spent over $700 million to provide military assistance to foreign governments. In 1978, Americans spent over $700 million playing Bingo (U.S. Bureau of the Census, 1979). The point is that we are a wealthy nation, and if we chose to do so we could more than amply provide for the needy elderly.

There has also been much discussion recently about returning responsibilities to the states and to "the private sector." Although state, local, and philanthrophic organization involvement and commitment are very important in an overall effort to meet the needs of the elderly, it would be a grave mistake to assume that we can do without strong and persistent leadership and financing at the national level. There are two important reasons for this fact. First, experience in delivering services to the elderly is not evenly distributed throughout the states. Some states have a great deal of experience, and some have relatively little. For service delivery to be of the highest possible quality, our *best* experience and practices need to be widely adopted, and the best way to do so is through a standardized national structure. The "Aging Network"—made up of local Area Agencies on Aging, local service providers, State Units on Aging, the Administration on Aging Regional Offices, and the federal Administration on Aging—has been a very vital part of the improvement that has occurred in service delivery to the elderly since 1970. Second, the federal government has vastly greater power and resources than state or local area governments. For example, the tax revenues that flow to the federal government are substantially higher than those available to all state and local governments combined. In 1976, the federal government collected over $200 billion in taxes, states collected about $90 billion, and local governments collected about $65 billion. The "private sector"—private philanthropy funds collected by churches, United Way campaigns, and so on—amounted to only $24 billion. Thus it should be clear that local governments and the private sector have relatively few resources compared to the national government. In addition, state and local governments must support activities such as education, transportation, fire protection, and law enforcement that the federal government plays only a very minor role in financing.

We need a national effort to effectively meet the future needs of the elderly. For example, between 1980 and the year 2000, the need for residential space in nursing and personal care homes will double. We are not going to be able to handle a problem of this magnitude at the local or state level. It will require the application of national resources.

The Future

For individuals, growing older is even more likely to be a positive experience in the future than it is now. People entering later life will be better educated, which will give them more resources for directing their own lives. They may also be in better health as a result of reductions in smoking, greater amounts of exercise, and more emphasis on preventive aspects of health care. Most will have more economic resources than those entering the older population today.

At the same time, the needy old will probably get needier. As the average age of the older population increases, the prevalence of serious disability will probably increase. Thus, although the need for services to the general population of older people may remain relatively stable or even decline, this situation may be more than offset by a dramatic increase in those who need long-term care, whether in a community setting or in institutions.

To cope with the dramatic increase in the very old, we will need to develop ways to involve more retired people in the caregiving process. In each community, we need a network of paid and voluntary services to ensure that if we are in the minority for whom aging means a drastic loss of functional capacity, we can count on someone being there to care for us. Being helpless *and* abandoned is the greatest fear people have about growing old. If older people are to have real security, we must do all we can to minimize this fear.

Demographic trends for the future ensure that preparing for a career in gerontology will be a solid investment. For example, the U.S. Senate Special Committee on Aging (1973) estimated that between 1970 and 1980 there would be 20,000 *new* positions for managers of retirement housing; 25,000 *new* positions for licensed practical nurses and 8,000 *new* positions for registered nurses to handle the increased need for nursing home care; 17,000 *new* positions for recreation program specialists serving the elderly. This increase is in addition to the several hundred thousand positions that already existed in gerontology-related fields.

In 1970, 20 million older people were living in the United States. By 1980, there were 24 million. By 1990, there will be 28 million, and by the year 2020, there will be 40 million! With the older population growing so fast, there is little chance that interest in aging will lessen. In fact, during the coming decades planning, administering, and delivering services to older people may well be one of the fastest growing areas of employment in America.

Glossary

accommodation: Altering one's behavior to more nearly conform to the demands of an external situation.

acculturation: The process of learning a culture.

acute condition: An illness or injury that is expected to be temporary.

adaptation: The process of adjusting oneself to fit a situation or environment.

age discrimination: The overt denial of opportunity based on age.

age norms: Norms tied to the life course that tell people of a given age what is allowed or not allowed for someone of that age.

aged: People age 65 or older.

ageism: Prejudice based on age.

aging (adj.): In the process of becoming old. Does not imply that the person *is* old.

aging (n.): The physical, psychological and social processes that over time cause changes in a person's functional capacities and that influence social definitions about a person's capacities, interests, and opportunities.

anticipation: Identifying in advance the rights, obligations, prerequisites, resources, and outlook of a position one will occupy in the future.

Area Agency on Aging (AAA): Local agencies charged with planning and coordinating services to older people and with providing information and referral. Older Americans Act funds flow to local community agencies through the AAA's.

assimilation: An internal process in which new experience is modified in the process of perception so as to fit better with already-existing ideas.

attachments: One-way bonds reflecting the perceiver's view of ties to people, environments, or objects.

case management: Looking at the totality of a person's needs and resources and developing an integrated treatment plan. (See also *long-term care.*)

chronic condition: An illness or injury that is expected to be long-term or permanent.

chronological age: The number of years a person has lived.

compensation: The processes whereby aging people or others around them offset
detrimental effects of aging.

conflict management: A mental process that changes our perceptions of conflicts
from negative to positive by altering the context in which the conflict is
viewed. Includes techniques such as altruism, humor, sublimation, anticipation, and suppression.

consolidation: Adapting to role or activity loss by redistributing time and energy to
roles and activities that remain.

continuity, external: Living in familiar environments and interacting with familiar
people.

continuity, internal: The persistence of a personal structure of ideas based on
memory.

decision demand: A type of norm that requires people to choose a course of action
within a specified time period and *from* an age-linked field of possibilities.

dementia: An organic brain disease characterized by mental confusion, poor memory, incoherent speech, and poor orientation to the environment.

disability, major: A condition that causes restriction in a major area of life such as
employment, child care, or housework.

disability, minor: A condition that causes restriction of activities, but not in major
areas such as employment, child care, or housework.

disengagement: Adapting to role or activity loss by withdrawal.

disengagement, differential: Adapting to loss by withdrawal in selected areas of
life. (See also *consolidation*.)

disengagement, societal: A process whereby people who reach an arbitrary age are
no longer encouraged to seek positions they are qualified for or are not encouraged to remain in positions they are functioning well in.

dying trajectory: The speed with which a person dies, the rate of decline in functioning.

elderly: People age 65 or older.

exchange resources: Resources such as wealth, information, approval, skill, or
reputation that actors can offer in a social exchange.

exchange theory: A theory of social interaction that assumes the main motive of
interaction is to increase rewards while incurring the least possible cost.

functional age definition: The use of attributes such as appearance, mobility,
strength, or mental capacity to assign people to broad age categories such as
middle age or old age.

gerontology, social: See social gerontology.

habituation: The process of learning not to pay attention to stimuli we encounter
over and over.

hospice: An organization that delivers services to dying persons and their families.

human development: The evolution of the human mind, including its patterns of thought, emotion, perception, memory, temperament, and so on, but constituted as an interactive whole.

independence: The capacity to rely on oneself.

later maturity: A life cycle stage socially defined or typified by energy decline; awareness of sensory loss; onset of chronic health problems; difficulty in remaining future-oriented; recognition that one's time is growing short; loss of social contacts through retirement, widowhood, and movement of children; and freedom from responsibilities such as work or child rearing.

life course: An ideal sequence of events people are expected to experience and positions they are expected to occupy as they mature and move through life.

life expectancy: The *average* length of time a group of individuals of the same age will live, given current mortality rates. Life expectancy can be computed from any age, but is most often computed from birth.

life span: The length of life that is biologically possible for a given species.

life stages: Broad age categories loosely based on ideas about effects of aging. Examples include middle age, later maturity, and old age.

long-term care: Long-term management of illness or disability.

maturation: The process of development. Can be physical, psychological, or social.

maturity: A quality of being fully grown. Physical maturity usually occurs much earlier than psychological and/or social maturity. Indeed, many contend that psychological development is never complete in the sense that physical development is.

Medicaid: A comprehensive health care program for the poor. Funds both acute and long-term care.

Medicare: A program of national health insurance for persons covered by Social Security and age 65 and over. Funds primarily acute care.

middle age: A stage of the life cycle socially defined or typified by energy decline; shifting from physical to mental activities; feeling of having reached a goal or plateau in one's career; awareness that life is finite; shrinking of family as children leave home; entry of women into the labor force; employment troubles; and feelings of restlessness, of not getting anywhere. (See also *later maturity, old age.*)

midlife: Middle age.

norms: Socially agreed-upon standards used to define behavior as acceptable or unacceptable.

nursing home: A facility that provides personal care plus health care such as administering medication.

old age: A stage of the life cycle socially defined or typified by increasing frailty and disability; much introspection and concern over the meaning of life; distinct awareness of approaching death; financial and physical dependency; isolation, boredom, and loneliness. (See also *middle age, later maturity.*)

Older Americans Act: Legislation which created a national network of services and programs for older people. It also provides funds for research, training, and model projects.

older people: People age 65 or older.

older person: Conceptually, an individual in the later maturity or old age stages of the life cycle. Socially, people are usually classified as older if they are chronologically 65 or older. Legally, there are several chronological ages that are used to define people as *old*, beginning as early as 45. (See also *later maturity, old age*.)

pension: A periodic payment to a person or his or her family, given as a result of previous on-the-job service.

pension, job-related: Retirement pensions available only through a specific position of employment and administered by a work organization, union, or private insurance company.

pension, retirement: Income received by retired persons by virtue of having been employed at least a minimum number of years in the past on a job covered by a pension system. (See also *job-related pension*.)

personal care home: A facility that provides meals, housekeeping services, and assistance with tasks such as dressing or bathing. Nursing and medical care are not provided.

personal effectiveness: The capacity to influence the conditions of one's life.

personality: The unique pattern of attitudes, values, beliefs, habits, mannerisms, and preferences that allows us to think of ourselves and others as individuals.

relationships: Reciprocal bonds of interdependence, affection, or belonging.

relative appreciation: A favorable attitude toward oneself or one's situation based on a comparison to others whose characteristics or situations are less fortunate.

rest home: See *personal care home*.

retirement: The period following a career of job holding, in which job responsibilities and often opportunities are minimized and in which economic support comes by virtue of having held a job for a minimum length of time in the past.

retirement community: A community whose residents are primarily retired persons.

retirement community, de facto: A retirement community that results from large-scale migration of retired households to small towns in certain regions of the country.

retirement community, full-service: A retirement community that offers its residents a continuum of services and levels of care.

role relationship: The ground rules that define what the players of reciprocal social roles can expect from one another.

selective appreciation: A recognition that people offer more in some situations than in others and an emphasis on areas where their potential contribution is the highest.

self: A person's awareness of his or her own nature and characteristics. The person as an object of his or her own awareness.

senility: An archaic term formerly used as a general term for mental infirmities thought to be the result of aging.

skilled nursing facility: A facility that provides hospital-quality nursing care around-the-clock.

social gerontology: A subfield of gerontology dealing with the developmental and group behavior of adults, and with the causes and consequences of having older people in the population.

social roles: The expected or typical behavior associated with positions in the organization of a group.

Social Security: Generally used as s colloquial term referring to the general public retirement pension administered by the federal government. Technically, Social Security also provides a number of other types of benefits to survivors and disabled people. It also administers Medicare.

socialization: The processes through which a group recreates in its members the distinctive way of life of the group.

SSI: Supplemental Security Income, a federal program of public assistance to indigent older people.

stereotype: A composite of inaccurate and derogatory beliefs about a category of people.

substitution: Adapting to loss by substituting a new role or activity for the one lost.

support system: The total of a person's relationships that involve the receiving of assistance and that are viewed by both the giver and receiver as playing a significant part in maintaining the psychological, social, and physical integrity of the receiver.

theory: A set of interrelated principles and definitions used conceptually to organize observations, information, or communication about a particular aspect of reality.

typology: A set of two or more mutually exclusive categories. Typologies specify relevant characteristics of each category and are used to identify differences and to make comparisons.

vulnerability: The actual or perceived probability that one may experience loss or harm.

References

Adams, Bert N.
1968   Kinship in an Urban Setting. Chicago: Markham.

Antunes, George E., Fay L. Cook, Thomas D. Cook, and Wesley G. Skogan
1977   Patterns of personal crime against the elderly: Findings from a national survey. The Gerontologist 17:321–27.

Arenberg, David
1968   Concept problem solving in young and old adults. Journal of Gerontology 23:279–82.

Atchley, Robert C.
1969   Respondents vs. refusers in an interview study of retired women. Journal of Gerontology 24:42–47.
1971a   Retirement and leisure participation: Continuity or crisis? The Gerontologist 11(1, part 1):13–17.
1971b   Disengagement among professors. Journal of Gerontology 26:476–80.
1971c   Retirement and work orientation. The Gerontologist 11(1, part 1):29–32.
1974   The meaning of retirement. Journal of Communications 24:97–101.
1975a   Dimensions of widowhood in later life. The Gerontologist 15:176–78.
1975b   The life course, age grading, and age-linked demands for decision making. Pp. 261–78 in Nancy Datan and Leon H. Ginsberg (eds.), Life-Span Developmental Psychology: Normative Life Crises. New York: Academic Press.
1975c   Sex differences among middle-class retired people. Pp. 22–31 in Robert C. Atchley, Research Studies in Social Gerontology. Oxford, Ohio: Scripps Foundation.
1976   The Sociology of Retirement. Cambridge, Mass.: Schenkman.
1977   Predictors of morale in later life. Paper presented at the annual meeting of the Gerontological Society, November, San Francisco.
1980a   Age and suicide: Reflection of the quality of life? Pp. 141–61 in S. G. Haynes and M. Feinleib (eds.), Epidemiology of Aging. Washington, D.C.: U.S. Government Printing Office.
1980b   The Social Forces in Later Life. 3rd ed. Belmont, Calif.: Wadsworth.

1981   Age discrimination. Pp. 320–36 in M. E. Olsen and M. Micklin (eds.), Hand-
              book of Applied Sociology. New York: Praeger.

1982   The process of retirement. In Maximiliane Szinovacz (ed.), Women's Retire-
              ment. Beverly Hills, Calif.: Sage Publications.

Atchley, Robert C., and Sheila J. Miller

1975   Housing of the rural aged. Pp. 95–143 in Robert C. Atchley (ed.), Environ-
              ments and the Rural Aged. Washington, D.C.: Gerontological Society.

1980   Older people and their families. Annual Review of Gerontology and Geriat-
              rics. 1:337–69. New York: Springer.

Atchley, Robert C., Suzanne R. Kunkel, and Carl Adlon

1978   An evaluation of preretirement programs: Results from an experimental
              study. Oxford, Ohio: Scripps Foundation.

Atchley, Robert C., Linda Pignatiello, and Ellen Shaw

1979   Interactions with family and friends: Marital status and occupational differ-
              ences among older women. Research on Aging 1:83–94.

Babic, Anna L.

1972   The older volunteer: Expectations and satisfactions. The Gerontologist 12:87–
              89.

Back, Kurt W.

1971   Metaphors as a test of personal philosophy of aging. Sociological Focus 5:1–8.

1976   Personal characteristics and social behavior: Theory and method. Pp. 403–31
              in Robert H. Binstock and Ethel Shanas (eds.), Handbook of Aging and the
              Social Sciences. New York: Van Nostrand Reinhold.

Back, Kurt W., and Carleton S. Guptill

1966   Retirement and self-ratings. Pp. 120–29 in Ida H. Simpson, and John C.
              McKinney (eds.), Social Aspects of Aging. Durham, N.C.: Duke University
              Press.

Bahr, S. J.

1973   Effects of power and division of labor on the family. Pp. 167–185 in Lois W.
              Hoffman and I. F. Nye (eds.), Working Mothers. San Francisco: Jossey-Bass.

Ballweg, John A.

1967   Resolution of conjugal role adjustment after retirement. Journal of Marriage
              and the Family 29:277–81.

Baltes, Paul B., and G. Labouvie

1973   Adult development of intellectual performance. Pp. 157–219 in Carl Eisdorfer
              and M. Powell Lawton (eds.), The Psychology of Adult Development and
              Aging. Washington, D.C.: American Psychological Association.

Barfield, Richard E., and James Morgan

1969   Early Retirement: The Decision and the Experience. Ann Arbor: Institute of
              Social Research, University of Michigan.

1978   Trends in planned early retirement. The Gerontologist 18:19–23.

Bart, Pauline B.

1971   Depression in middle-aged women. In V. Gornick and B. K. Moran (eds.),
              Women in a Sexist Society. New York: Basic Books.

Baxandall, Rosalyn, Linda Gordon, and Susan Reverby

1976   America's Working Woman. New York: Random House.

Belbin, E., and R. Meredith Belbin

1969   Selecting and training adults for New York. Pp. 66–81 in A. T. Welford (ed.),
              Decision Making and Age. New York: Karger.

Benedict, Robert

1972   A profile of the Indian aged. Pp. 51–57 in Minority Aged in America. Occa-
              sional Papers in Gerontology, No. 10. Ann Arbor: University of Michigan-
              Wayne State University Institute of Gerontology.

Bengston, Vern L., and Dean Black
1973   Intergenerational relations and continuities in socialization. Pp. 208–34 in P. B. Baltes and K. W. Schaie (eds.), Life-Span Developmental Psychology: Personality and Socialization. New York: Academic Press.

Bennett, Ruth
1980   Aging, Isolation and Resocialization. New York: Van Nostrand Reinhold.

Berg, W. B., L. Atlas, and J. Zeiger
1974   Integrated homemaking services for the aged in urban neighborhoods. The Gerontologist 14:388–93.

Better Housing League of Cincinnati
1978   Housing for Older Americans in Hamilton County, Ohio. Cincinnati: Better Housing League.

Birren, James E.
1964   The Psychology of Aging. Englewood Cliffs, N.J.: Prentice-Hall.

Birren, James E., and K. Warner Schaie (eds.)
1977   Handbook of the Psychology of Aging. New York: Van Nostrand Reinhold.

Bixby, Lenore E.
1976   Retirement patterns in the United States: Research and policy interaction. Social Security Bulletin 39(8):3–19.

Blau, Peter M.
1964   Exchange and Power in Social Life. New York: Wiley.

Blau, Zena S.
1961   Structural constraints on friendship in old age. American Sociological Review 26:429–39.

Blenkner, Margaret
1965   Social work and family relationships in later life with some thoughts on filial maturity. Pp. 46–59 in Ethel Shanas and Gordon F. Streib (eds.), Social Structure and the Family. Englewood Cliffs, N.J.: PrenticeHall.

Bornstein, P. E., P. J. Clayton, J. A. Halikas, W. L. Maurice, and E. Robins
1973   The depression of widowhood after thirteen months. British Journal of Psychiatry 122:561–66.

Botwinick, Jack
1978   Aging and Behavior. 2nd ed. New York: Springer.

Boyd, Rosamonde R.
1969   The valued grandparent: A changing social role. Pp. 90–102 in Wilma Donahue (ed.), Living in the Multigenerational Family. Ann Arbor: University of Michigan-Wayne State University Institute of Gerontology.

Bracey, H. E.
1966   In Retirement. Baton Rouge: Louisiana University Press.

Brickel, Clark M.
1980   A review of the role of pet animals in psychotherapy and with the elderly. International Journal of Aging and Human Development 12:119–128.

Brim, Orville
1968   Adult socialization. Pp. 182–226 in John Clausen (ed.), Socialization in Society. Boston: Little, Brown.

Britton, Joseph H., and Jean O. Britton
1967   The middle-aged and older rural person and his family. Pp. 44–74 in E. Grant Youmans (ed.), Older Rural Americans. Lexington: University of Kentucky Press.

Brody, Stanley J.
1973   Comprehensive health care for the elderly: An analysis. The continuum of medical, health, and social services for the aged. The Gerontologist 13:412–18.

Brown, A. S.
1974   Satisfying relationships for the elderly and their patterns of disengagement.
               Gerontologist 14:258–62.

Brown, Robert G.
1960   Family structure and social isolation of older persons. Journal of Gerontology
               15:170–74.

Brubaker, Timothy H., and Charles Barresi
1980   Social workers' levels of knowledge about old age and perceptions of service
               delivery to the aged. Research on Aging 1:213–31.

Bultena, Gordon, and Vivian Wood
1969a   The American retirement community: bane or blessing? Journal of Gerontol-
               ogy 24:209–17.
1969b   Normative attitudes toward the aged role among migrant and nonmigrant
               retirees. The Gerontologist 9(3, part 1):204–208.

Burnside, Irene M.
1981   Falls: a common problem in the elderly. Pp. 549–59 in Irene M. Burnside
               (ed.), Nursing and the Aged. New York: McGraw-Hill.

Butler, Robert N., and Myrna I. Lewis
1973   Aging and Mental Health. St. Louis, Mo.: Mosby.

Cantor, Marjorie H.
1980   The informal support system: its relevance in the lives of the elderly. Pp. 131–
               46 in Neil G. McClusky, and E. F. Borgatta (eds.), Aging and Society: Current
               Research and Policy Perspectives. Beverly Hills, Calif.: Sage Publications.

Carp, Frances M.
1968   Some components of disengagement. Journal of Gerontology 23:382–86.
1976   Housing and living environments of older people. Pp. 244–71 in Robert H.
               Binstock and Ethel Shanas (eds.), Handbook of Aging and the Social Sci-
               ences. New York: Van Nostrand Reinhold.
1978–79   Effects of the living environment on activity and use of time. Aging and
               Human Development 9:75–91.

Chiriboga, David, and Majda Thurnher
1975   Concept of self. Pp. 62–83 in Marjorie F. Lowenthal, Majda Thurnher, and
               David Chiriboga and Associates, The Four Stages of Life. San Francisco:
               Jossey-Bass.

Cijfer, E.
1966   An experiment on some differences in logical thinking between Dutch medi-
               cal people, under and over the age of 35. Acta Psychologica 25:159–71.

Clark, Margaret, and Barbara Anderson
1967   Culture and Aging. Springfield, Ill.: Thomas.

Clemente, Frank, and Jon Hendricks
1973   A further look at the relationship between age and productivity. The Geron-
               tologist 13:106–10.

Comfort, Alex
1976   Age prejudice in America. Social Policy 7(3):3–8.

Corso, John F.
1977   Auditory perception and communication. Pp. 535–53 in James E. Birren and
               K. Warner Schaie (eds.), Handbook of the Psychology of Aging. New York:
               Van Nostrand Reinhold.

Cottrell, Fred, and Robert C. Atchley
1969   Women in Retirement: A Preliminary Report. Oxford, Ohio: Scripps Founda-
               tion.

Cousins, Norman
  1968   Art, adrenalin, and the enjoyment of living. Saturday Review April 20, pp. 20–24.

Crane, D.
  1965   Scientists at major and minor universities. American Sociological Review 30:699–714.

Cuber, John F., and Peggy Harroff
  1965   The Significant Americans. New York: Appleton-Century-Crofts.

Cumming, Elaine, and William E. Henry
  1961   Growing Old: The Process of Disengagement. New York: Basic Books.

Cutler, Stephen J.
  1974   The effects of transportation and distance on voluntary association participation among the aged. International Journal of Aging and Human Development 5:81–94.
  1975   Age differences in voluntary association memberships. Paper presented at the meeting of the Gerontological Society in Louisville, Kentucky, October 29.
  1976   Age profiles of membership in sixteen types of voluntary associations. Journal of Gerontology 31:462–70.
  1977   Aging and voluntary association participation. Journal of Gerontology 32(4):470–79.

De Beauvoir, Simone
  1972   The Coming of Age. New York: Putnam's.

Dennis, Wayne
  1960   Long-term constancy of behavior. Journal of Gerontology 15:195–96.
  1966   Creative productivity between the ages of 20 and 80 years. Journal of Gerontology 21:1–8.

Douglass, Richard L.
  1982   Heating or eating? The crisis of home heating, energy costs and well-being of the elderly in Michigan. Ann Arbor: University of Michigan Institute of Gerontology.

Dowd, James J.
  1975   Aging as exchange: A preface to theory. Journal of Gerontology 30(5):584–94.
  1980   Exchange rates of old people. Journal of Gerontology 35:596–602.

Drake, St. Clair, and Horace Cayton
  1962   Black Metropolis. New York: Harper & Row.

DuBois, W. E. B.
  1915   The Philadelphia Negro. New York: Holt, Rinehart, & Winston.

Elias, Merrill F., and Penelope Elias
  1977   Motivation and activity. Pp. 357–83 in James E. Birren and K. Warner Schaie (eds.), Handbook of the Psychology of Aging. New York: Van Nostrand Reinhold.

Emerson, R. M.
  1962   Power-dependence relations. American Sociological Review 27:31–41.
  1972   Exchange theory. Part 1: A psychological basis for social exchange. Pp. 38–57 in Joseph Berger, M. Zeldich, and B. Anderson (eds.), Sociological Theories in Progress. Vol. 2. Boston: Houghton Mifflin.
  1972   Exchange theory. Part 2: Exchange relations and network structures. Pp. 58–87 in Joseph Berger, M. Zeldich, and B. Anderson (eds.), Sociological Theories in Progress. Vol. 2. Boston: Houghton Mifflin.

Engen, Trygg
  1977   Taste and smell. Pp. 554–61 in James E. Birren and K. Warner Schaie (eds.), Handbook of the Psychology of Aging. New York: Van Nostrand Reinhold.

Epstein, Seymour
    1980   The self-concept: A review and the proposal of an integrated theory of per-
                    sonality. Pp. 82–132 in E. Staub (ed.), Personality: Basic Issues and Current
                    Research. Englewood Cliffs, N.J.: Prentice-Hall.

Erikson, Erik H.
    1963   Childhood and Society. New York: Norton.

Estes, Carroll
    1979   The Aging Enterprise. San Francisco: Jossey-Bass.

Farrell, Michael P., and Stanley D. Rosenberg
    1981   Men at Midlife. Boston: Auburn House.

Feifel, Herman, and R. Jones
    1968   Perceptions of death as related to nearness to death. Proceedings of the 76th
                    Annual Convention of the American Psychological Association 3: 545–46.

Fischer, David H.
    1978   Growing Old in America. New York: Oxford University Press.

Fiske, D. W.
    1974   The limits for the conventional science of personality. Journal of Personality
                    42:1–11.

Fozard, James L. and Gordon D. Carr
    1972   Age differences and psychological estimates of abilities and skill. Industrial
                    Gerontology 13:75–96.

Friedmann, Eugene A., and Robert J. Havighurst (eds.)
    1954   The Meaning of Work and Retirement. Chicago: University of Chicago Press.

Fries, James F.
    1980   Aging, natural death, and the compression of morbidity. New England Jour-
                    nal of Medicine 300:130–135.

Garfield, C.A.
    1974   Psychothanatological concomitants of altered state experience. Unpublished
                    doctoral dissertation, University of California at Berkeley (as cited in Kalish,
                    1976).

George, Linda K., and George L. Maddox
    1977   Subjective adaptation to loss of the work role: A longitudinal study. Journal
                    of Gerontology 32(4):456–62.

Glenn, Norval D., and Michael Grimes
    1968   Aging, voting, and political interest. American Sociological Review 33:563–75.

Glick, Ira O., Robert S. Weiss, and C. Murray Parkes
    1974   The First Year of Bereavement. New York: Wiley.

Gordon, Chad, Charles M. Gaitz, and Judith Scott
    1976   Leisure and lives: Personal expressivity across the life span. Pp. 310–41 in
                    Robert H. Binstock and Ethel Shanas (eds.), Handbook of Aging and the
                    Social Sciences. New York: Van Nostrand Reinhold.

Gordon, Gerald
    1966   Role Theory and Illness. New Haven, Conn.: College and University Press
                    Services.

Graebner, William
    1980   A History of Retirement. New Haven, Conn.: Yale University Press.

Green, Mark R., H. C. Pyron, O.V. Manion, and H. Winkelvoss
    1969   Pre-Retirement Counseling, Retirement, Adjustment and the Older Em-
                    ployee. Eugene: Graduate School of Management, University of Oregon.

Greenwald, Anthony
   1980   The totalitarian ego: Fabrication and revision of personal history. American
                 Psychologist: 35:603–18.

Harris, Adella J., and Jonathan F. Feinberg
   1977   Television and aging: Is what you see what you get? The Gerontologist
                 17:464–67.
Harris, Charles S.
   1978   Fact Book on Aging: A Profile of America's Older Population. Washington,
                 D.C.: National Council on the Aging.
Harris, Louis
   1965   Pleasant retirement expected. Washington Post, November 28, p. 6.
Harris, Louis, and Associates
   1975   The Myth and Reality of Aging in America. Washington, D.C.: National
                 Council on Aging.
Havighurst, Robert J.
   1963   Successful aging. Pp. 299–320 in Richard H. Williams, Clark Tibbits, and
                 Wilma Donahue (eds.), Processes of Aging. Vol. 1. New York: Atherton
                 Press.
   1973   Social roles, work, leisure, and education. Pp. 598–618 in C. Eisdorfer and
                 M. P. Lawton (eds.), The Psychology of Adult Development and Aging.
                 Washington, D.C.: American Psychological Association.
Havighurst, Robert J., Bernice L. Neugarten, and Sheldon S. Tobin
   1963   Disengagement, personality, and life satisfaction. Pp. 319–24 in P. From
                 Hansen (ed.), Age with a Future. Copenhagen: Munksgaard.
Haynes, Suzanne G., Anthony J. McMichael, and Herman A. Tyroler
   1978   Survival after early and normal retirement. Journal of Gerontology 33:269–78.
Hickey, Tom, and Richard S. Douglass
   1981   Neglect and abuse of older family members: Professionals' perspectives and
                 case experiences. The Gerontologist 21:171–76.
Heidbreder, Elizabeth M.
   1972   Factors in retirement adjustment: White-collar/blue-collar experience. Indus-
                 trial Gerontology 12:69–79.
Hellebrandt, Frances A.
   1978   The senile dement in our midst: A look at the other side of the coin. The
                 Gerontologist 18:67–70.
Hess, Beth
   1972   Friendship. Pp 357–93 in Matilda White Riley, Marilyn Johnson, and Anne
                 Foner (eds.), Aging and Society. Vol. 3: A Sociology of Age Stratification.
                 New York: Russell Sage.
Hill, Reuben
   1965   Decision making and the family life cycle. Pp. 113–39 in Ethel Shanas and
                 Gordon F. Streib (eds.), Social Structure and the Family. Englewood Cliffs,
                 N.J.: Prentice-Hall.
Hill, Robert
   1978   A demographic profile of the black elderly. Aging 287–88:2–9.
Hochschild, Arlie Russell
   1975   Disengagement theory: A critique and proposal. American Sociological Re-
                 view 40(5):553–69.
Holmes, Thomas H., and M. Masuda
   1974   Life change and illness susceptibility. Pp. 45–72 in Barbara S. Dohrenwend
                 and Bruce P. Dohrenwend (eds.), Stressful Life Events: Their Nature and
                 Effects. New York: Wiley.

Homans, George F.
1961   Social Behavior: Its Elementary Forms. New York: Harcourt Brace & World.
Horn, John L.
1970   Organization of data on life-span development of human abilities. Pp. 424–467 in L. R. Goulet and Paul B. Baltes (eds.), Life Span Developmental Psychology: Research and Theory. New York: Academic Press.
Howie, Lonnie J., and Thomas F. Drury
1978   Current estimates from the Health Interview Survey: United States, 1974. Vital and Health Statistics, Series 10, No. 126. Washington, D.C.: National Center for Health Statistics.

Ingraham, Mark H.
1974   My Purpose Holds: Reactions and Experiences in Retirement. New York: TIAA/CREF [Teacher's Insurance and Annuity Association/College Retirement Equities Fund].

Jaffe, A.J., and Jeanne Clare Ridley
1976   The extent of lifetime employment of women in the United States. Industrial Gerontology 3:25–36.
James, William
1890   Principles of Psychology. New York: Dover.
Johnson, Elizabeth S., and Barbara J. Bursk
1977   Relationships between the elderly and their adult children. The Gerontologist 17:90–96.
Johnson, S. K.
1971   Idle Haven: Community Building Among the Working-Class Retired. Berkeley: University of California Press.

Kahana, Eva
1973   The humane treatment of old people in institutions. The Gerontologist 13:282–89.
Kalish, Richard A.
1967   Of children and grandfathers: A speculative essay on dependency. The Gerontologist 7:65–69.
1976   Death and dying in a social context. In Robert Binstock and Ethel Shanas (eds.), Handbook of Aging and Social Sciences. New York: Van Nostrand Reinhold.
Kamerman, S. B.
1976   Community services for the aged: The view from eight countries. The Gerontologist 16:529–37.
Kapnick, Philip J., Jay S. Goodman, and Elmer E. Cornwell
1968   Political behavior in the aged: Some new data. Journal of Gerontology 23:305–10.
Kasschau, Patricia L.
1974   Reevaluating the need for retirement preparation programs. Industrial Gerontology 1:42–59.
Kastenbaum, Robert J.
1969   Death and bereavement in later life. Pp. 28–54 in A. H. Kurscher (ed.), Death and Bereavement. Springfield, Ill.: Thomas.
1980–1981   Habituation as a model of human aging. International Journal of Aging and Human Development 12:159–70.
Kastenbaum, Robert J., and Sandra E. Candy
1973   The 4% fallacy: A methodological and empirical critique of extended care

facility population statistics. International Journal of Aging and Human Development 4:15–21.

Kay, D. W. K.
1972   Epidemiological aspects of organic brain disease in the aged. In C. M. Gaitz (ed.), Aging and the Brain. New York: Plenum.

Kayne, Ronald C.
1976   Drugs and the aged. Pp. 436–51 in Irene M. Burnside (ed.), Nursing and the Aged. New York: McGraw-Hill.

Kelley, George A.
1955   The Psychology of Personal Constructs. New York: Norton.

Kerckhoff, Alan C.
1966a   Family patterns and morale in retirement. Pp. 173–92 in Ida H. Simpson and John C. McKinney (eds.), Social Aspects of Aging. Durham, N.C.: Duke University Press.
1966b   Norm-value clusters and the strain toward consistency among older married couples. Pp. 138–59 in Ida H. Simpson and John C. McKinney (eds.), Social Aspects of Aging. Durham, N.C. Duke University Press.

Kleemeier, Robert W. (ed.)
1961   Aging and Leisure. New York: Columbia University Press.

Koff, Theodore H.
1982   Long-Term Care: An Approach to Serving the Frail Elderly. Boston: Little, Brown.

Kohlberg, L.
1973a   Continuities in childhood and adult moral development revisited. Pp. 179–204 in Paul B. Baltes and K. Warner Schaie (eds.), Life-Span Developmental Psychology: Personality and Socialization. New York: Academic Press.
1973b   Stages and aging in moral development—some speculations. The Gerontologist 13:497–502.

Kovar, Mary Grace
1977   Health of the elderly and use of health services. Public Health Reports 92(1):9–19.

Kronus, Sidney
1971   The Black Middle Class. Columbus, Ohio: Merrill.

Kübler-Ross, Elizabeth
1969   On Death and Dying. New York: Macmillan.

Kunkel, Suzanne R.
1979   Sex differences in adjustment to widowhood. Unpublished masters thesis, Miami University (Oxford, Ohio).

Lambing, Mary L. B.
1972   Leisure-time pursuits among retired blacks by social status. The Gerontologist 12:363–67.

Lando, Mordechai E.
1976   Demographic characteristics of disability applicants: Relationships to allowances. Social Security Bulletin 39(5):15–23.

Lawton, M. Powell
1972   Assessing the competence of older people. Pp. 122–43 in Donald P. Kent, R. Kastenbaum, and S. Sherwood (eds.), Research Planning and Action for the Elderly. New York: Behavioral Publications.
1978   Leisure activities for the aged. Annals of the American Academy of Political and Social Sciences 438:71–80.

Lee, Anne S.
1974   Return migration in the United States. International Migration Review 8:283–300.

Lee, Gary R.
1978   Marriage and morale in later life. Journal of Marriage and the Family 40:131–
               39.

Levinson, Daniel J., C. M. Darrow, E. B. Klein, M. H. Levinson, and B. McKee
1978   The Seasons of a Man's Life. New York: Knopf.

Lieberman, Morton
1975   Adaptive processes in late life. Pp. 135–59 in Nancy Datan and Leon H.
               Ginsberg (eds.), Life Span Developmental Psychology: Normative Life
               Crises. New York: Academic Press.

Liebow, Elliot
1967   Tally's Corner. Boston: Little, Brown.

Lipman, Aaron
1961   Role conceptions and morale of couples in retirement. Journal of Gerontology
               16:267–71.
1962   Role conceptions of couples in retirement. Pp. 475–85 in Clark Tibbits and
               Wilma Donahue (eds.), Social and Psychological Aspects of Aging. New
               York: Columbia University Press.

Litwak, Eugene
1960   Occupational mobility and extended family cohesion. American Sociological
               Review 25:9–21.

Livson, Florine B.
1976   Patterns of personality development in middle-aged women: A longitudinal
               study. International Journal of Aging and Human Development 7:107–15.

Longino, Charles F., Jr.
1981   Retirement communities. Pp. 391–418 in F. J. Berghorn and D. E. Schafer
               (eds.), The Dynamics of Aging. Boulder, Colo.: Westview Press.

Longino, Charles F., Jr., and G. C. Kitson
1976   Parish clergy and the aged: Examining stereotypes. Journal of Gerontology
               31:340–45.

Lopata, Helena Z.
1973   Widowhood in an American City. Cambridge, Mass.: Schenkman.
1975   Support systems of elderly urbanites: Chicago of the 1970's. The Gerontolo-
               gist 15:35–41.

Louis, Arthur M.
1968   America's centimillionaires. Fortune 77:152–57.

Lowenthal, Marjorie F.
1964   Social isolation and mental illness in old age. American Sociological Review
               29:54–70.

Lowenthal, Marjorie F., and Paul L. Berkman
1967   Aging and Mental Disorder in San Francisco. San Francisco: Jossey-Bass.

Lowenthal, Marjorie F., and David Chiriboga
1975   Responses to stress. Pp. 146–62 in Marjorie F. Lowenthal, Majda Thurnher,
               and David Chiriboga, The Four Stages of Life. San Francisco: Jossey-Bass.

Lowenthal, Marjorie F., and Clayton Havens
1968   Interaction and adaptation: Intimacy as a critical variable. American Socio-
               logical Review 33:20–31.

Lowenthal, Marjorie F., and Betsy Robinson
1976   Social networks and isolation. Pp. 432–56 in Robert H. Binstock and Ethel
               Shanas (eds.), Handbook of Aging and the Social Sciences. New York: Van
               Nostrand Reinhold.

Lowenthal, Marjorie F., M. Thurnher, and D. Chiriboga
1975   The Four Stages of Life. San Francisco: Jossey-Bass.

McFarland, Ross A.
    1973   The need for functional age measures in industrial gerontology. Industrial Gerontology 19:1–19.

McKain, Walter C., Jr.
    1969   Retirement Marriage. Storrs: University of Connecticut Agriculture Experiment Station.

McTavish, Donald G.
    1971   Perceptions of old people: A review of research, methodologies and findings. The Gerontologist 11(4, part 2):90–101.

Mallan, Lucy B.
    1974   Women born in the early 1900's : Employment, earnings, and benefit levels. Social Security Bulletin 37(3):3–25.

Marquis Academic Media
    1978   Sourcebook on Aging. Chicago: Who's Who.

Masters, William H., and Virginia Johnson
    1966   Human Sexual Response. Boston: Little, Brown.

Menninger, Karl
    1938   Man Against Himself. New York: Harcourt Brace & World.

Millard, Peter H., and Chriss Smith
    1981   Personal belongings—a positive effect? The Gerontologist 21:85–90.

Miller, Marv
    1978   Geriatric suicide: The Arizona study. The Gerontologist 18:488–95.

Miller, Sheila J.
    1982   Older women and disabilities. Oxford, Ohio: Scripps Foundation.

Miller, Stephen J.
    1965   The social dilemma of the aging leisure participant. Pp. 77–92 in Arnold M. Rose and Warren A. Peterson (eds), Older People and Their Social World. Philadelphia: Davis.

Mishara, Brian L., and Robert Kastenbaum
    1980   Alcohol and Old Age. New York: Grune & Stratton.

Moberg, David O.
    1972   Religion and the aged family. Family Coordinator 21:47–60.

Morgan, James N.
    1962   Income and Welfare in the United States. New York: McGraw-Hill.

Motley, Dena K.
    1978   Availability of retired persons for work: Findings from the retirement history study. Social Security Bulletin 41(4):18–28.

Mulkay, M. J.
    1971   Functionalism, Exchange, and Theoretical Strategy. New York: Schocken.

Nadelson, Theodore
    1969   A survey of the literature on the adjustment of the aged to retirement. Journal of Geriatric Psychiatry 3:3–20.

Nagi, Saad Z.
    1965   Some conceptual issues in disability and rehabilitation. Pp. 100–03 in Marvin B. Sussman (ed.), Sociology and Rehabilitation. Washington, D.C.: American Sociological Association.

National Center for Health Statistics
    1959   Health Statistics. Series B, No. 9. Washington, D.C.: National Center for Health Statistics.

Nesselroade, John R., K. Warner Schaie, and Paul B. Baltes
    1972   Ontogenetic and generational components of structural and quantitative change in adult cognitive behavior. Journal of Gerontology 27:222–28.

Neugarten, Bernice L. (ed.)
1964   Personality in Middle and Late Life. New York: Atherton Press.

Neugarten, Bernice L.
1968   Middle Age and Aging. Chicago: University of Chicago Press.
1977   Personality and aging. Pp. 626–49 in James E. Birren and K. Warner Schaie
              (eds.), Handbook of the Psychology of Aging. New York: Van Nostrand
              Reinhold.

Neugarten, Bernice L., and Nancy Datan
1973   Sociological perspectives on the life cycle. Pp. 53–69 in Paul B. Baltes and K.
              Warner Schaie (eds.), Life-Span Developmental Psychology: Personality and
              Socialization. New York: Academic Press.

Neugarten, Bernice L., Joan W. Moore, and John C. Lowe
1965   Age norms, age constraints, and adult socialization. American Journal of
              Sociology 70:710–17.

Newell, David S.
1961   Social structural evidence for disengagement. Pp. 37–74 in Elaine Cumming
              and W. E. Henry (eds.), Growing Old. New York: Basic Books.

Oliver, David B.
1971   Career and leisure patterns of middle-aged metropolitan out-migrants. The
              Gerontologist 11(4, part 2):13–20.

Palmore, Erdman
1971   Why do people retire? Aging and Human Development. 2:269–83.
1976   Total change of institutionalization among the aged. The Gerontologist
              16:504–07.

Palmore, Erdman, and K. Manton
1973   Ageism compared to racism and sexism. Journal of Gerontology 28:363–69.

Parkes, C. M.
1972   Bereavement. New York: International Universities Press.

Parnes, Herbert S., Aril V. Adams, Paul Andrisani, Andrew I. Kohlen, and Gilbert Nestel
1975   The Pre-retirement Years: Five Years in the Work Lives of Middle-Aged Men.
              Manpower Research Monograph No. 15. Washington, D.C.: U.S. Depart-
              ment of Labor.

Parnes, Herbert S., and Randy King
1977   Middle-aged job losers. Industrial Gerontology 4:77–96.

Parnes, Herbert S., and Gilbert Nestel
1981   The retirement experience. Pp. 155–96 in H. S. Parnes (ed.), Work and Re-
              tirement: A Longitudinal Study of Men. Cambridge, Mass.: M.I.T. Press.

Peck, R. C.
1968   Psychological developments in the second half of life. Pp. 88–92 in Bernice L.
              Neugarten (ed.), Middle Age and Aging. Chicago: University of Chicago
              Press.

Pollman, A. William
1971   Early retirement: A comparison of poor health to other retirement factors.
              Journal of Gerontology 26:41–45.

Powers, Edward A., Patricia Keith, and Willis H. Goudy
1975   Family relationships and friendships. Pp. 67–90 in Robert C. Atchley (ed.),
              Environments and the Rural Aged. Washington, D.C.: Gerontological Soci-
              ety.

Pratt, Henry J.
1977   The Gray Lobby. Chicago: University of Chicago Press.

Reno, Virginia P.
1971   Why men stop working at or before age 65. Social Security Bulletin 34(4):3–17.

Riegel, Klaus F.
1975   Adult life crises: a dialectic interpretation of development. Pp. 99–128 in
               Nancy Datan and Leon H. Ginsberg (eds.), Life Span Developmental Psy-
               chology: Normative Life Crises. New York: Academic Press.
1976   The dialectics of human development. The American Psychologist 31:689–
               700.

Riley, Matilda W., and Anne Foner
1968   Aging and Society. Vol. 1: An Inventory of Research Findings. New York:
               Russell Sage.

Riley, Matilda W., Marilyn Johnson, and Anne Foner
1972   Aging and Society. Vol. 3: A Sociology of Age Stratification. New York:
               Russell Sage.

Roberts, Jean
1968   Monocular-binocular visual acuity of adults: United States, 1960–1962. Vital
               and Health Statistics, Series 11, No. 30. Washington, D.C.: National Center
               for Health Statistics.

Rokeach, Milton
1973   The Nature of Human Values. New York: Free Press.

Roman, Paul, and Philip Taietz
1967   Organizational structure and disengagement: The emeritus professor. The
               Gerontologist 7:147–52.

Rosen, Benson, and Thomas H. Jerdee
1976a   The nature of job-related stereotypes. Journal of Applied Psychology 61:180–
               83.
1976b   The influence of age stereotypes on managerial decisions. Journal of Applied
               Psychology 61:428–32.

Rosenberg, George S.
1970   The Worker Grows Old. San Francisco: Jossey-Bass.

Rosenberg, Morris
1964   Society and the Adolescent Self-Image. Princton, N.J.: Princeton University
               Press.

Rosow, Irving
1967   Social Integration of the Aged. New York: Free Press.
1974   Socialization to Old Age. Berkeley: University of California Press.

Ross, Hugh
1968   Protective services for the aged. The Gerontologist 8(1, part 2):50–53.

Ryder, Robert G.
1968   Husband-wife dyads versus married strangers. Family Process 7:233–38.

Sainer, J., and M. Zander
1971   Guidelines for older person volunteers. The Gerontologist 11:201–04.

Sarason, Seymour B.
1977   Work, Aging, and Social Change: Professionals and the One Life-One Career
               Imperative. New York: Free Press.

Saunders, Cicely
1976   St. Christopher's hospice. Pp. 516–23 in E. S.Shneidman (ed.), Death: Cur-
               rent Perspectives. Palo Alto, Calif.: Mayfield.

Schaie, K. Warner, and I. A. Parham
1976   Stability of adult personality traits: Fact or fable? Journal of Personality and
               Social Psychology 34:146–58.

Schmidhauser, John
    1968   The political influence of the aged. The Gerontologist 8(1, part 2):44–49.

Schuerman, Laurell E., Donna Z. Eden, and David A. Peterson
    1977   Older people in women's periodical fiction. Educational Gerontology 2:327–51.

Schulz, James H.
    1973   The economic impact of an aging population. The Gerontologist 13:111–18.
    1974   The economics of mandatory retirement. Industrial Gerontology 1:1–10.
    1976   The Economics of Aging. Belmont, Calif.: Wadsworth.

Seelbach, Wayne C.
    1977   Gender differences in expectations for filial responsibility. The Gerontologist 17:421–25.

Settin, Joan M.
    1978   Some thoughts on diseases presented as senility. The Gerontologist 18:71–72.

Shanas, Ethel
    1962   The Health of Older People: A Social Survey. Cambridge, Mass.: Harvard University Press.
    1977   National Survey of the Aged: 1975. Chicago: University of Illinois, Chicago Circle.
    1979   The family as a social support system in old age. The Gerontologist 19:169–74.

Shanas, Ethel, and George L. Maddox
    1976   Aging, health, and the organization of health resources. Pp. 592–618 in Robert H. Binstock and Ethel Shanas (eds.), Handbook of Aging and the Social Sciences. New York: Van Nostrand Reinhold.

Shanas, Ethel, and Marvin B. Sussman (eds.)
    1977   Family, Bureaucracy, and the Elderly. Durham, N.C. Duke University Press.

Shanas, Ethel, Peter Townsend, Dorothy Wedderburn, Henning Friis, Paul Milhøj, and Jan Stehouwer
    1968   Older People in Three Industrial Societies. New York: Atherton Press.

Sheehy, Gail
    1976   Passages: Predictable Crises of Adult Life. New York: Dutton.

Sheppard, Harold L.
    1976   Work and retirement. Pp. 286–309 in R. H. Binstock and Ethel Shanas (eds.), Handbook of Aging and the Social Sciences. New York: Van Nostrand Reinhold.

Sherman, Edmund, and E. S. Newman
    1977–1978   The meaning of cherished personal possessions for the elderly. International Journal of Aging and Human Development 8:181–92.

Shock, Nathan W.
    1977   Biological theories of aging. Pp. 103–15 in James E. Birren and K. Warner Schaie (eds.), Handbook of the Psychology of Aging. New York: Van Nostrand Reinhold.

Shock, Nathan W., and A. H. Norris
    1970   Neuromuscular coordination as a factor in age changes in muscular exercise. Pp. 92–99 in D. Brunner and E. Jokl (eds.), Physical Activity and Aging. New York: Karger.

Sill, John S.
    1980   Disengagement reconsidered: awareness of finitude. The Gerontologist 20:457–62.

Simpson, Ida H., and John C. McKinney (eds.)
    1966   Social Aspects of Aging. Durham, N.C.: Duke University Press.

Simpson, Ida H., Kurt W. Back, and John C. McKinney
    1966a   Continuity of work and retirement activities, and self-evaluation. Pp. 106–19 in Ida H. Simpson and John C. McKinney (eds.), Social Aspects of Aging. Durham, N.C.: Duke University Press.
    1966b   Orientation toward work and retirement, and self-evaluation in retirement. Pp. 75–89 in Ida H. Simpson and John C. McKinney (eds.), Social Aspects of Aging. Durham, N.C.: Duke University Press.

Smith, Madorah E., and Calvin Hall
    1964   An investigation of regression in a long dream series. Journal of Gerontology 19:66–71.

Sohngen, Mary
    1977   The experience of old age as depicted in contemporary novels. The Gerontologist 17:70–78.

Social Security Administration
    1975   Social Security Around the World. Washington, D.C.: U.S. Government Printing Office.
    1981   The income and resources of the elderly in 1978. Social Security Bulletin 44:12:3–11.

Sommers, Tish, and Laurie Shields
    1979   Problems of the displaced homemaker. Pp. 86–106 in Ann F. Cahn (ed.), Women in Midlife—Security and Fulfillment. Washington, D.C.: House Select Committee on Aging.

Spence, Donald L., and Thomas Lonner
    1971   The "empty nest": A transition within motherhood. Family Coordinator 20:369–75.

Starr, Bernard D., and M. B. Weiner
    1981   Sex and Sexuality in the Mature Years. New York: Stein & Day.

Sterne, Richard S., James E. Phillips, and Alvin Rabushka
    1974   The Urban Elderly Poor: Racial and Bureaucratic Conflict. Lexington, Mass.: Heath.

Streib, Gordon F.
    1976   Social stratification and aging. Pp. 160–85 in Robert H. Binstock and Ethel Shanas (eds.), Handbook of Aging and the Social Sciences. New York: Van Nostrand Reinhold.

Streib, Gordon F., and Clement J. Schneider
    1971   Retirement in American Society. Ithaca, N.Y.: Cornell University Press.

Streib, Gordon F., and Ruth B. Streib
    1975   Communes and the aging. American Behavioral Scientist 19:176–89.

Sudnow, David
    1967   Passing On: The Social Organization of Dying. Englewood Cliffs, N.J.: Prentice-Hall.

Sussman, Marvin B., and Lee Burchinal
    1962   Parental aid to married children: Implications for family functioning. Marriage and Family Living 24:320–32.

Taietz, Philip
    1975   Community complexity and knowledge of facilities. Journal of Gerontology 30:357–62.

Thaler, Margaret
    1956   Relationships among Wechsler, Weigle, Rorschach, EEG findings and abstract-concrete behavior. Journal of Gerontology 11:404–09.

Thomae, Hans (ed.)
1975   Patterns of Aging: Findings from the Bonn Longitudinal Study of Aging. New York: Karger.

Thomas, L. Eugene
1977   Motivations for mid-life career change. Paper presented at the annual meeting of the Gerontological Society, September, San Francisco.

Thompson, Gayle B.
1973   Work versus leisure roles: An investigation of morale among employed and retired men. Journal of Gerontology 28:339–44.

Thompson, Wayne E.
1956   The impact of retirement. Unpublished doctoral dissertation, Cornell University.

Thurnher, Majda
1975   Family confluence, conflict, and affect. Pp. 24–47 in M. F. Lowenthal, M. Thurnher, and D. Chiriboga (eds.), The Four Stages of Life. San Francisco: Jossey-Bass.

Tissue, Thomas L.
1971   Social class and the senior citizen center. The Gerontologist 11:196–200.

Troll, Lillian E.
1971   The family of later life: A decade review. Journal of Marriage and the Family 33:263–90.
1972   The salience of members of three-generation families for one another. Paper presented at the Annual Meeting of the American Psychological Association, September, Honolulu.
1975   Early and Middle Adulthood. Monterey, Calif.: Brooks/Cole.
1982   Continuations: Adult Development and Aging. Monterey, Calif.: Brooks/ Cole.

Troll, Lillian E., Sheila J. Miller, and Robert C. Atchley
1979   Families in Later Life. Belmont, Calif.: Wadsworth.

U.S. Bureau of the Census
1976   Demographic aspects of aging and the older population in the United States. Current Population Reports, Series P-23, No. 59. Washington, D.C.: U.S. Government Printing Office.
1977   Marriage, divorce, widowhood, and remarriage by family characteristics: June, 1975. Current Population Reports, Series P-20, No. 312. Washington, D.C: U.S. Government Printing Office.
1978   1976 survey of institutionalized persons: A survey of persons receiving long-term care. Current Population Reports, Series P-23, No. 69. Washington D.C.: U.S. Government Printing Office.
1979   Statistical Abstract of the United States. Washington, D.C.: U.S. Government Printing Office.

U.S. Bureau of Labor Statistics
1980   Budgets for an urban family of four, a retired couple and a retired individual. Bulletin 1570–80. Washington, D.C.: U.S. Government Printing Office.

U.S. Commission on Civil Rights
1977   The Age Discrimination Study. Washington, D.C.: The Commission on Civil Rights.

U.S. Department of Labor
1979   Age Discrimination in Employment Act of 1967: Activities Under the Act During 1978. Washington, D.C.: U.S. Department of Labor.

U.S. General Accounting Office
1977   The Well-Being of Older People in Cleveland, Ohio. Washington, D.C.: U.S. Government Printing Office.

U.S. Senate Special Committee on Aging
   1965   Frauds and Deceptions Affecting the Elderly. Washington, D.C.: U.S. Gov-
                 ernment Printing Office.
   1973   Training Needs in Gerontology. Washington, D.C.: U.S. Government Print-
                 ing Office.

Vaillant, George E.
   1977   Adaptation to Life. Boston: Little, Brown.

Vinick, Barbara H.
   1979   Remarriage. Pp. 141–243 in Ruth H. Jacobs and Barbara H. Vinick, Re-
                 Engagement in Later Life: Re-Employment and Remarriage. Stamford,
                 Conn.: Greylock.

Wantz, Molly S., and John E. Gay
   1981   The Aging Process: A Health Perspective. Cambridge, Mass.: Winthrop.

Weisman, Avery D.
   1972   On Dying and Denying. New York: Behavioral Publications.

Weiss, Alfred D.
   1959   Sensory functions. Pp. 503–42 in James E. Birren (ed.), Handbook of Aging
                 and the Individual. Chicago: University of Chicago Press.

Welford, Alan T.
   1959   Psychomotor performance. Pp. 562–613 in James E. Birren (ed.), Handbook
                 of Aging and the Individual. Chicago: University of Chicago Press.

Wells, Thelma J., and Carol A. Brink
   1981   Urinary incontinence: Assessment and management. Pp. 519–48 in Irene M.
                 Burnside (ed.), Nursing and the Aged. New York: McGraw-Hll.

Wershow, Harold J.
   1977   Reality orientation for gerontologists: Some thoughts about senility. The
                 Gerontologist 17:297–302.

West, Howard
   1971   Five years of Medicare—a statistical review. Social Security Bulletin 34(12):17–
                 27.

Whitbourne, Susan K., and Comilda S. Weinstock
   1979   Adult Development: The Differentiation of Experience. New York: Holt,
                 Rinehart, & Winston.

Wilder, Charles S.
   1971   Chronic conditions and limitations of activity and mobility: United States,
                 July 1965 to June 1967. Vital and Health Statistics, Series 10, No. 61. Wash-
                 ington, D.C.: National Center for Health Statistics.
   1973   Limitation of activity due to chronic conditions: United States, 1969 to 1970.
                 Vital and Health Statistics, Series 10, No. 80. Washington, D.C.: National
                 Center for Health Statistics.
   1974   Acute conditions: Incidence and associated disability: United States, July 1971
                 to June 1972. Vital and Health Statistics, Series 10, No. 88. Washington, D.C.:
                 National Center for Health Statistics.

Wilder, Charles S.
   1977   Health characteristics of persons with chronic activity limitations: United
                 States, 1974. Vital and Health Statistics, Series 10, No. 112. Washington,
                 D.C.: National Center for Health Statistics.

Wilder, Mary H.
   1972   Home care for persons 55 years and over: United States, July 1966 to June
                 1968. Vital and Health Statistics, Series 10, No. 73. Washington, D.C.: Na-
                 tional Center for Health Statistics.

Wilensky, Harold
    1964   Life cycle, work situations and participation in formal associations. Pp. 213–
                    42 in Robert W. Kleemeier (ed.), Aging and Leisure. New York: Oxford
                    University Press.
Williams, Richard H., and Claudine Wirths
    1965   Lives Through the Years. New York: Atherton Press.
Woehrer, Carol E.
    1978   Cultural pluralism in American families: The influence of ethnicity on social
                    aspects of aging. Family Coordinator 27:329–39.

Zimberg, Sheldon
    1974   The elderly alcoholic. The Gerontologist 14:221–24.
Zuckerman, Harriet, and Robert K. Merton
    1972   Age, aging, and age structure in science. Pp. 292–456 in Matilda W. Riley,
                    Marilyn Johnson, and Anne Foner (eds.), Aging and Society. Vol. 3: A Soci-
                    ology of Age Stratification. New York: Russell Sage.

Index